Dirty Money

The State of the Federation

Series editor: Christian Leuprecht

The State of the Federation series provides timely commentary and perspectives on critical issues affecting Canadian federalism. Since 1985 it has reviewed events on the federal-provincial agenda. Books in the series offer retrospective and prospective assessments of emerging policy from the vantage points of Canadian and comparative federalism, intergovernmental relations, and multilevel governance, paying particular attention to the overlap with Canadian politics and society writ large. Authored by leading scholars and practitioners from government and business, chapters in each volume are integrated thematically.

Dirty Money
Financial Crime in Canada
Edited by Christian Leuprecht and Jamie Ferrill

Canada at 150
Federalism and the Democratic Renewal
Edited by Elizabeth Goodyear Grant and Kyle Hanniman

Canadian Federalism and Infrastructure
Edited by John R. Allan, David L.A. Gordon, Kyle Hanniman, André Juneau, and Robert A. Young

Aboriginal Multilevel Governance
Edited by Martin Papillon and André Juneau

Regions, Resources and Resiliency
Edited by Loleen Berdahl, Carolyn Hughes Tuohy, and André Juneau

The Changing Federal Environment
Rebalancing Roles?
Edited by Nadia Verrelli

Shifting Power
The New Ontario and What It Means for Canada
Edited by Matthew Mendelsohn, Joshua Hjartarson, and James Pearce

Carbon Pricing and Environmental Federalism
Edited by Thomas J. Courchene and John R. Allan

Dirty Money

Financial Crime in Canada

EDITED BY
CHRISTIAN LEUPRECHT AND JAMIE FERRILL

Published for the Institute of Intergovernmental Relations
School of Policy Studies, Queen's University
by
McGill-Queen's University Press
Montreal & Kingston | London | Chicago

ISBN 978-0-2280-1904-6 (cloth)
ISBN 978-0-2280-1905-3 (paper)
ISBN 978-0-2280-1988-6 (ePDF)
ISBN 978-0-2280-1989-3 (ePUB)

Legal deposit third quarter 2023
Bibliothèque nationale du Québec

Printed in Canada on acid-free paper that is 100% ancient forest free (100% post-consumer recycled), processed chlorine free

Funded by the Government of Canada   Financé par le gouvernement du Canada

Canada Council for the Arts   Conseil des arts du Canada

We acknowledge the support of the Canada Council for the Arts.
Nous remercions le Conseil des arts du Canada de son soutien.

Library and Archives Canada Cataloguing in Publication

Title: Dirty money : financial crime in Canada / edited by Christian Leuprecht and Jamie Ferrill.
Other titles: Dirty money (Montréal, Québec)
Names: Leuprecht, Christian, 1973- editor. | Ferrill, Jamie, editor.
Description: Series statement: State of the federation | Includes bibliographical references.
Identifiers: Canadiana (print) 20230190855 | Canadiana (ebook) 2023019088X | ISBN 9780228019053 (paper) | ISBN 9780228019046 (cloth) | ISBN 9780228019893 (ePUB) | ISBN 9780228019886 (ePDF)
Subjects: LCSH: Money laundering—Canada. | LCSH: Commercial crimes—Canada.
Classification: LCC HV6771.C3 D57 2023 | DDC 364.16/80971—dc23

In memory of the late Arthur J. Cockfield IV (1967–2022), professor, colleague, teacher, friend, mentor, and a preeminent authority on comparative and international tax law, e-commerce, privacy, and legal ethics, with a global reputation for his expertise in tax avoidance and financial crime.

Contents

Acknowledgements

The late Art Cockfield and I conceived this volume in our joint efforts to raise the profile of the insidious and pervasive nature of financial crime in Canada and transnationally. This project is part of a joint Insight Grant entitled Invisible Underworld: Inhibiting Global Financial Crime, funded by the Social Sciences and Humanities Research Council of Canada (grant number 435-2019-1333), and the Institute of Intergovernmental Relations at Queen's University. Art's expertise in tax law, evasion, and avoidance was unique, not just in Canada but globally. Among the most referenced tax law scholars in the world, his work was frequently cited by the Supreme Court of Canada. He became known to the general public as a distinguished subject expert in his field through numerous newspaper columns, featured articles, and a novel, *The End*. The Canadian government, the World Bank, and several other public and private sector stakeholders frequently sought him out to consult on such issues as combatting international tax evasion and other forms of cross-border financial crime. Particularly notable was his consultancy to the International Consortium of Investigative Journalists (ICIJ), initially in 2013 regarding tax haven data leaks that would explode into the Panama Papers. Among his seminal publications was the co-authored book *International Taxation in Canada* (LexisNexis 2006, 4th ed. 2018). Canada's Supreme Court, calling Cockfield a "learned author," would cite it thirteen times in *Canada v. Alta Energy Luxembourg SARL*, its 2021 decision so eagerly anticipated by the international tax community worldwide.

When Art passed unexpectedly on 9 January 2022, we had already agreed on the contributors and Art had drafted his own contribution on tax evasion and aggressive tax avoidance, which appears posthumously in this volume. Art and I had already engaged a co-editor, Dr. Jamie Ferrill, a Canadian political sociologist and former federal law enforcement officer, who is now the Discipline Lead for Financial Crime at the Australian Graduate School of Policing and Security at Charles Sturt University in Canberra, Australia. Her scholarly and editorial talents would prove integral in seeing this volume through, and I am forever grateful to her for her collegiality, expertise, support, and friendship. She encouraged me to persist with this project and inspires me to carry on Art's legacy in raising awareness about the deleterious effects of financial crime and tax evasion.

The volume brings together foremost scholars and practitioner-scholars studying financial crime in Canada. I thank them for being so cooperative and great to work with, notwithstanding requests for revisions and delays in publication. Special shout out to Jeff Simser and Denis Meunier for their incisive support in reviewing material, to John Jacobson for his reflections, as well as to current and former members of the intelligence and law enforcement community for their input. Among the sixteen chapters, half are co-authored by women, seven of whom are emerging scholars, and six chapters have women as lead authors. Ten authors have backgrounds as practitioners: in law enforcement, intelligence, and private practice. That is, the volume seeks to bridge superior professional expertise with excellence in research. That is indispensable in a subfield that is not only highly complex and difficult to study, but which strives to have an impact in policy and practice. Indeed, many of the contributors to this volume have already been highly influential. Contributors are drawn from the six most populous provinces from right across this country. That is important for a subfield whose harms affect local communities everywhere, and to educate and train a new generation of scholars and practitioners. Finally, authors come from backgrounds in law, political science, criminology, and sociology, making this volume genuinely interdisciplinary, which is indispensable in a subfield as varied as financial crime. I am not aware of another volume in a country of comparable size that brings together as diverse a set of home-grown talent. That bodes well for a bright and sustainable future for this subfield, and suggests that the field is evolving, and changing rapidly. The concerted effort in this volume to muster this breadth of expertise holds out hope that it is possible to make inroads against one of the most pervasive and insidious crimes global crimes facing our society.

Since 1985 the IIGR's State of the Federation series has been purveying timely research on matters of fiscal federalism, social policy, constitutional and institutional change, Indigenous governance, healthcare reform, the environment, and demographic diversity, to name but a few of the many topics covered over the years; the series was ahead of its time in generating important policy innovation and more informed public discourse on issues of intergovernmental relations affecting the federation. This latest volume in the Series introduces financial crime as novel areas in the study of intergovernmental relations, comparative federalism, and multilevel governance. Far from pretending to have the last word, it aims to change the way people behave, by changing the way they think, and change the way they think, by giving them the language to talk about financial crime. In keeping with my mentor and eminence grise of the IIGR, its late director Ronald L. Watts, a towering figure in comparative federalism and constitutional politics whose influence and legacy continues to resonate across the globe, the volume also intends to foster a new generation of scholars.

As director of the Institute of Intergovernmental Relations, now in its seventh decade, I am grateful for the decades-long relationship with McGill-Queen's University Press in publishing and revitalizing the State of the Federation series. I thank Emily Andrew and Phil Cercone for this enthusiasm and support for this particular book project, Filomena Falocco and colleagues Elli Stylianou, Roy Ward, and Kate Fraser for enabling it, Jennifer Roberts and Andy Black for helping to market the book, and Kathleen Fraser and Elena Goranescu for coming up with the cover design. The IIGR's stalwart administrative assistant, Mary Kennedy, helped the many moving parts that underpin a volume coalesce, and Anne Holley-Hime worked her usual magic on copyediting and laying out each chapter. I should also acknowledge the support of the director of the School of Policy Studies, Warren Mabee, and the Associate Dean, Research, Social

Sciences and Humanities, of the Faculty of Arts and Sciences at Queen's University, for their support for the IIGR.

All would have been for naught had Jamie Ferrill not stepped into the fray after Art's death left me stunned and dumbfounded about how the research and this project could possibly go on without his loyal and trusted collaboration. In a moment of shock and darkness, Jamie came alongside to help make the seemingly impossible, possible. As an exemplary scholar, dedicated educator, and committed mentor, Art would have been delighted by the way this volume came together, and the promise it and especially its younger contributors hold. I hope you will enjoy reading this volume and will take away as much as I have from this collection of exceptionally insightful chapters. May this volume stand the test of time as a memorial in honour of Art and his work.

Christian Leuprecht
Kingston, March 2023

Dirty Money

Introduction

Jamie Ferrill, Christian Leuprecht, and Jeffrey Simser

This is a book about financial crime in Canada. There may not be a public safety issue in Canada with as great a mismatch between prominence and severity on the one hand, relative to the ponderous bureaucratic and political inaction that reflects perfunctory public debate on the other. Public consciousness of financial crime and its consequences will put pressure on politicians and policy makers to act. In other words, the book aims to change the way people behave by changing the way they think about financial crime. And it aims to change public and political thinking by changing the language people use to talk about financial crime. To this end, this volume raises public awareness about the extent of financial crime in Canada. It builds greater appreciation for the social harms it causes. It aims to raise the level of informed debate with the hope of spurring decision-making. The book intends to build confidence among policy makers, politicians, and the public alike by translating financial crime and its consequences into the vernacular, and to generate more scholarship – the last book on financial crime in Canada dates back some fifteen years!

Contributions to this volume reveal the vast expanse of Canada's financial underworld: how financial criminals operate, the channels they use, how they suborn banks and institutions, and how Canada's system emboldens them to conduct brazen crimes with impunity. The volume paints a picture: of financial crime and its corrosive effects on communities, democratic institutions, and prosperity. Dirty money drives up the cost of housing, aggravates gang violence and related shootings, is behind the synthetic opioids that manifest in an overdose epidemic, enables human trafficking and other forms of gross exploitation, finances nuclear weapons proliferation by rogue states, and helps malicious countries evade international sanctions while enabling foreign interference in Canada's democratic institutions by hostile state and non-state actors (e.g., Cooper 2021). Financial fraud bilks seniors of their retirement savings and ransomware costs companies billions in losses annually. The public bears the costs: through higher prices, taxation (lost revenue and increased fiscal costs for law enforcement), and rising insurance premiums.

This book brings together scholars with public (international, federal, provincial, and local) and private sector expertise intent on remedying the many deficiencies in the Canadian system. They chart future domestic policy and research as well as the underlying international regime. It contextualizes Canadian issues in a broader global perspective and draws links between domestic and international threat vectors. Since Canada is integrated into the global financial system, weaknesses in its domestic regime has international consequences, such as emboldening transnational organized crime and state capture. Financial crime bears considerable political and economic risk. Loss of confidence in countries and their financial systems has implications for investments, credit, supply chains, bilateral agreements, and so on.

The structure of this introduction mirrors the structure of the book. First, it frames the problem and its enablers. Hampering financial crime deters real crime. The more expensive it is to launder money, the less profitable real crime becomes. But instead of hampering financial crime, Canada's financial regime (in)advertently enables it. Law is intensely domestic, especially in this domain. Canada's legislation has sharp edges with fundamentally wrong tradeoffs between financial privacy and the collective good of Canadian society. Ideological narratives that demonize wealth in general rather than crime specifically are a major impediment to tighter regulation. Concomitantly, civil forfeiture is a powerful legal device in the hands of a well-funded and ambitious prosecutor looking to build a reputation of cases won.

Much of today's financial crime and anti-money laundering legislation was written for a bygone Westphalian era of domestic jurisdiction. Countries cannot solve the problem of financial crime alone. Criminals coordinate across borders to commit crime and launder the proceeds. In the absence of a coordinated response across borders, individual countries' own efforts will be largely ineffective. The bordering processes of globalization enhance criminogenic asymmetry: transnational organized crime has professionalized and perfected the art of optimizing for weaknesses across jurisdictions (Shelley 2018). Technological innovation such as cryptocurrency has proven an accelerant of globalization as an enabler of illicit transnational flows. The global illicit economy is estimated to account for about US$2.2 trillion, or 3.6 percent of the global GDP per year (World Economic Forum 2015). Some figures peg it closer to 10 percent of global GDP (The High-Level Panel on International Financial Accountability Transparency and Integrity for Achieving the 2030 Agenda 2020). Although the extent of illegal financial outflows and capital flight from China is a matter of debate, undoubtedly China's illicit economy is worth tens of billions of dollars annually (e.g., Kessler and Borst 2013). All this money needs a road to its wrongful owner. Financial crime is that road.

Second, in light of persistent failures to contain transnational financial crime, the book describes how to interrogate the data. Methodologically and empirically, that turns out to be a major challenge. The illicit international political economy is hidden and opaque, which makes it difficult to detect, especially within any one sovereign jurisdiction (Andreas 2004; Ryner 2006; Hudson 2005, 2013, 2019). Money laundering as a business has perfected the art of making transactions in any one jurisdiction appear perfectly legal (Teichman 2017); so, identifying problematic trends requires a transnational aperture that national intelligence and enforcement organizations tend to lack.

Third, it introduces the politics of financial crime and emerging issues. Russia's invasion of Ukraine confirmed that containing problematic financial flows is fundamentally a matter of political will (Drezner, Farrell, and Newman 2021). Expeditious legislative change is possible when a government deems it in its interest. Instead of the political fortunes of any one government, however, imperatives of financial crime should be driven by the common good of society.

Fourth, the book grapples with different approaches to contain financial crime. These include improved intelligence capacity and increased enforcement action to deter against Canadian jurisdictions being leveraged to perpetrate global financial crime. But what is the intended effect: to capture and possibly return financial proceeds of crime, or is it to trap (prevent movement of) the proceeds so they lose their value? The book concludes with recommendations related to financial crime from the perspective of Canadian federalism. In particular, it focuses on striking a better balance between democratic imperatives of financial secrecy and combating the global financial enablers of a panoply of heinous local crimes.

The Problem: Financial Crime in the Canadian Federation

Financial crime in its many forms is shorthand: including but not limited to predicate offences, money laundering, and terrorist financing (King, Walker, and Gurulé 2018), aggressive tax avoidance (Zucman 2015; Saez and Zucman 2019; Harrington 2020), and corruption (Shelley 2014). Terrorist financing falls outside the scope of this volume.[1] By contrast, tax evasion and avoidance are a recurring theme.[2]

For a brief explanation of the core concept that informs this book, the Cullen Commission on Money Laundering in British Columbia (herein referred to as the Cullen Commission) quotes the co-authors of this introduction:

Money laundering requires moving value acquired as the result of a crime (the "predicate offence") to a setting in which the criminals can use it freely; in other words, money laundering tries to break the connection between the crime and the use of the value it produced. Using a chain (or better still a network) of movements makes it more difficult to find and demonstrate the connection. There is a fundamental asymmetry between criminals and law enforcement because adding more complexity to the chain is relatively easy for criminals but disproportionately increases the effort to follow the chain for law enforcement. Each link in the chain is detectable in principle because the movement of value creates data that can be captured and analyzed using data-analytic techniques. However, there are several kinds of links that do not leave a trace, and so break the chain required to prosecute the offence of money laundering (Cullen 2022, 93).

FINTRAC summarizes a variety of forms money laundering can take (Table 1.1). The money laundering regime is generally premised on precursor crime. The conventional money laundering model has criminals place their ill-gotten gains in the financial system, concealing their origins by layering them, and then integrating the cleaned money back into the financial system. Transnational financial crime leverages money laundering as a business to obfuscate financial flows across jurisdictions. Financial intelligence units (FIUs) tend to limit their lens to their respective state jurisdiction. Professional money launderers – aided and abetted by accountants, lawyers, tax planners, real estate agents, etc. – specialize in making flows and transactions appear perfectly legal to authorities in any one jurisdiction. Only the transnational combination of patterns is suspicious, but because mandates tend to end at state borders, agencies remain oblivious to global deviant flows.

Transnational in character, financial crime has global reach: it enables authoritarianism, human rights abuses on a vast scale, and state capture by corrupt elites and transnational criminals. Financial crime enables malevolent actors, ranging from kingpins in drug trafficking organizations to kleptocrats and state officials, intent on evading international sanctions. It shifts economic power from the market, government, and citizens to criminals. In today's global economy, countries whose financial reputation is tarnished find it difficult to obtain loans and attract foreign investment.

In the words of Canada's former Minister of Finance Bill Morneau testifying before a committee of Parliament: "To put it bluntly, these things [money laundering and terrorist financing] are a threat to the safety and security of Canadians" (Standing Committee of Finance 2018). Indeed, financial crime poses just as great a threat to national security as crimes that receive far more attention and resources from government, law enforcement, and intelligence: financial crime and its precursors inflict extensive social harms on society's most vulnerable in local communities across the country on a daily basis. Insofar as financial crime erodes trust,

Table 1.1: Types of Money Laundering

Structuring and Smurfing

- Cash purchases by one or many individuals of Electronic Fund Transfers (EFTs) that fall under the reporting threshold.
- Currency exchanges under $10,000 from CAD to USD or vice versa.
- Cash purchase of money orders or bank drafts under $1,000 (which does not require identification) that are payable to third parties.
- Depositing a large number of $20 bills totaling under $10,000.

Refining

- Exchanging small-denomination bills for larger ones (e.g., $20 bills for $100 bills).

Commingling

- Financial transactions suspected to be a mix of legitimate business revenue and criminal proceeds.
- Businesses acting as fronts to make financial transactions appear more legitimate, often indicated by multiple entities sharing a common address.
- Holding numerous business bank accounts and conducting various transfers between accounts; funds are then moved to one account and bank drafts are purchased.

Source: FINTRAC (2019).

the economic and political power wielded by financial crime weakens the social fabric, collective ethical standards, rule of law, and ultimately undermines democratic institutions. Its precursors undermine the lives of ordinary people, the integrity of businesses, the economic prosperity, the government, and trust in the rule of law. That is, it incurs social and political costs that cut to the very heart of democratic values. Organized financial crime infiltrates financial and political institutions. It acquires control of large sectors of the economy through investment or bribes to public and government officials. It enables the underground economy, which undermines taxation, customs control, the financial system, rule of law, and raises questions of credibility and transparency. That, in turn, diminishes the tax revenue collected by the government, widens the tax gap (Department of Finance Canada 2023; Canada Revenue Agency 2021), and undermines the government's capacity to provide welfare to its citizens, which ultimately weakens the foundations of democracy.

Canada is a preferred destination to launder ill-gotten gains with impunity. Numerous investigations that ultimately went nowhere have revealed weak legislation and an under-resourced enforcement regime that is manifestly not fit for purpose. Chances of getting caught are almost nil, civil and criminal asset forfeiture is weak, and penalties are negligible. That is the gist from a panoply of recent public revelations, studies, commissions, and inquiries about financial crime in Canada, its expanse and prominence. Canada lacks in interagency, interdepartmental, and international cooperation, coordination, and collaboration. Government (in) action is complicated by intergovernmental governance and asymmetries that are a function of Canada's federal system.

Data and Evidence: Financial Crime in Canada

Globalization has proven an accelerant for financial crime (Legrand and Leuprecht 2021). Criminals adapt their strategies according to emerging economic trends to turn a profit and avoid detection by law enforcement (Dupuis and Gleason 2021). Ergo, financial crime is notoriously difficult to measure: It is illicit and, therefore, opaque. It is often disguised as legitimate in appearance and only a full picture of associated transnational transactions reveals their illicit nature and criminal intent (Leuprecht et al. 2019). In short, financial crime in Canada is a mystery: although endemic, we know little about it. Unless, and until that changes, behaviour, thinking, and discourse about financial crime are unlikely to change.

The Cullen Commission was the most comprehensive effort yet to pull back the curtain. Media reports of bags of cash being laundered in casinos – allegedly due to weak cash controls – initially led the provincial government to commission Peter German (a contributor to this volume) to author reports on the gambling and real estate sectors respectively. Subsequent video capture of those bags of cash led the government to answer political messaging (by BC's provincial political opposition) by appointing a commission. However, the provenance of the hockey bags of currency that were so prominently promoted by the media around 2018 has never been definitively determined. The locally generated cash was likely part of a cross border value transfer involving drugs, precursor chemicals, and wealthy gamblers.

The Cullen Commission heard extensive evidence but was unable to quantify the volume of money laundering other than to speculate that it was significant and to affirm Professor Langdale's theory about a "Vancouver Model" explaining the triangular movement of money that filters overseas and domestic funds into Vancouver's real estate (German 2021; Sanger 2019). In 2016, $36.8 billion of residential real estate changed hands in Vancouver's lower mainland. In 2019, 11 percent of condos in Metro Vancouver were owned by non-resident investors (Canada Mortgage and Housing Corporation 2019). There are two memos in the second German report from the RCMP responding to media reports about $1 billion being laundered through BC real estate. Although $1 billion would be too small an amount to distort Vancouver's housing market upwards, where retail markets for illicit trade are richer – as the Cullen Commission substantiates for Vancouver – the impact is stronger.

Not to put too fine a point on just how complex and understudied the problem is, and how inconclusive the underlying evidence, the Cullen Commission's *Final Report*, released in June 2022, comprises more than 1,800 pages. It postulates pervasive money laundering in real estate and gaming, along with its enablers in financial institutions, and the corporate and professional sectors. The 101 recommendations encourage governments, law enforcement, regulators, and professions to take strong and decisive action (Cullen 2022). Justice Cullen's report concludes that Canada's intelligence and law enforcement posture along with the federal anti-money laundering (AML) regime is woefully inadequate.

The Politics of Financial Crime in Canada

Since 1989 the Financial Action Task Force (FATF) has been the driver behind multilateral standards that have given rise to global anti-money laundering practices. Over 200 countries around the world have since committed to the FATF's recommendations – but much of the system is more performative than effective. The system is messy, complicated, and inchoate. How good are standards and their implementation really when global financial crime remains pervasive? At best, FATF sets minimum standards; a bar too low for any country that is serious about curtailing financial crime. To get serious about financial crime, Canada would need to go well beyond FATF.

Yet, Canada is struggling even to do the bare minimum. Between 2011 and 2015 Canadian authorities only led thirty-five prosecutions and obtained twelve convictions of single-case money laundering cases (FATF 2016, 50, Table 6). Civil forfeiture has been a persistent challenge: In 2023, the British Columbia Court of Appeal overturned a decision by a trial court and ordered the forfeiture of three Hells Angels clubhouses, in a case that started in 2007 and is likely to continue on to the Supreme Court of Canada (Simser 2023). Law enforcement and prosecutorial agencies are seemingly unable to turn copious intelligence produced by the Financial Transactions and Reports Analysis Centre of Canada (FINTRAC) into criminal intelligence that meets the requisite evidentiary threshold.

Few countries exceed the FATF standards; one reason for this is that financial institutions want to remain competitive with those in other jurisdictions in attracting clients and turning a profit. There is resistance to FATF raising its standards as that increases compliance costs to financial institutions. Canada's compliance system, for instance, is already quite expensive: private industry spends roughly $6.8 billion a year on compliance. The FATF's approach has been to raise standards globally and conduct Mutual Evaluation Reports to pressure each country on technical standards *and* how effective a country has been at implementing them. In effect, special interest groups and professionals pressure governments to slow-roll or not implement reforms as, for instance, has long been the case for beneficial ownership registries in Canada (Kenney 2022). Their campaign for privacy on corporate opacity for sometimes legitimate clients thus inadvertently bolsters organized crime, kleptocrats, tax evaders, and the like.

Structure of the Book

The book has five sections: enablers of financial crime, persistent failures, emerging issues in financial crime, containing financial crime, and financial crime in Canadian federalism.

The first section addresses financial crime's enablers by way of critical introductions to Canadian federalism. Peter German's chapter surveys what makes Canada so hospitable and attractive to transnational organized criminals. German explores why understanding money laundering is important to every Canadian and its manifestation in everyday life. He addresses why money laundering is essential to the success of organized criminal groups and corrupt regimes while at the same time posing a major risk of detection for these groups. The chapter delves into the nature of the laundromat in Canada. It outlines money laundering in the context of Canadian organized crime, what the laundromat looks like, and how it can be exploited by intelligence, law enforcement, and government to take down the intended beneficiaries: transnational organized criminal groups.

The late Arthur Cockfield's chapter on tax evasion and aggressive tax avoidance – a posthumous publication that was written before his passing – reviews financial data leaks. These are among the few threads of evidence on financial crime in Canada and abroad, which Cockfield knew intimately because he was repeatedly called on as an advisory by the International Council of Investigative Journalists. Cockfield's contribution on offshore tax evasion and international money laundering summarizes the main revelations associated with Canada. He illustrates typologies of cross-border structures, the role of professionals such as lawyers in creating the structures in the first place, and how the greatest beneficiaries of the offshore world are the ultra-rich, who engage in aggressive tax avoidance by stashing their fortunes in tax havens. He touches on related Canadian reforms with an emphasis on global tax transparency measures and concludes by noting some of the empirical, methodological, and theoretical challenges associated with using leaked data.

Christian Leuprecht and Jamie Ferrill broach the state of financial crime in Canada. The chapter lays out the implications of money laundering, including discussions surrounding the global standards set by the FATF and initiatives specific to Canada's anti-money laundering and counter-terrorism financing regime. For purposes of illustration, their critical case study draws on federal and provincial enforcement measures against contraband tobacco and cigarettes, illuminating the vast sums of money the illicit trade generates that need to be laundered. It compares enforcement efforts among select provinces and contrasts Canadian efforts with those in the United States before offering an international assessment of the incentives that drive the illicit trade in contraband and associated money laundering. The chapter finds that in theory there are some efforts by federal and provincial governments to address the identified problems. In practice, lacklustre results are a function of meagre resources and insufficient policy attention devoted to the issue.

Sanaa Ahmed offers a critical assessment of the Canadian state's vociferous, publicly articulated opposition to money laundering against the country's growing reputation as a premier money laundering destination. Ahmed interrogates the seeming disconnect between the state's averred commitments and actually delivering on them. If the state is indeed opposed to laundering, why isn't it able to impede, let alone contain, the phenomenon? This chapter contends that money laundering persists because the state is materially invested in its occurrence. She addresses factors that allow the Canadian state seemingly to tighten the screws while benefitting materially from lax regulation: running with the hare, hunting with the hounds.

The section that follows examines persistent failures and provides critical perspectives on federal and provincial intelligence and enforcement. Denis Meunier asks: is Canada a leader or laggard in combatting money laundering? He links Canada's federal, provincial, territorial, and private-sector efforts to international standards to prevent, detect, investigate, prosecute, and recover assets from money laundering activities. While "following the money" has been the mantra in the global fight against money laundering, states the world over are falling well short. FATF standards have created a global framework for combating money laundering, terrorist financing, and proliferation, but gaps and vulnerabilities are aplenty. These are exacerbated by Canada's own shortfalls in meeting those standards, especially lack of transparency of beneficial owners of corporations and trusts. Meunier identifies key gaps for the FATF and Canada to address and measures the FATF and Canada could adopt to do better.

Garry Clement recounts money laundering investigations in Canada from 1982 to the present. Illustrating this history with stories from earlier eras, he explains the impetus for legislative changes regarding the proceeds of crime. Drawing on his extensive experience in the public and private sectors, he shows how Canada has failed to maintain a commitment to ensuring effective, efficient, and proactive money laundering enforcement. Clement's suggestions to improve practices in Canada come with a stark warning: the government must recognize that a failure to demonstrate resolve to combat organized crime activities, notably money laundering, further enshrines Canada's reputation as a weak link in the enforcement chain among democratic countries.

Is it possible to have an effective money laundering enforcement regime without a strong administrative regulator? Katarzyna (Kasia) McNaughton's chapter casts doubt. Based on data gathered as part of her comparative dissertation of financial intelligence units (FIUs) across different jurisdictions, the chapter investigates the origins, structure, and limitations of the Financial Transactions and Reports Analysis Centre of Canada (FINTRAC) in the Canadian anti-money laundering framework. Her contribution is based on legal and content analysis of publicly available sources and supported by data obtained through fieldwork that included extensive semi-structured interviews. FINTRAC was designed as an administrative (rather than an investigative) FIU, with a legal mandate that has been narrowly defined and construed, which makes FINTRAC an outlier among its international peers, not only in the way it is structured but, compared to the US or UK for instance. The chapter raises serious questions about the effectiveness of a Canadian financial intelligence regime that generates very few money laundering charges, prosecutions, and convictions.

The next section addresses emerging Issues in financial crime, focusing on challenges in multilevel governance. Caroline Dugas, Pierre-Luc Pomerleau, and David Maimon seek to explain money laundering activities through underground banking operations within the Canadian context, while discussing the modus operandi of criminal organizations that employ casinos and real estate transactions to support these illegal activities. The chapter identifies the Toronto and Vancouver regions as scenes of serious investigations of illegal activities and underground banking structures, focusing on the E-Pirate project and Project Collector. Moreover, it shares various recommendations from both scholars and practitioners to reduce the use of underground banking for criminal activities.

John Cassara examines the least understood, recognized, and enforced money laundering methodology: trade-based money laundering (TBML). He provides a definition of TBML, explores the magnitude of the problem, the variety of ways it poses a threat, and the various ways it is carried out. Usefully providing examples and case studies, he provides insight into the incredibly insidious nature of TBML along with current countermeasures and approaches to fighting it, including a focus on data and technology affordances. Linking to the observations and findings of the Cullen Commission, the chapter explores the vulnerabilities specific to Canada and British Columbia highlighting capital flight, the black market peso exchange, and misuse of the international gold, precious metals, diamonds, and gems industries. Finally, eight recommendations are put forward to tackle this widespread threat.

Todd Hataley and Jamie Ferrill discuss the potential for the Canada–United States trade stream to be exploited by organized crime by investigating the intersection of TBML with organized crime (OC). By exploring the potential links between OC and the Canada–United States cross-border trade stream, the chapter illuminates vulnerabilities in the trade stream. Just as the trade stream has access points that can be exploited, OC have certain characteristics and tactics that would draw them towards TBML as a form of money laundering. The chapter finds that public-private partnerships, advancing the study and investigation of TBML, and a better understanding of the evolution of OC tactics and methodologies in terms of TBML will be critical to effective enforcement activity.

Concluding this section, Stephen Schneider then explores two interrelated fields within the study of organized crime. The first is concerned with the ongoing debate over the nature, scope, and very existence of task specialization within organized crime groups and mafia-style criminal organizations specifically. The second is related to the growing literature concerned with particular tasks carried out by what has been variously called the "professional money launderer," the "money laundering specialist," or the "third-party money launderer." This chapter explores both of these issues by examining a Canadian case study: the Montréal Mafia, in which members and associates appear to specialize in money laundering. While these individuals were instrumental in laundering the vast illicit proceeds generated by the Montréal Mafia, they were also involved in revenue-generating crimes such as gambling, loansharking, market manipulation, and drug trafficking.

The following section looks at containing financial crime, focusing on innovation in multilevel governance. Caitlyn Jenkins, Christian Leuprecht, and Rhianna Hamilton apply socio-technical systems theory to crypto-laundering analysis and utilize this lens to inform analysis and policy recommendations as they pertain to Canada's crypto-laundering regime. The chapter provides an overview of how current Canadian investigative agency and regulatory body responses have responded to crypto-laundering using socio-technical systems thinking as a basis. This chapter finds that the main impediments to effective crypto-laundering mitigation within the Canadian regime are lacking mechanisms to engage in multi-jurisdictional investigations made increasingly essential by the transnational and non-state-based nature of crypto-laundering. It identifies that there is a broader need for technical understanding of how cryptocurrency operates to see any substantial change in our ability to uncover and effectively prosecute cases.

Pamela Simpson and Cameron Field address public-private partnership opportunities in the Canadian anti-money laundering and regulatory landscape. They detail information-sharing frameworks within public-private partnerships and explore the strengths and weaknesses of information-sharing processes within identified partnerships. The chapter then proposes international frameworks that Canada could adopt to enhance information-sharing processes within public-private partnerships, specifically drawing on the American examples of the Bank Secrecy Act and sections of the PATRIOT Act. With the lens on a relatively new public-private partnership, the Counter Illicit Finance Alliance of British Columbia (CIFA-BC), the chapter identifies certain strengths of such partnerships and provides recommendations to enhance the efficiency and quality of data shared within them.

Michelle Gallant's chapter provides novel suggestions regarding how provincial and territorial law could inform a global money laundering strategy. Drawing specifically on provincial civil forfeiture regimes, provincial piercings of corporate opacity, and the regulation of lawyers, the chapter links these pieces to the realization of transnational aspirations. Canada's domestic approach towards money laundering continues to be shaped by transnational money laundering ordering and the need to align domestic regulation with precepts forged in international forums, which gives rise to the importance of exploring the provincial pieces of the global strategy.

The final section addresses financial crime in Canadian federalism, exploring federal and provincial policy options. Here, Jeffrey Simser examines Canada's intergovernmental policy response to money laundering. The chapter begins by illuminating some of Canada's money laundering vulnerabilities. To this end, it offers an explanation of the Vancouver Model: the money laundering and Communist Party of China espionage-meets-influence-meets-corruption typology that in many ways gave birth to the Cullen Commission. His chapter explains how vast amounts of money have been laundered through an informal value transfer system, specifically targeting casinos in British Columbia. It then goes on to outline prevention and detection via policy devices, followed by examining the remedial and enforcement mechanisms that can aid in investigating and disrupting money laundering. Finally, policy options are proposed. The chapter highlights the importance of information gateways and intergovernmental policy interactions, aptly stating that policy responses are only as strong as the system as a whole.

Conclusion

Financial crime is highly adaptive and dynamic. It reaches across a range of activities and actors: assets that are hidden offshore, the public health crisis created by drug addiction, threats to democratic institutions, fraud and cyber threats faced by small business and ordinary citizens, and violent extremism in the form of terrorism. The sheer magnitude of the economic power that accrues from financial crime spawns corrosive effects across the globe. With statutory reviews and an international evaluation on the horizon, there is a window of opportunity for the Government of Canada to become an agent of reform and change.

Financial crime undermines Canada's democratic values and the rule of law, Canada's standing in the international community, and Canada's place in the global economy. The book frames this problem in terms of threats that financial criminals pose to Canadian society, including to the tax and financial systems, and international trade. The Cullen Commission, the Rouleau Emergencies Act Inquiry (2022), and Québec's Charbonneau Commission (2015) have shed light on systemic inadequacies, such as ponderous bureaucratic inaction, an unfit-for-purpose regulatory, monitoring, and reporting system, as well as myriad cracks in the system that criminals and their enablers are exploiting. A recurring theme across the chapters is the extent to which current practices, processes, legislation, and/or organizations that are meant to tackle financial crime in Canada are insufficient and inefficient.

A robust anti-financial crime architecture is premised on resolve and leadership by government and the private sector. Indeed, recent sanctions on Russian financial interests and assets suggest that deterring financial crime is a matter of political will: enacting legislation and enforcing it, and a better balance between financial intelligence administration and production, and actionable evidence and effective money laundering enforcement capacity. Reporting requirements imposed on private businesses, including banks, are stringent, costly, and somewhat performative. That problem is not uniquely Canadian. For reporting entities around the world, monitoring and compliance is a net cost; so, it is in their best interest to do what they must to meet their obligations and protect their reputation, not necessarily what they could or should do.

By mapping the legislative and regulatory challenges that Canada faces, this book hopes to lower sunk costs that impede timely, effective, and efficient decision-making. Canada's fight against financial crime begins at home: with the federal and provincial governments. The bewildering number of Canadian governments, agencies, and organizations that supposedly have a mandate to deal with matters of financial crime is remarkable: there are thirteen (as detailed in Jeffrey Simser's conclusion to this volume). They are complemented by provincial, territorial, and local authorities, including governments, crown attorneys, courts, and law enforcement agencies as well as the private sector. This volume covers financial crime across the Canadian federation, situating federal, provincial, local, intergovernmental, and public-private multilevel governance in the broader global context of a phenomenon that is inextricably transnational.

Much can be done to mitigate the extensive and persistent harm that financial crime causes; that is, to detect, disrupt, and investigate illicit in-, out-, and through-flows and enhance the capacity to arrest and prosecute financial criminals to interdict and deter the flow of dirty money and confiscate ill-gotten gains. The Cullen Commission reinforced that the federal regime is left wanting, with vast financial intelligence production that produces limited results, and public-private cooperation that is lacking. Between 2019 and 2021, more than $220 million was provided by the federal government to increase resourcing for law enforcement, enable inter-agency cooperation and collaboration, and revise legislation to address current challenges. Funding increases for FINTRAC and to a Public Safety Canada Financial Crime Coordination Centre (FC3) amounts to a tacit endorsement of the stakes this book raises. FC3 is a five-year pilot to coordinate intelligence and law enforcement personnel to tackle significant financial crime threats. Still, these measures are distressingly homeopathic compared to how entrenched and insidious the problem of financial crime is in Canada.

Deficiencies identified by Beare and Schneider in their 2007 book persist: a dearth of useful data to inform effective AML programs that could contain financial crime to preserve the integrity of businesses and institutions. Since Beare and Schneider's book, globalization, blockchain technology, and the advent of cryptocurrency have been obscuring financial crime further (Leuprecht, Jenkins, and Hamilton 2022; Tiwari, Ferrill and Mehrotra 2022).

Yet, law enforcement agencies need to be appropriately postured to parlay financial intelligence into actionable criminal intelligence and collect evidence for disruption and possible prosecution. Canada also needs to be more agile: prosecution is costly and difficult. Criminal and civil asset forfeiture should, in principle, be much easier, but that is a function of effective processes and practices surrounding financial and criminal intelligence, all of which Cullen and the FATF have flagged. FINTRAC and law enforcement need timely access to reliable beneficial ownership information of trusts and corporations, which is (as of yet) unavailable federally and across the thirteen provincial and territorial jurisdictions (see Gallant's chapter in this volume). As governments grapple with financial crime, better data collection and funded research helps policy makers understand the challenges to be met. Research and disclosures inform evidence-based solutions, which in turn close key information gaps to enable timely, effective, and efficient decision-making.

Together, these chapters explore the insidious nature of money laundering on a global scale, with a discrete focus on the inner workings of domestic policy and practice. Politicians, practitioners, and academics the world over are coming to the realization that money laundering is a sinister national security threat with implications for the country's economic and social well-being. The time is ripe for policy and legislative changes, improvements to practice, and an increase in capabilities across all sectors and levels of government to tackle it.

Notes

1 Two decades ago, jurisdictions the world over hastily grafted terrorist financing onto extant money laundering legislation. That, however, has proven tenuous: Money laundering and terrorist financing operate according to different logics. While money laundering has been a focus of law enforcement for over a century, the United Nations' Palermo Convention in 2000 was a shotgun wedding between money laundering and terrorist financing. After 2001, terrorist financing was added to the FATF remit.

2 Aggressive tax avoidance blurs the lines of illegality and criminality. It refers to taxpayers who not only spend lavishly to comply with the law – a tax increase on high-income earners brought in by the federal Liberal government was supposed to raise $38 billion in new tax revenue, but tax receipts actually declined by $4 billion as a result – but also aggressively push the boundaries

to avoid meeting their obligations. How much people are required to pay predictably has behavioural consequences: The top 1 percent in Canada pay 21 percent of all income tax collected, the top 10 percent pay 53 percent (Statistics Canada 2022). Tax evasion erodes public services and shifts a fiscal burden on wage earners whose packets are deducted at source.

References

Andreas, P. 2004. "Review: Illicit International Political Economy: The Clandestine Side of Globalization." *Review of International Political Economy* 11, no. 3: 641–652. https://www.tandfonline.com/doi/abs/10.1080/09692290420 00252936.

Beare, M., and S. Schneider. 2007. *Money Laundering in Canada: Chasing of Dirty and Dangerous Dollars.* Toronto: University of Toronto Press.

Canada Mortgage and Housing Corporation. 2019. New Insights on Non-resident Ownership and Participation in BC, ON and NS Housing Markets.

Canada Revenue Agency. 2021. *Overall Federal Tax Gap Report: Estimates and Key Findings for Non-Compliance, Tax Years 2014 to 2018.*

Charbonneau, F., and R. Lachance. 2015. *Rapport final de la commission d'enquête sur l'octroi et la gestion des contrats publics dans l'industrie de la construction.* http://www.bv.transports.gouv.qc.ca/mono/1175409.pdf.

Cooper, S. 2021. *Wilful Blindness: How a Network of Narcos, Tycoons and CCP Agents Infiltrated the West.* Toronto: Optimum Publishing International.

Cullen, A. 2022. Commission of Inquiry into Money Laundering in British Colombia. Final Report. Vancouver: Cullen Commission. https://cullencommission.ca/files/reports/CullenCommission-FinalReport-Full.pdf.

Department of Finance Canada. 2023. Updated Assessment of Inherent Risks of Money Laundering and Terrorist Financing Canada. https://www.canada.ca/en/department-finance/programs/financial-sector-policy/updated-assessment-inherent-risks-money-laundering-terrorist-financing-canada.html.

Drezner, D. W., H. Farrell, and A. L. Newman. 2021. *The Uses and Abuses of Weaponized Interdependence.* Washington, DC: Brookings.

Dupuis, D., and K. Gleason. 2021. "Money Laundering with Cryptocurrency: Open Doors and the Regulatory Dialectic." *Journal of Financial Crime* 28, no. 1: 60–74. doi: 10.1108/JFC-06-2020-0113.

Financial Action Task Force (FATF). 2016. *Mutual Evaluation Report: Canada.* https://www.fatf-gafi.org/media/fatf/documents/reports/mer4/MER-Canada-2016.pdf.

German, P. 2021. "Editorial." *Journal of Money Laundering Control* 24, no. 2: 213–214, https://doi.org/10.1108/JMLC-01-2021-0004.

Harrington, B. 2020. *Capital without Borders: Wealth Management and the One Percent.* Cambridge, MA: Harvard University Press.

Hudson, R. 2005. *Economic Geographies: Circuits, Flows and Spaces.* Sage: London.

———. 2013. "Thinking through the Relationships between Legal and Illegal Activities and Economies: Spaces, Flows and Pathways." *Journal of Economic Geography* 14, no. 4: 775–795.

———. 2019. "Economic Geographies of the (Il)Legal and the (Il)Licit." In *A Research Agenda for Global Crime*, 1–27. Cheltenham: Edward Elgar Publishing. https://doi.org/10.4337/9781786438676.00007.

Kenney, M. 2022. "Businesses Deserve Privacy, Too: The Case Against Public Registers for Company Ownership." *The Globe and Mail*, 22 December. https://www.theglobeandmail.com/business/commentary/article-businesses-deserve-privacy-too-the-case-against-public-registers-for/.

Kessler, M., and N. Borst. 2013. "Did China Really Lose $3.75 Trillion in Illicit Financial Flows?" Washington, DC: Peterson Institute for International Economics. https://www.piie.com/blogs/china-economic-watch/did-china-really-lose-375-trillion-illicit-financial-flows.

King, C., C. Walker, and J. Gurulé. 2018. *The Palgrave Handbook of Criminal and Terrorism Financing Law.* Cham: Springer.

Legrand, T., and C. Leuprecht. 2021. "Securing Cross-Border Collaboration: Transgovernmental Enforcement Networks, Organized Crime and Illicit International Political Economy." *Policy and Society* 40, no. 4: 565–586. https://doi.org/10.1080/14494035.2021.1975216.

Leuprecht, C., A. Cockfield, P. Simpson, and M. Haseeb. 2019. "Tracking Transnational Terrorist Resourcing Nodes and Networks." *Florida State University Law Review* 46, no. 2: 289–344. https://qspace.library.queensu.ca/handle/1974/29837.

Leuprecht, C., C. Jenkins, and R. Hamilton. 2022. "Virtual Money Laundering: Policy Implications of the Proliferation in the Illicit Use of Crytocurrency." *Journal of Financial Crime*, September 19. https://www.emerald.com/insight/content/doi/10.1108/JFC-07-2022-0161/full/html.

Rouleau, P. S. 2022. *Report of the Public Inquiry into the 2022 Public Order Emergency.* Ottawa. https://publicorderemergencycommission.ca/final-report/.

Ryner, J. M. 2006. "International Political Economy: Beyond the Poststructuralist/Historical Materialist Dichotomy." In *International Political Economy and Poststructural Politics*, edited by M. De Goede, 139–156. London: Palgrave Macmillan.

Saez, E., and G. Zucman. 2019. *The Triumph of Injustice: How the Rich Dodge Taxes and How to Make Them Pay.* New York: W.W. Norton.

Sanger, T. 2019. Opacity - Why Criminals Love Canadian Real Estate. Transparency International. https://static1.squarespace.com/static/5df7c3de2e4d3d3f-ce16c185/t/5e1e357c8460a6689db1c5f8/1579038078911/opacity.pdf.

Shelley, L. 2014. *Dirty Entanglements: Corruption, Crime and Terrorism.* Cambridge: Cambridge University Press.

————. 2018. *Dark Commerce: How a New Illicit Economy is Threatening Our Future*. Princeton: Princeton University Press.

Simser, J. 2023. *Civil Forfeiture in Canada*. Toronto: Canada Law Book.

Standing Committee of Finance, Canada. 2018. Meeting No. 163, June 20. https://parlvu.parl.gc.ca/Harmony/en/PowerBrowser/PowerBrowserV2/20180620/-1/29632.

Statistics Canada. 2022. *High Income Tax Filers in Canada*. https://www150.statcan.gc.ca/t1/tbl1/en/tv.action?pid=1110005501&pickMembers%5B0%5D=1.1&pickMembers%5B1%5D=3.5&cubeTimeFrame.startYear=2016&cubeTimeFrame.endYear=2020&referencePeriods=20160101%2C20200101.

Teichmann, F. M. J. 2017. "Twelve Methods of Money Laundering." *Journal of Money Laundering Control* 20, no. 2: 130–137. https://doi.org/10.1108/JMLC-05-2016-0018.

The High-Level Panel on International Financial Accountability Transparency and Integrity for Achieving the 2030 Agenda. 2020. *FACTI Panel Interim Report*. https://uploads-ssl.webflow.com/5e0bd9edab846816e263d633/5f6b-91b197c6c0d8904089c2_FACTI_Interim_Report_ExecutiveSummary.pdf.

Tiwari, M., J. Ferrill, and V. Mehrotra. 2022. "Using Graph Database Platforms to Fight Money Laundering: Advocating Large Scale Adoption." *Journal of Money Laundering Control*. [Ahead of print]. https://www.emerald.com/insight/content/doi/10.1108/JMLC-03-2022-0047/full/html.

World Economic Forum. 2015. "State of the Illicit Economy Briefing Papers." www3.weforum.org/docs/WEF_State_of_the_Illicit_Economy_2015_2.pdf.

Zucman, Gabriel. 2015. *The Hidden Wealth of Nations: The Scourge of Tax Havens*. Chicago: The University of Chicago Press.

Enabling Financial Crime: Critical Introductions to Canadian Federalism

2

Washing Money in the Canadian Laundromat

Peter M. German[1]

Canada is a vast country, spreading from Atlantic to Pacific to Arctic. It is sparsely populated by indigenous people and a mosaic of immigrants, who predominantly reside near its southern border. Living in one of the world's most desirable countries, Canadians can be a smug lot. They know they sit on a bounty of riches, including vast natural resources, plentiful lakes and oceans, a strong economy, and world class financial institutions. They possess democratic governments, a national health system, modern highways, strong educational institutions, and a diversity of religions, cultures, and ethnicities. They and their country are the envy of billions of people in today's world.

For many years, Canada punched above its weight in terms of diplomacy, peacekeeping, and international assistance. Canadian politicians occasionally lectured other nations about bad behaviour and their failure to uphold human rights. As a member of the Financial Action Task Force (FATF) and the Organisation for Economic Co-operation and Development (OECD), Canada has participated in the shunning and listing of countries deemed not to be doing their share in terms of money laundering prevention. Nevertheless, Canada's own scorecard is not without blemish.

However, before considering Canada's record in combatting money laundering, it is important to first understand organized crime and why Canada presents such an appealing and welcoming place for criminals to live and play. It is also important to understand why money laundering is important to every Canadian and how it manifests itself in daily lives.

Transnational Organized Crime

In 1876, Canada's minister of justice stood up in the House of Commons and declared that a "carnival of crime [was] beginning on our border" (Corbett 1990). "Organized crime" and "transnational organized crime" were not part of the lexicon of the day. For Edward Blake it was those perfidious Americans who seemed always to be ignoring the international border by allowing pernicious groups such as the whiskey traders in the west and the Fenians in the east to violate Canadian sovereignty.

Little could Blake have imagined that the horse and buggy world of his day would give rise to a global village in which airplanes crisscrossed the skies and an invisible internet snaked around the world, that international travel would be described in terms of hours, not weeks, and that money would be transmitted between continents in a series of zeros and ones.

More than 100 years after Blake's prophetic statement, the Honourable Ray Hnatyshyn, later a governor general of Canada but then its minister of justice, stood in the same House of Commons and stated:

> Increasingly, we are seeing the effects of criminal organizations operating both from within and without this country that are totally dedicated to the commission of crime for profit. These organizations take advantage of modern communications, transportation, and corporate structure to frustrate the reach of national legal systems to amass illicit and illegal wealth. (House of Commons Debates 1987, 8888)

Hnatyshyn's pronouncement belayed a foreboding of what was to come. When he spoke in 1987, Canadians had become much more mobile than in the past; however, the internet had yet to reach the public domain, social media was not part of the discourse, and letters were still the preferred method of communication. Ten years later, everything had changed. Courier companies competed with Canada Post, facsimile machines had replaced Telex machines, personal computers were rolling out to the masses, word processing software had taken hold, and most of all, the internet had become a reality. This evolution was just as pronounced in the criminal underworld, particularly that of financial crime.

Those who studied organized crime as part of a criminology program pre-1990, may as well shelve their hardback textbook under the history category or place it in the bin for the next library book sale. Organized crime has adapted well to the new world. Their traditional structures have given way to modern enterprises: organizations have diversified and adapted, intense rivalry between groups has increasingly been replaced by cooperation and collaboration, domestic boundaries have been cast aside, and technology has been embraced to instantaneously hide their identity.

Compartmentalization of organized crime into traditional groups based upon their geographic, cultural, or ethnic origins, such as East European, Russian, Asian, Chinese, Iranian, Vietnamese, Italian, or Irish, is fast disappearing, with integration being the watchword for many organized crime networks. This is particularly true when considering second and third generation gang members who retain fewer ties to their homeland than previous generations. It also conveniently ignores the reality that these organizations operate within Canada and are composed of Canadians. We even see crime groups that flaunt the fact they are Canadian, such as outlaw motorcycle gangs.

Although most crime groups may not be controlled from abroad, the existence of familial connections overseas does provide opportunities for collaboration with trusted networks of like-minded individuals, as well as a sanctuary from Canadian authorities should there be a need. Most importantly, organized crime groups which exist in ethnic diasporas can rely on established networks that are based on trust. Prime examples are the Cosa Nostra, the 'Ndrangheta, and Chinese Triads. It should never be assumed, however, that these organizations have the support of their diasporas. In fact, many of these groups prey upon people in their own communities.

Organized crime is not unique to one country, one race, one ethnicity, or even one continent. It is a worldwide phenomenon that, due to current technology and transportation systems, can operate internationally with relative ease. It knows no allegiance to the rule of law, is amorphous and increasingly not commodity specific.

Organized crime is about making money and using money for the benefit of the organization and its members. These groups develop allegiances wherever necessary to further this goal; with politicians, public servants, revolutionary groups, terrorist networks, other organized crime groups, and even ordinary citizens who wish to make a "quick dollar." Organized crime uses people as instruments, whether to procure, transport, or sell illegal substances, or to launder the proceeds of their crime.

When crime groups cross international borders they are referred to as transnational organized crime. The fact that they are international in scope necessitates a degree of sophistication which may not be the case for domestic groups. It is infinitely more difficult for law enforcement to track criminals outside of a country. Furthermore, criminal law is country-specific, such that transnational organized criminals are only prosecuted if they commit an offence against a nation's domestic laws.

Transnational organized crime groups are flexible and will continue to form and reform, while the response by governments typically operates with much less flexibility. Some forms of organized crime are quite complex; however, complexity can also lead to managerial difficulties for the syndicates and is not necessarily the preferred option. The ideal criminal enterprise is one that produces high value with low risk.

Transnational organized crime groups are not only a criminal threat but may also be a destabilizing force in the countries where they transact business. The threat level increases exponentially if the syndicate is linked to a terrorist group or carries out its activities at the behest of a rogue regime.

Organized crime is characterized by global linkages; the fluid and ever-changing nature of its operations; its sophistication, including a high degree of coordination, planning, technical knowledge, and business acumen; the global mobility of its members; and the financial strength of organizations which can cross with ease between legal and illegal markets. The infiltration of organized crime in overseas diasporas allows these syndicates to rapidly move into new markets and exploit vulnerabilities.

Many organized crime groups function like multi-national corporations, using transport and business networks to trade commodities such as methamphetamines, precursor chemicals, counterfeit goods, and illegal migrants, for cash and commodities. Asian and Middle Eastern criminal groups affiliate with European and North American groups to facilitate the flow of illegal commodities, with the profits being transferred via banks and money transfer services in Dubai, Hong Kong, London, and elsewhere. One constant among organized crime groups is the making of money, their raison d'être.

Today, this ability to transfer money in an instant to a correspondent party in a distant land, or to use a cryptocurrency machine to transfer virtual currency unseen by regulators or law enforcement, has helped transform the landscape. Nevertheless, certain key concepts continue to describe the process followed by criminals and their organizations when moving money.

Money Laundering

Most crime is committed for profit, and all but simple street crime will require that the proceeds of illegality be disguised in some fashion to allow the perpetrator to "clean" his or her dirty money. Money laundering is the term used to describe this process. It is a necessary element of the crime cycle, allowing criminals to process large sums of illegally obtained money. It is the "back office" of profit-driven crime and its objective "is to make it difficult if not impossible to trace funds back to their illegal or fraudulent source" (Bank of China 2015, para. 160). This is not easy, however, due to the sheer weight and bulk of cash, the risk of detection that cash poses, and the dangers created by transporting large sums.

The process of money laundering can be quite complex; however, for definitional purposes is almost always divided into three stages: placement of the dirty money in the legitimate financial system, layering the money by moving it through other financial vehicles to disguise its origin, and integrating it back into the legitimate economy. Each stage can manifest itself in a plethora of ways. The three stages are equated to the three cycles of washing and drying clothes, giving the word "laundering" a meaning quite unintended by its Latin origin, lavare, or to wash.

Placement the "wash cycle" has traditionally been the most vulnerable stage for money launderers because cash is a bulky commodity in large quantity. It generally occurs through over-the-counter deposits or exchanges at a bank, currency exchange, or other legitimate financial institution. If this process is structured, by using low-level members of criminal organizations to deposit or exchange relatively small amounts of money at various institutions, it is referred to as "smurfing" (Malarek 1989, 163).

Placement may also occur through back door deposits, or by using a legitimate business, such as a currency exchange, a travel agency, a casino, or virtually any cash-based enterprise, as a "front." In *R. v. Trac*, the Ontario Court of Appeal described placement as "the injection of cash generated through criminal activity into the legitimate, commercial mainstream through the deposit of that cash with a reputable deposit-taking institution" (*R. v. Trac 2013*, para. 84).

The layering stage, or "spin cycle," typically involves transferring funds from one financial vehicle to another, or through multiple layers of often complex financial transactions, in the hope of disguising their origin and thereby avoiding detection. This may involve the purchase and sale of assets, wiring money to anonymous accounts, the use of shell companies, investing in securities, or purchasing bank drafts or money orders, to name but a few of seemingly endless alternatives. Oftentimes moving money out of a jurisdiction, including internationally, occurs in the spin cycle.

In the integration stage, or "dry cycle," funds are repatriated or reintegrated without fear that their origin will be detected. This process can be relatively simple or as complex as human imagination and technology permit. The ultimate beneficiary may be the criminal actor, a crony, a family member, or a creditor and can involve the purchase of luxury goods, vehicles, boats, precious stones, or real estate, to name but a few.

The advent of the internet significantly affected the movement of legitimate and dirty money around the world, both domestically and internationally. In the short span of approximately twenty-five years, we have seen a never-ending series of new and innovative technologies which leverage the internet. These include personal computers, mobile phones, electronic funds transfers, automated cash dispensers, "cloud-based" applications and storage, remote servers, encrypted devices, and many others. Although the intent behind all these innovations is not new, that being the ability to communicate and transfer data, the rapidity of movement which they provide, represents a paradigmatic shift in how we transact business.

Organized Crime and Money Laundering

The trafficking of illegal drugs is a familiar topic to Canadians and likely the most relevant example to readers of the importance of money laundering to a criminal organization. Drug trafficking organizations are typically structured akin to a bureaucracy or a military hierarchy, with the head of the organization at the top of a pyramid and street-level dealers at the bottom. Complex trafficking organizations can in fact be bifurcated, with the drug sales handled quite independently from the proceeds of that activity; in essence, two parallel pyramids reporting to the same boss. Those at the bottom are disposable to the organization and often paid a pittance by comparison to the sales which they generate. These low-level traffickers are often referred to as "dial-a-dopers," neighborhood drug suppliers who respond to orders received by mobile phone, email, or text.

Although street-level drug sales can be accomplished using digital currency, cash remains the most prevalent form of payment, and $20 bills are the most common denomination (*R. v. Chan 2019*, para. 35). Cash must find its way into the financial system by being deposited in a bank or other financial institution or being exchanged at a cash-intensive business. Digital currency finds its way into the system much faster than cash and can therefore begin the layering process almost immediately.

Laundering the proceeds of drug trafficking is not an optional exercise for traffickers within a drug organization. This is because of the difference between the proceeds of crime and the profits of crime. These are not terms without distinction. In the context of a drug organization, every trafficker buys stock from a supplier who is generally one link higher in the organization. That supplier must be paid. In many, if not most cases, drugs are supplied on credit, meaning that the supplier waits for repayment. The street trafficker's profit can be as little as a few percentage points of the value of the drugs or may simply be an hourly wage.

Often the cash generated by drug sales will weigh more than the drugs it purchased. Depositing large sums of cash, particularly in denominations of $20, is difficult to do without raising suspicion. The methods by which drug traffickers seek to conceal or transfer funds or other valuable property vary over time. However, despite this fact and the onrush of technological advances, more traditional methods for the movement of money do not disappear. The following are the primary methods, or schemes used by drug traffickers to conceal or transfer funds or other valuable property in Canada.

Bulk movement of cash. The bulk movement of cash and other monetary instruments is the traditional means by which illegal monies are transferred between people and places. For example, a large quantity of money can be moved by car, truck, plane, cargo container, or mail. The route taken will generally be that of least resistance in terms of monitoring and detection. The downside to the bulk movement of money is the fact that cash is bulky and creates suspicion in large amounts. Furthermore, it poses potential safety risks. This can lead to the structuring of cash deposits, in which large sums of money are sub-divided and deposited by "smurfs" in multiple financial institutions, or accounts.

Cash-intensive businesses. Businesses that are cash-intensive offer a convenient venue for the placement of illegal funds. The key is to find a business that either does not have financial reporting requirements or where anti-money laundering regulatory scrutiny is low. This can include travel agencies, auction houses, vehicle and boat dealers, marijuana dispensaries, or even government offices which accept cash in payment of taxes and other charges.

Electronic funds transfer. Today, the inter-jurisdictional movement of money is largely accomplished through electronic funds transfers between financial institutions, and by the advent of a plethora of consumer-based services, such as e-transfers. These transfers utilize mainstream institutions and require that money has already entered the legitimate financial system. They operate with great speed and transactions are literally accomplished within seconds. They do, however, leave a "digital trail" which may be available to investigators, provided that the financial entity stores its records in Canada, or in another jurisdiction which is accessible to Canadian investigators.

Offshore havens. Funds obtained illegally are often moved to destinations outside Canada which contain bank secrecy laws that prevent foreign authorities from following the assets as they change form and location. The use of offshore company formation agents, accountants and attorneys facilitate the continued layering of these monies. The countries which serve as offshore havens can be large or small; however, the opaque nature of laws and their lip service or outright unwillingness to action international requests for information allows them to operate with a certain impunity.

Money service businesses (MSBs). Money transmitters exist throughout Canada. They permit an individual to send money to domestic or international destinations for a fee. The money moves with great speed. Many MSBs are standalone businesses, while others are contained within corner stores and other locations. All must be registered and file reports with Canada's financial intelligence agency, the Financial Transactions and Reporting Centre, although there is little enforcement of non-compliance with registering and reporting. Provincial licensing of MSBs is not required in Canadian provinces, other than in Québec.

Informal value transfer systems or underground banking. Unregistered MSBs, often located in ethnic communities with ties abroad, can effectuate a transfer of money without any actual movement of funds. These entities, often referred to as hawalas, informal remittance businesses, or underground or shadow bankers, are ancient in origin and operate based on familial or collegial ties between individuals in two countries, one of whom obtains funds from a client and arranges for a colleague in another country to deliver an equivalent amount, less a commission, to the same person or to his or her designate. The transactions occur after a phone call, a text message, or an email exchange between the shadow bankers. Informal records are maintained at both origin and destination and accounts are settled over time. These businesses are typically efficient and operate with great speed.

Cryptocurrency. Bitcoin and many other forms of cryptocurrency, sometimes referred to as virtual, digital, or electronic currency, offer a new and unparalleled opportunity to convert funds into digital cash, for retrieval elsewhere in the world. Cryptocurrency ATMs are found in many Canadian cities and abroad. Cryptocurrency can be used to fund point of sale and other transactions, both legal and illegal. The anonymity of their underlying technology makes them ideal conduits for the transfer of money. They operate with great speed and do not leave a readily accessible digital trail, making their entry and exit points, the inputting or receiving of cash, their principal vulnerabilities.

Trade-based activity. Inserting illegal commodities into the legal movement of trade can be accomplished in simple or complex ways. In its simplest form, it involves illegal cargo being included in a legal shipment. Variants include businesses paying for legitimate products or invoices with illegally obtained, or disguised funds. More complex forms include the insertion of illegally obtained money in trade through over- and under-invoicing, false invoicing, and similar commercial transactions. Recently, the purchase of luxury cars, with cash or other untraceable monetary payments, oftentimes for export, has highlighted this activity (German 2019, part 3).

In summary, the transfer of money through various financial vehicles and between jurisdictions is an effective strategy by which drug traffickers can launder the proceeds of their activity, with the intent of frustrating its recovery by authorities and individuals. There are numerous methodologies available, depending on the character of the funds, and the degree of anonymity and transactional speed required.

The Geopolitics of Money Laundering

Environmental factors play a significant role in terms of what opportunities are available to a person intent on laundering money or disguising a money trail. Canada is largely defined by its geography and climate. The country is primarily composed of a thin ribbon of people stretching for 4,400 miles from St. John's, Newfoundland to Victoria, BC. The east-west corridor defies economic sense, as Canada's trade is predominantly north-south with the United States. Seattle is a three-hour drive from Vancouver, Detroit is a bridge or tunnel away from Windsor, and Montréal is a few hours from New York's interstate highways.

The anomaly of Canadian geography is quite consistent, however, with its historical roots in the British and French empires, two colossi who fought for dominance over an unspoiled land of mountains, trees, lakes, and hardy Indigenous folk who had lived there for a millennium. Despite its artificial construct and harsh climate, Canadians have made their country work. In fact, its land mass is the second greatest of any country in the world and its border with the United States is the longest, undefended border in the world.

If we push past the gloss and beauty of Canada, we soon realize that what makes Canada a desirable place to live, also makes it desirable for organized crime, both domestic and international. Although the ingredients of this desirability differ according to region, the net result is the same.

As an example, Vancouver is a metropolitan area with a climate that is mild by comparison to most of Canada. While the great bulk of Canada lives under a blanket of snow for five months of the year, Vancouverites complain vehemently when they face more than a few days of snow during a winter season. Its airport and seaport facilitate travel and cargo shipments around the world, but primarily to the burgeoning markets of Asia. Vancouver possesses world-class banking, communications, and high-tech sectors. Large and long-standing diasporas are also present and provide traditional and familial ties to foreign nations. There is also a smorgasbord of financial service businesses, both regulated and unregulated, which provide services to clients, including the transmission of money. Most importantly, it sits directly above Canada's border with the United States.

All these factors, which make Vancouver a desirable place to live, also make it desirable for organized crime. To these, we can add a fair and comparatively liberal criminal justice system, an aversion to long prison sentences, and a slow and cumbersome investigative and prosecutorial process. The relevance of environmental factors is readily apparent when

we again examine the most obvious form of organized crime in Canada
– drug trafficking.

During the past decade, British Columbia witnessed large sums of
money, much of which was the proceeds of drug trafficking, being laundered through registered and unregistered MSBs. Some unregistered
transmitters served a dual function, doubling as a conduit for wealthy
people who wished to transfer large sums of money from Asia to Canada
but could not do so through traditional banking systems due to their
home country's currency restrictions (German 2018, ch. 20).

The Human Toll

Today, it is estimated that over 1,000 addicts die on the streets and in the
homes of Greater Vancouver every year due to overdoses, with no end in
sight. It is a shocking indictment of a society in which the average standard of living is among the highest in the world. The urgency of the problem is not lost on anyone who travels down Hastings Street as it meets
Main, but it can also be found in the suburbs and in smaller communities
east and north. The same can be said of most large Canadian cities and
of many remote locations.

The response to the ongoing drug crisis has largely moved away from
enforcement and supply reduction to finding medical solutions to drug
addiction, often referred to as harm reduction. That term, however, clearly implies that harm continues. Organized crime is resilient. As drugs are
legalized or made available without penalty, it will turn to more potent
drugs, cheaper drugs, more accessible drugs, or simply switch commodities.
Human trafficking and counterfeit goods are both lucrative alternatives.

The desire to be safe in one's home, places of work and worship, and
during leisure activity, is almost universal and resonates with municipali-
ties and their police departments. As a result, law enforcement invariably
prioritizes violent crime. It was not until recently that Canadians realized
the hidden toll that money laundering takes on lives. In British Columbia, a light was shone upon the money laundering problem by Attorney
General David Eby, who drew a connection between overdose deaths and

the illegal profits of drug enterprises (Smyth 2018). His clear and cogent linkage of cause and effect resonated with the public and made money laundering a mainstream topic of discussion in that province and with the federal government.

Corruption and Money Laundering

However bad the situation may be on the gritty downtown streets of our major cities, Canada's challenges pale by comparison to the plight of many countries in the world. Once again, money laundering is the tool that permits this to occur.

In recent decades, the world community has recognized that corruption in the Developing World is a huge impediment to the forward movement of nations. Although no state is immune from corrupt practices, where institutions are guided by legal processes, its impact is minimized. Where the checks and balances do not exist or are not enforced, people in positions of power are free to benefit personally from their office (Rubin 1999, 2–3). Former US Secretary of State Madeline Albright once commented that "corruption is not capitalism's natural product, but its perversion" (Albright 1999). Corruption has emerged as a global menace.

Public corruption is the abuse of government office for private gain. It involves a transaction between two parties, one of whom holds a public position, for their mutual benefit or advantage (Rose-Ackerman 1999, 113). Typically, the parties are of unequal bargaining power. Corruption is anathema to the rule of law, which Western democracies view as the cornerstone of good government. Without an elected legislature, an opposition, a transparent bureaucracy, a free press, and an independent judiciary, corruption will thrive; its impact unfairly affecting the most vulnerable in society.

Grand corruption is an extension of this criminality – the odious use of public office for personal gain, in which leaders seek to expand their personal wealth, or that of family members and cronies, at the expense of the general population. They do this through various bribery and corruption schemes which have the effect of robbing the national bank or treasury of assets. The common term for such persons is kleptocrats. At the base level, they are nothing more than common thieves. Kleptocrats come in every colour and are of every race and religion. They share many features in common. They are morally bankrupt, enamoured by power for the sake of power, loyal to family and friends, and disloyal to virtually all others. Kleptocrats live lavish lifestyles at home – palaces, vehicles, parties, and money – while also moving money out of their respective countries, to safe havens in the developed world. Names such as Suharto, Marcos, Mobutu, Abacha, Milosevic, Duvalier, and so many more of the past and present, are well known to observers of this phenomenon.

Corrupt practices can spread throughout a government bureaucracy, in which public servants, police, and the military may exact tribute in return for doing tasks that they are already paid to perform. The ripple effect is found in private industry which, in its attempt to satisfy the demands of public officials, will develop its own corrupt practices with respect to contracts and tenders. Eventually, corruption becomes a way of life, accepted by the public as a necessary evil to obtain basic services. Jack Blum notes that corruption is contagious: "If the bosses are stealing, the employees feel that they can steal with impunity," thereby creating a culture of corruption (Blum 2000). It is a self-replicating amoeba that will increase exponentially.

By obtaining political power, kleptocrats acquire a form of legitimacy which serves to veil their criminal activity and their efforts to launder their profits. Where power is concentrated in the hands of a few, where the rule of law is flawed, if government is structurally weak and not transparent, if civil society and the media are wanting, or where a culture of corruption has developed as a way of doing business, the impact can be horrendous. There is insufficient money left in government coffers for healthcare, education, housing, and basic social services. Not surprisingly, the poor suffer disproportionately.

Corruption is often facilitated by organized crime. The business of corruption has also adapted to modern systems, with money laundering being a prime example. Money can be wired offshore in nanoseconds, frustrating audit trails, and allowing hoarding in foreign countries. Trade barriers have been relaxed and borders seldom present the difficulties which they did in past years. Don Semesky, the architect of the U.S. Drug Enforcement Administration's ambitious goal of seizing and restraining US$ 1 billion annually in proceeds of crime, states that the number one requirement of drug traffickers is corruption. It paves the way for their business (Semesky 2009).

An incontrovertible fact remains. Money that should remain within the Developed World, which represents the toil and struggle of the peoples of those lands, has found its way into financial institutions that fuel the most powerful economies of the world, including Canada. It is only in recent decades, through regional and other instruments focused on corruption, culminating in the UN Convention Against Corruption of 2003, that nations of the world have finally taken the fight against corruption to the global level (UN General Assembly 2003).

Summary

Money laundering is a tool of organized crime. It is also a tool for corrupt regimes around the world. The injury and damage which flows from profit-driven crime is enormous and hard to quantify. Clearly, it affects all members of the public, but some disproportionately. It is not just a local or national problem, as its sweep is international, facilitated by the ability of money to be transmitted across borders and oceans. It is a real challenge for law enforcement, for legislators, and for every member of the public.

Nevertheless, it can also be the Achilles heel of criminals, as money must be cleansed to be of use. By "following the money," law enforcement can attack organized crime where it is most vulnerable. But to do so, an "all of government" strategy is required. Private industry must also do its share through rigorous reporting of suspicious and other transactions. Recognizing the problem is a crucial first step. Managing it is better than ignoring it. Stopping it must be the goal.

Note

1 Peter M. German, 2021. My sincere appreciation to Jeffrey Simser, Esq., for his review of a draft of this chapter.

References

Albright, Hon, and Madeline Albright. 1999. "Conference on Fighting Corruption and Safeguarding Integrity Among Justice and Security Officials." Remarks, Washington, DC, February 24.

Bank of China v. Fan. 2015. BCSC 590.

Blum, Jack A. 2000. "Multilateral Assistance to Nigeria and the Recovery of Misappropriated Nigerian Assets." Statement to the U.S. House of Representatives Committee on Banking and Financial Services Subcommittee on Domestic and International Monetary Policy, May 25.

Corbett, W. H. 1990. Foreword to Law Enforcement in the Global Village. Ottawa: Supply and Services Canada, quoting Blake to the Earl of Carnarvon, Colonial Secretary. Aug. 7, 1876.

German, Peter M. 2018. Dirty Money: An Independent Review of Money Laundering in Lower Mainland Casinos. Vancouver, Province of British Columbia. https://news.gov.bc.ca/files/Gaming_Final_Report.pdf.

———. 2019. *Dirty Money – Part 2: Turning the Tide – An Independent Review of Money Laundring in B.C. Real Estate, Luxury Vehicle Sales & Horse Racing*. Vancouver, Province of British Columbia. https://news.gov.bc.ca/files/Dirty_Money_Report_Part_2.pdf.

House of Commons Debates (Canada). Sept. 14, 1987.

Malarek, Victor. 1989. Merchants of Misery. Toronto: Macmillan.

R. v. Chan. 2019. ONSC 2785.

R. v. Trac. 2013. ONCA 246.

Rose-Ackerman, Susan. 1999. Corruption and Government. Cambridge University Press.

Rubin, Robert. 1999. "Conference on Fighting Corruption and Safeguarding Integrity Among Justice and Security Officials." Statement, Washington, DC, February 24.

Semesky, Donald. 2009. "Asset Forfeiture Global Conference." Remarks, Hollywood, Florida, April 15.

Smyth, Mike. 2018. "Eby Exposes a 'Devil's Triangle.'" *The Province*, June 28.

UN General Assembly. 2003. UN Convention Against Corruption. UN General Assembly Resolution 58/4. Oct. 31.

3

What Do Tax Haven Data Leaks Tell Us About Canadian Financial Crime?

Arthur Cockfield

Introduction

This chapter provides a snapshot of what recent tax haven data leaks tell us about Canadian financial crime with an emphasis on offshore tax evasion and international money laundering (Cockfield 2016a). A number of important revelations began with earlier thefts of bank account data in Liechtenstein and Switzerland, leading to a series of mega-leaks, all of them ultimately obtained by the International Consortium for Investigative Journalists (ICIJ). These mega-leaks revealed the inner workings of both the offshore world of tax havens and the onshore world of financial secrecy in places such as Canada. It is a tale of crooks and millionaires, sometimes both, and how a complacent political culture, enabled by an asleep-at-the-wheel public, has created a perfect storm of perks that encourage global financial crime.

Part one of this chapter introduces some of the main revelations associated with Canada while part two teases out lessons concerning typologies of cross-border structures, the role of advisors such as lawyers in creating the structures in the first place, and how the greatest beneficiary of the offshore world may be the filthy rich, those in the top 0.01 percent of wealth, who have stashed their fortunes in tax havens for decades. Part three touches on related Canadian reforms with an emphasis on global tax transparency measures such as the Common Reporting Standard. The final part concludes by noting some of the empirical, methodological, and theoretical challenges associated with using leaked data.

Revelations from the Leaks

The following analysis focuses on two Canadian crimes – offshore tax evasion and international money laundering – as revealed by the tax haven data leaks (Cockfield 2017a). It does not include a discussion of terrorist financing because the leaks have not revealed ties to this crime, at least vis à vis Canada.

Earlier Leaks

Before discussing the mega-leaks, which involved much more detailed and extensive information about global financial crimes, two of the earlier leaks that had implications for Canadian policymakers are outlined.

The story begins with an unhappy bank clerk in Liechtenstein. One of the first leaks to gain any media and public attention involved the theft of a CD containing information from about 1,400 offshore bank accounts held by customers of LGT Bank in Liechtenstein. In August 2007, a bank clerk at this bank stole the CD and then sold it to an individual who in turn sold the information to German law enforcement authorities. The Germans then shared this information with governments, including Canada's. The leak revealed that 182 Canadians had maintained a bank account with LGT Bank, which led to the first extensive Canada Revenue Agency (CRA) audit of undisclosed accounts held within a foreign country.

The details concerning this development are available because the matter was reviewed by the Auditor General of Canada and a summary of the findings was subsequently published in the Auditor General's 2013 annual report (the author served as a legal consultant to the Office of the Auditor General of Canada with respect to this review and report; Auditor General of Canada 2013). For five years, the CRA conducted its investigation, which led to the imposition of fines and penalties on 23 taxpayers in the amount of roughly $25 million. No cases were referred by the CRA's criminal investigation program to the federal prosecutor for prosecution.

One of the main lessons from this experience was that the CRA resources were well deployed in this first trial run of a mass audit of allegedly undisclosed offshore income. The government "turned a profit" in the sense that the sanctions imposed on the taxpayers exceeded the government's related costs. Similar efforts by the CRA in the future might equally bear fruit.

Another leak occurred at roughly the same time as the Lichtenstein leak. This one took place in 2007 when a banker agreed to provide information to US authorities about Americans who maintained secret bank accounts with UBS Bank in Geneva. A subsequent Senate investigation revealed the scale of UBS's operations where hundreds of trips took place from Switzerland to Canada and the United States to market anonymous accounts to high net worth individuals. The Swiss bankers travelled to Toronto, Montréal, and Vancouver and told the wealthy individuals they could hide their fortunes in bank accounts and that Canadian authorities would never be the wiser.

The US government ultimately pressured the Swiss government to force UBS Bank to transfer information concerning roughly 4,000 US account holders so the US could prosecute the criminals. In turn, the US government fined UBS Bank USD$780 million. The Internal Revenue Service also published the names of the taxpayers who were prosecuted for maintaining undisclosed offshore accounts. The US government also started a program, called the "Swiss Bank Program," to sanction other banks for prior misdeeds. As of 2016, sixteen Swiss banks paid fines of USD$4 billion to the US government and eighty other Swiss banks had disclosed tax-related crimes in efforts to settle the matter (United States Department of Justice 2016). The Senate investigation revealed that Canadians held roughly $5 billion in one of the Swiss banks, which led to a request by the Canadian government to acquire the relevant information. The Swiss government refused to provide any information to Canadian authorities.

One of the main lessons from this experience is that Canada cannot go it alone to investigate offshore tax cheats as it does not have the political leverage to force foreign governments to cooperate. Canada's efforts with respect to catching offshore tax evaders continue to rely on global cooperative efforts such as the Common Reporting Standard, discussed below.

Mega-Leaks

Unlike the earlier leaks, beginning in 2012 a series of mega-leaks were ultimately obtained by the ICIJ, a Washington, DC-based organization that coordinates global reporting investigations. Instead of mere account information, the leaks contained millions of documents that often provided highly detailed profiles of individuals and intermediaries engaged in global financial crimes. In terms of the data size, for instance, the first leak, labelled "Offshore Leaks," was revealed to the public in April 2013 and contained 2.5 million documents involving 70,000 taxpayers. Measured at 260 gigabytes, the total size of the leaked files obtained by the ICIJ is more than 160 times larger than the leak of U.S. State Department documents by WikiLeaks in 2010. The author served as a legal consultant to the Canadian Broadcasting Corporation (CBC) beginning in 2012 to explain to journalists what the leaked data meant.

Offshore leaks revealed that roughly 4,500 Canadians maintained offshore bank accounts within tax havens although there is no information concerning how many were actually engaged in tax evasion (i.e., the purposeful non-disclosure of offshore income).

CBC journalists also helped track down the money trail relating to the Sergei Magnitsky affair. Mr. Magnitsky was a Moscow tax lawyer who investigated a large-scale financial scam and published a report implicating Russian government officials in the scam. Magnitsky was promptly arrested and jailed for roughly a year before being beaten to death by prison guards, according to a Russian human rights report. The Russian government put Magnitsky on trial – after he was dead – and convicted him of stealing the monies in question. However, Offshore Leaks revealed that the husband of one of the allegedly corrupt prison officials sent millions of dollars offshore to be hidden in a web of corporations (Canada House of Commons 2013). Because the offshore service provider that did the transaction was owned by a Toronto millionaire at the time, the file was sent to Canadian journalists. Despite the evidence of government corruption, the Russian government continues to maintain that Magnitsky, not its own civil servants, was the culprit.

In reaction to these developments, the United States passed the first "Magnitsky Act" that freezes any US-based assets and denies entry to government officials who are thought to be guilty of human rights violations such as the ones that took place regarding Magnitsky. In 2017, Canada passed its own version of the Magnitsky Act (called the Justice for Victims of Corrupt Foreign Officials Act) and has since taken action against officials based in Venezuela, Yemen, Saudi Arabia, Russia, South Sudan, and Myanmar. The leak highlighted how corrupt government officials and members of organized crime steal money from their own governments and then transfer and hide the money offshore.

This initial leak also gave a sense that global financial criminals were using Canada as a base for their operations in part because of lax enforcement of related criminal laws. These criminals used Canada to "snow wash" money, a distinctively Canadian term for money laundering, as they sought to place, layer, and integrate the dirty money within Canada's conventional financial system (see Peter German's chapter).

Another revelation from the initial mega-leak involved a prominent Canadian class action lawyer. The media coverage (including a special CBC episode of *The National* where I provided commentary; *The National* 2013) alleged that this lawyer was sending cash and cheques offshore to a phony non-resident trust structure that he had set up – without disclosing the fund transfers or any related investment income (Zalac et al. 2013). One of the trust beneficiaries was his spouse who at the time was a senator (she has since retired; CBC 2013). The materials accessed by the CBC seemed to show that the lawyer had restructured his offshore holdings on several occasions to provide the luster of compliance.

The Panama Papers of 2016 caused a significant media splash in Canada and around the world. The leak detailed over 11.5 million documents and evidence of more than 214,000 offshore entities. Non-resident taxpayers were taking advantage of Canadian corporate laws to launder their dirty money. Foreign criminals were filing information tax returns with the CRA that indicated "no activity to report" along with no tax payable. In other cases, foreign criminals took advantage of the fact that Canadian laws generally did not require the disclosure of beneficial owners of assets (that is, the actual human beings who are the ultimate owners of an asset). For instance, until recent reforms (touched on below), foreigners could own "bearer shares" under federal or provincial corporate laws. For bearer shares there is no corporate registry that discloses the shareholder and their name; rather, bearer shares are owned by the individual who has physical possession of the share certificate, hence affording anonymous ownership.

The Bahamas Leak of 2016 was taken from the Bahamian corporate registry and revealed the existence of "thousands" of Canadian-owned companies. Three Canadian banks – Royal Bank of Canada, CIBC, and Scotiabank – were reported to have administered almost 2,000 Bahamian companies since 1990. The leaked evidence, however, did not provide evidence of any illegal activities.

The Paradise Papers of 2017 was the biggest leak to date and revealed information about 3,300 Canadian individuals and entities in the offshore world (Ouellet 2017). The leak revealed how, like the situation with UBS Bank, lawyers working for the law firm Appleby made trips to Canada to solicit new clients; in 2012 alone, the firm secured 127 new accounts from Canadians. Three former Canadian prime ministers turned up in the leak: Brian Mulroney, Jean Chrétien, and Paul Martin (Ouellet 2017). The chief fundraisers to the Liberal Party of Canada and Prime Minister Justin Trudeau were also identified as deploying non-resident trusts. In all of these cases, there was no evidence of criminal wrong-doing as it is legally permissible for Canadians to transfer and hold monies offshore – as long as they disclose the assets and any related income.

Another tax haven scandal generated probably as much attention as the Panama Papers: the Isle of Man/KPMG affair (Chashore et al. 2016). KPMG, one of the world's Big Four accounting firms, had set up an aggressive tax plan that they marketed to high net worth individuals who mainly lived in British Columbia. The taxpayers were also provided with two legal opinions that the tax plan was legal. Under the plan, wealthy investors would gift a portion of their fortunes to a corporation based in the Isle of Man, a tax haven in the Irish Sea between England and Ireland. In March 2016, the CBC published reports that indicated the CRA had entered into overly generous settlement agreements with taxpayers and one unhappy taxpayer went to the media with their complaints.

Part of the controversy surrounded the fact that no sanctions were levied against the tax advisors, the accountants, and lawyers, who had set up and then marketed the plan in the first place. Unless advisors are penalized in situations where they provide reckless or grossly negligent tax advice, they will continue to market aggressive schemes that constitute non-compliant tax avoidance (Section 163.2(2)).

Lessons from the Leaks

Typologies

Taking a sample of taxpayer files primarily drawn from offshore leaks, the author set out typologies of offshore structures and analyzed them (Cockfield 2017a). All of the structures involved Canadian connections and in many cases were developed by Canadian tax advisors. The structures enabled offshore tax evasion and/or international money laundering as terrorist financing schemes were less apparent.

The structures generally followed the three main elements of international money laundering: placement, layering, and integration. On client instructions, an entity is formed, either by a law firm or an offshore service provider. The entity is normally either a corporation (a business entity) or a trust (a legal entity) depending on planning needs. Steps are then taken to mask the beneficial owner of the underlying assets held within the entities. Nominee directors or shareholders could be used. Then steps are taken to bring the monies back to Canada so they can be injected into the conventional financial system.

The study of these structures, however, poses certain challenges. First, the structures constantly change in response to changing client needs or efforts to comply (or subvert) legal reforms. Accordingly, a particular structure designed for a particular place and time will have little applicability elsewhere or in some other period.

Taxpayers use these entities for two main criminal purposes: first, the entities are used to hide the identities of the actual human beings who are engaged in the crimes and, second, the entities provide a lustre of compliance should tax or law enforcement officials begin an audit or investigation of an individual's offshore dealings. Because taxpayers use these same entities in tax havens for legitimate personal or business purposes it can be very difficult for investigators to distinguish between legal and illegal activities.

Prior to the mega-leaks, there was little information on offshore service providers such as what finance and trust companies actually do to facilitate offshore evasion. The gap in the writings can be largely explained by the secretive nature of tax haven activities that shielded them from outside scrutiny (Chaikin and Hook 2018).

Much of the information from the ICIJ financial data leak comes from the memos to files written by the workers at the offshore service provider. To encourage compliance and presumably to create a record that would help insulate them from liability, offshore service providers would write down client instructions as well as any telephone comments they made to clients where they asserted concerns about the file. At times, clients would request services that the offshore service providers thought may not comply with domestic or international regulations; in such cases, the client was asked to enter into an indemnity agreement whereby the client would pay for any losses the offshore service provider incurred as a result of the transaction. In this way, clients were allowed to engage in non-compliant transactions.

A resident (parent) corporation can also set up a related corporation based in a tax haven. Then, the parent corporation "cooks the books" to fabricate payments made to the tax haven corporation to launder ill-gotten gains and reduce taxable income in a high-tax country. For instance, a phoney management fee paid by the parent corporation (in the high-tax country) to the subsidiary in the tax haven can be used to create a deduction and hence reduction in tax, as well as a corresponding inclusion of this fee in a country that does not impose an income tax. Legitimate businesses are often used to facilitate these illegal outcomes by adding fictional revenues to make it look like the inflated earnings came from legal activities. The legitimate business is also used to help hide the fact that monies were illegally earned.

A trust is a legal entity designed to provide certain benefits to individuals (i.e., "beneficiaries"). A trust is set up by an individual or organization (i.e., "settlor") that bestows the trust with an asset such as a cash amount. The individuals or companies that maintain legal title to the asset are generally called trustees. Hence, there is a legal separation between the legal title owner of the asset and the beneficiary. Trustees are normally vested with the power to make decisions concerning how trust assets are invested and to ensure that the trust agreement (sometimes called the trust indenture or trust deed) provisions are followed. In some countries, trustees also have fiduciary duties (that is, duties of utmost loyalty imposed by statute or common law) to pursue the interests of the beneficiaries.

In many instances, the usage of non-resident trusts is perfectly legal. For instance, a legal structure sometimes referred to as a "granny trust" involves a foreign person (e.g., a wealthy grandmother in the United Kingdom) setting up a trust for the benefit of an individual living in another country (e.g., her grandson in Canada). Because the monies originate offshore, there will generally be no taxation of the trust assets when they are distributed to a trust beneficiary, although this beneficiary would have to disclose the existence of the trust or any interest in the trust when he or she files a Canadian tax return. Consistent with the legal nature of granny trusts, if funds originate offshore, it may be possible to have the trust pay out the capital tax-free to the recipient back home. Some of the scams revealed by the ICIJ data leak thus had two components: getting undeclared cash and other assets offshore so that they appear to originate in a foreign country, and creating a granny trust structure to clean up the monies and return them home on a tax-free basis.

Most trusts within the ICIJ data leak had sophisticated structures that involved several individuals other than the trust settlor. This settlor would normally (but not always) be an individual residing in a jurisdiction outside of the country where the beneficiaries live. A common trust would work as follows. A settlor transfers legal title to donated assets to an offshore trustee. The trustee would be a corporation formed by the offshore service provider. Its tasks were to enforce the provisions of the trust, which in turn dictated that these tasks would be exclusively perfunctory in nature. That is, the trustee is solely interested in compliance with the trust agreement and with all relevant local laws and regulations. Under this structure, the trustee and the settlor are given no legal powers to exercise any meaningful management discretion over the trust's assets. This discretion is provided to another individual who is a (seemingly) neutral third party who may be called a protector or a director of the trust. Because the settlor, beneficiary, and trust protector appear to be different individuals the trust seems to be a legitimate trust that might pass the initial "smell test" and escape further scrutiny by outside auditors or law enforcement authorities.

In addition, the leaks revealed that criminals sometimes set up more complicated offshore structures involving multiple entities – a process I call "layering the cake." For instance, the trust can hold the shares in a nominee, shell, or holding corporation (based in the same offshore jurisdiction or another one) that in turn owns all of a Canadian taxpayer's assets. This corporation, whose directors are controlled by the Canadian taxpayer, borrows the assets from the trust so that it owes them back. When the Canadian taxpayer needs money, he calls his local lawyer and instructs him to have the offshore corporation pay back $1 million owed to the trust. The trust assets can be distributed to the Canadian. The lawyer then calls the trustee (i.e., the offshore trust company) and tells it that the trust beneficiary has made a request for money – sometimes called a "list of wishes."

The trustee contacts the protector living offshore and tells this person of the request (as discussed below, this protector can be another lawyer). The protector then instructs the trustee to disburse the needed $1 million to the named beneficiary (i.e., the Canadian taxpayer). All of these instructions can be conducted over the telephone as long as oral instructions are permissible under a provision of the trust indenture. The trust settlor who created the trust agreement in the first place may have called for oral instructions under the view that there would be no written records of the trust disbursements, hampering law enforcement investigations.

In summary, analysis of the leaks has revealed a number of vulnerabilities in the international financial system vis á vis global financial crime, including (a) offshore service providers often did little to no due diligence to identify the source of an investor's funds as required by FATF international "know your customer" regulations as well as similar domestic implementing legislation; (b) for a successful prosecution, a criminal investigation must determine that the monies originated from illicit activities, and there was generally no record of such origin maintained by the offshore service provider (which likely wishes to remain intentionally ignorant to create plausible deniability); (c) offshore service providers enter into indemnity agreements whereby the investor assumes all liability for any outside government or creditor lawsuits thereby allowing the offshore service provider to continue to provide services that do not comply with relevant international or domestic laws; (d) complex offshore structures involving layers of corporations, trusts, and other entities make it difficult for law enforcement authorities to determine whether global financial crimes are being committed; (e) trust agreements that permit oral instructions for trust disbursements are used to reduce the risk of a paper trail that identifies trust financial activities; and (f) offshore service providers (such as one that was the subject of the Offshore Leaks data leak) can quickly close down, inhibiting any investigations.

Role of Intermediaries

The leaks also shone a spotlight on the role played by intermediaries within the offshore world: accountants, bankers, lawyers, and real estate brokers (German 2017, 2019).

A number of steps were taken to tighten up the world where non-residents invest in Canadian real estate. In British Columbia, for instance, the Land Owner Transparency Act, which came into effect in 2020, makes information about the beneficial ownership of BC real estate publicly available by creating a searchable registry of individuals who hold, directly or indirectly, beneficial interests in BC real estate through, among others, corporations, trusts, or partnerships.

Bankers are subject to tax transparency measures such as the Common Reporting Standard, which impose information collection obligations on banks, including know-your-customer standards set out under federal anti-money laundering and anti-terrorist financing laws (see below).

Also of interest were the ways that lawyers and accountants facilitate transactions that mask the identities of beneficial owners as well as some of the activities undertaken by the hidden individuals. The leaks provided evidence that these actors played a critical role in enabling large-scale global financial crimes to take place. For instance, the Panama Papers were drawn in large part from the databanks of Mossack Fonseca, a now-defunct Panamanian law firm. Similarly, the Paradise Papers of 2017 were drawn in part from the records of Appleby in Bermuda; this global law firm had its tentacles in many of the world's tax havens. In both cases, the lawyers created offshore entities like corporations and trusts, took steps to anonymize the identity of beneficial owners and re-structured transactions where necessary to supposedly comply with legal changes like new disclosure requirements.

Like bankers, accountants and lawyers have some information collection obligations to protect against crime and terrorist financing. Accountants, in particular, maintain and, if needed, pass on to law enforcement information concerning client billings.

The issue surrounding lawyer collection obligations concerning monies paid for legal services is complex and thorny (Unger 2013). From an international law perspective, there is no law that can compel a lawyer in a particular country to maintain or disclose records for anti-money laundering and anti-terrorist financing purposes. Instead, recommendations are issued by the FATF concerning these obligations. Since at least 2002, the FATF has recommended that governments pass laws to ensure lawyers collect, maintain, and disclose information concerning client billings to government regulators. The step is thought necessary to guard against the use of lawyers as willing or unwilling dupes who are being paid with crooked dollars.

In peer reviews, the FATF has highlighted the ongoing non-compliance by two countries that refuse to abide by the disclosure recommendation: Canada and the United States. Both of these countries are constitutional democracies with Constitutions that guarantee certain fundamental rights to citizens – in this case, the right in a free and democratic society to have an impartial lawyer who can keep client secrets and resolutely advocate on a client's behalf. This is important because even if the federal governments of these two countries pass laws to mandate lawyer disclosures of client information these laws may be struck down by courts as being unconstitutional.

Such was the fate of post-9/11 efforts by the Canadian federal government to force lawyers to maintain and, in narrow circumstances, disclose client billing records to the government. The Federation of Law Societies (*Canada v. Federation of Law Societies of Canada 2015*), a body that regulates Canadian law schools, went to court and successfully challenged the law on the basis that it did not comply with the Canadian *Charter of Rights and Freedoms*. A unanimous Supreme Court of Canada agreed that the law violated the Charter because it undermined a lawyer's ability to be neutral and independent-minded in providing legal advice to clients (that is, the federal law interfered with a lawyer's commitment to a client's cause, which the Court found to be a principle of fundamental justice; Cockfield 2016a; 2016b). The Department of Finance subsequently redrafted a new law that sought to follow the Court's guidance with respect to narrowing the breadth of the disclosure obligations.

The Filthy Rich

The CRA estimates that in 2014 the government lost between $0.8 billion and $3 billion in tax revenues because of hidden offshore accounts maintained by Canadians (Canada Revenue Agency, n.d.). The methodology deployed by the CRA is consistent with that used by other researchers who try to examine the impact of criminal offshore activities (mainly by indirectly observing cross-border bank flows then working backward to figure out how many illicit flows are taking place).

While this chapter focuses on Canadian matters, researchers have deployed a different methodology concerning Scandinavian taxpayers that suggests the approach used by the CRA and others is flawed. Professors Alstadsaeter, Johannesen, and Zucman (2017) instead deploy real-world data gleaned from tax haven leaks, which generates much higher estimates of revenue losses generated when the truly wealthy engage in offshore tax evasion. The authors had come up with an ingenious way to test the under-reporting of income and wealth by "ultra high net-worth" individuals. The paper's shocking conclusion: The top 0.01 percent of the wealthiest households in Scandinavia, on average, engage in criminal tax evasion to dodge 25 percent of their income tax liability. Prior studies had shown the "regular rich" in the top 1 percent only evaded 5 percent of their income taxes. The general population, in contrast, is thought to evade 0.6 percent of their taxes via offshore investments.

The paper's data drew from two main tax haven data leaks. This one was taken from HSBC Switzerland in 2007 and came to be known by the name of the "Falciani List" after Hervé Falciani, the bank employee who initially obtained the list or, alternatively, the "Lagarde List" after Christine Lagarde who at the time was the French minister of finance who received the list. This list contained the names and bank records of 30,000 taxpayers. After the French government acquired the list, it shared it with governments around the world, including Canada and the United States. Somewhat unusually, this list did not just specify the owners of bank accounts, it also set out the beneficial owners of business entities like corporations that in turn owned the bank accounts. In addition to the Falciani/Lagarde List, the authors also reviewed data obtained from the Panama Papers, which also revealed undisclosed offshore accounts maintained by super-rich Scandinavian taxpayers.

Working with the study authors, the tax authorities of Denmark, Sweden, and Norway then matched the account with taxpayers within their countries. After a lengthy investigation, the Danish and Norwegian tax authorities concluded that 90 to 95 percent of the taxpayers from the

Lagarde List had not reported, or paid taxes on, their income. The governments took the position that this non-reporting was not the result of legal tax avoidance, but rather criminal tax evasion.

The study also found that it was the wealthiest members of society that in many cases were the real problem: the top 0.01 percent (in this case, individuals with USD$45 million and more in wealth). This group of super-rich people were thirteen times more likely to hide assets in HSBC Switzerland compared to the bottom half of the top 1 percent (who owned between USD$2 million and USD$3 million in wealth). In other words, filthy rich people committed the crime of tax evasion at a much greater rate when compared to the merely rich. The study found that identified taxpayers hid roughly 40 percent of their wealth within tax havens.

The authors of the study also noted that using entities like corporations to shield their wealth was a more sophisticated way to engage in offshore tax evasion, instead of directly owning a bank account. This view is consistent with the findings noted above: corporations, limited liability partnerships, foundations, trusts, etc. are used to create a multi-layer cake that makes it very difficult for law enforcement to understand what is really taking place.

Finally, the authors also mention that 14 percent of the top 0.01 percent of the wealthiest households disclosed assets in a tax amnesty program offered by Scandinavian governments between 2009 and 2015. These tax dodgers, on average, hid almost one-third of their wealth, which is lower but consistent with the study's finding that they dodged 40 percent of their wealth.

The study is somewhat surprising because prior research has shown that Scandinavian countries have some of the highest taxpayer compliance rates in the world. If the level of criminal activity was so extensive for the Scandinavian ultra-high net worth individuals, it could be even greater for most other countries.

In fact, this is the same conclusion that professors Alstadsaeter, Johannesen, and Zucman came to in their earlier study that relied on data on bank account deposits from the Bank for International Settlements (the data did not cover securities like shares in which the bulk of tax haven wealth is found; Alstadsæter et al. 2017). This data is probably not as reliable as directly observing taxpayer behaviour through tax haven data leaks but is nevertheless helpful in estimating the amount of crime taking place.

Through this different methodology, the authors estimate that tax havens hold hidden wealth worth about 10 percent of global gross domestic product (Zucman 2017). In the United States, Great Britain, France, and Spain, the ultra-high net worth households (that is, those at the top 0.01 percent of wealth) hides between 30 and 40 percent of their wealth in tax havens. The study also revealed that many of the wealthiest individuals in Russia, Venezuela, Saudi Arabia, and the United Arab Emirates stash much greater amounts offshore.

These findings are consistent with a 2018 study by economists Juliana Londono-Velez and Javier Ávila-Mahecha titled *Can Wealth Taxation Work in Developing Countries? Quasi-Experimental Evidence from Colombia.* (Londoño-Vélez and Ávila-Mahecha 2018). The authors reviewed taxpayer behaviour in Colombia and found that the wealthiest 0.01 percent is twenty-four times as likely to be named in the Panama Papers than the wealthiest 5 percent. Two-fifths of the top 0.01 percent of income earners disclosed illegal offshore assets after a voluntary disclosure program was announced, with an 800 percent increase of such disclosures after the release of the Panama Papers. Again, the richest of the rich were far more likely to stash their monies offshore in comparison with other well-off taxpayers.

This is more real-world evidence, in this case involving Colombian taxpayers, that the truly wealthy use the offshore world's services to conceal their wealth from their own governments. The limited social science data suggests that many of the wealthiest members of society have committed criminal offences by hiding a portion of their fortunes offshore where it grew tax-free, potentially for generations – while at the same time honest taxpayers were paying their taxes and funding services used by the tax cheats. The Canadian government should consider participating in similar studies that look at tax haven data leaks and try to discern actual real-world taxpayer behaviour. Such studies may also show that revenue losses associated with offshore tax evasion may be higher than the losses estimated under the CRA's methodology. It should be possible for researchers to participate in this study although steps will need to be taken so that the government should only be aware of the identities of actual taxpayers to preserve taxpayer privacy.

Legal and Policy Reforms

There have been a series of international legal and policy reforms since the 1990s that have strived to inhibit offshore tax evasion (Cockfield 2017b, 2018). The Canadian federal government has ramped up its policy response since the Finance Standing Committee hearings that began in 2012 and lasted until 2017. The Finance Standing Committee produced two reports on the issue of offshore tax evasion and aggressive international tax planning. The reports also set out sixteen of the author's recommendations drawn from testimony and five different hearings; some of the proposals (such as embedding Justice tax litigators with CRA audit units) have already been implemented (Canada House of Commons 2013; 2016).

The government is trying to address the "tax gap" created by offshore tax evasion and non-compliant tax planning through the stricter enforcement of tax laws. In recent federal budgets, the Liberal administration has dedicated an extra $1 billion toward tax enforcement resources, with most of the monies dedicated to transfer-pricing audits. A further $600 million was promised in the November 30, 2020 fall economic statement.

While there are many different proposed solutions, this part briefly touches on tax transparency measures used to inhibit offshore tax evasion.

These measures date back to the late 1990s when the OECD tried to inhibit "harmful tax competition" and created a blacklist of tax haven countries. The OECD identified a lack of effective tax information sharing from these tax havens to OECD countries as the main culprit. In 2002, the OECD created a model tax information exchange agreement (TIEA), which envisioned agreements between OECD countries and tax haven countries. But the "information on request" basis of this model was soon found deficient: the resident country usually does not have sufficient information to make the request in the first place (the OECD model protocol to the TIEA, published in 2015, contemplates the addition of automatic and spontaneous tax exchanges). Canada has entered into TIEAs with twenty-four countries, and it has, in addition, ninety-four bilateral tax treaties, many of which have provisions for the automatic exchange of tax information.

From 2013 onward, the OECD and the G-20 emphasized that the automatic exchange of tax information needed to be the new global standard, and this standard is being implemented through the Common Reporting Standard (CRS). The CRS mandates an "internationally agreed standard" by which countries require their financial institutions to obtain information on accounts held by non-residents and – under applicable TIEAs or bilateral treaties – to automatically report that information to the account holders' local authorities.

Under this system, Canadian law requires Canadian financial institutions to identify non-resident account holders and to report specified information to the CRA, which shares this information with the tax authority of the country where the account holder resides. Canada's partners in the CRS provide the CRA, in turn, with information concerning Canadian residents who have foreign accounts. Armed with this information, the CRA can check to see whether the Canadian resident has disclosed all income connected to its offshore holdings. Most developed countries participate in the CRS, with the glaring exception of the United States.

It could be argued that the CRS has as many holes as Swiss cheese. At times, certain structures appear to comply with CRS requirements while still maintaining the anonymity of beneficial owners of assets. For instance, a structure may involve the setting up of a paying agent within a non-participating regime such as the United States; since the United States does not participate in the CRS there is no obligation under domestic US law to disclose the beneficial owner. Another apparent loophole involves setting up structures so that non-residents can use foreign trusts as long as these trusts hold assets outside of the country where the trust is formed; domestic legal implementation of CRS normally does not require beneficial owner disclosure in this circumstance. Another gambit that doesn't require disclosure involves setting up the paying agent and the reporting bank within the same jurisdiction. And we have not even started a discussion of the exotic entities like foundations that governments can set up to get around listed entities that require disclosure to the home jurisdiction of the beneficial owner.

Recently, the federal and provincial governments have taken additional steps to promote tax transparency. These steps include the addition of beneficial ownership disclosure requirements to the Canada Business Corporations Act (CBCA) and the elimination of bearer shares from the CBCA and some provinces' business corporation laws. Canada and the provinces may need to take additional steps, such as creating a national registry of the beneficial owners of businesses and legal entities. The government should also promote the adoption of a multilateral taxpayer bill of rights, to ensure the protection of taxpayers (Cockfield 2010). If governments have confidence that their taxpayers' rights will be respected, they are more likely to engage in effective exchanges with other countries.

Conclusion

The previous analysis discussed revelations from tax haven data leaks such as the Panama Papers with a focus on Canadian stories found within the leaks. The leaks show how Canadians engage in offshore tax evasion and international money laundering while Canada itself often serves as a base for global financial criminals with offshore advisors touting the benefits of setting up corporations and other entities within Canada, including the apparent lax enforcement regime.

The leaks provide a wealth of detailed information about the behaviour of specific taxpayers as well as how advisors sometimes facilitate global financial crime. Nevertheless, the use of the leaks is not without problems, owing to empirical, methodological, and theoretical challenges.

From an empirical perspective, the use of specific taxpayer anecdotes, which are drawn from the leaks, can be problematic. Different types of review biases may skew overall research results if researchers focus on specific cases that are in fact aberrational. Moreover, laws and regulations governing cross-border financial transactions are subject to change, which means that the structures identified in the leaks may no longer be effective. These structures may need to be revised to ensure compliance or at least have the lustre of compliance. The leaks themselves provided evidence of decades-old structures being updated from time to time in response to global regulatory developments.

In terms of methodological challenges, reviewing specific taxpayer cases derived from the leaks does little to assess the scale of the overall problem of global financial crime. As mentioned, traditional approaches have tried to assess the scale of the problem by indirectly observing other market indicators such as capital flows to give a sense of the amount of money associated with criminal activities taking place. A potentially superior approach, discussed in the last part on the "filthy rich," would involve combining real-world evidence gleaned from the leaks and matching this against overall compliance efforts.

Finally, there are ongoing theoretical challenges. The leaks show that criminals engage in offshore tax evasion and/or international money laundering yet writings in this area are normally compartmentalized into tax crimes or financial crimes. Few efforts thus far address offshore tax evasion, international money laundering, and terrorist financing in a holistic fashion under the broader category of global financial crime. Because we have different legal regimes covering these different crimes (although money laundering and terrorist financing are normally covered by the same legislation) it allows criminals to exploit the legal gaps. Instead, we need both a theory to understand how these crimes can be combined along with legal and policy solutions that follow this combined approach. Nascent efforts in this area – such as the 2015 use by the OECD and G20 of the FATF definitions for beneficial owners for purposes of the Common Reporting Standard – should bear fruit by allowing investigators to better target and disrupt offshore criminal schemes.

As researchers gain a more robust understanding of the potentials and limits of different scholarly approaches, they will more accurately assess the nature and severity of global financial crime along with best practices to counter it.

References

Alstadsaeter, Annette, Niels Johannesen, and Gabriel Zucman. 2017. "Tax Evasion and Inequality." Working Paper No. 23772, NBER.

Auditor General of Canada. 2013. "Main Points—What We Found." In *Offshore Banking—Canada Revenue Agency: 2013 Fall Report of the Auditor General of Canada*. Ottawa: Office of the Auditor General of Canada.

Canada (Attorney General) v. Federation of Law Societies of Canada. (2015). S.C.J. No. 7, 2015 SCC 7.

Canada. House of Commons. 2013. "Tax Evasion and the Use of Tax Havens, Report of the Standing Committee on Finance." 41st parl., 1st sess., May 2013.

———. 2016. "The Canada Revenue Agency, Tax Avoidance and Tax Evasion: Recommended Actions, Report of the Standing Committee on Finance." 42d parl., 1st sess., October 2016.

Canada Revenue Agency. n.d. "International Tax Gap and Compliance Results for the Federal Personal Income Tax System." https://www.canada.ca/en/revenue-agency/corporate/about-canada-revenue-agency-cra/tax-canada-a-conceptual-study/tax-compliance.html.

CBC. 2013. "Senator Wants Answers on Colleague's Role on Offshore Account." *CBC News*, April 4. https://www.cbc.ca/news/politics/senator-wants-answers-on-colleague-s-role-in-offshore-account-1.1414741.

Chaikin, David, and Gordon Hook, eds. 2018. *Corporate Trust Structures: Legal and Illegal Dimensions*. North Melbourne: Australian Scholarly Publishing Pty. Ltd.

Chashore, Harvey et al. 2016. "Canada Revenue Offered Amnesty to Wealthy KPMG Clients in Offshore Tax 'sham'." *CBC News*, March 8.

Cockfield, Arthur J. 2010. "Protecting Taxpayer Privacy under Enhanced Cross-Border Tax Information Exchange: Toward a Multilateral Taxpayer Bill of Rights." *University of British Columbia Law Review* 42: 419–471.

———. 2016a. "Big Data and Tax Haven Secrecy." *Florida Tax Review* 18, no. 8: 483–539, 510–17.

———. 2016b. *Introduction to Legal Ethics*, 2nd ed., 259–263. LexisNexis.

———. 2017a. "Examining Canadian Offshore Tax Evasion." *Canadian Tax Journal* 65: 651–680.

———. 2017b. "How Countries Should Share Tax Information." *Vanderbilt Journal of Transnational Law* 50: 91.

———. 2018. "Shaping International Tax Law in Challenging Times." *Stanford Law Journal of International Law* 54: 223–240.

German, Peter. 2017. "Dirty Money: An Independent Review of Money Laundering in Lower Mainland Casinos" conducted for the Attorney General of British Columbia.

————. 2019. "Dirty Money, Part 2: Turning the Tide – An Independent Review of Money Laundering in B.C. Real Estate, Luxury Vehicle Sales & Horse Racing." Attorney General of British Columbia.

Londoño-Vélez, Juliana, and Javier Ávila-Mahecha. 2018. "Can Wealth Taxation Work in Developing Countries? Quasi-Experimental Evidence from Colombia." https://eml.berkeley.edu/~saez/course/londono-wealth2018.pdf.

Ouellet, Valérie. 2017. "More Than 3,000 Canadian Names in the Paradise Papers." *CBC*, November 6. https://www.cbc.ca/news/business/paradise-papers-canada-connection-1.4386126.

The National. 2013. "Merchant of Secrecy Broadcast." *CBC*, April 2. https://www.cbc.ca/news/thenational/the-merchant-of-secrecy-1.437266.

Unger, Brigitte. 2013. "Introduction." In *Research Handbook on Money Laundering*, edited by Brigitte Unger and Daan van der Linde. Cheltenham: Edward Elgar.

United States. Department of Justice. "Offshore Compliance Initiative (2009–2016)." www.justice.gov/tax/offshore-compliance-initiative.

Zalac, Fréderic, et al. 2013. "Senator's Husband Put $1.7M in Offshore Tax Haven." CBC News, April 3. https://www.cbc.ca/news/canada/senator-s-husband-put-1-7m-in-offshore-tax-havens-1.1329197.

Zucman, Gabriel. 2017. *The Hidden Wealth of Nations*, 2nd ed. Chicago: University of Chicago Press.

4

Taken to the Cleaners:
How Canada Can Start to Fix
Its Money-Laundering Problem

Christian Leuprecht and Jamie Ferrill

Introduction

Governments across Canada are increasingly concerned about the amount of money being laundered within and through the country. As of late, there has been a flurry of activity by federal and provincial governments and agencies on this issue. It necessarily calls for a whole-of-government and, indeed, international effort, for money laundering and its insidious effects transcend provincial and national boundaries. Effects include serious social harms from gun violence to escalating property prices, the undermining of financial systems, reputational risk for the State, and the criminalization of society. Ultimately, money laundering and its associated precursor crimes transfers economic power from the market, government, and citizens to criminals.

This chapter takes stock of current Canadian efforts to address money laundering. In recent years, the government of British Columbia commissioned four reports that detail the extent and sophistication of the money laundering in BC's real estate market, casinos, and other sectors (German 2018, 2019; Maloney, Somerville, and Unger 2019; Perrin 2018). The reports prompted the provincial government to set up the Cullen Commission on Money Laundering in British Columbia (2019) whose *Final Report* comprised 101 recommendations. Also, the Ontario government committed to tackling the issue in its November 2019 *Economic Outlook and Fiscal Review* (Ontario, Ministry of Finance 2019a, 123).

Federally, in *Budget 2019,* the Government of Canada made several commitments to contain financial crimes, including money laundering and terrorist financing. In June 2019, federal ministers met with their provincial and territorial counterparts to discuss approaches to preventing financial crime. Following the meeting, a Department of Finance Canada news release emphasized four initiatives on which there was consensus, including an "intention" to provide $10 million to the RCMP, in addition to current budget commitments, for the force to invest in the infrastructure and tools needed to pursue complex financial crimes (Canada, Department of Finance 2019a). $24 million was also pledged to establish the Financial Crime Coordination Centre (FC3).

Still, capacity to tackle money laundering in Canada remains limited, as confirmed by the Cullen Commission. Canada is compensating by cooperating with its major trading partners and allies to develop and expand multilateral frameworks such as the Financial Action Task Force (FATF). This chapter starts by surveying those global efforts and standards, then looks at Canada's anti-money laundering (AML) initiatives, which includes Canada's overall AML regime, Canada's most recent National Risk Assessment, the global FATF evaluation of Canada's efforts, Canada's response to shortcomings identified in that evaluation, and new initiatives the federal government has launched in the meantime.

The chapter then lays out the implications of money laundering in Canada. It uses federal and provincial enforcement measures against contraband tobacco and cigarettes as a critical case study because of the vast sums of money that illicit trade generates, which then often need to be laundered. The chapter closes on a comparison of enforcement efforts among select provinces and reflections on illicit cannabis as a rapidly emerging accelerant of money laundering.

Its conclusions are mixed. In theory, there is some good will by federal and provincial governments to address the problem. In practice, lacklustre results are a function of meagre resources and insufficient policy attention devoted to the issue. There is good reason to doubt the federal government's commitment to ensuring that law enforcement can effectively investigate, arrest, and convict suspects involved in financial crime.

Money Laundering

Money laundering is driven by organized crime groups (OCGs) that make use of sophisticated schemes to avoid detection by national law enforcement, intelligence, and regulatory agencies. Often transnational in nature, they rely on different economic sectors, financial procedures, and methods to mask their illegally acquired funds. Ultimately, these processes and schemes are designed to make transactions in any one jurisdiction appear perfectly legal.

As government entities do not have the full picture across borders, they are at an asymmetric disadvantage in uncovering the illicit nature of these funds. The complex nature and transnational linkages of the transactions often only comes to light when law enforcement and regulatory agencies conduct exhaustive investigations of diverse financial records that identify and expose illegal activity. It follows that only a transnational, or rather genuinely global, approach will cut to the crux of the problem.

Global Standard: Financial Action Task Force

In 1989, the Group of Seven Nations (G7) initiated the FATF of which Canada is a founding member. With Finance as the lead department, Canada contributes both expertise and funding to the FATF.

The initial focus of the FATF was to develop policies and establish best practices to combat money laundering; eventually, its mandate grew to encompass terrorism financing and proliferation financing. The FATF monitors progress of member countries in implementing its 40 Recommendations. A key requirement is for countries to identify and assess money laundering and terrorist financing risks within their own jurisdiction. This information can be used in the development of mitigation strategies and to assess each country's capacity against the global standards set by the FATF. While the publication of such risk assessments is not mandated, there is no question that sharing them highlights global challenges associated with money laundering and terrorism financing.

The FATF provides detailed guidelines for undertaking a risk assessment. They include producing a matrix to break down criminal activity into levels of threat, developing strategies to address the identified risks, and conducting an environmental scan to examine potential vulnerabilities in the political, economic, social, legislative, and technological sectors. Since criminals are bound to exploit any and all available vulnerabilities, an honest examination of the different sectors within each country will provide intelligence as to where the country should focus its resources and/or develop initiatives to mitigate adverse outcomes, such as the loss of tax revenue. In Canada, the last national risk assessment was completed in 2015 and is publicly available.

Further to these guidelines, the FATF also conducts evaluations of member nations. Currently in its fourth round, FATF mutual evaluations are peer reviews; member nations assess each other and provide an analysis of the efficacy of the financial system and its vulnerabilities. Based on effectiveness and technical compliance, the evaluations involve an expert team that completes a technical review, sets the parameters or scope of the assessment, conducts an on-site visit, completes a draft report to address technical compliance and effectiveness, engages in discussion and review with the assessed country, and puts forward the final report to the FATF. The FATF Plenary reviews and discusses those findings, makes recommendations, and adopts the final report. These mutual evaluation reports are reviewed by the FATF global network, and then made public (FATF 2021).

Canadian Anti-Money Laundering Initiatives

Canada's AML/ATF Regime

Through the Financial Transactions and Reports Analysis Centre (FIN-TRAC) and the Proceeds of Crime (Money Laundering) and Terrorist

Financing Act (PCMLTFA), Canada's federal government has now had an anti-money laundering and anti-terrorist financing (AML/ATF) regime, led by the Department of Finance, that dates back two decades. The latest iteration of the PCMLTFA came into force on June 1, 2021. It introduced a revised operating framework including mandatory reporting to FINTRAC (Osler 2021). The regulatory burden includes building, instituting, and overseeing a compliance program subject to biennial audits and FINTRAC examinations, which must also address all relevant ongoing regulatory requirements including, but not limited to, client identification, transaction reporting, and record keeping procedures (CPA 2022). The regime consists of both funded and non-funded federal partners.[1] It is supported by other federal departments, provincial financial sectors and other regulators, and provincial and municipal law enforcement agencies. A parliamentary review of the PCMLTFA is expected to launch in 2023.

From the private sector, 31,000 Canadian financial institutions and designated non-financial businesses and professions (DNFBPs) known as reporting entities have reporting obligations to the regime under the PCMLTFA to support its initiatives. Since its inception in June 2000 to the end of fiscal year 2018/2019, almost CA$1.1 billion in federal funding had been allocated to the AML/ATF regime. The eight funded regime participants received a total of CA$72 million in the last fiscal year (Canada, Department of Finance 2018a). Figure 4.1 contains a summary and breakdown of the recent performance and annual commitments of select AML/ATF regime members.

The objective of the AML/ATF regime is "to detect and deter money laundering and the financing of terrorist activities and to facilitate the investigation and prosecution of money laundering and terrorist financing offences" (Canada, Department of Finance 2018a). The regime is regularly reviewed to ensure it remains effective, addresses emerging risks, and maintains Canada's international leadership in the fight against money laundering and terrorist financing. Reviews are informed by various evaluations, consultations, assessments of money laundering and terrorist financing risks, as well as international considerations, includ-

Figure 4.1: Selected Members of Canada's AML/ATF Regime Reported on Their Performance in the Government of Canada's Departmental Performance Reports 2018/2019

- Department of Finance Canada received $244,000 in 2018/2019 and uses the funds to participate as a member of the FATF and other groups. This year it will update the 2015 money laundering and finance terrorism risk assessment. Overall, its performance is based on its participation in various meetings.

- Financial Transactions and Reports Analysis Centre of Canada (FINTRAC) is Canada's Financial Intelligence Unit and the centrepiece of Canada's AML regime. Headquartered in Ottawa, it received over $45 million in 2018/2019. The centre's overall performance is based on the number of investigations that are supported by FINTRAC disclosures. In the 2018/2019 fiscal year, FINTRAC received more than 28 million financial transaction reports.

- Royal Canadian Mounted Police (RCMP) received over $11 million in 2018/2019. Its overall performance is based on the percentage of criminal operations completed that have a money laundering component, the number of training sessions it provides, and the meetings it attends.

- Canada Revenue Agency (CRA) received about $8 million in 2018/2019. It reviews all disclosures received from FINTRAC and identifies targets with identifiable tax and collection potential. By March 2019 it will reportedly strengthen operational relationships with AML/ATF regime partners. Its performance is based on the number of Joint Force Operations (JFO) completed.

- Canada Border Services Agency (CBSA) received about $3.7 million in 2018/2019. Its performance is based on the number of intelligence products produced and the number of JFOs it conducts with the RCMP and other federal departments.

Note: all figures are in Canadian dollars.

Source: Government of Canada, Department of Finance (2018b).

ing the activities of the FATF and the actions of G7 partners (Canada, Department of Finance 2018a).

2015 AML/ATF National Risk Assessment

In 2015, the federal government undertook a whole-of-government initiative to develop and publish a combined national risk assessment for both money laundering and terrorist financing, in part to address the requirements in the FATF guidelines. The report, *Assessment of Inherent Risks of Money Laundering and Terrorist Financing in Canada* (Canada, Department of Finance 2015), categorized various money laundering threats, identified key participants in such activities and pinpointed ten groups posing the highest risk for terrorist activities in the country.

The money laundering threat was assessed by evaluating twenty-one different criminal activities most associated with generating proceeds of crime that may be laundered in Canada. Of these, nine activities were considered very high risk: capital markets fraud, commercial (trade) fraud, corruption and bribery, counterfeiting and piracy, illicit drug trafficking, mass marketing fraud, mortgage fraud, third-party money laundering, and tobacco smuggling and trafficking. OCGs and professional money launderers are the key actors associated with money laundering in Canada. Professional money launderers are rarely involved in the activity that generates the proceeds of crime but are sought out by OCGs due to the sizeable profits that the illicit trade in drugs and tobacco generates.

To determine the terrorist financing threat, the AML/ATF regime assessed ten terrorist groups as well as foreign fighters (those who travel abroad to support terrorist groups).[2] Although the threat of terrorist financing may not figure as prominently in Canada as elsewhere in the world, the most recent *Report on the Terrorism Threat* to Canada cautions: "Internationally, Canada continues to face exposure to terrorism financing risks" (Public Safety Canada 2019a, 19). Connections to conflict zones such as Syria and Iraq "present a high risk for the Canadian financial system's exposure to terrorist financing activity" (Public Safety Canada 2019a, 19), which includes raising, collecting, and transmitting funds to listed terrorist entities. Specifically, "Daesh, AQ [al-Qaida] and Hizballah continue to be the main concern. [...] Hizballah has a diversified funding structure and global reach that allows it to obtain funds from sympathetic individuals, businesses and charities, including via domestic support from Canada" (Public Safety Canada 2019a, 19). Criminal convictions related to terrorist financing in Canada include Hizballah and the Tamil Tigers (Leuprecht et al. 2017).

Global Report Card on Canada's AML/ATF Regime

Following the 2015 *Assessment of Inherent Risks of Money Laundering and Terrorist Financing in Canada,* the International Monetary Fund (IMF) supported the FATF in conducting a mutual evaluation of the effectiveness of Canada's AML/ATF regime and its compliance with the FATF's 40 Recommendations. The final report, published in 2016, offered multiple recommendations on strengthening Canada's AML/ATF regime.[3]

The FATF mutual evaluation showed that Canada is exposed to significant money laundering risks both domestically and abroad. Canada's AML/ATF regime achieved good grades in some areas, but others required improvements to be more effective (FATF 2016). The FATF evaluation indicated that Canada's recovery of the proceeds of crime was relatively low and inadequate relative to Canada's main money laundering risks. Québec was credited with being significantly more effective at confiscating the proceeds of crime than were other jurisdictions in Canada. The FATF recognized provincial and municipal governments in Québec for having clear priorities that identify assets for confiscation, especially in cases involving OCGs; this approach resulted in greater asset forfeiture in Québec than in other jurisdictions in Canada (see the Québec section below). The FATF recommended that Canada review the priorities of law enforcement agencies to align them better with the findings of its own 2015 risk assessment.

The 2016 FATF mutual evaluation also highlighted the apparent disconnect between money laundering risks identified in the 2015 assessment and actual law enforcement activity. The FATF assessors determined that although law enforcement agencies in Canada generally agreed with the findings in the 2015 risk assessment, their prioritization processes, particularly those of the RCMP, were not compliant with the findings of the 2015 risk assessment. While resources were directed at illicit drug offences, "other instances of high-threat predicate offenses [i.e., those offenses that give rise to money-laundering activities], especially fraud, corruption, counterfeiting, tobacco smuggling, and related ML ... are not adequately ranked in the prioritization process and, consequently, are not pursued to the extent that they should" (FATF 2016).

The federal government at the time had committed to providing law enforcement with funding to address money laundering threats. However, the agencies that the FATF assessors studied pointed out competing priorities that prevented them from targeting other aforementioned money laundering risks. As a result, the FATF recommended increasing efforts to detect, pursue, and prosecute cases of money laundering related to high-risk predicate offenses other than drugs and fraud, notably, corruption and tobacco smuggling.

On the topic of prosecutorial effectiveness, the FATF evaluation found Canada's rate of conviction for money laundering to be low. This deficiency was also noted in a March 2018 annual report submitted by the US Department of State's Bureau of International Narcotics and Law Enforcement Affairs (2018). The document largely echoed the FATF's findings and recommended that Canada step up enforcement and prosecution.

Among other recommendations, the FATF evaluation repeatedly pointed out that FINTRAC should be afforded more authority, and that it is insufficient for law enforcement to submit information to FINTRAC only on a voluntary basis. It suggested that challenges around developing actionable intelligence were due to FINTRAC's lack of rigorous information sharing practices. This comment by the FATF is noteworthy for the voluntary information regime whereby FINTRAC discloses information proactively as the most effective way for law enforcement to gain access to FINTRAC data. Heretofore law enforcement had viewed most disclosures as unactionable intelligence.

Canada's Commitments

Canada's performance in the 2016 FATF mutual evaluation prompted policy changes and legislative amendments to Canada's PCMLTFA. In an enhanced follow-up report in 2021, the FATF improved Canada's ratings for politically exposed persons, wire transfers, and a number of anti-laundering measures. The regulations are now more aligned with international standards and the FATF's recommendations. The PCMLTFA is now more relevant to the sectors that are most vulnerable to money laundering and terrorist financing. These changes are intended to strengthen Canada's AML/ATF regime and close the gaps identified in the 2016 FATF evaluation.

The federal Department of Finance has stated its intent to update Canada's 2015 AML/ATF risk assessment in consultation with the public and private sectors and addressing the operational challenges that AML/ATF regime partners face, particularly those who are responsible for investigating and prosecuting threats of money laundering. The federal government also announced its commitment to the international AML/ATF standards and to advancing an integrated domestic response to combat money laundering and terrorist financing (Canada, Department of Finance 2019a, 2019b).

Canada's updated AML/ATF risk assessment had been expected in 2019 but has not yet been released. Upon completion, whether it will introduce significant changes from Canada's 2015 risk assessment, modify the criminal activities that will be prioritized, and discuss whether law enforcement authorities will shift their priorities to include the threats identified as "very high" risk remains to be seen. Methods and criteria used to support the assessment will be subject to scrutiny to ensure that they have not been modified in such a way as to do nothing more than support the status quo of existing operational priorities as a way of avoiding further scrutiny by the international community.

New Initiatives

On paper, the 2021 amendments to the PCMLTFA regulations and the 2018/2019 priorities of the AML/ATF regime are aligned with FATF guidelines and recommendations. Yet in practice, it is unclear how the shortcomings identified in the 2016 FATF mutual evaluation will be addressed.

For example, the FATF evaluation made specific mention of tobacco smuggling and the need to prioritize "very high" threats other than illicit drugs. FATF assessors indicated that "confiscation results do not adequately reflect Canada's main ML risks, neither by nature nor by scale" (FATF 2016, 36). They also noted that prosecutions related to tobacco smuggling were not currently being calculated separately (they are embedded in a catch-all "others" category), which makes it difficult to gauge how effective they really are.

Performance reports to date have made little specific mention of how AML/ATF regime members approached the "very high" risks identified in the 2015 national risk assessment. A scan of criminal operations completed by FINTRAC yields only one operation that involved the illicit trade in tobacco. Project OTremens, which concluded on November 9, 2017, was a high-level project led by the RCMP in which FINTRAC was a partner: an Italian organized crime file that saw the arrest of several high-profile targets with several offences, including drugs, illicit tobacco, and about 3 million contraband cigarettes (FINTRAC 2018, 7).

When federal and provincial officials met in June 2019 to address money laundering and terrorist financing, the federal government issued a press release that focused on efforts to combat financial crimes in Canada (Canada, Department of Finance 2019a). In a separate joint statement, delegates "agreed that governments should intensify efforts to investigate and prosecute financial criminals, and recover proceeds of crime using criminal and civil processes" (Canada, Department of Finance 2019b). It identified vulnerable sectors as "including real estate, casinos, money services, businesses and the legal profession." The joint statement also referred to the "integrated plan to combat money laundering and terrorist financing" in the federal budget for 2019, which includes:

- Strengthening federal policing operational and investigative capacity by providing up to $68.9 million over five years, beginning in 2019–20, and $20.0 million per year ongoing, to the Royal Canadian Mounted Police.
- Creating four new dedicated real estate audit teams through $50 million over five years to the Canada Revenue Agency.
- Strengthening operational capacity, including increased compliance examinations and enforcement in the real estate sector, through $16.9 million over five years, and $1.9 million per year ongoing, for the Financial Transactions and Reports Analysis Centre of Canada. (Canada, Department of Finance 2019b. See also Canada, Department of Finance 2019c)

CASE Study: Money Laundering and Contraband Tobacco

The 2015 AML/ATF national risk assessment identified tobacco smuggling and trafficking as one of nine activities rated as a "very high threat" based on sophistication, capability, scope of use of financial institutions, and estimated dollar value of the proceeds of crime. Tobacco smuggling and trafficking ranked ahead of identity theft and fraud, robbery and theft, human smuggling, and firearms smuggling and trafficking, as money laundering threats in Canada. Although tobacco smuggling is lucrative precisely because it evades federal and/or provincial tax payments, tax evasion and tax fraud curiously rated as "medium" money laundering threats.

The 2015 risk assessment identifies four key areas that generate the proceeds of crime from the illicit tobacco trade in Canada:

1. manufacturing operations based on Aboriginal reserves (identified as the largest source of the illicit tobacco trade in Canada),
2. counterfeit cigarettes imported from overseas (primarily China),
3. cigarettes produced legally and sold tax-free, and

4. "fine cut" tobacco imported illegally, mostly by Canadian-based manufacturers.

The 2015 risk assessment further notes significant involvement by organized crime in smuggling and trafficking illicit tobacco across the Canada–US border. It identifies these groups as among the most "sophisticated and threatening in Canada" (Canada, Department of Finance 2015).

Given the substantial proceeds of crime associated with the illicit trade in tobacco in Canada, criminals use economic sectors, financial products, and other methods to launder their money. The 2015 assessment draws particular attention to structuring, refining, and commingling.

Money Laundering Methods

The report provides an example of a group involved in drug trafficking, counterfeiting, tobacco smuggling, and human trafficking, which used deposit-taking financial institutions (DTFI) to launder money. This type of money laundering involves using ATMs to deposit cash amounts under the $10,000 reporting threshold into various personal and business accounts held at multiple DTFIs. The money is moved through bank drafts or cheques to individual businesses and then transferred to other individuals or businesses through domestic wire transfers or international electronic fund transfers.

Despite the very high level of threat identified in 2015, tobacco smuggling is conspicuously absent from recent communiqués and reports on anti-money laundering initiatives. Over the past four years, the federal government partners tasked with detecting and deterring money laundering activities have not published any significant results of steps taken to mitigate this risk.

The United States has called on Canada to be more proactive in combatting the illicit trade in tobacco, as has the international community through the FATF. Yet Canada's poor performance does not appear to be associated with its 2015 assessment, but rather in its overall implementation. The "very high" threat of money laundering in the 2015 assessment notwithstanding, Canadian law enforcement authorities have not responded in kind. According to the 2016 FATF evaluation, law enforcement agencies, specifically the RCMP, had other operational priorities and few resources available to devote to threats listed by the AML/ATF regime.

The federal and British Columbia governments have focused on AML initiatives related to real estate, casinos, luxury cars, and other sectors identified in the recent BC reports and especially in the Cullen Commission's final report. The manufacturing and distribution of contraband tobacco in Canada has notably been absent from any discussion until the release of the Cullen Commission final report where it received a brief mention. Despite its demonstrable involvement in money laundering, little effort has been made thus far to follow the proceeds of this crime. Major law enforcement initiatives in Ontario and Québec (see the "law enforcement actions" listed below) have dismantled tobacco smuggling rings but have not followed the money trail to investigate where the profits go.

Enforcement

Efforts to renew Canada's Federal Tobacco Control Strategy (FTCS) and the *Assessment of Inherent Risks of Money Laundering and Terrorist Financing in Canada* notwithstanding, Canada's federal government has taken very little concrete action to address the country's role in the illicit tobacco trade, its international impact, and laundering associated proceeds of crime.

Canada Revenue Agency

The Canada Revenue Agency's Criminal Investigations Program (CIP) has investigators who are responsible for looking into suspected cases of tax evasion, fraud, and other serious violations of tax laws. According to the CRA website, the CIP prioritizes significant cases of tax evasion with an international element. The CIP also looks at sophisticated and organized tax schemes aimed at defrauding the government and significant cases involving income tax and/or GST/HST tax evasion, including the underground economy. All these criteria are aligned with the trafficking and smuggling of contraband tobacco. However, the key results for the CRA's criminal investigations provide no breakdown of criminal markets or any indication that the illicit trade in tobacco is a priority for the CIP.

RCMP

When the old Federal Tobacco Control Strategy expired in 2018, the RCMP removed all traces of it from its website. It has not been replaced with a new strategy, nor do the RCMP's 2018/2019 and 2019/2020 departmental performance plans make any substantive mention of the FTCS or tobacco smuggling. Despite RCMP funding dedicated to combatting contraband tobacco (via the FTCS or the AML/ATF regime), the force lacks a strategy to deal with the illicit trade in tobacco.

Law Enforcement Actions

Owing to the many variables involved and conflicting public reporting, the potential money-laundering value of assets forfeited during seizures is difficult to determine. By way of example, should the value be calculated strictly as a function of goods seized during a raid, or should a value be extrapolated for the time the ring was in operation?

Police sometimes estimate values, but how robust these are is difficult to gauge because sources and methods are not disclosed and thus impossible to triangulate. Nonetheless, the sample of cases below is meant to convey an impression of the staggering sums that criminal operations end up needing to launder.

Project Cairnes. In June 2020, Project Cairnes, a 24-month tobacco smuggling investigation led by the Contraband Tobacco Enforcement Team (CTET) of the OPP, resulted in the arrests of sixteen people were charged with 218 offenses centred around "Traditional Organized Crime" that developed and ran an illicit cigarette factory on a southern Ontario Aboriginal reserve. These cigarettes fuelled a trans-Canadian supply chain of illicit products with tobacco moving west into BC and illicit cannabis returning. Cairnes resulted in the seizure of 11.5 million cigarettes with a street value of $2.6 million in British Columbia or

$942,000 in Ontario, 1,714 lbs of cannabis with a street value of $2.5 million, 1.14 kg of cocaine, 1.3 kg of fentanyl, over $236,000 in currency, and seven vehicles.

Projects Olios and Median. On June 26, 2019, the Sûreté du Québec (SQ) issued a communiqué with an update on the contraband tobacco network that was dismantled in 2018 as part of projects Olios and Median (Sûreté du Québec 2019). These two investigations mobilized about fifty police officers from different organizations that led to the arrest of sixteen individuals. Project Olios was led by the SQ and resulted in the seizure of 15,535 kg of contraband tobacco. The SQ collected evidence that showed an estimated 632,000 kg of tobacco was imported into Canada in forty-eight shipments between June 24, 2016 and December 22, 2017, defrauding the federal and provincial governments of an estimated $178 million in unpaid taxes.

Project Median was led by the Service de police de la Ville de Montréal (SPVM) and collected intelligence that showed individuals smuggled approximately 446,500 kg of tobacco between January 2017 and March 2018 in about thirty shipments, which amounts to an estimated $110 million tax fraud. The sixteen people who were arrested as part of projects Olios and Median appeared before the courts; all have been released under conditions pending further proceedings.

Project Cendrier. A 2017 investigation, Project Cendrier (RCMP 2017) targeted individuals involved in contraband tobacco, the production and trafficking of cannabis, and the trafficking of cocaine in Québec's Valleyfield region. Cendrier resulted in the arrest of more than thirty individuals involved in various smuggling activities. Over 230 kg of cocaine destined for the Montréal market and nearly $320,000 were seized. In conjunction with Cendrier operations, an investigation targeting the trafficking of tobacco through the Port of Valleyfield and using the Lac Saint-François waterway led to the arrest of seven individuals in March 2017.

Project Mygale. In 2016, a nearly two-year investigation led by the SQ, dubbed Project Mygale, identified 158 truckloads of raw tobacco smuggled into Canada (Lau 2016). More than sixty arrests were made, and police seized more than 52,800 kg of tobacco valued at $13.5 million, more than US$3 million in cash, CA$15 million in cash and more than 800 kgs of cocaine. Police allege that between August 2014 and March 2016, more than 2 million kg of tobacco was illegally imported into Canada, worth about $530 million.

Project Lycose. In November 2014, Project Lycos (Public Safety Canada 2019b; Gonthier 2014), an 18-month tobacco smuggling investigation led by the SQ, resulted in the arrests of twenty-eight people, including Montréal's Italian Mafia and native organized crime. Police said the tobacco was imported into Canada through the Lacolle border crossing or through the Akwesasne Mohawk reserve. At the time, the SQ claimed that it was one of the largest operations ever to target the underground tobacco trade in North America, ending a tax evasion scheme worth upwards of $30 million. Lycose resulted in the seizure of approximately 40,000 kg in tobacco, which would have produced an estimated $10 million tax loss.

Provincial Government Actions

Québec

International and domestic organizations have commended Québec's approach to combatting the illicit trade in tobacco. The Québec strategy, known as ACCES Tabac (Sécurité publique Québec 2013), brings together the Sûreté du Québec, the Service de police de la Ville de Montréal, other Québec police forces, and provincial departments and agencies, as well as the RCMP, the CRA, and the CBSA.

Québec's cooperative enforcement measures were introduced in Bill 59, which empowers local police to launch and prosecute contraband investigations (Leuprecht 2016). In Ontario, by contrast, only officials from the Ministry of Finance, members of the OPP Contraband Tobacco Enforcement Team (CTET), which has been authorized by the Minister of Finance (or delegate) to exercise the same powers Ministry of Finance investigators exercise under Ontario's Tobacco Tax Act, or the RCMP have the authority to conduct full contraband tobacco investigations. Bill 59 also ensures that in Québec, sufficient resources are dedicated to contraband tobacco and that ACCES Tabac continues to receive annual funding. In 2016–2017, the Ministère des Finances du Québec allocated $50.4 million to fight tax evasion – $13.2 million of which went to AC-CES Tabac. For 2017–2018, the budget to fight tax evasion was reportedly $51.7 million, of which $13.7 million went to ACCES Tabac. According to Québec's economic action plan, the return per dollar invested in the strategy was $9.90 (Québec 2018).

The FATF and other groups credit the Québec government for providing enough funding to allow its agencies to target sectors where the risk of tax evasion is highest. According to Québec's latest *Economic Plan*, its focus on tax evasion has helped reduce tax losses. The province gives credit to its intensified efforts to fight tobacco smuggling, "which has reduced the underground economy in this sector by one half since 2009" (Québec 2018). In 2015–2016, the province received $180 million from legal tobacco revenues, and in 2016–2017 that amount increased to $186.5 million.

ACCES Tabac targets all activities related to tobacco smuggling, from the supply of raw materials to the sale of tobacco products to consumers. Between April 1, 2017 and January 31, 2018, this team made fifty-three arrests and conducted forty-five searches, which resulted in the seizure of 36,143 kg of loose tobacco, 6,250 baggies containing 200 cigarettes each, 32 vehicles, and one boat (Leuprecht et al. 2019). These seizures represent the equivalent of more than 37.4 million cigarettes.

Starting in 2022, Québec plans to inject $190 million over the next five years to improve its tools to ensure tax fairness, including $15 million that will be used in its fight against economic crimes. According to the Ministry of Finance, tax losses were $5.3 billion across the province in 2019 (Genois Gagnon 2022). Québec seems focused on the construction and crypto markets although acknowledges significant black markets in alcohol, cannabis, and tobacco. While each sector has, and appears to have maintained a dedicated task force, the relative size and focus of the Québec government seems to be shifting to crypto and other parts of the underground economy.

Ontario

The Ontario Ministry of Finance is the lead agency for regulating and enforcing tobacco regulations in the province. The OPP's aforementioned CTET, established in 2016, is currently composed of ten officers and one analyst. Compared to Québec, however, that is a disproportionately meagre investment in absolute terms, let alone for a province and economy almost twice the size of Québec. Despite the limitations of financial and human resources, CTET has had some success, but that pales in comparison with the aforementioned achievements of the JFOs in Québec under ACCES Tabac.

The provincial government's *2018 Ontario Economic Outlook and Fiscal Review*, entitled *A Plan for the People*, announced a commitment to compliance measures to address illegal tobacco (Ontario, Ministry of Finance 2018). These measures included adding penalty and offense provisions for failing to notify the Ministry of Finance of the destruction of raw leaf tobacco, exploring the implementation of automated "track and trace" technology to monitor the movement of raw leaf tobacco, expanding the size of the OPP CTET, and establishing a grants pilot project that would make funding available to law enforcement in support of tobacco investigations. While these promises appeared positive on paper, they lacked timelines for implementation. Early in 2019 the Ontario government announced that it would increase funding to CTET from $2 million to $10 million, but this promise has yet to materialize.

Half a year later, the 2019 Ontario Budget (Ontario, Ministry of Finance 2019b) made no mention of contraband and no provision for the commitments made in the 2018 *Economic Outlook*. Some articles speculated that the Ford government is backing off because it is too politically sensitive a topic to broach with Indigenous communities (Bonokoski 2019). The 2019 *Economic Outlook and Fiscal Review* (Ontario, Ministry of Finance 2019c) issued in November revealed the province's new nomenclature for contraband; it dropped the phrase "illegal tobacco" in favour of the term "unregulated tobacco," and made vague promises to "consult public health stakeholders, industry and retail associations, as well as First Nation partners" on the issue.

The Ontario government's approach appears to be shifting towards reconciliation and away from enforcement. Ontario most recently stated it is looking at "modernizing the raw leaf tobacco oversight program through the adoption of advanced technologies" as well as "collaborating with federal partners on strengthening border enforcement and combatting tobacco smuggling" (Ontario, Ministry of Finance 2022). However, unregulated trade appears to be the true focus "strengthening First Nation partnerships by focusing on economic development, business regulation and community safety" and "working closely with cigar wholesalers to strengthen guidance regarding on-reserve sales." This is consistent with the "FACT" framework whose primary purpose is to establish a regulatory system on reserves with revenue generation. It effectively authorizes and entrenches lower-price products on reserves as a way to boost economic activity. This builds on Ontario's pilot projects at Akewsasne and with the Chippewas of the Thames First Nation Indian Reserve No. 42.

Other Provinces

Manitoba continues to lead in the fight against the illicit trade. This goes for intelligence-led disruption of supply chains as well as persistent and aggressive retail compliance and undercover retail purchases. Manitoba has achieved several successes through its Ministry of Finance Special Investigations Unit (MoF SIU). It has reported multiple seizures of large volumes of contraband moving west from Ontario. This has done much to deter and limit growth of the illicit market in the province and is notable considering the overall budget and limited resources of the MoF SIU.

This is against the backdrop of significant and increasing flow of volume from Ontario and Québec going westward. The flow includes all prairie provinces and increasingly has a market in BC that has grown from obscurity to pervasive. The trend is expected to increase and accelerate in the near future as "tribe to tribe" trade is being permitted (amid ongoing court cases), which the FACT framework has set for rapid implementation.

The significance of the Ministry of Finance's success is attributable to its illicit tobacco strategy being intelligence-led. The ministry has refined the art of combining intelligence-gathering with solid senior leadership within the SIU. The province's law enforcement outreach program is pan-Canadian, as it participates in many JFOs. The SIU's seizure successes have been complemented by a program for retail compliance inspections that are meant to ensure that the black market is blocked from areas that were once dominated by contraband tobacco sales.

New Brunswick briefly had a nine-member task force that was proving effective at protecting the province and the rest of Atlantic Canada from an influx of illicit tobacco, but it was shut down in 2019 by the newly elected government.

Conclusion

AML initiatives have been receiving significant attention from governments and regulatory bodies in Canada and around the world. With governments in Canada – both federal and provincial – losing vast amounts of potential tax revenue, coupled with national and international efforts to reduce smoking rates, and given that illicit tobacco ranks among the highest threat risks for money laundering, Canada could be far more aggressive in controlling and combatting the illicit cigarette trade.

Without comprehensive and cohesive policies across departmental and political jurisdictions, Canada perpetuates high smoking rates domestically and runs the risk of being labelled as a major international source of contraband tobacco.

Two federal initiatives would go a long way toward mitigating the impact of the illicit trade in tobacco in Canada and abroad, along with its associated money laundering threats, specifically:

1. to emulate the United States in creating a Canadian Tobacco Ombudsman to coordinate efforts among relevant agencies and regulatory bodies and ensure effective focus a common goal; and
2. to introduce legislation similar to the Combating the Illicit Trade in Tobacco Products Act (CITTPA) currently being considered in the United States, which would allow Canada's federal government to impose sanctions on foreign players that are involved in the illicit tobacco trade.

These two steps would help to curtail the associated proceeds of crime from being laundered, support public health and safety initiatives, and reduce smoking rates in Canada.

Finally, to address the shortcomings identified by the FATF evaluation of the government's 2015 risk assessment, law enforcement agencies in Canada will have to bolster their efforts to combat money laundering or there will continue to be a considerable risk to Canada's financial and economic stability. The most effective way to dismantle criminal organizations is to target their infrastructure and pursue the forfeiture of their assets. Most serious criminal organizations are motivated by profit; removing that incentive is the ultimate deterrent.

In the wake of media attention and heightened international scrutiny of money laundering and terrorist financing, Canadian federal and provincial governments have redoubled their efforts to strengthen the legal and enforcement regime. However laudable in theory, the actual resources and policy attention detailed in this study cast doubt on the federal government's commitment to ensuring that law enforcement can effectively investigate, arrest, and convict suspects involved in financial crime.

Notes

1 The funded partners are the Department of Finance Canada, the Department of Justice Canada, the Public Prosecution Service of Canada (PPSC), the Financial Transactions and Reports Analysis Centre of Canada (FINTRAC), the Canada Border Services Agency (CBSA), the Canada Revenue Agency (CRA), the Canadian Security Intelligence Service (CSIS), and the Royal Canadian Mounted Police (RCMP). The non-funded partners are Public Safety Canada, the Office of the Superintendent of Financial Institutions Canada, and Global Affairs Canada.
2 The ten assessed, in addition to the foreign fighters, include: Al Qaeda in the Arabian Peninsula, Al Qaeda Core, Al Qaeda in the Islamic Maghreb, Al Shabaab, Hamas, Hizballah, Islamic State of Iraq and Syria, Jabhat Al-Nusra, Khalistani extremist groups, and remnants of the Liberation Tigers of Tamil Eelam.
3 The FATF assessment was conducted for the International Monetary Fund and was adopted by the FATF at its June 2016 plenary meeting.

References

Bonokoski, Mark. 2019. *"Bonokoski: Will the Big Premiers' Meeting Stamp Down on Illegal Smokes?"* *Toronto Sun*, June 29. https://torontosun.com/opinion/columnists/bonokoski-will-the-big-premiers-meeting-stamp-down-on-illegal-smokes.

Bureau of International Narcotics and Law Enforcement Affairs. 2018. *2018 INCSR – Volume II: Money Laundering and Financial Crimes*. Government of the United States, Department of State, March 17. https://www.state.gov/2018-incsr-volume-ii-money-laundering-and-financial-crimes-as-submitted-to-congress/.

Canada, Department of Finance. 2015. *Assessment of Inherent Risks of Money Laundering and Terrorist Financing in Canada*. Government of Canada. https://www.fin.gc.ca/pub/mltf-rpcfat/index-eng.asp.

———. 2018a. *Departmental Plan 2018–19: Supplementary Information Tables*. Government of Canada. https://www.fin.gc.ca/pub/dp-pm/2018-2019/st-ts03-eng.asp.

———. 2018b. *Reviewing Canada's Anti-Money Laundering and Anti-Terrorist Financing Regime*. https://www.canada.ca/en/department-finance/programs/consultations/2018/canadas-anti-money-laundering-anti-terrorist-financing-regime.html.

———. 2019a. "Government of Canada Leads National Response to Money Laundering and Terrorist Financing." News Release. Government of Canada, June 13. https://www.canada.ca/en/department-finance/news/2019/06/government-of-canada-leads-national-response-to-money-laundering-and-terrorist-financing.html.

———. 2019b. *Joint Statement – Federal, Provincial and Territorial Governments Working Together to Combat Money Laundering and Terrorist Financing in Canada*. Government of Canada, June 14. https://www.fin.gc.ca/n19/19-065-eng.asp.

———. 2019c. *Budget 2019: Investing in the Middle Class*. Government of Canada, March 19. https://www.budget.gc.ca/2019/docs/plan/toc-tdm-en.html.

Chartered Professional Accountants (CPA) Canada. 2022. *A Guide to Comply with Canada's Anti-Money Laundering and Anti-Terrorist Financing (AML/ATF) Legislation*. March. https://www.cpacanada.ca/-/media/site/operational/ex-executive/docs/03002-ex_aml-guidelines-en.pdf.

Cullen Commission. 2019. *Commission of Inquiry into Money Laundering in British Columbia*. https://cullencommission.ca/.

———. 2016. *Anti-Money Laundering and Counter-Terrorist Financing Measures – Canada, Fourth Round Mutual Evaluation Report*. FATF/OECD. https://www.fatf-gafi.org/publications/mutualevaluations/documents/mer-canada-2016.html.

———. 2021. *Mutual Evaluations*. FATF/OECD. https://www.fatf-gafi.org/publications/mutualevaluations/more/more-about-mutual-evaluations.html?h-f=10&b=0&s=desc(fatf_releasedate).

Financial Transactions and Reports Analysis Centre of Canada (FINTRAC). 2018. *Annual Report 2017-2018*. Government of Canada. https://www.fintrac-canafe.gc.ca/publications/ar/2018/ar2018-eng.pdf.

Genois Gagnon, Jean-Michel. 2022. "Crimes économiques, travail au noir dans la construction, cannabis, tabac et alcool. Québec veut accélérer sa bataille contre les activités illicites et la dissimulation de revenus chez des particuliers et des entreprises." *Le Journal du Québec* 25 March. https://www.journaldequebec.com/2022/03/25/la-chasse-aux-fraudes-en-tous-genres-va-sintensifier.

German, Peter M. 2018. *Dirty Money: An Independent Review of Money Laundering in Lower Mainland Casinos Conducted for the Attorney General of British Columbia*. Peter German & Associates Inc. https://news.gov.bc.ca/files/Gaming_Final_Report.pdf.

———. 2019. *Dirty Money – Part 2: Turning the Tide – An Independent Review of Money Laundering in B.C. Real Estate, Luxury Vehicle Sales & Horse Racing*. Peter German & Associates Inc. https://news.gov.bc.ca/files/Dirty_Money_Report_Part_2.pdf.

Gonthier, Valérie. 2014. "Contrebande de tabac : 28 arrestations dans le cadre du projet Lycose." *Journal de Montréal*, April 30. https://www.journaldemontreal.com/2014/04/30/vaste-operation-visant-la-contrebande-de-tabac-2.

Lau, Rachel. 2016. "Quebec, U.S. Police, RCMP Bust Drug, Illegal Tobacco Ring with Ties to Bikers, Reserves." *Global News*, March 30. https://globalnews.ca/news/2607530/quebec-u-s-police-rcmp-bust-drug-illegal-tobacco-ring-with-ties-to-bikers-reserves/.

Leuprecht, Christian. 2016. *Smoking Gun: Strategic Containment of Contraband Tobacco and Cigarette Trafficking in Canada*. Macdonald Laurier Institute. https://www.macdonaldlaurier.ca/files/pdf/MLILeuprechtContrabandPaper-03-16-WebReady.pdf.

Leuprecht, Christian, Olivier Walther, David B. Skillicorn, and Hillary Ryde-Collins. 2017. "Hezbollah's Global Tentacles: A Relational Approach to Convergence with Transnational Organized Crime." *Terrorism and Political Violence* 29, no. 5: 902–921.

Leuprecht, Christian, Arthur Cockfield, Pamela Simpson, and Masseh Haseeb. 2019. "Tackling Transnational Terrorist Resourcing Nodes and Networks," *Florida State University Law Review* 46, no. 2: 290–344.

Maloney, Maureen, Tsur Somerville, and Brigitte Unger. 2019. *Combatting Money Laundering in BC Real Estate*. Expert Panel on Money Laundering in BC Real Estate. https://news.gov.bc.ca/files/Combatting_Money_Laundering_Report.pdf.

Ontario, Ministry of Finance. 2018. *A Plan for the People: Ontario Economic Outlook and Fiscal Review. 2018 Background Papers*. Government of Ontario. https://www.fin.gov.on.ca/fallstatement/2018/fes2018-en.pdf.

———. 2019a. *A Plan to Build Ontario Together: 2019 Ontario Economic*

Outlook and Fiscal Review. Government of Ontario. http://budget.ontario.ca/2019/fallstatement/pdf/2019-fallstatement.pdf.

———. 2019b. *2019 Ontario Budget: Ontario's Plan to Protect What Matters Most.* Government of Ontario. http://budget.ontario.ca/2019/index.html.

———. 2019c. *A Plan to Build Ontario Together: 2019 Ontario Economic Outlook and Fiscal Review.* Government of Ontario. http://budget.ontario.ca/2019/fallstatement/pdf/2019-fallstatement.pdf.

———. 2022. *Fall Economic Statement. Annex: Details of Tax Measures and Other Legislative Activities.* https://budget.ontario.ca/2022/fallstatement/annex.html.

Osler. 2021. *Anti-Money Laundering in Canada. A Guide to the June 1, 2021 Changes.* https://www.osler.com/osler/media/Osler/reports/anti-money-laundering/Anti-money-laundering-in-canada-guide.pdf.

Perrin, Dan. 2018. *Real Estate Regulatory Structure Review. Perrin, Thorau and Associates Ltd. for B.C. Ministry of Finance.* https://news.gov.bc.ca/files/Real_Estate_Regulatory_Structure_Review_Report_2018.pdf.

Public Safety Canada. 2019a. *2018 Public Report on the Terrorism Threat to Canada.* Government of Canada. https://www.publicsafety.gc.ca/cnt/rsrcs/pblctns/pblc-rprt-trrrsm-thrt-cnd-2018/index-en.aspx.

———. 2019b. *Evaluation of the Akwesasne Organized Crime Initiative.* Government of Canada. Available at *https://www.publicsafety.gc.ca/cnt/rsrcs/pblctns/2018-19-kwssn-rgnzd-crm-vltn/index-en.aspx.*

Québec. 2018. *The Québec Economic Plan: Additional Information 2018-2019.* Gouvernement du Québec, March. http://www.budget.finances.gouv.qc.ca/budget/2018-2019/en/documents/AdditionalInfo_18-19.pdf.

Royal Canadian Mounted Police (RCMP). 2017. "Investigation Cendrier: Several Arrests for Trafficking Illegal Tobacco." News Release, December 12. RCMP. http://www.rcmp-grc.gc.ca/en/news/2017/investigation-cendrier-arrests-trafficking-illegal-tobacco.

Sécurité publique Québec. 2013. *Lutte contre le commerce illégal du tabac: Actions concertées pour contrer les économies souterraines – Tabac.* Government of Quebec. https://www.securitepublique.gouv.qc.ca/police/phenomenes-criminels/fraude/acces-tabac.html.

Sûreté du Québec [SQ]. 2019. "*Démantèlement d'un réseau de contrebande de tabac.*" Press Release, June 26. Sûreté du Québec. https://www.sq.gouv.qc.ca/communiques/demantelement-dun-reseau-de-contrebande-de-tabac/.

5

Running with the Hare, Hunting with the Hounds: The Canadian State and Money Laundering

Sanaa Ahmed

Introduction

From relative obscurity, "money laundering"[1] and launderers have risen to notoriety in Canada in the last eight years. Despite an ostensibly well-regulated financial sector and strict adherence to global AML regulation, Canada has been making headlines as a premier onshore destination for laundered monies from across the world (Oved 2016). In 2015, a government-initiated enquiry into corruption within the construction industry in Québec showed the intimate linkages between mafia-type criminal organizations and domestic politicians, big business and service industry professionals (lawyers, accountants, etc.).[2] Between 2016 and 2017, the Panama and Paradise papers revelations blew the lid off a vibrant, Canadian-made money laundering operation rather poetically referred to as "snow-washing" (Cribb and Oved 2017).[3] By the end of 2017, casinos in British Columbia were running laundering operations sophisticated enough to merit their own name – the "Vancouver Model" – while the ongoing fentanyl crisis was also producing a steady stream of illicit monies. In the background, there were also reports of $10 billion having been laundered in Alberta in 2015, reports of how laundered monies had fuelled the meteoric rise of real estate markets in Toronto and Vancouver, as well as a scandal about a Canadian bank being involved in money laundering.[4] Meanwhile, the Tax Justice Network (TJN) data for 2020 shows that inbound flows to Canada have caused other jurisdictions' tax losses worth $8 billion (Tax Justice Network 2021). It is unclear from the TJN data whether this figure also includes money lost through capital flight from other economies to Canada. Clearly, Canada is no stranger to laundering.

That said, the country also boasts a seemingly strong AML regime. Canada was among the founding members of FATF in 1989 and is also a member of the Asia/ Pacific Group (APG) on Money Laundering (FATF n.d.).[5] As recently as 2016, the country was commended by the FATF for the strength of its anti-money laundering and counter-terrorism financing (AML/CTF) regime (FATF n.d.).[6] Within Canada, money laundering is currently governed by fifteen different laws and regulatory instruments,[7] with responsibility for their implementation and enforcement assigned to various organs and institutions of the state. At the federal level, Canada currently has twelve agencies tasked with AML enforcement and prosecution while there are approximately fourteen within each province.[8] However, the extent of money laundering in Canada has cast long shadows over the purported efficacy of these laws, regulations, and agencies in impeding or preventing laundering.

Some of the problems are apparent: first, Canada relies on a definition of laundering that closely follows the one used by FATF, which positions criminality at the heart of what is seen as laundering.[9] This reduces the scope of what can be prosecuted as a laundering offence. Tax abuse of the sort revealed by the Panama and Paradise Papers, for example, would generally not qualify. Second, further reducing the number of successful laundering prosecutions is the paucity of investigative and/or prosecutorial ability. In 2018, for example, the RCMP publicly confessed it had no expertise to conduct sophisticated financial or corporate investigations. Corroborating this was a 2019 newspaper report citing Statistics Canada data as showing that 86 percent of money laundering charges filed between 2012 and 2017 never made it to trial because they were withdrawn or stayed (Oved 2019).[10] Third, regulatory and/or legislative missteps haven't helped the state's anti-laundering cause. In 2019, the federal government *seemingly* cracked down on beneficial ownership by setting up a public registry at the federal level that was meant to have persons with more than 25 percent beneficial interest disclose the same. But not only did the initiative ignore the fact that 90 percent of corporations are registered provincially – not federally – it also ignored the fact that 25 percent is too high a limit to catch anything worthwhile (Oved and Cribb 2017). The final blow comes from shifting political priorities: early in 2020, for example, the RCMP disbanded its Financial Crimes Unit in Ontario since the "new" priorities were national security, transnational serious and organized crime, and cybercrime (Oved 2020). Unsurprisingly then, there have been fewer than fifty laundering convictions in Canada in the last ten years (Maloney et al. 2019, 22–3).[11]

While it is tempting to ascribe the inadequacy of existing laws and institutions to legislative and institutional inefficiency or incompetence, to do so would be reductionist at best and willful oversight at worst. More simply: a few errors in judgment or miscalculation could potentially be explained away but an entire *series* of chronological missteps by the executive, the legislature, *and* the judiciary throw the role of the state into sharp relief. The more germane question then becomes: how are the state's normative commitments and pronouncements against laundering to be reconciled with its slew of seemingly contradictory policies, regulations, and in/action? Given the state's demonstrated and repeated inability to deliver on its promises, how reasonable is the presumption that the Canadian state *wants* to prevent or even contain laundering? And, indeed, if non-prevention is the aim, what will this achieve? To phrase the foregoing differently: who benefits from and wants laundering to continue unabated? And where does the state stand on this?[12] But every answer about what the state wants or does (or doesn't), begins with one question: who is "the state"?

The present chapter begins by unpacking what is understood as the state. The AML project appears to have an omnipotent state as its locus.

But to understand how social change is effected, one must look away from the structures and institutions of power (such as the state) to *what drives them* instead. Why does the state make the choices it does? Mann's "IEMP model" describes the *sources* of power that effect social control – ideological, economic, military, and political power (Mann 2012, 1).[13] In a similar vein, this chapter locates the logic animating the state within its engagements with other actors and structures. As a corollary to the foregoing, the state's opposition to laundering is not taken as received; instead, the very presumption is challenged by asking: cui bono? The second part drills deeper and takes up the question of whether private benefit can be segregated from public. That is, given the significance of laundering to the Canadian political economy,[14] can the interests of the state be ontologically distinct from those of the domestic political and economic elite? The third part shows how AML laws and regulations operate within the larger framework of public policy and in consonance with a host of other governmental policies on issues as varied as immigration, corporate taxation, and surveillance capitalism. The conclusion offers some preliminary thoughts on Canada's future with respect to money laundering.

State, Power and the IEMP Model

The state's *purported* centrality to the AML regulatory project owes to the link between laundering and crime. As with other crimes, the criminalization of laundering has assigned prime responsibility for its regulation to the state. Accordingly, in most jurisdictions around the world, money laundering features in the penal code as well as laundering-specific legislation. But, as discussed below, this notion of state centrality is inherently problematic. First, locating money laundering within a criminal law context encourages the import of ideas and concepts that have little relevance from a financial crime perspective. Second, by masking the actual processes of governmental decision-making, the myth of state centrality makes invisible the interests, roles, and significance of other actors.

Take the example of assault or homicide. In both cases, the state jealously guards its monopoly on violence as well as the responsibility for the maintenance of public order in the Hobbesian sense. Accordingly, the state extracts its vengeance from transgressors by imposing punishments. The problem with applying this fundamental principle of criminal justice to money laundering is that it imports – without adequate justification – the associated notion of a powerful, benevolent but disinterested arbiter to the AML regulatory project. The Hobbesian governance project pursues peace for the benefit of all: all citizens choose to forego certain rights/invest certain rights in the person of the sovereign in exchange for an objective collectively determined to be the most valuable. The political covenant is undertaken with a specific, intended outcome: peace. Even so, the sovereign only ever represents the will of the majority; the sovereign never acts for their own benefit (MacPherson 1968, 150).[15] While the modern state also *ostensibly* represents the will of the majority (at least in liberal democracies), the complexity of the decision-making process renders the eventual decision less than truly representative of the desires of the electorate. This is because, unlike Hobbes' sovereign, the modern state is both actor and place in the money laundering project (Mann 1993, 56).

What does this mean? Starting from the unexceptional position that all regulation is an expression of some interest, the law generally codifies the interests of those who have power. Since power is no zero-sum game and everyone has some power (Hobbes 1640, 26), what is notionally understood as the state is thus revealed as a *place* where ideological, economic, military, political, and judicial powers[16] interact and influence each other as well as what is understood as "state policy."[17] As Mann contends, the eventual direction of a regulation or a policy crafted by the state, is actually negotiated between the various sources and networks of power within the polity besides geopolitical concerns. A state's decision to wage war, for example, is a *political* decision that is further shaped by its military's propensity for adventurism. Yet the decision is also profoundly influenced by economic power actors (these would potentially include defence contractors looking to sell arms, government and military functionaries looking to make money off these deals, traders and businesses seeking new markets etc.). While no singular source of power has determinacy, each source of power brings its own pressure to bear on what is eventually characterized as a state decision. This is the state as *place*, where the state may *own* a decision, but the decision is not solely determined by the interests of the state, independent of other actors within the polity.

That said, how are the state's interests to be ring-fenced? For example, most states presumably want higher tax revenues and the consequent ability to fund public goods. But where tax cuts are essential to the promotion of domestic industries and improved employment statistics, *both* options – the tax hike (which benefits citizens) and the tax cut (which benefits businesses) – can be seen as promoting the interests of the state. The interests of a state are thus fluid and are influenced by its various constituencies (that is, the citizens who benefit from public goods, the industries being promoted, and the people finding jobs) as well as the exigencies of the time (for example, promoting industry is deemed more important in a recession).

Yet Mann's state also manifests an autonomy, an identity independent of its multiple networks of power (Mann 1993, 86). Mann and Kennedy both agree that the position of an actor/structure and their specific interests are *the ossifications of earlier conflict and power battles* (Kennedy 2018, 79). The point is significant: the positions, interests, and objectives assumed by a state (or any power actor, structure, or institution, for that matter) evolved during previous encounters with power. So, for example, the pro-capitalist tilt of the Canadian state is not *received* as present-day pressure from the economic elite but is the *result* of the state's earlier interactions with economic, ideological, and political power. That is, the state as an *actor* is internally transformed by the encounter such that its own objectives become initially entwined, but eventually independent of the external power. Facilitating business, for example, makes sense for the state because, in previous interactions with economic power, the state realized that doing so furthers its political leverage among the economic elite, creates political capital (through the provision of employment opportunities for the citizens), and often generates economic revenue in the form of greater tax revenues. Due to this internal transformation, facilitating business became a "state objective" much the way crime control is.

However, one crucial difference remains: peace/crime control is a *collectively determined* objective, where the sovereign acts for and on behalf of the citizens who have delegated their power to the sovereign to do something they *all* want. But facilitating business is neither a collectively determined objective nor desired by all; here is something the state does *for itself* and *some* of its constituencies. This recognition militates against the image promoted by *Leviathan* – and criminal law – of the sovereign as a disinterested arbiter. This sovereign – the modern state – is clearly interested and deeply invested in the outcomes it promotes.

What does the above mean in the context of money laundering? While a detailed discussion follows, three points are key. First, situating the modern state at the centre of the AML regulatory project imputes to the state autonomy and a puissance unsubstantiated by ground realities. The modern state is not the sole driver of regulation, and the influence of its constituencies is significant, if not always determinative. Theoretically, this should not matter: a state with a conflict of interest *ought* not to have complete regulatory autonomy. However, indulging in the pretense that the state – as a unitary, monolithic power – is the locus of decision-making allows for making invisible the interests and identities of those who drive its decisions. As long as the state remains the cynosure, the drivers of its decisions – who also stand to benefit from the same – can remain hidden. To put it another way: the question of cui bono does not arise or is forestalled *because* the fiction that the state creates policies and regulations alone and in a vacuum is so powerful.

Second, treating money laundering like any other crime allows this "compromised" or impressionable state to assume the mantle of neutrality. Aside from when it cedes to the influence of others, historically, the state has also looked to use AML regulation for its own ends: as a political tool in line with foreign policy objectives (Beare and Woodiwiss 2014, 546), as a domestic law enforcement policy tool (Kilchling 2014, 657–9), or even as a bid to increase the arbitrary powers available to law enforcement agencies Naylor 2004, 11). At times the regulation has followed state greed – for confiscated assets (Kilchling 2014, 659) or tax evasion dollars (Levi 2014, 420–1); at other times, the regulation has been used to construct a multimillion-dollar "compliance industry" and to facilitate its growing "exports" of training and education initiatives (Beare 2003, xv–vi). Most significantly, in onshore havens as well as offshore ones, laundering activity has helped sustain the real economy (Ahmed, 2023). To categorize laundering as a criminal offence is to allow the state complete discretion in how to enforce laws, prosecute, and adjudge crimes *that it benefits from materially*. And, if the state so desires, *to choose not to do anything at all*, especially where laundering is the lifeblood of the domestic political economy. The key point is, that every decision to focus (or not) on a particular set of offences or crimes, to fund (or defund) certain departments and units, is animated by a passionate underlying logic even when this is not apparent.

Third, the criminal categorization also enables the state to assume an air of studied opposition to the practice of laundering without ever needing to prove it. Even in the absence of evidence, the state is presumed to oppose laundering as fervently as it opposes homicide. Significantly, this presumption of opposition structures what can be thought, said, and done. For example, the idea that the state may want to facilitate and promote laundering – a perfectly legitimate hypothesis, given the multiple ways the state stands to benefit from the same and the many ways the state fails in its prosecution and enforcement duties – begins to sound as ridiculous as the idea that the state may wish to encourage homicide. The effect? Even the critical scholars see the advantages accruing to the state – the powers for LEAs, the confiscated assets etc. – as serendipitous by-products of the regulatory regime and not the state's primary objective. As such, there is no sustained interrogation of those who do benefit from laundering, both within the state and without.

Recognizing this state-sized blind spot will change many of the questions in the field. Canada's drive against drug trafficking and corruption is a good example. The question being asked is whether the existing laundering regulation is enough to stop drug traffickers and corrupt persons. But perhaps the question that needs to be asked is, who does this focus on drugs and corruption benefit? Who or what offences does one stop seeing when one zooms in on drug-related offences? Or, to put this in a fairly pragmatic way, could Canada ever have attained success as an onshore haven for illicit monies from trade-based malpractices if its entire enforcement and prosecution might have not been directed against fentanyl peddlers and smugglers in the first place?

Private vs. Public?

While recognition of the state's role in laundering is the first step, the attendant second step is sequestering the state from its non-state influences and adequate problematization of its role. Without this, the apportionment of responsibility – or, conversely, blame – for the thriving laundering business becomes inordinately difficult. As such, it is critical to determine the extent of the state's actual involvement in regulation, to understand why the state made the choices it did, and how it chose its prescriptive and/or proscriptive measures. Further, it is equally important to know who else the AML/CTF regime helped and how much AML regulation was driven by private/non-state interests as opposed to public interests.

Unfortunately, these questions have drawn little scholarly attention for the most part, which has left intact the tangled mess of public and private benefits. The issues were mostly subsumed by the focus on the criminogenic character of laundering. Conventional criminology suggested that only criminals benefitted from crime, and the same logic was applied to laundering. As such, the question of material benefits accruing to the state did not arise. Further, as the Hobbesian guarantor of peace, the state was seen as fully engaged with and responsible for the processes of regulation, its choices implicitly understood to be governed by the imperatives of crime control. With such an expansive role for the state, there was little space left for others; consequently, as discussed above, the question of other beneficiaries was neither articulated nor their contribution recognized.[18] But the point that merits heavy underscoring is that this making invisible – of the material interests of the state, of the roles played by others – is neither passive nor inadvertent.

Scholars have long discussed the centrality of invisibility to the construction of an edifice of power.[19] More recent scholarship details the advantages of invisibility: for example, how "expertise" provides plausible deniability regarding the agency of individual decision-makers or, in the context of war and law, how the process of abstraction allows actors to make decisions without having to assume responsibility for the same (Kennedy 2018, 111, 275). But Althusser's critical contribution is that invisibility, too, is constructed (2015, 36).[20] The invisible becomes so *because* it is "repressed from the field of the visible." It goes unperceived because the *function* of the field of knowledge "is not to see them, to forbid any sighting of them." As such, argues Althusser, the invisible does not exist *outside* the visible but is "the *inner darkness of exclusion*, inside the visible itself" (emphasis in original; 2015, 24–5).

In the realm of AML regulation, the criminalization of laundering paved the way for making its beneficiaries invisible, both state and non-state. Criminalization set up a bright line between public and private in the AML regulatory space where none existed. Deeming the activity "criminal" instantly transformed laundering into a matter of public interest and pitched perpetrators against the state. Preventing laundering and protecting the public from laundering and its effects was categorized as a task for the state. The idea that the state could be cavalier about this responsibility or that the state could be interested in propagating and/or facilitating laundering thus became as inconceivable as the idea that a state could encourage other crimes. This allowed for, as Bourdieu puts it, the profit of saying while denying it by the way it is said. That is, the repressed elements (here, the material interests of the state) are concealed by integrating them into a network of relations (here, the relationship between the state and criminal law) which modify their value without modifying their substance (Bourdieu 1991, 142–3). The invisibility of the state's interests allowed it to protect and promote these interests while maintaining the fiction of proscription.

On the other hand, the sole responsibility of the state for laundering regulation also drew attention away from the *fact* of the blurred distinction between the public and the private.[21] While the "free market" is not and has never been truly free of state intervention or regulation, the post-neoliberalism state has its priorities visibly aligned with those of the market.[22] These "joint" priorities are articulated by the state through actions/reactions vide law and public policy but, increasingly, through inaction at both.[23] This is seen in the direction of specific governmental policy on, for example, immigration (discussed below) or investment but also in whether the RCMP is provided, for example, funding for hiring forensic accountants. But the point worth reiterating is that this regulation is *co-authored* by non-state actors. The notion of solo responsibility overlooked the co-option of the state by the sources of power and the influence of their historical interaction on the decisions of the state. The result was a key misunderstanding about how decisions are made within the state.

In practice, the blurring of the public-private/state-corporation distinction is what enables the neoliberal deployment of social power (that is, mutually reinforcing ideological, economic, *and* political power) to reinforce what is ultimately accepted as the natural order of things. More simply: a win-win policy that caters to the interests of all the sources of power and draws support from all as the consensus decision. This collective support – and not solo authorship by the state – is what ensures the widespread acceptance of a policy or regulation as necessary, even if not natural. As Kennedy articulates, the context for making a decision is neither a subjective preference nor an objective necessity; it is the settled outcome of "background work" or *the social construction of interests and facts relevant for decision making* (2018, 112–4). That is, a power actor's decisions stem from how it perceives and characterizes facts and its own interests to its multiple audiences. Since the public and private sectors are both involved in this construction, the interests of both have become irrevocably entwined over time.

Take the example of money laundering as an industry within the broader Canadian political economy.[24] While the Panama Paper's disclosures in 2016 brought Canada's snow-washing industry into the public eye, the jurisdiction's reputation as an onshore destination is of far older provenance and consequently, its roots in the political economy run deep. To most eyes, the advantages of promoting laundering accrue to the private sector, the wealthy global and Canadian investors who have money to hide, and the bankers, accountants, lawyers, casinos, etc., who help them navigate beneficial corporate and/or land ownership schemes and advise them on tax abuse, trade-related malpractices, and loopholes in the system. However, the gains of laundering for the Canadian state are also substantial.

While the Canadian economy is among the ten largest economies of the world (IMF 2021, 105),[25] certain structural characteristics render the economy particularly susceptible to illicit financial flows. First and foremost is the way the Canadian economy is financed. A look at the pre-pandemic numbers[26] through the conventional Keynesian Savings equals Investment lens shows the household savings rate at a low 2 percent of GDP[27] and revenues comprising just 17 percent of GDP.[28] A 2018 report by the Canada Revenue Agency (CRA) showed that wealthy Canadians had stashed between $76 billion and $241 billion in various onshore and offshore havens, which was causing tax revenue losses worth some $3 billion annually. According to the OECD's website on 18 July 2022, not only is Canada's tax-to-GDP ratio of 33.5 percent for 2019 very low by developed country standards,[29] but it is also excessively so for a welfare state. The economy is not fuelled by "excess" dollars swilling around in the system because Canada does not make enough to support itself.

Predictably, the shortfall is met through government borrowing or the incurrence of public debt.[30] Canada's gross debt in the third quarter of 2019 had ballooned to slightly over 136 percent of its GDP.[31] Of course, this level of indebtedness would be difficult to sustain without the easy availability of cheap debt, which lets Canadian federal and provincial governments enjoy virtually unlimited access to finance without suffering any of the usual consequences (high interest rates, large debt repayments, inflationary spirals, for example). The key interest rate in Canada, for example, remained below 2.25 percent between October 2008 and June 2022.[32] Needless to say, such low rates would not have been possible had the supply of money been constrained. Also noteworthy is the fact that for a highly indebted government, Canada pays less than 7 percent of federal government revenue in interest expenses (Statistics Canada 2022).[33] However, even unending streams of money must originate *somewhere*.

The data shows that domestic savings and revenue together are insufficient for the spending needs of the government. That leaves only financial inflows into Canada, which are derived from a mix of activities that are licit (for example, capital flight and business investment), illicit (for example, white collar crime and tax evasion) and on the fringes of legality (for example, tax avoidance and trade-related malpractices).

Canada's dependence on external inflows is rendered all the more complete because of the other structural peculiarity of the economy: its continuing dependence on real estate, rentals, and leasing as well as construction for economic growth. The top three contributors to the Canadian economy in terms of the percentage of GDP remain real estate, rentals, and leasing (13 percent of GDP); manufacturing (10 percent) and construction (7 percent). Taken together, the real estate and construction sector account for 20 percent of GDP (Statistics Canada 2023). This is significant because, as a general rule, the more advanced economies have moved away from the production of lower-value goods towards the provision of higher-value services as a driver of growth.[34] However, even this figure is a hugely conservative estimate since it does not pick up the elements related to real estate and construction within other sectors of the economy such as manufacturing,[35] wholesale,[36] retail,[37] and finance and insurance,[38] professional, scientific, and technical services.[39] As the details in the footnotes show, real estate and construction drive much of the activity within an economy in terms of both output and job creation.

This assertion is borne out by the growth figures for Canada. According to Statistics Canada, in 2019, the GDP grew by 2 percent, a decrease from 3.2 percent in 2017.[40] The growth rate fell because of the decline in business investment in non-residential construction due to the completion of major construction projects in several provinces and territories as well as the downward pressure on housing activity following the implementation of heightened mortgage rules and higher interest rates. Statistics Canada's province-wise breakdown of growth also showed that the most growth came from real estate activity as well as construction-related activities.[41] It would not be an overstatement here to conclude that continued *and substantial* investment in these industries is *essential* to the welfare of the Canadian economy.

Fortunately, then, real estate and rental leasing happens to be the top industry for business investors, both immigrant and non-immigrant. The Business Immigration Program survey conducted by the Evaluation Department in 2014 found that real estate and rental leasing accounted for 27.9 percent of businesses operated by non-immigrants and for 29.5 percent of businesses operated by business immigrants. The breakdown for each of the three classes of business immigrants was even more revealing: real estate and rental leasing accounted for 48.8 percent of businesses operated by investors, 25.6 percent of businesses operated by entrepreneurs and 22.4 percent of businesses operated by self-employed persons (Evaluation Department 2014, 43).

The foregoing has a significant bearing on what the role of the state is or ought to be. First, the influx of "laundered monies" – whether through beneficial corporate/land ownership schemes, business immigration programs or a studied governmental indifference to tax abuse and trade-related malpractices – helps the state stay afloat because ordinary, middle-class Canadians clearly do not save enough to finance investment. Encouraging and facilitating this inflow is thus of great importance to the state. Second, Canada derives most of its economic growth from real estate and construction-related activities. Even if the bulk of investment in these industries derives from laundered monies, the positive impact on incomes and employment justifies the state promoting the same. In both these situations, the interests of the state can be seen as clearly dovetailing with those of the private sector. This is why the idea of public interests as distinct from private interests does not hold water anymore.

Tombs corroborates such a reading. He invokes Gramsci and Poulantzas to contend that the distinction between public and private spaces is a juridical one sustained by the apparatuses of the state (2012, 173).[42] Dubbing the state as invariably "capitalist," Tombs maintains that this state values profit above social values and challenges the "false assumption" that the state is oppositional and external to corporations (2012, 171–2, 176) or that the state and the power elite are "ontologically distinct" (Kauzlarich, Mullins, and Matthews 2003, 242). In a similar vein, Pistor also maintains that the role of regulatory agencies is to reproduce the social conditions necessary to sustain the capitalist social order (2019, 3–5).

As the above shows, criminalizing laundering and holding the state alone responsible for regulation allowed the fictitious "the state" to eclipse the role of all others in devising policies and the AML architecture that benefitted them all. A jointly helmed project was solely ascribed to the state. Not only were the interests and roles of the other beneficiaries made invisible, but even the material interests of the state were also overlooked. Since the state was not *seen* as a direct beneficiary of laundering, the myth of its impartiality remained undisturbed. This vindicates Kennedy's stance that background work is at its best when it is least visible and has become internalized as a way of thinking (2018, 115–6). Further, as the ostensibly disinterested arbiter, the state also got to control the dominant narrative in public policy and in the mainstream media without challenge.

Laundering as Public Policy

To understand how AML laws and regulations fit into the Canadian public policy framework, the state's historical response to laundering incidents and events is a starting point. However, it is far more important to look at governmental policy in seemingly unrelated areas such as immigration (or corporate taxation and surveillance capitalism, for that matter) to figure out how the state really approaches laundering.

In the last decade, every revelation about Canada's laundering problem – such as the casinos, and the Panama and Paradise Papers – has triggered waves of public opprobrium and calls for greater regulatory oversight. However, the linkages between the events were never mounted into a more meaningful discussion of money laundering in Canada. Why, for example, is the sizeable financial crime policing apparatus in Canada unable to detect, apprehend, or prosecute the launderers? Is the apparatus responsible for these failures, either because of its systemic design flaws and/or its operational inefficiencies? If so, who is to be held accountable and how? Or is continued laundering evidence of a flawed public policy? If so, how is this to be remedied?

Without clear answers to any of these questions, public discourse on laundering focused on the purported laxity of regulation of casinos and the housing and drugs markets while policing and other issues receded into the background. Simultaneously, the state announced seemingly ambitious but essentially unquantifiable policy responses to the issue of laundering: "rooting out" corruption, increasing regulatory "oversight" at the casinos, "tackling" the opioids crisis and making housing "affordable" for "ordinary Canadians." The accompanying regulatory initiatives were just as whimsically conceived and often, entirely inadequate to their task. For example, there was little explication of how corruption in the Québec construction industry would be rooted out or who would do this when most of the stakeholders and actors (including regulators and politicians) were in on the game. Similarly, when the extent of snow-washing through shell companies was unearthed, the then finance minister initially refused to institute a public register containing ownership details of corporations and, subsequently, instituted one at only the federal level.[43] Given that most corporations are incorporated provincially (Oved and Cribb 2017, 18 July),[44] the exercise was doomed to failure. In another instance, the BC government commissioned a series of reports into laundering in the province[44] and in 2019, came up with legislation mandating transparency in land ownership[45] and, subsequently, corporate ownership.[46] However, the laws as they stand are unlikely to have the kind of impact on either housing prices or corporate transparency that champions of transparency would have hoped for.[47] Meanwhile, it is significant that Manulife, the bank at the centre of money laundering-related fines, did not lose its licence.

The above policy responses and regulatory initiatives are unsurprising to critics of Canada's money laundering policies who have long argued that there is little political or corporate will to combat laundering and investigate white-collar crime, particularly once the story disappears from news cycles (Beare 2018b, 514).[48] This lack of will manifests itself more in action (or inaction[49]) than in words, more in on-the-ground institutional arrangements than in political statements. While the attitudes of Crown prosecutors or politicians shuttering the Financial Crimes Unit in Ontario are some examples, some of the clearest indicators of such "arrangements" lie within broader governmental policy in seemingly unrelated areas. One such example is that of Canadian immigration policy.

Since the 1990s, the federal government and Québec have concurrently been running immigration programs specifically designed to draw foreign capital into Canada. The program logic was to have foreign investors make up for the lack of Canadian capital by financing industries and/or businesses that would both generate income and provide employment (Evaluation Division 2014, 2, 73).[50] The 2016 census data compiled by Statistics Canada shows the number of economic migrants to Canada between 1980 and 2016 was 2,994,135,[51] of which 284,840 (or 9.5 percent) were applicants under business programs while 331,800 (or 11 percent) had applied under provincial and territorial nominee programs.[52] Investors were asked to make a one-time capital contribution of either $400,000 (pre-2010) or $800,000 (post-2010) to the Canadian economy in the form of a five-year, interest-free loan. While bringing funds from their home countries to Canada was a precondition for business immigration, even the economic migrants who were workers (2,357,225[53] or 78.7 percent) or provincial/territorial nominees brought funds for their resettlement costs, etc. Between 2007 and 2011 alone, Canada attracted $6.42 billion under just its federal and Québec immigrant investor program (Evaluation Division 2014, 47).[54]

But the most important point to note here is that *the economic migration program does not seem to have had any stipulations regarding the source or origin of funds in the home country.*[55] This is not to imply that *all* economic migrants to Canada were kleptocrats, corrupt government officials, or drug traffickers who brought in pools of filthy lucre from their countries of origin. But the *absence* of stipulations clearly indicates that the cleanliness of the money was *not* a priority for the Canadian state. The idea appears controversial initially, but it makes imminent sense upon further reflection: once it is in the system, dirty money behaves just like clean money. Banks and casinos make profits off even laundered monies, pay their employees and use this money to grow their businesses and make more jobs. The lawyers, accountants, and government officials who deal with this money – to conduct real estate transactions or set up shell companies – plough this money back into the economy, through both their own consumption and by paying federal and provincial taxes on this income. The governments also reap corporate taxes and fees for many of these transactions. Why would *any* government – let alone a cash-strapped government such as the Canadian government – worry about the origins of this money?

While the federal investor program was discontinued in 2014, the pool of ready money was too attractive to dismiss. Consequently, provinces continued to have their own investor and entrepreneurial streams. Now, the federal government has included ambitious immigration targets in its efforts to stimulate the moribund pandemic economy. It will be interesting to see if the government imposes a "cleanliness" requirement on funds being brought in by the new immigrants. This is particularly because most indicators – especially the Panama and Paradise Papers findings as well as the 2020 Tax Justice Network figures – suggest that Canada is still not unduly worried about the cleanliness of inflows, whether from immigration or from investment. The paucity of domestic savings and tax revenue have rendered the state dependent on external monies and by all accounts, the state is not looking this gift horse in the mouth.

The above shows that flailing governmental/corporate desire to "combat" money laundering is not born of lethargy or apathy: the significant political and economic benefits of laundering necessarily *obviate* every desire to extinguish the phenomenon. While *laundering* regulation is often strengthened, its efficacy depends on the network of other laws and regulations in the field. As long as immigration policies, for example, are designed to encourage the influx of illicit funds, laundering in Canada is unlikely to stop. Similarly, just as long as corporate taxation in Canada remains lower relative to other countries with similar features, Canada will remain an attractive destination for funds from corporate malpractices. More simply: the torpor of Canadian public policy is among the requisite features of vibrant onshore destinations and thus, is more likely to be systemic rather than serendipitous. The laundering industry does not flourish because laundering regulation is *weak*; regulation is weak *because* the industry is strong.

Conclusion

The various government-sponsored reports on money laundering seem to suggest that the federal and provincial governments are desperate to stop laundering. The fact of the various reports commissioned is, somehow, supposed to indicate the seriousness of the government's resolve. However, none of these reports addresses the core political economy issue: can Canada do without illicit financial flows? Opponents of laundering – including the normatively inclined among the report authors – often cite runaway housing prices as evidence of how laundering is hurting "ordinary" Canadians. Dirty money from abroad, so the argument goes, is pricing Canadians out of the housing market. The argument that gets negligible traction comparatively is that the same money is also a steady source of finance for a borrowing-prone government, is funding investment in various industries, is providing jobs and income for "ordinary" Canadian plumbers, masons, carpenters, realtors, mortgage brokers, and accountants *and* is helping gird up Canadian growth figures.

The primary problem with the criminalization approach to laundering is that it ignores the less-than-palatable imperatives of the state. It cannot synthesize the conflicting responsibilities of the state: to keep housing prices low but also find cheap funds that will invigorate the Canadian economy. This is perhaps why the Canadian state uses one set of policies (laundering regulation) to appease the cheap housing lobbyists and another set of policies (investment and immigration policies) to protect its own interests and mollify those who have come to rely on laundered monies for their livelihood. Since the state is incapable of articulating and owning these disparate, conflicting sets of commitments, the actual and the stated public policy objectives and positions assumed by the Canadian state will remain riven by a disjuncture. However, this will not affect ground realities and is unlikely to disrupt the laundering business at all. And while this disjuncture remains, Canada will remain open for snow-washing.

Notes

This chapter stems from research conducted as a Killam postdoctoral fellow at the Schulich School of Law, Dalhousie University from 2019 to 2021. The author wishes to acknowledge the generosity of the Killam Foundation in funding this project.

1 The global regulator for money laundering – the Financial Action Taskforce on Money Laundering and Terrorism Financing (FATF) – defines laundering as the processing of the proceeds of criminal acts to disguise their illegal origin so that criminals may enjoy these profits without jeopardizing their source. According to FATF, only drugs and arms trafficking, smuggling, sex work, embezzlement, insider trading, bribery, and computer fraud schemes qualify as crimes proper. Tax-related matters are specifically excluded. However, the FATF definition has many critics. They advocate for the more expansive term illicit financial flows (IFFs), which captures methods, practices and crimes that aim to transfer money or capital from one country to another, in contravention of national or international laws or their spirit. The term thus covers a range of practices, including tax abuse (evasion and avoidance), trade-related malpractices (including transfer pricing and Base Erosion Profit Shifting), white-collar crime (including political, corporate, and criminal corruption), capital flight as well as proceeds of informal economies. In this chapter, "money laundering" and "IFFs" are used interchangeably, unless context suggests otherwise. The politics of the usage of the term money laundering is beyond the scope of this text.

2 The Charbonneau Commission, officially called the Commission of Inquiry on the Awarding and Management of Public Contracts in the Construction Industry, was a public inquiry into corruption in the management of public construction contracts in Québec. For critical reads on the report, see Beare (2018a, 2018b).

3 The term riffs off the original "laundering" phrase with a nod to both the pristine reputations of Canada and its financial regulators as well as the Canadian winter.

4 The bank was eventually identified as Manulife but was only fined for laundering money.

5 The stated function of the APG is to "ensure the adoption, implementation and enforcement of internationally accepted anti-money laundering and counter-terrorist financing standards[.] ... The effort includes assisting countries and territories of the region in enacting laws to deal with the proceeds of crime, mutual

legal assistance, confiscation, forfeiture and extradition; providing guidance in setting up systems for reporting and investigating suspicious transactions and helping in the establishment of financial intelligence units." (FATF 2016) While the list of members includes several countries seen as recalcitrant and thus, in need of such assistance, presumably the same does not apply to countries such as Canada, the US, Australia, and New Zealand, which are also FATF members, and can be reliably presumed to be the ones *providing* assistance.

6   Canada's major failing was seen as its inability to demand that lawyers and Québec notaries report their clients for money laundering. In 2015, the Supreme Court of Canada had prevented lawyers from reporting on grounds that the practice would lead to breach of client-attorney privilege. (FATF 2016).

7   These include the Criminal Code of Canada, Proceeds of Crime (Money Laundering) and Terrorist Financing Act 2000, Mutual Legal Assistance in Criminal Matters 1985, Income Tax Act 1985, OSFI Act 1985, Canada Business and Corporations Act 1985, Seized Property Management Act 1993, United Nations Act 1985, Proceeds of Crime (Money Laundering) and Terrorist Financing Suspicious Transaction Reporting Regulations, Proceeds of Crime (Money Laundering) and Terrorist Financing Regulations, Cross-border Currency and Monetary Instruments Reporting Regulations, Proceeds of Crime (Money Laundering) and Terrorist Financing Registration Regulations, Proceeds of Crime (Money Laundering) and Terrorist Financing Administrative Monetary Penalties Regulations, Regulations Implementing the United Nations Resolutions on the Suppression of Terrorism 2001 and United Nations Al-Qaida and Taliban Regulations 1999.

8   The federal agencies include the Canada Border Services Agency, the Canada Revenue Agency, CSIS, Department of Finance, Department of Justice, Financial Transactions and Reports Analysis Centre of Canada (FINTRAC), Public Prosecution Service of Canada, RCMP, Statistics Canada, Canada Mortgage and Housing Corporation, Bank of Canada and the Office of the Superintendent of Financial Institutions. The provincial agencies include the RCMP (except in Ontario and Québec), municipal police, Crown counsel (e.g., BC Crown Counsel), Civil Forfeiture Office, MoF Revenue Division, Office of the Chief Information Officer (BC), Land Title and Survey Authority (BC), BC Assessment, real estate regulators, financial sector regulators, securities regulators, Financial Institutions Commission (BC), professional regulators (e.g., Law Society of Ontario, Notaries Public, Chartered Professional Accountants, etc.) as well as lottery/gambling regulators.

9   The Criminal Code states: "S 462.31 (1) Every one commits an offence who uses, transfers the possession of, sends or delivers to any person or place, transports, transmits, alters, disposes of or otherwise deals with, in any manner and by any means, any property or any proceeds of any property with intent to conceal or convert that property or those proceeds, knowing or believing that, or being reckless as to whether, all or a part of that property or of those proceeds was obtained or derived directly or indirectly as a result of (a)

the commission in Canada of a designated offence; or (b) an act or omission anywhere that, if it had occurred in Canada, would have constituted a designated offence." Section 2(1) of the PCMLFTA, on the other hand, simply defines a "money laundering offence" as "an offence under subsection 462.31(1) of the Criminal Code".

10 The article says this is because Crown prosecutors end up using the laundering charges as a bargaining chip and withdrawing charges after successful plea negotiations with the accused.

11 Interestingly, the authors say that while terrorism financing is generally prioritized over laundering, even the police see civil forfeiture as an easy alternative to criminal prosecution for money laundering.

12 Perhaps even more interesting would be the question of whether laundering is possible without the complicity and the connivance of the state but that is another article entirely!

13 While Mann relies on standard understandings of "economic" and "ideological" power, his segregation of military and political power merits further explication. To Mann, military power is focused, furious, lethal violence exercised by armies, terrorists, paramilitaries, and criminals. Political power, on the other hand, is the centralized, territorial regulation of social life, through law and rule-governed political deliberations in centralized courts, councils, assemblies, and ministries. Unlike Weber who thinks any organization (including NGOs, corporations, and social movements) can have political power, Mann sees the state as the only spatial and institutionalized form of centralized, territorial power. However, Mann fails to evaluate judicial power as a source of social power; this is an unfortunate omission.

14 For a detailed discussion of the centrality of money laundering to the Canadian political economy vide domestic capital and domestic businesses, see Ahmed (2023).

15 Although the process Hobbs describes is clearly the delegation of authority, he insists this exercise of collective power is not delegation. He claims that the subjects do not *give* the sovereign the right to punish; they *choose* not to exercise their own right to do so, thereby strengthening the sovereign's right (354).

16 The use of the word "powers" – instead of actors – is deliberate here as most actors draw on multiple sources of power simultaneously. For example, the state, the military establishment, and the economic elite all have *some* economic power, depending on the nature of their economic interests, in addition to their political power. The formulation of "state policy" is thus a two-tiered negotiation: first, between the actors (for example, the influence of the economic elite on decision-making by the state), and second, between the relational interests of these actors (for example, how do the economic interests of the state stack up against the economic interests of the military on foreign policy issues?).

17 As used here, "state policy" is a catchall for governmental policies, regulations, and laws.

18 Tsingou's 2010 study of the political economy of laundering remains an exception.

19 These include Max Weber, Pierre Bourdieu, Michel Foucault, and Steven Lukes.

20 Althusser argues that both the subject (the knower) and the object of study predate knowledge; as such, both already define a certain fundamental field. The real object, he contends, comprises an essential and an inessential part; knowledge is the process of abstraction (from the realm of objects to that of ideas) designed to purge the inessential real as well as every trace of its operation.

21 Kennedy takes the comparatively extreme position that there is no difference between public and private power (2018, 44).

22 As described above, some of these priorities are aligned due to the influence of other sources of power on the state; yet others become aligned due to the state's previous encounters with power that result in the internal transformation of the objectives of the state.

23 This shows up as state or policy capture (that is, the influence large corporations have on public policy in both domestic and global markets); regulatory capture (that is, the "outsourcing" or privatization of regulatory policy in particularly those industries where public officials lag behind private actors in terms of knowledge and expertise); and the active undermining of regulation by the state itself through the deliberate lack of enforcement of the same regulation. See Steve Tombs (2018) as well as Steve Tombs and David Whyte (2015).

24 "Political economy" is understood here as the interrelationships of individuals, governments, as well as public policy.

25 In Oct 2019, Statistics Canada put the size of the GDP at 2012 chained prices at \$1.9 trillion. "Historical (real-time) releases of gross domestic product (GDP) at basic prices, by industry, monthly (x1,000,000). https://www150.statcan.gc.ca/t1/tbl1/en/tv.action?pid=3610049101.

26 For the purposes of consistency and accuracy of comparison, pre-pandemic figures are used throughout the chapter for the most part. This is because exponential government spending in the wake of the pandemic has worsened the debt situation for both the federal and provincial governments. In the budget announced in April 2021, for example, after announcing a slew of spending measures aimed at resuscitating the pandemic economy, Finance Minister Chrystia Freeland estimated the size of the 2020–2021 deficit at \$354.2 billion and said she expected the federal debt to peak at 51.2 percent of GDP in 2021–22 before declining to 49.2 percent of GDP in 2025–26. (Reuters 2021)

27 The figure is for the fourth quarter of 2019. Statistics Canada. "Current and capital accounts - Households, Canada, quarterly." https://www150.statcan.gc.ca/t1/tbl1/en/tv.action?pid=3610011201.

28 Revenues include both taxes (individual, corporate, and others) as well as non-tax revenue such as social contributions; revenue from grants; property income, sales of goods and services; fines, penalties and forfeits; voluntary transfers other than grants; as well as miscellaneous revenue (for example, auto premia, drugs plan premia and other revenue not classified elsewhere).

Statistics Canada. "Canadian government finance statistics for the federal government (x1,000,000)." https://www150.statcan.gc.ca/t1/tbl1/en/tv.action?pid=1010001601.

29 Comparatively, the OECD average tax-to-GDP ratio for 2019 was 33.8 percent. Of a total of thirty-seven countries, Canada ranked twenty-first.

30 *Public debt* is defined here as the debt incurred by the federal government as distinguished from the debt of provincial governments and/or municipal organizations (Britannica n.d.).

31 Canada's gross debt position (domestic debt plus foreign debt) in the third quarter of 2019 was $2,491,758 million (or $ 2.49 trillion) while the size of its GDP (chained at 2012 dollars) in October 2019 was $ 1.98 trillion. Statistics Canada. "General government gross debt, quarterly (x 1,000,000)." https://www150.statcan.gc.ca/t1/tbl1/en/tv.action?pid=3610046701. The debt-to-GDP ratio is the former figure expressed as a percentage of the latter. However, the debt-to-GDP ratio varies according to the methodology used by various authors. In a January 2020 op-ed, the Fraser Institute's Jake Fuss and Milagros Palacios put the size of the combined federal-provincial net debt-to-GDP ratio for 2019–20 at 64.3 percent (2020) while Bank of Canada governor Stephen Poloz put the figure at 90 percent in his December 2019 address in Toronto (2019). Meanwhile, Philip Cross at the Macdonald Laurier Institute cites the Bank for International Settlements and says Canada's debt-to GDP ratio is 305.7 percent (2020). However, use of the debt-to-GDP ratio as a measure of a country's ability to service its debt is also fraught with problems and many economists prefer debt per capita figures to explain the extent of the problems of debt. This is because, first, GDP is too complex and too difficult to measure accurately. Second, debt is paid off from revenues a country generates and not the value of the total amount of goods and services produced by a country. For a neat explainer, see the Investopedia website. At $335 billion for the year 2018, Canada's revenues account for just 12 percent of total debt. Statistics Canada. "Canadian government finance statistics for the federal government (x1,000,000)." https://www150.statcan.gc.ca/t1/tbl1/en/tv.action?pid=1010001601&pickMembers%5B0%5D=3.2.

32 Since July 2022, the government has progressively been increasing the key interest rate, which stood at 3.25 percent in September 2022. For historical data, use the Key Interest Rate tool on the Bank of Canada website.

33 For 2018, this amount was $23 billion.

34 A useful comparison emerges when one looks at the sectoral breakdown of other countries higher than Canada in GDP rankings. The top two contributors to US growth, for example, are healthcare and technology. China, meanwhile, has progressively deindustrialized since 2011 and the share of the services sector in the coming decade is pitched at 65 percent of value added while industrial activity is expected to fall to 30 percent of value added (Zhu, Zhang and Peng 2019, 30). While manufacturing in both Japan and Germany account for a large chunk of GDP (20 percent each), the goods produced are high-value en-

gineering-oriented, R&D-led industrial products in Japan's case and high-value capital goods in Germany's. (https://tradingeconomics.com/germany/indicators; https://tradingeconomics.com/japan/gdp-from-manufacturing).

35 These would include the manufacture of furniture and related products for kitchens and bathroom cabinets and vanities; veneer, plywood and engineered wood products; millwork (mouldings, parquet flooring, stairwork); sawmills (lumber, etc.); wood preservatives; structural wood products; particle boards and fibreboard mills; wood windows and doors; pre-fab wood buildings; petroleum refineries' products (such as asphalt); asphalt paving, roofing and shingles; adhesives, resins and synthetic rubbers, chemicals, paints, coatings, plastic plumbing; plastic window and door manufacturing; plumbing fixtures; clay building material and refractory manufacturing (tiles); glass and glass products (including fiberglass installations and windows); cement and concrete products; gypsum products (drywall, ornamental and architectural plaster work); all other non-metallic mineral products (dimension stone for buildings, dry-mix concrete, stucco and stucco products, tiles); steel products; copper products (copper wires, tubing); architectural and structural metals; hardware (hinges, locks, etc.); spring and wire products; turned product and crew; nuts and bolts; metal valves; construction machinery; sawmill and woodworking machinery; rubber and plastics machinery; ventilation, heating and air-conditioning equipment; metalworking machinery; electrical equipment, appliances and components (bulbs, tubes, lighting fixtures); furniture and related products; household and institutional furniture and kitchen cabinets; wood kitchen and cabinets and countertops; upholstered household furniture; other wood household furniture; household furniture (except wood and upholstered); institutional furniture; office furniture; other furniture-related products; mattresses; and blinds and shades. Statistics Canada. "North American Industry Classification System (NAICS) Canada 2017 Version 3.0." https://www23. statcan.gc.ca/imdb/p3VD.pl?Function=getVD&TVD=1181553.

36 These would include merchants dealing in linen, drapery, and textile furnishings (for institutional buyers such as hotels, hospitals, offices, etc.); floor coverings; other home furnishings; building material and supplies; electrical, plumbing, heating and air-conditioning equipment and supplies; lumber, millwork, hardware, and other building material supplies; construction and forestry machinery, equipment and supplies. Statistics Canada. "North American Industry Classification System (NAICS) Canada 2017 Version 3.0. https:// www23.statcan.gc.ca/imdb/p3VD.pl?Function=getVD&TVD=1181553.

37 These would include retailers providing furniture, home furnishings, fittings (doors, windows, etc.), building material and supplies (hardware, paints, etc.). Statistics Canada. "North American Industry Classification System (NAICS) Canada 2017 Version 3.0." https://www23.statcan.gc.ca/imdb/p3VD.pl?Function=getVD&TVD=1181553.

38 These would include financial intermediaries (credit unions, banks, mortgage brokers), insurers, reinsurers (such as property reinsurance carriers) as well as

mortgage funds.

39 These would include lawyers, accountants, architectural design services etc.

40 "Gross domestic product (GDP) at basic prices, by industry, monthly, growth rates (x 1,000,000)." https://www150.statcan.gc.ca/t1/tbl1/en/tv.action?pid=3610043402&pickMembers%5B0%5D=2.1&pickMembers%5B1%5D=3.1&cubeTimeFrame.startMonth=12&cubeTimeFrame.startYear=2019&referencePeriods=20191201%2C20191201.

41 Statistics Canada. 2019. "Provincial and territorial economic accounts, 2018." In *The Daily*, 7 November. https://www150.statcan.gc.ca/n1/daily-quotidien/191107/dq191107a-eng.htm.

42 Also see Sassen who talks of how global processes are embedded in what she calls "national strategic spaces": state institutions, territories, and infrastructure (2006, 381, 403).

43 After the 2019 amendments to the Canada Business Corporations Act, companies must disclose true ownership to both shareholders and creditors. However, this information is (a) only provided about individuals who own more than 25 percent of voting or all shares outstanding, and (b) is not available publicly. https://www.ic.gc.ca/eic/site/cd-dgc.nsf/eng/cs08216.html.

44 These include the two Peter German reports, the Expert Commission on Money Laundering in BC Real Estate as well as the Cullen Commission enquiry.

45 This is the Land Ownership Transparency Act (LOTA). Meanwhile, in its 2019 budget, Québec promised to begin consultations regarding the setting up of a public beneficial ownership registry and was followed by BC in early 2020 (St. Denis 2019, 13 June).

46 In 2019, the BC legislature amended the British Columbia Business Corporations Act and Business Corporations Regulation to mandate greater transparency in corporate ownership. The amendments took effect in October 2020. See https://www.bclaws.gov.bc.ca/civix/document/id/oic/oic_cur/0169_2020.

47 Space constraints preclude a detailed discussion of the reasons here but the primary problems with the laws are that the additional information about ownership is, first, required only about individuals who own more than 25 percent of the interest in a property or more than 25 percent of the voting shares or all shares outstanding, and second, this information is not available publicly. Additionally, the law does not set out specifically what happens in cases where individuals control corporations through legal entities and/or other individuals. See https://www.bclaws.gov.bc.ca/civix/document/id/oic/oic_cur/0169_2020.

48 Beare contends that street crimes and/or crimes involving visible signs of violence have always been accorded greater political priority than what she scathingly refers to as "*so-called* 'victim-less' [emphasis added]" crimes such as corruption or white-collar crime.

49 The "inaction" piece refers to the fact that governments act *even when they choose not to act*, that inaction is as valid a policy response as action. See, generally, Pearce 1976, who develops the idea of an "imaginary social order"

to explain why the behaviour of police, state, and corporation diverges from their stated priorities.

50 In its program logic model for the Business Immigration Program (Appendix A), the report specifically sees the investor immigrants category as providing "low-cost capital for provincial investment."

51 "2016 Census of Population, Statistics Canada Catalogue no. 98-400-X2016202." https://www12.statcan.gc.ca/census-recensement/2016/dp-pd/dt-td/Rp-eng.cfm?LANG=E&APATH=3&DETAIL=0&DIM=0&FL=A&-FREE=0&GC=0&GID=0&GK=0&GRP=1&PID=110558&PRID=10&P-TYPE=109445&S=0&SHOWALL=0&SUB=0&Temporal=2017&THEME=120&VID=0&VNAMEE=&VNAMEF=.

52 "Immigrant population by selected places of birth, admission category and period of immigration, Canada, provinces and territories, census metropolitan areas and areas outside of census metropolitan areas" 2016 Census. https://www12.statcan.gc.ca/census-recensement/2016/dp-pd/dv-vd/imm/index-eng.cfm.

53 "Immigrant population by selected places of birth, admission category and period of immigration, Canada, provinces and territories, census metropolitan areas and areas outside of census metropolitan areas." 2016 Census. https://www12.statcan.gc.ca/census-recensement/2016/dp-pd/dv-vd/imm/index-eng.cfm.

54 The other two categories available under the Business Immigration Program are entrepreneurs and self-employed persons.

55 Interestingly, the replication of the Canadian immigration strategy more recently by EU countries such as Cyprus, Portugal, and Malta have drawn vehement criticism by developed countries for "selling" citizenship in exchange for wads of "dirty money" (Goodley and Pegg 2021).

References

Ahmed, Sanaa. 2023 (forthcoming). "The political Economy of Money Laundering in Canada." In *Big Policing and Big Crime: All About Big Money?* edited by Tonita Murray, Elizabeth Kirley, and Stephen Schneider. Toronto: University of Toronto Press.

Althusser, Louis, Etienne Balibar, Roger Establet, Pierre Macherey, and Jacques Ranciere. 2015. *Reading Capital*, translated by Ben Brewster and David Fernbach. London: Verso.

Baxi, Upendra. 2005. "Market Fundamentalisms: Business Ethics at the Altar of Human Rights." *Human Rights Law Review* 5:1. Oxford: Oxford University Press.

Beare, Margaret E. 2018a. "Shadow Boxing Against the Crimes of the Powerful." In *Revisiting Crimes of the Powerful*, edited by Steve Bittle, Laureen Snider, Steve Tombs, and David Whyte, 45–59. Abingdon-on-Thames: Routledge Press.

———. 2018b. "Entitled Ease: Social Milieu of Corporate Criminals." *Critical Criminology: An International Journal*, Special issue "Crimes of the Powerful: The Canadian Context." 509–526.

————. 2019. "Canada: Internal Conspiracies — Corruption and Crime". In *Handbook of Organized Crime and Politics*, edited by Felia Allum and Stan Gilmore, 189–208. Cheltenham: Edward Elgar Publishing Ltd.

Beare, Margaret E., ed. 2003. *Critical Reflections on Transnational Organised Crime, Money Laundering, and Corruption*. Toronto: University of Toronto Press.

Beare, Margaret E., and Michael Woodiwiss. 2014. "U.S. Organised Crime Control Policies Exported Abroad." In *The Oxford Handbook on Organised Crime*, edited by Letizia Paoli. Oxford: Oxford University Press.

Bourdieu, Pierre. 1991. *Language and Symbolic Power*, edited by John B. Thompson, translated by Gino Raymond, and Matthew Adamson. Cambridge: Harvard University Press. [Symbolic]

Britannica. n.d. https://www.britannica.com/topic/government-budget/Government-borrowing#ref26345.

Canada (Attorney General) v. Federation of Law Societies of Canada. 2015. https://scc-csc.lexum.com/scc-csc/scc-csc/en/item/14639/index.do.

Cribb, Robert, and Marco Chown Oved. 2017. "Snow Washing: Canada Is the World's Newest Tax Haven." *Toronto Star,* 25 January. https://projects.thestar.com/panama-papers/canada-is-the-worlds-newest-tax-haven/.

Cross, Philip. 2020. "Philip Cross: The 2010s Were a Lost Decade of Debt." *Financial Post*, 8 January. https://business.financialpost.com/opinion/philip-cross-the-2010s-were-a-lost-decade-of-debt#comments-area.

Evaluation Division. 2014. "Evaluation of the Federal Business Immigration Program." https://www.canada.ca/content/dam/ircc/migration/ircc/english/pdf/pub/e2-2013_fbip.pdf.

FATF. "Asia/Pacific Group on Money Laundering (APG)." https://www.fatf-gafi.org/pages/asiapacificgrouponmoneylaunderingapg.html
————. "Canada." https://www.fatf-gafi.org/countries/#Canada

Fuss, Jake, and Milagros Palacios. 2020. "Canadian Governments Should Get Serious About Bringing Down Debt." *The Globe and Mail*, 15 January. https://www.theglobeandmail.com/business/commentary/article-canadian-governments-ought-to-get-serious-about-bringing-down-debt/.

Goodley, Simon, and David Pegg. 2021. "Malta Still Selling Golden Passports to Rich Stay-Away 'Residents'." *The Guardian*, 23 April. https://www.theguardian.com/world/2021/apr/23/malta-still-selling-golden-passports-to-rich-stay-away-residents.

Global Financial Integrity. 2015. *Illicit Financial Flows from Developing Countries: 2004–2013*. http://www.gfintegrity.org/wp-content/uploads/2015/12/IFF-Update_2015-Final-1.pdf.

————. September 2015. *Illicit Financial Flows: The Most Damaging Economic Condition Facing the Developing World*. https://www.scribd.com/document/281848024/Illicit-Financial-Flows-The-Most-Damaging-Economic-Condition-Facing-the-Developing-World.

Hobbes, Thomas. 1640. *Elements of Law, Natural and Politic* (available for download at HeinOnline) at https://home.heinonline.org.

International Monetary Fund (IMF). 2021. World Economic Outlook: Managing Divergent Recoveries. https://www.imf.org/en/Publications/WEO/Issues/2021/03/23/world-economic-outlook-april-2021.

Kauzlarich, David, Christopher W. Mullins, and Rick A. Matthews. 2003. In *Contemporary Justice Review* 6, no. 3: 241–254.

Kennedy, David. 2018. *A World of Struggle: How Power, Law and Expertise Shape Global Political Economy*. Princeton: Princeton University Press.

Kilchling, Michael. 2014. "Finance-Oriented Strategies of Organised Crime Control." In *The Oxford Handbook on Organised Crime,* edited by Letizia Paoli. Oxford: Oxford University Press.

Levi, Michael. 2014. "Money Laundering." In *The Oxford Handbook on Organised Crime*, edited by Letizia Paoli. Oxford: Oxford University Press.

MacPherson, C.B., ed. 1968. *Thomas Hobbes: Leviathan*. London: Penguin.

Maloney, Maureen, Tsur Somerville, and Brigitte Unger. 2019. Combatting Money Laundering in BC Real Estate: Expert Panel on Money Laundering in BC Real Estate. https://www2.gov.bc.ca/assets/gov/housing-and-tenancy/real-estate-in-bc/combatting-money-laundering-report.pdf.

Mann, Michael. 1993. *The Sources of Social Power Volume 2: The Rise of Classes and Nation-States, 1760 – 1914)*. New York: Cambridge University Press.

———. 2012. *The Sources of Social Power Volume 4: Globalisations, 1945 – 2011*. New York: Cambridge University Press.

Naylor, R. T. 2004. *Wages of Crime: Black Markets, Illegal Finance and the Underworld Economy*. Montreal: McGill-Queen's University Press.

Oved, Marco Chown. 2016. "Corporate Secrecy Makes Canada a Haven for White-Collar Crime, Says Report." Toronto Star, December 7. https://www.thestar.com/news/world/2016/12/07/report-corporate-secrecy-makes-canada-a-haven-for-white-collar-crime.html.

———. 2019. "In Canada, Nearly All Accused Money Launderers Get Their Charges Dropped." Toronto Star, 26 December. https://www.thestar.com/news/investigations/2019/12/26/in-canada-nearly-all-accused-money-launderers-get-their-charges-dropped.html?rf.

———. 2020. "The RCMP Is Shutting Down Its Financial Crimes Unit in Ontario. Here's Why Former Top Mounties Says It's a Mistake." Toronto Star, 15 January. https://www.thestar.com/news/investigations/2020/01/15/the-rcmp-is-shutting-down-its-financial-crimes-unit-in-ontario-heres-why-former-top-mounties-says-its-a-mistake.html.

Oved, Marco Chown, and Robert Cribb. 2017. "Ottawa Vows to Lift Corporate Secrecy in Bid to Stop Tax Evasion and Money Laundering." Toronto Star, 18 July. https://www.thestar.com/news/canada/2017/07/18/corporate-secrecy-to-be-lifted-to-help-stop-tax-evasion-and-money-laundering.html.

Pearce, Frank. 1976. *Crimes of the Powerful: Marxism, Crime and Deviance.* London: Pluto Press Limited.

Pistor, Katharina. 2019. *The Code of Capital: How Law Creates Wealth and Inequality.* Princeton: Princeton University Press.

Poloz, Stephen S. 2019. "Big Issues Ahead – the Bank of Canada's 2020 Vision." Remarks by Mr. Stephen S. Poloz, Governor of the Bank of Canada, 12 December, at Empire Club of Canada, Toronto. https://www.bis.org/review/r191220d.pdf.

Reuters. 2021. "Takeaways-Canada 2021 Budget in Numbers." *Yahoo Finance,* 19 April. https://finance.yahoo.com/news/takeaways-canada-2021-budget-numbers-201120275.html.

Sassen, Saskia. 2006. *Territory, Authority, Rights: From Medieval to Global Assemblages.* Princeton: Princeton University Press.

St. Denis, Jen. 2019. "Fight Against 'Nefarious' Money Laundering Gets $10 Million Federal Boost for RCMP." Toronto Star, 13 June. https://www.thestar.com/vancouver/2019/06/13/fight-against-nefarious-money-laundering-gets-10-million-federal-boost-for-rcmp.html.

Statistics Canada. 2022. Canadian government finance statistics for the federal government (x1,000,000). https://www150.statcan.gc.ca/t1/tbl1/en/tv.action?pid=1010001601&pickMembers%5B0%5D=3.2.

Statistics Canada. 2023. Gross domestic product (GDP) at basic prices, by industry, monthly (x 1,000,000). https:// www150.statcan.gc.ca/t1/tbl1/en/tv.action?pid=3610043401.

Tax Justice Network. 2021. Country Profile 2021: Canada." https://taxjustice.net/country-profiles/canada/.

Tombs, Steve. 2012. "State-Corporate Symbiosis in the Production of Crime and Harm." *State Crime* 1.2: 170–195.

———. 2018. In *Revisiting Crimes of the Powerful: Marxism, Crime and Deviance*, edited by Steve Bittle, Laureen Snider, Steve Tombs, and David Whyte. Abingdon-on-Thames: Taylor & Francis Group.

Tombs, Steve, and David Whyte. 2015. *The Corporate Criminal: Why Corporations Must Be Abolished.* Abingdon-on-Thames: Routledge.

Tsingou, Eleni. 2010. "Global Financial Governance and the Developing Anti-Money Laundering Regime: What Lessons for International Political Economy?" *International Politics* 47, no. 6: 617–637.

Zhu, Min, Longmei Zhang, and Daoju Peng. 2019. "China's Productivity Convergence and Growth Potential—A Stocktaking and Sectoral Approach." Working Papers. International Monetary Fund. https://www.imf.org/en/Publications/WP/Issues/2019/11/27/Chinas-Productivity-Convergence-and-Growth-Potential-A-Stocktaking-and-Sectoral-Approach-48702.

Persistent Failures:
Critical Perspectives on Federal and Provincial Intelligence and Enforcement

6

Canada: Combating Money Laundering – Leader or Laggard?

Denis Meunier

Introduction

While Canada's fight against money laundering begins at home, it is inexorably linked to evolving international threats, global rules, and cooperative efforts to address the problem. Its domestic efforts are tied not only to the federal, provincial, and territorial legislative and regulatory frameworks and the private sector's preventative contribution and its own investments to address the problem, but also to the international standards for preventing, detecting, investigating, prosecuting, and recovering the assets from laundering money.

While "following the money" has been the mantra of Canadian financial crime sleuths and their counterparts the world over, all are falling short of their goal to arrest the problem. So, what is the international context in which Canada's anti-money laundering regime operates? Are there gaps and vulnerabilities in the international standards set by the Financial Action Task Force (FATF)? How does Canada's anti-money laundering regime rate against the FATF standards? What are some of the key gaps Canada must address? What could the FATF, and Canada, do better?

This chapter describes some of the actions the FATF and Canada are taking to address money laundering, outlining key international obligations, challenges, and Canada's current record of effectiveness with its successes and shortcomings, as well as key initiatives to be more effective at combating money laundering.

Making Dirty Money and Money Laundering: Two Intertwined Processes

There are many ways to make dirty money. Their outcome has an official name: generating proceeds of crime.

Illicit narcotics can be peddled, taxes evaded, humans trafficked, illegal gambling conducted, people and goods smuggled, bribes offered and accepted, wildlife trafficked, cybercrimes committed, environmental crimes perpetrated, counterfeit goods sold, illegal gaming set up, only to name a few criminal indictable offences from which proceeds of crime can be acquired.

Generating the proceeds of crime is a process itself, and laundering the proceeds is another process. Two intertwined processes each with five common characteristics:

1. They both involve high volumes of dirty money. Enormous amounts of proceeds of crime are generated which are then transformed, through laundering, into clean money.
2. They both require several people, organized groups, or networks to be successful.
3. There is most often a transnational connection to them.
4. They make use of professional enablers.
5. They use corporations and trusts to cover their tracks.

The Process of Generating Proceeds of Crime

In the case of commodity-related crimes (drugs and wildlife trafficking, smuggling of goods, counterfeit goods, etc.) and human-related crimes (human smuggling and trafficking) the process of criminally generating proceeds involves several steps and intermediaries collaborating in business to engage in both domestic and transnational activities. In the case of commodity-related crimes those activities could include manufacturing, importing, transforming, storing, transporting, exporting, wholesaling, retailing, and regulating the market of the illicit commodities (e.g., through threats and intimidation, assaults, arson, murder).

When it comes to non-commodity and non-human related crimes, such as phone frauds, romance scams, phishing, securities, real estate, mortgage, payment card, and other frauds they may require fewer steps and intermediaries from predicate offence to laundered money, but a process is nonetheless established to successfully pull off the scheme between collaborators, often located in another country.

The Process of Laundering the Proceeds of Crime

So, what do most criminals and organized crime groups do with dirty money once acquired? They need to make use of or hide that illicit wealth; enter in the process of money laundering.

Members of criminal organizations need to eat, sleep, shelter, and enjoy life like others. They use the money to buy goods, services, real estate, businesses, and investments; they transfer and move it and hide its origin to make the funds appear legitimate and avoid it being traced back to their illegal source by law enforcement. They launder their dirty money.

Criminals don't have corporate pension plans. They create their nest eggs by laundering their money through various techniques, quite often by co-mingling dirty money with legitimate income through legitimate businesses, trusts, and investment vehicles. The most sophisticated criminals hire professional money launderers who, through various means and using a risk-based approach, are beating the slim odds of getting caught with the loot, undetected, unpursued, unscathed, and one step ahead of a slow-paced criminal justice system.

Assuming John Doe, the criminal, has cash from drug sales; he can easily buy groceries, concert tickets, meals in restaurants, gas for his vehicle, clothing, and many other consumables and services without raising much suspicion about the source of funds. However, the greater the prosperity of the underworld business ventures, the greater the risk of being scrutinized for questionably sourced wealth when an ostentatious lifestyle has been adopted. Placing substantial amounts of cash into the legitimate financial pipeline becomes riskier without expert help. In such circumstances, money laundering techniques and professional enablers must be used to mask the source of funds and the source of wealth.

Because Canada's Criminal Code distinguishes between the offences of possessing the proceeds of crime and laundering them, John Doe, if caught red-handed trafficking narcotics with only a stash of cash in his hands, could face charges of drug trafficking and possession of the proceeds of crime when caught, but likely not money laundering.

However, if John Doe is caught using, depositing, or transferring the illegal proceeds linked to drug trafficking into or from his bank account,[1] he can also be charged with money-laundering because of the clearer nexus between the source of funds, the possession of the proceeds of crime, and the laundering of dirty money.

Generating proceeds of crime and laundering them are two, interdependent processes feeding each other, each in a repeating cycle. Combined, they wreak societal, health, financial, economic, and political havoc in their wake. When the fruits of criminals' labours are allowed to remain untouched, unbroken in their cycle, they incentivize further criminal activity. Seizing and forfeiting the proceeds of crime and preventing dirty money from being laundered disrupts criminal enterprises and decreases the risk of engaging in criminal economic activity.

The United Nations defines money laundering as "any act or attempted act to disguise the source of money or assets derived from criminal activity." Similarly adopted by one of its agencies, the United Nations Office on Drugs and Crime (UNODC), goes a bit further by defining it as a process "…by which a person conceals or disguises the identity or the origin of illegally obtained proceeds so that they appear to have originated from legitimate sources." An essential feature of money laundering is the fact that it is a "process" whereby "dirty money" – produced through criminal activity – is transformed into "clean money," the criminal origin of which is difficult to trace.

Canada's financial intelligence unit, the Financial Transactions and Reports Analysis Centre of Canada (FINTRAC) further describes money laundering as a three-stage process where "1. *Placement* involves placing the proceeds of crime in the financial system. 2. *Layering* involves converting the proceeds of crime into another form and creating complex layers of financial transactions to disguise the audit trail and the source and ownership of funds. This stage may involve transactions such as the buying and selling of stocks, commodities, or property. 3. *Integration* involves placing the laundered proceeds back in the economy to create the perception of legitimacy. The money laundering process is continuous, with new "dirty" money constantly being introduced into the financial system." (FINTRAC 2022).

Because it is a three-phase "process" of placement, layering and integration, like the creation of proceeds of crime, it usually involves several persons or organizations (wittingly or unwittingly) at each phase to push the money through, using many different techniques, to gradually make the money appear legitimate and distant from its illegal source. In each of the three phases of this process, there are inherent transition points, characteristics, risks, and opportunities.

Creating that nest egg is what successful criminal enterprises attempt to do in this three-phase process, with some describing it as four stages (OECD 2019; Maloney, Somerville, and Unger 2019a), by integrating the proceeds of crime into the legitimate economy by investing, for example, in businesses, residential and commercial real estate, securities, and so on.

As Dirty Money Moves Through the Money Laundering Process, It Becomes More Difficult to Detect, Investigate and Prosecute

It becomes more difficult to connect the proceeds of, for example, drug trafficking activity when the dirty money has been through dozens of transformations, many offshore banks, and integrated into the purchase or development of commercial real estate back in Canada. All these transactions, across borders, makes it more arduous and costly for investigators to follow the money trail.

One of the most common and yet difficult ways to detect money laundering is co-mingling dirty money with legitimate funds. According to the Criminal Intelligence Services of Canada (CISC), 28 percent of the organized crime groups (OCGs) involved in money laundering "...are suspected of using private sector businesses to facilitate laundering or hiding their proceeds of crime" (CISC 2020). The three top suspected sectors are "...food/beverage services (e.g., restaurants and bars), automotive (e.g., vehicle sales and repair), and construction (e.g., new builds and renovations)."

Lots of Dirty Money

Globally, criminal endeavours generate a staggering amount of money. One of the earliest guesstimates of the amount of money laundered worldwide was published by Vito Tanzi (1996, iii), an economist with the International Monetary Fund (IMF). In his paper, it was estimated that anywhere from US$300 billion to US$500 billion was laundered annually.

In 1998, an estimate of between 2 percent to 5 percent of global Gross Domestic Product (GDP) was said to have been cited by the managing director of the IMF, as a "consensus range" of the likely scale of money-laundering transactions at the global level (Camdessus 1998). The World Bank also cited this estimate that same year in its own publication and reprised it in 2006 (Schott 2006).

A United Nations Office on Drugs and Crime (UNODC) study (UNODC 2011) showed that, excluding those funds derived from tax evasion, criminal proceeds amounted to 3.6 percent of global GDP, with 2.7 percent (or US$1.6 trillion) being laundered.

With a global GDP of US$88 trillion in 2020 (Statista 2022), and using the 2.7 percent figure, the scale of dirty money worldwide is nonetheless alarming at about US$2.37 trillion. If that figure of 2.7 percent were applied to the size of Canada's GDP in 2020 (about US$1.6 trillion), that would represent about US$43 billion laundered annually in Canada or approximately CAN$54 billion.

In Canada, the Expert Panel (Maloney, Somerville, and Unger 2019b) looking into money laundering in British Columbia conservatively estimated the scale of money laundering in Canada to be about $46.7 billion (2018) annually, representing about 2.1 percent of Canada's GDP or roughly 15 percent of Canada's total annual budgetary revenues of $323.4 billion in 2018–2019 (Finance Canada 2018).

No matter which estimate is used, $54 billion or $46.7 billion, the value of criminal proceeds laundered in Canada is enormous. It is equivalent to the size of Nova Scotia's GDP in 2018.

International Collaboration and Organized Crime

A globalized world delivers many economic and development benefits: increased air and marine travel to transport goods and people, communication through mobile phones, the internet, swift capital flows, bilateral and multilateral trade and investment agreements, trade and investment facilitation, increased immigration, new technologies, virtual currencies, and many other examples in the 2020 ITA report. Of the OCGs assessed, 33 percent (164 OCGs) "are reported as being active in the methamphetamine market" and 62 percent (313 OCGs) are assessed as "involved in some aspect of cocaine trafficking, with 71 groups involved in importation" (CISC 2021a).

While there is significant domestic manufacturing of methamphetamine in Canada, there is nonetheless international importing into the country and exporting from Canada (CISC 2021b). Mexico has become a key source of imported methamphetamine in Canada (CISC 2021c).

As for the domestic cocaine market, it relies on "imports from source countries (e.g., Bolivia, Columbia, and Peru)" (CISC 2021d) and must be smuggled into Canada. The networking of foreign cocaine suppliers, brokers as intermediaries, domestic importers, and downstream domestic traffickers, is descriptive of the transnational nature of the crime connections necessary for the marketing of this illicit commodity.

Imported drugs or precursor chemicals may traverse several international borders with the help of diverters, facilitators such as cargo handlers, corrupt officials, and transportation companies. Every hand-off in this chain is an opportunity for exploitation of weakness by law enforcement. Everyone along this chain needs to be paid somehow. A money trail, however well camouflaged, is nonetheless an opportunity for financial crime detection and investigation. Intelligence about these connections on the international money trail needs to be scrutinized and shared more effectively among trusted law enforcement professionals.

Like the cooperation and conspiracy involved in the smuggling of drugs, moving funds to pay for the narcotics must follow a certain route, albeit more circuitous than the one used for its smuggling. Paying for the illicit goods requires a step-by-step process with the involvement of several individuals and businesses with more than one person generating the proceeds of the crime and ultimately, laundering the money, by accessing the financial system using intermediaries. That chain, from the generation of the proceeds of crime to its cleaning, involves a transnational connection (German, this volume) in most financial crimes using professional enablers who create legal structures and pathways for their clients' getaway cars. Notwithstanding this challenge, the evolution of crypto-currencies, used as a means of shifting payments surreptitiously outside the formal banking system, has been making it difficult for investigators to uncover the money trail in money-laundering cases. More needs to be done to equip the investigators through knowledge, technological tools, international support, and cooperation to bridge this growing gap (Jenkins, Hamilton, and Leuprecht, this volume).

Professional Enablers in Laundering Money

Lawyers, notaries, accountants, financial experts, and others with the know-how to create holding companies in complex sets of structured corporations, trusts, partnerships, and shell corporations are the enablers sought out by criminals. Professional money launderers may suggest a plethora of methods and techniques such as the black market peso exchange (FATF 2020), the similar but more complex "Vancouver Model" (Lindsay 2020) studied by the Cullen Commission, previous adaptations of these schemes (Hall 2004) or any other number of methods including the use of legal professionals (FATF 2013a).

Professional money launderers have gained the attention of anti-money laundering experts for some time, culminating with the FATF's report (FATF 2018) on their characteristics, methods, business models and networks, supporting mechanisms, and other actors. FINTRAC followed suit with its own operational alert on a similar topic at the same time while the Government of Canada included a series of measures and increased resource allocations in its 2019 Budget to address growing concerns about money laundering including those from professional money launderers (Finance Canada 2019a; Cooper 2019).

Corporations, Trusts, and Other Legal Arrangements Are the Get-Away Cars for Laundered Money

The concealment of the identity of the owners/controllers of corporations and trusts is a well-known and common means of laundering dirty money. In its simplest form, hiding beneficial ownership is registering a corporation with someone else's name and keeping the real owner anonymously hidden. This is perfectly legal and has been for decades, if not centuries in most countries. This seems so obvious, to misuse private corporations and trusts, that it boggles the mind as to why this has been allowed to exist. Basically, a private corporation can register a "strawman" (nominee) who could be a lawyer or anyone else acting as an administrator of the corporation without any ownership of the company, with a majority shareholder as another corporation, or another person remaining anonymous. There are reports (Cribb and Oved 2017) of individuals registered as administrators of hundreds of companies in Canada and elsewhere, acting as paper pushers for anonymous corporate owners. Leaks like the Panama Papers (ICIJ 2016), the Paradise Papers (ICIJ 2017), and the FINCEN Papers (ICIJ 2020) are just some illustrations of how anonymous owners and facilitators can hide or ease the movement of illicit wealth.

The Regulatory Environment

The FATF

The FATF is an inter-governmental organization formed in 1989. In 1990 it produced a list of 40 Recommendations to address money laundering globally. The FATF also evaluates countries, through mutual evaluation reports, and holds countries to account for meeting those standards. Since its inception, these standards have evolved to include measures to combat the financing of terrorist activities and the proliferation of weapons of mass destruction. These recommendations have become the anti-money laundering and anti-terrorism financing (AML/ATF) standards that more than two hundred jurisdictions around the world are expected to meet.

As the FATF standards (FATF 2012–2022a) continue to be updated, they cover seven broad categories of measures that countries are expected to adopt in their own national legislation. The measures are comprehensive and cover the following, with a preponderance of Recommendations focusing on prevention (15) and powers and responsibilities (10):

1. AML/ATF policies and coordination,
2. money laundering and confiscation,
3. terrorist financing and financing of proliferation,
4. preventive measures,
5. transparency and beneficial ownership of legal persons and arrangements,
6. powers and responsibilities of competent authorities and other institutional measures, and
7. international cooperation.

The measures contain both *criminal law* and *administrative (civil) law* concepts. As examples of administrative law, there are standards that cover the use of a risk-based approach to compliance (Recommendation No. 1), ensuring reporting entities subject to the AML/ATF laws are obliged to meet certain requirements (preventive measures), providing competent authorities such as regulators and supervisors with sufficient powers to effectively supervise, examine, and sanction reporting entities (powers and responsibilities). As examples of the use of criminal law concepts, there are rules about instituting criminal law provisions by countries (such as requiring a country's legislation to define money laundering and terrorist financing offences), detection mechanisms (creation of financial intelligence units and requirements for reporting entities to provide information to them), investigation and prosecution (powers and responsibilities), confiscation of assets (money laundering and confiscation) and extradition and mutual legal assistance (international cooperation).

Canada's AML/ATF Regime

Canada has progressively been ratcheting the effectiveness of its AML/ATF regime since 2000 with the enactment of its Proceeds of Crime (Money Laundering) Act[2] and the creation of FINTRAC in that same year. Over the years many amendments have been added to the legislation and included regulations tightening the loopholes, and in 2019 even adding a "recklessness" provision to the Criminal Code's definition of money laundering.[3] But the FATF's 2016 Mutual Evaluation of Canada's AML/ATF regime was not a glowing report. In fairness, the FATF did identify some of Canada's regime strengths. However, the FATF listed several serious weaknesses that coincide with common global vulnerabilities. Despite progress since the year 2000, overall Canada is not a leader, and on many key fronts, such as beneficial ownership transparency, is a laggard (Meunier 2018).

What Is Missing Globally and Domestically?

Today, laundering dirty money is a criminal offence just about anywhere you live on the planet. But this would not have happened globally if it were not for international collaboration on rulemaking and standards. In 1989, Canada with other countries was a founding member of the FATF, the global money laundering and terrorist financing watchdog. The creation of the FATF and the issuance of its AML/ATF standards was a game-changer. Through its evolving incremental policymaking and mutual evaluations of countries' AML/ATF regimes, it puts pressure on all countries to implement these rules. While the FATF standards and their mutual evaluations have been crucial in moving the AML/ATF ball forward globally, criminals have adapted and moved faster.

Canada, despite being a founder, has been slow in adopting many of the international standards into its own domestic legislation. For example, it was only in the year 2000, eleven years after the introduction of the FATF global rules in 1989, that FINTRAC was created, to prevent and detect money laundering, and since 2001, the detection of terrorist activity financing. And as indicated earlier, Canadian jurisdictions as a whole are still not fully compliant with transparency of beneficial ownership rules for corporations, trusts, and other legal structures eighteen years after the standards were set.

Canada's AML/ATF regime operates based on three interdependent pillars: (i) policy and coordination; (ii) prevention and detection; and (iii) investigation and disruption, with different federal government departments and agencies participating in its implementation. This approach is appropriate as it mirrors the FATF's conceptual framework established in its standards.

The five common characteristics to the two intertwined processes of generating proceeds of crime and laundering money were identified earlier in the chapter. These characteristics also correspond to global and domestic weaknesses. So, what's missing globally or domestically in Canada to be more effective in countering money laundering?

There are five significant shortfalls in both the FATF's standards, and Canada's laws, regulations, and practices. While these processes

1. produce and transform extraordinarily high volumes of dirty money into clean money, there are no recent or periodically updated estimates by the FATF or Canada of the amount of money laundered;

2. require several people, organized groups, or networks to be successful, the FATF does not offer a standard to address criminal organizations per se nor does Canada effectively prosecute large criminal organizations;

3. most often have a transnational connection to them; the mechanisms to pursue transnational criminals are ineffective;

4. make use of professional enablers, in Canada these facilitators, specifically lawyers and Québec notaries, are not effectively regulated or supervised, and

5. corporations and trusts are used to generate proceeds of crime and cover criminals' tracks, it is only recently that the FATF has introduced a strengthened requirement for effective international

beneficial ownership transparency (FATF 2022). There is a lack of global and domestic access and interoperability for publicly accessible beneficial ownership registries of legal persons and legal arrangements (e.g., trusts).

No Recent Estimates of Money Laundered

No Global Estimate

Without updated global estimates serving as a gauge to assess progress on attacking money laundering, how can we know if the strategies used worldwide are producing the right outcomes?

While economists and researchers have argued about the proper methodology for measuring the size of the global money laundering (ML) problem for years, what seems more important than getting the perfect measuring stick is evaluating whether, over time, using the same methodology, the problem is growing faster or slower relative to each jurisdiction's GDP or the global GDP. Using the same methodology consistently should identify that the trend of ranges is more important than the absolute number itself. A country-by-country measurement, as subsets of the global estimate, would be useful in focusing global action and measures on those countries that generate proceeds of crime and those that benefit by laundering them.

As a result, the FATF should work with other international organizations to periodically publish trend analyses and estimates of global money laundering with breakdowns on a country-by-country basis. Canada should encourage such an initiative. While Canada has resisted for decades the call for the measurement of a tax gap (CRA 2022) domestically, it finally relented in 2016 by producing some estimates. The same previous resistance to the estimation of the tax gap should be avoided in attempting to measure the domestic money laundering problem and its trend. Rather, such measurement and longitudinal analysis should be supported by Canada and promoted at the FATF by adding such a measurement and analysis requirement to the FATF's Recommendation No. 33 dealing with statistics (FATF 2012–2022c).

No Canadian Estimate of Money Laundering

An Expert Panel's report on money laundering in the real estate sector in British Columbia (Maloney, Somerville, and Unger 2019c) provided, an estimate for Canada that was "...generated on the basis of economic analysis and modelling and the first estimate of money laundering over time." The report went on to say "the Panel conservatively estimates annual money laundering activity in 2015 in Canada at $41.3 billion ($46.7 billion for 2018) ... However, it must be stressed that the inherent secrecy of an activity designed to hide the true nature of financial transactions, together with the lack of reliable, internationally consistent data, means that there is no definitive way to measure money laundering activity. The methodology used is likely to generate an estimate of money laundering near its lower bound." (Maloney, Somerville, and Unger 2019d).

Soon after its release, criticism was heard from various quarters about either the methodology or the estimate itself. The province that generated the greatest amount of laundered money (i.e., Alberta; Hunter and Hager 2019) was more vociferous than others, questioning the data used in the model. Rather than questioning the Expert Panel's estimate of the size of the money laundering problem in Canada and by province or region,[4] it would be more helpful if the federal government, provinces, and territories worked collaboratively to come up with periodic national/provincial/territorial estimates for the same reasons the FATF should produce a worldwide estimate of ML periodically: diagnose the size of the problem and adjust and devise strategies to minimize the harm it causes.

Addressing Criminal Organizations

Lack of An FATF Standard on Criminal Organizations

The FATF's Standards require countries to criminalize money laundering based on the Vienna Convention and the Palermo Convention (the United Nations Convention against Transnational Organized Crime [UNTOC]), and terrorist financing on the basis of the Terrorist Financing Convention.[5] The UNTOC, for its part, requires countries to criminalize organized crime groups and provides definitions for terms such as "organized criminal group," "structured groups," "transnational" offence and other related terms (UNODC 2003).

What has fallen between the cracks is the lack of inclusion of a requirement in the FATF's Recommendations for countries to criminalize an "organized criminal group" using UNTOC's definition. Why is it important that the FATF include such a requirement in its Recommendations? The answer lies in the fact that the FATF has gained much influence over the years through the implementation of its processes for mutual evaluation, follow-ups and "grey-listing"[6] of non-compliers with its Recommendations. As a critical linchpin to the money laundering problem, the FATF should assess each country's effectiveness in combating organized criminal groups domestically and how well they cooperate internationally on their investigations, prosecutions, and asset forfeitures. By publishing its mutual evaluation reports since 2004, delinquent countries are called out publicly when they fail to adhere to the Recommendations. The FATF has incrementally and successfully been evaluating, applying consequences, and turning the screws on the implementation of AML/ATF requirements globally, something few other international bodies have done in their respective remit such as for the UNTOC.

In comparison, it is only since 2018 that there has been an effort on the UNTOC to move to the establishment of a mechanism for the review of its implementation.[7]

For over ten years the United Nations (UN) has identified transnational crime as "… a threat to peace and development, even to the sovereignty of nations" (UNODC 2010). Yet, while there are 167 signatories to the UNTOC, there is little information about the effectiveness and jurisdictional progress on combating organized crime groups.

Proliferation of Criminal Groups in Canada

In 2008, over 900 organized crime groups were identified in Canada, including approximately 300 street gangs (CISC 2009). In 2020 the CISC (CISC 2021c) and the Royal Canadian Mounted Police (RCMP) said that there are at least two thousand organized criminal groups (OCG) in Canada (Northcott 2021). The more than doubling of OCGs in Canada over the last twelve years is not only troubling because of their increase alone, but their consequential influence on our society and poor reflection on Canada's ability to contain or minimize the OCG threat. The expansion of criminal groups can reasonably be assumed to be associated with the growth of criminal markets, proceeds of crime, and money laundering. The expansion of the money laundering problem must be seen not only as a threat to the financial system, competition in the marketplace, or other economic factor, but rather as a threat to national and international security.

In 2011, the United States government's National Security Council released a report titled "Strategy to Combat Transnational Organized Crime: Addressing Converging Threats to National Security." The overarching message derived from the report is that "Transnational organized crime (TOC) poses a *significant and growing threat to national and international security* [my emphasis], with dire implications for public safety, public health, democratic institutions, and economic stability across the globe."

That was over ten years ago, in a different country. In 2018, Canada's Minister of Finance Bill Morneau, who at the time was responsible for Canada's AML/ATF legislation and testifying at a Parliamentary Committee reviewing the *Proceeds of Crime (Money Laundering) and Terrorist Financing Act* (PCMLTFA), made a similar statement. "Mr. Chair, before I wrap up, I'd like to assure the committee that these concerns, money laundering and terrorist financing, are concerns that the government takes very seriously. To put it bluntly, *these things are a threat to the safety and security of Canadians* [my emphasis], and the government knows that keeping Canadians safe has to be a top priority" (FINA 2018).

In February 2020, the Government of Canada stated at the Commission of Inquiry into Money Laundering in British Columbia that "Canada recognizes that money laundering and terrorist financing pose a significant *threat to domestic and global safety and security* [my emphasis] and can compromise the integrity and stability of the financial sector and the broader economy" (Government of Canada 2020).

Money is the lifeblood of organized crime groups. As the number of criminal groups in Canada has more than doubled in the last ten years, and likely the amount of proceeds of crime and money laundered has also increased to keep these two thousand criminal groups operating, there is a need to evaluate Canada's efforts to combat organized criminal groups and money laundering. Consequently, there is a burgeoning requirement to assess the extent to which Canada's national security been compromised due to the increase in OCGs over the years and whether Canada's efforts been successful or lacking.

Failure to Effectively Combat Transnational Crime Organizations

The FATF Provides a Partial Framework

As identified previously, the FATF Recommendations provide a comprehensive framework for the administrative and criminal regulation of ML/TF. However, the Recommendations could be improved by building into Recommendation 40 (other forms of international cooperation) a requirement for countries to exchange financial intelligence between Financial Intelligence Units (FIUs) within defined timelines and quality targets and report performance against those agreed expectations in mutual evaluation reports. Such public reporting would identify the FIUs that are significantly and consistently slow in responding to requests for information, provide poor quality, or no information at all.[8] The timeliness and quality of information exchanged are critical for analytical, investigative, prosecutorial, and asset forfeiture purposes. Pressure by the FATF on delinquent countries in providing effective and timely responses could accelerate the exchange of information process. Similar requirements could be applied to mutual legal assistance requests (Recommendations 37 and 38).

Canada Needs Reformed Legislation and More Resources Focused on Combating Organized Crime

Reformed Legislation Needed

Several experts on organized crime in Canada, including senior RCMP officers and David Eby, the then attorney general for British Columbia and now the premier of BC, have criticized Canada's lack of effective legislative tools, enforcement resources, and prosecutorial expertise in going after transnational crime organizations (Cooper 2021).

It has been suggested that the Racketeer Influenced and Corrupt Organizations Act, or RICO-style[9] legislation that has been successful in obtaining Mafia convictions in the USA should be considered in Canada (Clement, this volume). The RICO targets offenders working at the top levels of various kinds of criminal organizations. Another American law designed to go after heads of criminal groups that could be considered in Canada is the USA's Continuing Criminal Enterprise Statute[10] that targets only drug traffickers who are responsible for long-term and elaborate conspiracies.

An alternative legislative measure that would help in combating money laundering is an Unexplained Wealth Order (UWO) recently adopted in the UK and recommended by the BC Expert Panel (Maloney, Somerville, and Unger 2019e). It is early days for this form of reverse onus legislation in the UK, but it has been successful in the case of Zamira Hajiyeva, wife of a jailed banker, who lost her appeal against the UWO in December 2020 at the Supreme Court in the UK. The court "...announced that it had refused Hajiyeva's application for permission to appeal the UWO made against her by the National Crime Agency (NCA), asserting that her challenge to the UWO raised no arguable point of law" (McDermott Will & Emery 2021).

While the federal government announced additional resources to combat money laundering in its 2019 Budget (Finance Canada 2019b), it seems to have come to the party almost twenty years too late. The fact remains that since the 9/11 terrorist attacks in 2001, Canada has shifted many of its federal policing resources away from organized crime and money laundering investigations in favour of national security priorities, trading off the national security threat posed by transnational criminal organizations for the one posed by Al Qaeda, ISIL, and other terrorist groups. Ignoring a house on fire to fight a fire a kilometre away rather than calling in reinforcements to fight both fires does not make sense. It is also possible that the shift in policing resources over the years away from organized criminal groups has fostered an increase in the number of criminal groups in Canada from nine hundred to two thousand. Or perhaps OCGs are counted differently (i.e., with or without street gangs) or better, or maybe there is a greater demand for the illicit goods and services that produce proceeds of crime. The question remains to be answered.

More Resources Needed

There are both insufficient resources dedicated to the investigation and prosecution of money laundering cases involving organized crime. High-level criminal organizations hire expert lawyers and accountants, and other professionals to defend their cases, adding complexity and cost to the challenge for prosecutors.

As an example of a lack of resources in prosecution, prosecutors often negotiate plea deals with those accused of money laundering because of the time and effort involved in building a money laundering case. It is easier, under the guise of the "public interest" guideline, to accept a guilty plea for the predicate offense (e.g., drug trafficking, fraud) instead of a more difficult money laundering charge to prosecute despite potentially harsher consequences for the accused. However, with more resources available for prosecution, and a more dedicated pursuit of deterrence, specific and general, of ML offenders, these actions might be a more compelling boost to the "public interest" principle.

Poorly Supervised Enablers of Money Laundering

The FATF Requires Legal Professionals to Be Regulated For AML/ATF

Legal professionals are among the most sought-after enablers of money laundering and terrorist financing (FATF 2013b) because of their expertise and the solicitor-client privilege that exempts them from AML/ATF legislation in some jurisdictions. In Canada, they include lawyers and Québec notaries.

The FATF Recommendations compel countries to include them as obliged entities in national legislation (FATF 2012–2022b) recognizing their role as gatekeepers in preventing the abuse of their profession for illicit purposes. Ever since the Supreme Court of Canada's February 13, 2015, ruling to exempt lawyers and Québec notaries from the requirements of the PCMLTFA, the Government of Canada has yet to follow through on its commitment to revisit the PCMLTFA provisions and bring forward new ones for the legal profession that would be constitutionally compliant (Finance Canada 2015a). As a documented high-vulnerability rating (Finance Canada 2015b) to money laundering and terrorist financing in Canada, this gap has been outstanding for over twenty years. Canada needs to address this failure urgently (Clement, this volume).

Canada's Provincial and Territorial Jurisdictions Have Weak AML/ATF Supervisory Regimes Over Legal Professionals

Perhaps the most significant money laundering or terrorism financing risk for the legal profession occurs when a lawyer willfully participates in or facilitates the commission of a crime. In Canada, the investigation, prosecution, and conviction of lawyers for criminal offences are not uncommon practices. It is real and serious. The amounts of money laundered by lawyers runs into the millions of dollars. Some lawyers who have been convicted for ML in Canada were working directly with major organized crime groups. The legal profession is not immune to criminality and corruption of its own practitioners in Canada or globally. However, because they are part of the justice system, their willful involvement in criminal activity is that much more egregious and arguably deserves harsher treatment as some judges have noted in the sentencing of these criminals. There are several reported cases of criminal charges and convictions of money laundering by lawyers in Canada.[11]

Stephen Schneider (2016, 517) has written that Joseph Lagana, a Montréal lawyer, was arrested on August 30, 1995, along with fifty-six other people on hundreds of counts of money-laundering and drug trafficking offences. The author mentions that "...Lagana...along with a couple of junior lawyers in his law firm, had delivered at least $15 million in Canadian cash to the undercover storefront operation ...". Some estimates are of $91 million (Lamothe and Humphreys 2006). Schneider also mentions:

> ... Other services availed by lawyers were purchases of monetary instruments and arranging for overseas wire transfers. Lagana, who was described in court as the right-hand man of Vito Rizzuto and an intermediary with Columbian drug traffickers, confessed to laundering $47.4 million in drug proceeds and participating in a conspiracy to import 558 kilos of cocaine to Canada. He pleaded guilty in June 1995 and was sentenced to thirteen years in prison.

Much earlier Schneider (2004a, 65) had conducted an analysis using a sample of 149 cases from the RCMP's Proceeds of Crime closed files from 1993 to 1998 (with some files investigated in 2000). In his research, *lawyers were found to be involved unwittingly in 49.7 percent (74 cases)* of the 149 ML cases sampled.

The study showed the professionals that predominately came into contact with the proceeds of crime are deposit institution staff (101 cases), insurance agents or brokers (88 cases), *lawyers* (74 cases), real estate professionals (57 cases), automobile dealership staff (17 cases), 45 accountants (13 cases), currency exchange staff (7 cases), securities dealers and portfolio managers (5 cases) and another category.

It was observed, according to Schneider, that in most of the cases examined, the professionals were innocently implicated; however, in the case of lawyers, there were a smaller number of cases where the nature of the transaction was clearly suspicious (e.g., large amounts of cash to purchase big ticket items, using multiple bank drafts from different banks to personally finance the purchase of a home, requests that lawyers purchase assets on behalf of a client through cheques issued from legal trust accounts, incorporation of numerous companies carrying no legitimate business but have large amounts of cash deposited into corresponding bank accounts) but was nonetheless carried out.

He also noted that lawyers were used to conduct various financial transactions such as the facilitation of real estate transactions, incorporating companies, holding money in trust accounts, and handling cash on behalf of clients. Several synopses of sampled criminal cases were presented supporting his observations that lawyers were being used to launder the proceeds of crime. Schneider also indicated that:

> In short, the nature of the involvement of lawyers in money laundering will be dictated by the complexity and sophistication of the laundering operation itself. In rudimentary schemes, such as those simply involving the purchase of a home, a lawyer is not sought out by the money launderer, but instead is involved due to the necessity to involve legal professionals in real property transactions. In these cases, only a limited range of services are offered by the lawyer, and they are not necessarily in a position to detect a suspicious transaction or client. In larger, more complex laundering schemes, there appears to be a concerted effort by criminal offenders to seek out and involve lawyers. In these cases, lawyers are more actively involved in providing a range of services specifically tailored to money laundering and often appear to be in a position where there is a greater chance that they are cognizant of the criminal source of funds.

Considering these vulnerabilities, the Federation of Law Societies of Canada and its member societies across Canada have created and updated the rules that legal professionals across Canada must follow in their respective jurisdictions to prevent AML/ATF. The profession has not been inactive. However, given that the Supreme Court has supported the legal profession's case not to report to or be supervised by FINTRAC, it is expected that the profession would meet or exceed the standards set out in the PCMLTFA and its regulations to prevent misuse of the profession by money launderers and terrorist financiers. There continues to be shortfalls not only in their rules but also in their supervision and the transparency of their AML/ATF supervision.

For example, among the gaps in the regulations of the profession is the absence of requirements for a compliance program consisting of the appointment of a compliance officer, written AML/ATF policies and procedures, an up-to-date written training plan and program, risk assessments of clients and transactions, and independent review every two years of the effectiveness of the policies and procedures. This is a requirement for all reporting entities under the AML/ATF legislation in Canada and especially for the same activities that apply to both accountants and accounting firms and legal professionals under the FATF standards.

As for supervision and transparency, more could be done to demonstrate publicly how the various law societies supervise their members for AML/ATF purposes, with AML/ATF experts, how often, what the results are and what sanctions are applied. The rules and transparency of the supervisory regime for legal professionals are not at par with the domestic legislation and regulatory framework currently implemented by FINTRAC. Provinces and territories could do more to review and strengthen the governance of their law societies to meet international and federal AML/ATF standards and regulations (Gallant, this volume).

Lack of Beneficial Ownership Transparency

The FATF Must Close the Gap on Access to Beneficial Ownership Transparency

The FATF dedicates a separate category of recommendations or standards to be followed globally in dealing with the transparency of legal persons (e.g., corporations, partnerships) and legal arrangements (e.g., trusts).[12] If it were not for a globally recognized vulnerability, the FATF likely would not have identified the lack of beneficial ownership transparency as a serious issue in two of its 40 Recommendations in 2003 (now identified as Recommendations 24 and 25). These two FATF recommendations regarding beneficial ownership transparency require countries to take measures to prevent the misuse of legal persons (Recommendation 24) and legal arrangements (Recommendation 25) for money laundering or terrorist financing. They also require countries to ensure that adequate, accurate and timely information on beneficial ownership is made available to competent authorities. The FATF has progressed by consulting publicly on potential revisions and expansion of these two recommendations, including the consideration of more public access to beneficial ownership information (FATF 2022), but more could be done.

Canada Lags on Beneficial Ownership Transparency

Criminals and their professional enablers have known about the vulnerabilities of these legal structures for years, not just in Canada, but worldwide. Whether it was for tax evasion or money laundering purposes, criminals have sought professional assistance to guide them in search of anonymity and a hideout to stash their cash.

Canada has never fully met the FATF standard on beneficial ownership transparency. In its last mutual evaluation in 2016, Canada was rated as partially compliant with transparency of beneficial ownership on legal persons (Recommendation 24) and non-compliant with Recommendation 25 dealing with trusts. Canada was rated as having a "low level of effectiveness" when it comes to how Canada ensures that legal persons and arrangements are prevented from being misused for money laundering or terrorist financing and how it makes information on their beneficial ownership available to competent authorities without impediments. Canada has the worst rating possible on effectiveness and stands at the time of the evaluation in 2016 at the bottom of the list with 45 other countries including the USA,[13] a list that includes over 25 percent of least developed countries as of November 2021 (UN 2021). This has not been a badge of honour for Canada as it has gained an international reputation for "snow washing," a term coined to describe the process of making a company as clean as pure white snow (Cohen and Caldera 2021) to legitimize it for the purpose of cleaning dirty money.

In 2015, FINTRAC reviewed money laundering court cases. In a sample of forty cases, it identified the misuse of businesses, shell, or front companies (several in foreign jurisdictions) in seven[14] of those cases (17.5 percent) and comingling in six[15] of those cases (15 percent) as significant means to launder money.[16]

Until recently[17] all fourteen jurisdictions (federal, provincial, and territorial) in Canada facilitated the creation of corporations without a requirement to collect information about who the beneficial owner of it was; that is, not another legal person but a natural person, who significantly owns or controls a corporation. Some provinces, like Alberta and New Brunswick allow non-residents to register as corporate directors with no link to Canada.

It is clear from Canada's own 2015 Assessment of Inherent Risks of Money Laundering and Terrorist Financing in Canada (Finance Canada 2015c) that corporations (especially privately owned corporations) and trusts are rated as inherently *very highly* vulnerable to money laundering and terrorist financing. The reason for that vulnerability rating "... relates to the ability of these entities to be used to conceal beneficial ownership, therefore facilitating the disguise and conversion of illicit proceeds."

Thus, for Canada, this "very high vulnerability" rating does not get any higher as the two categories of corporations and trusts are among the highest in the twenty-seven categories rated at four levels (very high, high, medium, and low) in that risk assessment report. The very high inherent risk of corporations and trusts as cloaks for keeping beneficial owners anonymous and vehicles for money laundering has been known for decades, globally and in Canada.

Much earlier than the FINTRAC report, Schneider (2004b, 44–50) dedicated a whole section of his report on criminally controlled companies. He found that "Of the 149 POC [Proceeds of Crime] cases examined, 49 (32.9 percent) involved criminally-controlled companies." Schneider also cites numerous historical references to government reports in Canada and abroad of the predilection for organized crimes to make use of companies for the purposes of laundering money.

Domestically, the very high risk of abusing corporate structures has existed without serious mitigation, until 2019 when legislation was adopted at the federal level to force federally incorporated private companies to keep track of their beneficial owners. It is only recently, through pressure brought about by the media on the release of leaks such as the Panama Papers, the Bahamas Papers, the Paradise Papers (Cockfield, this volume), and money laundering scandals in British Columbia, and NGOs[18] demanding increased efforts on anti-tax evasion, anti-money laundering, anti-corruption, and beneficial ownership transparency, that

Canada has moved off the sofa, lying there for fifteen years, to address the problem of misuse of corporations for money laundering purposes. In Budget 2021, the federal government proposed "to provide $2.1 million over two years to Innovation, Science and Economic Development Canada to support the implementation of a publicly accessible corporate beneficial ownership registry by 2025." Later, in Budget 2022, with the invasion of Ukraine by Russia, it was announced that the deadline had been advanced to the end of 2023. These announcements are major steps forward in addressing the opacity of private corporation ownership in Canada and a long-awaited means of deterring criminals from using corporations to obfuscate the dirty money trail. It will only be effective if all provinces and territories cooperate to implement a pan-Canadian public registry of beneficial owners, which will be a challenge. In addition, Canada has yet to begin to effectively address the threat posed by express trusts, which criminals and their advisors have likely already been using as legal arrangements to bury and protect their assets.

Conclusion

The international community's rules are not keeping up to effectively combat money laundering. The reality is that the FATF only moves as fast as some of its key thirty-eight members: the USA, the European Union and its twenty-seven members and the United Kingdom (UK). That speed is slow given the nature of international relations, collaboration, coordination, and agreement. Moving the yardstick at the FATF is a laborious process full of compromises and dealmaking. To its credit, if it weren't for the FATF, little progress would have been made globally since 1989 on the AML/ATF front and in Canada especially. Canada has responded more expeditiously to international criticism by the FATF than it did to domestic pressure so far. Even today, Canada is only compliant with 11/40 recommendations and has 0/11 high level of effectiveness ratings on effectiveness measures.

Little stops any individual jurisdiction from meeting all the FATF's standards or demonstrating leadership by exceeding them. For example, while Canada is demonstrably a laggard on beneficial ownership transparency (Recommendations 24 and 25), the UK and the European Union have exceeded the FATF Standards on beneficial ownership transparency. They are among the world's leaders on this issue while Canada lags and has significant room to catch up with the front-runners on this issue in particular and needs to do more and do it better on so many other fronts in the fight against money laundering and terrorist financing.

Notes

1 The exact definition of money laundering is found in the Criminal Code of Canada at subsection 462.31.

2 The Proceeds of Crime (Money Laundering) Act became the Proceeds of Crime (Money Laundering) and Terrorist Financing Act in December 2001 after the 9/11 terrorist attacks in the USA.

3 Criminal Code S.462.31 (1) Every one commits an offence who uses, transfers the possession of, sends or delivers to any person or place, transports, transmits, alters, disposes of or otherwise deals with, in any manner and by any means, any property or any proceeds of any property with intent to conceal or convert that property or those proceeds, knowing or believing that, *or being reckless as to whether* [emphasis added], all or a part of that property or of those proceeds was obtained or derived directly or indirectly as a result of (a) the commission in Canada of a designated offence; or (b) an act or omission anywhere that, if it had occurred in Canada, would have constituted a designated offence. https://laws-lois.justice.gc.ca/eng/acts/c-46/page-96.html - h-123410

4 To apply the model to Canada, six regions were defined: BC, Alberta, Prairies (Saskatchewan and Manitoba), Ontario, Québec, and Atlantic (New Brunswick, PEI, Nova Scotia, and Newfoundland and Labrador).

5 FATF Recommendations 3 and 5 respectively.

6 The "grey list" describes jurisdictions called out by the FATF because of strategic deficiencies or subject to increased monitoring.

7 Reviews were scheduled to take place no later than six weeks after 16 October 2020; each year, one-third of the States parties is to be reviewed. The reviews are to be staggered over three consecutive years, with the start date for each group as follows: 1 December 2020, 1 November 2021, and 1 November 2022. https://www.unodc.org/documents/treaties/UNTOC/COP/SESSION_10/Resolutions/Resolution_10_1_-_English.pdf.

8 It is assumed here that reasonable terms of exchange would be developed and agreed upon based on each country's legislation.

9 "Passed in 1970, the Racketeer Influenced and Corrupt Organizations Act (RICO) is a federal law designed to combat organized crime in the United States. It allows prosecution and civil penalties for racketeering activity performed as part of an ongoing criminal enterprise. Such activity may include illegal gambling, bribery, kidnapping, murder, money laundering, counterfeiting, embezzlement, drug trafficking, slavery, and a host of other unsavory business practices. To convict a defendant under RICO, the government must prove that the defendant engaged in two or more instances of racketeering activity and that the defendant directly invested in, maintained an interest in, or participated in a criminal enterprise affecting interstate or foreign commerce. The law has been used to prosecute members of the mafia, the Hells Angels motorcycle gang, and Operation Rescue, an anti-abortion group, among many others." https://www.nolo.com/legal-encyclopedia/content/rico-act.html.

10 "Continuing criminal enterprise" For purposes of subsection (a), a person is engaged in a continuing criminal enterprise if – (1) he violates any provision of this subchapter or subchapter II the punishment for which is a felony, and (2) such violation is a part of a continuing series of violations of this subchapter or subchapter II – (A) which are undertaken by such person in concert with five or more other persons with respect to whom such person occupies a position of organizer, a supervisory position, or any other position of management, and (B) from which such person obtains substantial income or resources. https://www.law.cornell.edu/uscode/text/21/848.

11 Kenneth James (June 2012), Stanko Grmovsek (January 2010), Simon Rosenfeld (2009), Pierre Boivin, Québec lawyer (2008), *R. v. Root, 2008 ONCA 869, R. v. Shoniker, 2006 O.J. No. 5368, USA v. Martin G. Chambers, Federal Circuits, 11th Cir.* (June 24, 2005), Mr. Justice Robert Flahiff (2000), Joseph Lagana, 1995.

12 The FATF Recommendations 24 and 25.

13 List of 46 countries rated by the FATF as having a low level of effectiveness on beneficial ownership transparency as of March 9, 2021: Bangladesh, Belarus, Bhutan, Botswana, Burkina Faso, Cabo Verde, Cambodia, Canada, China, Costa Rica, Fiji, Ghana, Haiti, Honduras, Hungary, Iceland, Jamaica, Jordan, Latvia, Madagascar, Malawi, Mali, Mauritania, Mauritius, Mongolia, Morocco, Myanmar, Nicaragua, Palau, Pakistan, Panama, Peru, Philippines, Saint Lucia, Senegal, Seychelles, Solomon Islands, Sri Lanka, Thailand, Tunisia, Uganda, United Arab Emirates, United States of America, Vanuatu, Zambia, Zimbabwe.

14 *R. v. Dastani* (2013), *R. c. Halle* (2012), *R. v. Feuerwerker* (2011), *R. v. Black* (2009), *R. v. Boivin* (2008), *R. v. Drakes* (2006), *R. v. Rosenfeld* (2005).

15 *R. v. Chicoine* (2012) – Québec, *R. v. Dastani* (2013) – Ontario, *R. v. Kanagarajah et al.* (2012) – Ontario, *R. v. Lefebvre* (2007) – Québec, *R. v. Rathor* (2011) – British Columbia, *R. v. Tran* (2004) – British Columbia.

16 Obtained through an Access to Information Request – Review of Money Laundering Court Cases in Canada, November 2015.

17 The federal government requires, as of June 2019, the collection of beneficial ownership information for private corporations formed under the Canada Business Corporations Act (CBCA). Several provinces have since emulated similar provisions in their corporate business acts, but until the end of 2022, large jurisdictional outliers included Alberta and Ontario.

18 Non-governmental organizations like Transparency International Canada, Canadians for Tax Fairness and Publish What You Pay.

References

Camdessus, Michel.1998. "Money Laundering: The Importance of International Countermeasures – Address by Michel Camdessus." International Monetary Fund. Paris. http://www.imf.org/external/np/speeches/1998/021098.htm.

CISC (Criminal Intelligence Service Canada). 2009. Testimony before the House of Commons Standing Committee on Justice and Human Rights, March 11, 2009. https://www.ourcommons.ca/DocumentViewer/en/40-2/JUST/meeting-9/evidence.

———. 2020. National Criminal Intelligence Estimate on The Canadian Criminal Marketplace: Money Laundering and Fraud: 11–12. https://ag-pssg-sharedservices-ex.objectstore.gov.bc.ca/ag-pssg-cc-exh-prod-bkt-ex/1017%20-%20OR%20Criminal%20Intelligence%20Service%20of%20Canada%20National%20Criminal%20Intelligence%20Estimate%20on%20the%20Canadian%20Criminal%20Marketplace%20Money%20Laundering%20and%20Fraud%20-2020-.pdf.

———. 2021a. Public Report on Organized Crime in Canada 2020:12. https://publications.gc.ca/collections/collection_2021/scrc-cisc/PS61-39-2020-eng.pdf.

———. 2021b. Public Report on Organized Crime in Canada 2020:10. https://publications.gc.ca/collections/collection_2021/scrc-cisc/PS61-39-2020-eng.pdf.

———. 2021c. Public Report on Organized Crime in Canada 2020: 10. https://publications.gc.ca/collections/collection_2021/scrc-cisc/PS61-39-2020-eng.pdf.

———. 2021d. Public Report on Organized Crime in Canada 2020: 12. https://publications.gc.ca/collections/collection_2021/scrc-cisc/PS61-39-2020-eng.pdf.

Cohen, James, and Sasha Caldera. 2021. "Putting an End to Snow-Washing: The Case for a Publicly Accessible Corporate Registry of Beneficial Owners in Canada." *Journal of Financial Compliance*, 4, no. 4: 379–390.

Cooper, Sam. 2019. "Canada Proposes National Money Laundering Task Force in Budget 2019." *Global News,*19 March. https://globalnews.ca/news/5069141/2019-budget-money-laundering/.

———. 2021. "Canada Needs U.S.-Style Racketeering Laws, Current Organized Crime Laws Failing, B.C. AG Tells Feds." *Global News*, 19 August. https://

globalnews-ca.cdn.ampproject.org/c/s/globalnews.ca/news/8122106/canada-needs-u-s-style-racketeering-laws-current-organized-crime-laws-failing-b-c-ag-tells-feds/amp/.

CRA (Canada Revenue Agency). 2022. *Overall Federal Tax Gap Report: Estimates and Key Findings for Non-Compliance, Tax Years 2014-2018.* https://www.canada.ca/en/revenue-agency/programs/about-canada-revenue-agency-cra/corporate-reports-information/tax-gap-overview.html.

Cribb, Robert, and Marco Chown Oved. 2017. "Signatures for Sale – Paid to Sign Corporate Documents, Nominee Directors Serve to Hide Companies' Real Owners." *Toronto Star,* 26 January. https://projects.thestar.com/panama-papers/canada-signatures-for-sale/.

FATF (Financial Action Task Force). 2012–2022a. *International Standards on Combating Money Laundering and the Financing of Terrorism & Proliferation,* 5–6. Paris, France. www.fatf-gafi.org/recommendations.html.

———. 2012–2022b. *International Standards on Combating Money Laundering and The Financing of Terrorism & Proliferation. Recommendations 22 and 23.* Paris, France. www.fatf-gafi.org/recommendations.html.

———. 2012–2022c. *International Standards on Combating Money Laundering and The Financing of Terrorism & Proliferation. Recommendation 33.* Paris, France. www.fatf-gafi.org/recommendations.html.

———. 2013a. *FATF Report – Money Laundering and Terrorist Financing Vulnerabilities of Legal Professionals,* 37–76. Paris, France. https://www.fatf-gafi.org/media/fatf/documents/reports/ML%20and%20TF%20vulnerabilities%20legal%20professionals.pdf.

———. 2013b. *FATF Report – Money Laundering and Terrorist Financing Vulnerabilities of Legal Professionals,* 19–20. Paris, France. https://www.fatf-gafi.org/media/fatf/documents/reports/ML%20and%20TF%20vulnerabilities%20legal%20professionals.pdf.

———. 2018. FATF Report – *Professional Money Laundering,* 10–48. Paris, France. https://www.fatf-gafi.org/media/fatf/documents/Professional-Money-Laundering.pdf.

———. 2020. *Trade-Based Money Laundering – Trends and Developments,* 4. Paris, France. https://www.fatf-gafi.org/media/fatf/content/Trade-Based-Money-Laundering-Trends-and-Developments.pdf.

———. 2022. *FATF Public Statement on revisions to R. 24.* March 2022. Paris, France. https://www.fatf-gafi.org/publications/fatfrecommendations/documents/r24-statement-march-2022.html.

FINA (House of Commons Standing Committee on Finance). 2018. June 20, 2018,1245. https://www.ourcommons.ca/DocumentViewer/en/42-1/FINA/meeting-163/evidence.

Finance Canada. 2015a. *Assessment of Inherent Risks of Money Laundering and Terrorist Financing in Canada,* 32, footnote 31. https://www.canada.ca/content/dam/fin/migration/pub/mltf-rpcfat/mltf-rpcfat-eng.pdf.

————. 2015b. *Assessment of Inherent Risks of Money Laundering and Terrorist Financing in Canada*, 32, Table 3. https://www.canada.ca/content/dam/fin/migration/pub/mltf-rpcfat/mltf-rpcfat-eng.pdf.

————. 2015c. *Assessment of Inherent Risks of Money Laundering and Terrorist Financing in Canada*, 32, Table 3. https://www.canada.ca/content/dam/fin/migration/pub/mltf-rpcfat/mltf-rpcfat-eng.pdf.

————. 2018. *Budget 2018. Equality + Growth. A Strong Middle Class*, 319. https://www.budget.gc.ca/2018/docs/plan/toc-tdm-en.html.

————. 2019a. "Strengthening Canada's Anti-Money Laundering and Anti-Terrorist Financing (AML/ATF) Regime." In *Budget 2019. Investing in the Middle Class*, 199. https://www.budget.gc.ca/2019/docs/plan/toc-tdm-en.html.

————. 2019b. *Budget 2019. Investing in the Middle Class*, 183. https://www.budget.gc.ca/2019/docs/plan/chap-04-en.html.

FINTRAC 2022. "Money laundering" in Mandate. Updated 2022-03-12. https://www.fintrac-canafe.gc.ca/fintrac-canafe/1-eng.

Government of Canada. 2020. *Commission of Inquiry into Money Laundering in British Columbia*. Opening statement of the Government of Canada. Part 1, Overview: 2. https://cullencommission.ca/files/OpeningStatement-GovernmentOfCanada.pdf.

Hall, Neal. 2004. "B.C. Money-Laundering Scam Raked in $200 Million." *Vancouver Sun*, 17 June. http://www.mapinc.org/drugnews/v04/n895/a06.html.

Hunter, Justine, and Mike Hager. 2019. "Alberta Questioning B.C.'s Money-Laundering Report." *Globe and Mail*. 13 May. https://www.theglobeandmail.com/canada/article-alberta-questioning-bcs-money-laundering-report/.

ICIJ (International Consortium of Investigative Journalists). 2016. "The Panama Papers: Exposing the Rogue Offshore Finance Industry." https://www.icij.org/investigations/panama-papers/.

————. 2017. "Paradise Papers: Secrets of The Global Elite." https://www.icij.org/investigations/paradise-papers/.

————. 2020. "FinCEN Files. Global Banks Defy U.S. Crackdowns by Serving Oligarchs, Criminals and Terrorists." https://www.icij.org/investigations/fincen-files/global-banks-defy-u-s-crackdowns-by-serving-oligarchs-criminals-and-terrorists/.

Lamothe, Lee, and Adrian Humphreys. 2006. *The Sixth Family: The Collapse of the New York Mafia and the Rise of Vito Rizzuto*, 220. Toronto: John Wiley & Sons.

Lindsay, Bethany. 2020. "Vancouver Model for Money Laundering Unprecedented in Canada, B.C. Inquiry Hears." Canadian Broadcasting Corporation, 26 May. https://www.cbc.ca/news/canada/british-columbia/cullen-commission-money-laundering-bc-tuesday-1.5585890.

Maloney, Maureen, Tsur Somerville, and Brigitte Unger. 2019a. *Combatting Money Laundering in BC Real Estate, Expert Panel on Money Laundering in BC Real Estate*, 19. https://www2.gov.bc.ca/assets/gov/housing-and-tenancy/real-estate-in-bc/combatting-money-laundering-report.pdf.

————. 2019b. *Combatting Money Laundering in BC Real Estate, Expert Panel on Money Laundering in BC Real Estate*, 47. https://www2.gov.bc.ca/assets/gov/housing-and-tenancy/real-estate-in-bc/combatting-money-laundering-report.pdf.

————. 2019c. *Combatting Money Laundering in BC Real Estate, Expert Panel on Money Laundering in BC Real Estate*, 1. https://www2.gov.bc.ca/assets/gov/housing-and-tenancy/real-estate-in-bc/combatting-money-laundering-report.pdf.

————. 2019d. *Combatting Money Laundering in BC Real Estate, Expert Panel on Money Laundering in BC Real Estate*, 1–2. https://www2.gov.bc.ca/assets/gov/housing-and-tenancy/real-estate-in-bc/combatting-money-laundering-report.pdf.

————. 2019e. *Combatting Money Laundering in BC Real Estate, Expert Panel on Money Laundering in BC Real Estate*, 3. https://www2.gov.bc.ca/assets/gov/housing-and-tenancy/real-estate-in-bc/combatting-money-laundering-report.pdf.

McDermott Will & Emery. 2021. "Supreme Court Rejects Appeal to Overturn UK's First Unexplained Wealth Order." *Lexology*. https://www.lexology.com/library/detail.aspx?g=a0cfcad9-5b50-44b5-a8e6-e56a5b95faae.

Meunier, Denis. 2018. *Hidden Beneficial Ownership and Control: Canada as a Pawn in the Global Game of Money Laundering*. Toronto. C.D. Howe Institute. https://www.cdhowe.org/sites/default/files/attachments/research_papers/mixed/Final%20for%20advance%20release%20Commentary_519_0.pdf.

Northcott, Paul. 2021. "Just the Facts – Organized Crime." *Royal Canadian Mounted Police. RCMP Gazette*. https://www.rcmp-grc.gc.ca/en/gazette/just-the-facts-organized-crime.

OECD (Organisation for Economic Co-operation and Development). 2019. *Money Laundering and Terrorist Financing Awareness Handbook for Tax Examiners and Tax Auditors*. Paris: OECD. https://www.oecd.org/tax/crime/money-laundering-and-terrorist-financing-awareness-handbook-for-tax-examiners-and-tax-auditors.pdf.

Schneider, Stephen. 2004a. *Money Laundering in Canada: An Analysis of RCMP Cases*, 65. Toronto: Nathanson Centre for the Study of Organized Crime and Corruption, York University. https://ag-pssg-sharedservices-ex.objectstore.gov.bc.ca/ag-pssg-cc-exh-prod-bkt-ex/7%20-%20Money%20Laundering%20in%20Canada%20An%20Analysis%20of%20RCMP%20Cases%20March%202014.pdf.

————. 2004b. Money Laundering in Canada: An Analysis of RCMP Cases, 44–50. Toronto: Nathanson Centre for the Study of Organized Crime and Corruption, York University. https://ag-pssg-sharedservices-ex.objectstore.gov.bc.ca/ag-pssg-cc-exh-prod-bkt-ex/7%20-%20Money%20Laundering%20in%20Canada%20An%20Analysis%20of%20RCMP%20Cases%20March%202014.pdf.

————. 2016. *ICED: The Story of Organized Crime in Canada*, 517. Mississauga: John Wiley and Sons Canada, Ltd. First edition.

Schott, Paul Allan. 2006. Reference Guide to Anti-Money Laundering and Combating the Financing of Terrorism, 1–7. Washington: World Bank, Second edition. https://openknowledge.worldbank.org/bitstream/handle/10986/6977/350520Referenc1Money01OFFICIAL0USE1.pdf?sequence=1&isAllowed=y.

Statista. 2022. "Global Gross Domestic Product (GDP) at Current Prices from 1985 to 2027." https://www.statista.com/statistics/268750/global-gross-domestic-product-gdp/.

Tanzi, Vito. 1996. "Money Laundering and the International Financial System." *International Monetary Fund. Fiscal Affairs Department.* Working Paper. Abstract. https://www.elibrary.imf.org/doc/IMF001/04732-9781451847598/04732-9781451847598/Other_formats/Source_PDF/04732-9781451995251.pdf.

UN (United Nations). 2021. "List of Least Developed Countries (as of 24 November 2021)." Committee for Development Policy. https://www.un.org/development/desa/dpad/wp-content/uploads/sites/45/publication/ldc_list.pdf.

UNODC (United Nations Office of Drugs and Crime). 2003. United Nations Convention Against Transnational Organized Crime, Articles 2 and 3. https://www.unodc.org/documents/treaties/UNTOC/Publications/TOC%20Convention/TOCebook-e.pdf.

————. 2010. "Organized Crime Has Globalized and Turned into a Security Threat." https://www.unodc.org/unodc/en/press/releases/2010/June/organized-crime-has-globalized-and-turned-into-a-security-threat.html.

————. 2011. "Estimating Illicit Financial Flows Resulting from Drug Trafficking and Other Transnational Organized Crimes." Vienna: Research Report. https://www.unodc.org/documents/data-and-analysis/Studies/Illicit_financial_flows_2011_web.pdf.

7

Money Laundering Investigations in Canada 1982 to Present: Why Canada Is Failing

Garry Clement

One strong conclusion which flowed after Justice Cullen heard testimony over three years was that Canada's federal and provincial governments are ill-equipped to combat money laundering and financial crime. Based on the report findings it should be well evidenced that transnational organized crime has become a central issue in international affairs, an important factor in the global economy, and an immediate reality for Canadians. Examining the direct impacts of drug addiction, sexual exploitation, environmental damage, and a host of other scourges, it is clear organized crime has the capacity to undermine the rule of law and good governance, without which there can be no sustainable development. The initial impetus for the proceeds of crime legislation was to target organized criminals engaged in drug trafficking. A lofty goal and as history has demonstrated, a futile goal. As the legislation evolved the government included designated offences which resulted in the mandate to include the jurisdiction of the provinces, thereby requiring the provincial attorney generals to assume responsibility for offences not related to drug trafficking.

With the expanded legislative authorities both federal and provincial governments believed they had enacted sufficient legislation to ensure a well-defined ability to combat all aspects of money laundering. What was overlooked was the fact that money laundering investigations, like other financial crime investigations, are arduous, complex, and costly. This is combined with the need to have seasoned investigators and prosecutors who have a bent to deal with the financial arena.

In the early stages the only vehicle available was the integrated proceeds of crime units that at the outset had a mandate to look at all aspects of money laundering derived from financial crimes. The bulk of the cases, however, focused solely on drug crimes – seeing the units had federal Crown corporations embedded in the units. It was also found that money laundering cases were expensive, and thus for most police organizations, outside of their operational means to pursue cases. Provincial Crowns were for the most part inexperienced and lacked the will to delve into long, drawn-out money laundering cases.

For this reason, provincial governments, commencing with Ontario, began to investigate the aspect of civil forfeitures, which now have become the main provincial focus along with the concept of offence-related property. Both approaches reduce the economic burden found in substantive proceeds of crime cases and the need for highly sophisticated financial crime investigators.

My government investigative and private sector consulting experience has provided me with a rare opportunity to understand two very distinct perspectives. For more than thirty-four years, I had a law enforcement perspective. In that capacity, my perspective was government and investigation driven. For the last twelve years, in my current position as a consultant, my perspective has shifted to one that is industry and compliance driven. Having been a liaison officer in Hong Kong in 1991 through 1994 I witnessed firsthand the weaknesses in our immigration system wherein criminals were permitted to enter Canada virtually unimpeded and became sensitized to the threat posed by China.

I have given specific mention to China as my experience in the '90s caused me to opine that Canada, and in particular Vancouver, would become a transshipment destination from Asia for illicit drugs and remain attractive to transnational organized crime. Over the years efforts to alert the political elite failed, as there was a strong desire, dating back to Pierre

Elliott Trudeau, to have strong relationships with China. The Desmarais family in Québec spearheaded many of Canada's relationships which were eagerly endorsed by successive prime ministers.

Today this has given rise to a fentanyl pandemic; Canada being seen as a haven for transnational money laundering, our intellectual property being targeted, and Chinese Canadians being subject of surveillance by illicit Chinese police stations embedded in large Canadian cities.

In 2022, the Canadian Security Intelligence Service – Canada (CSIS) released a report highlighting the impact of organized crime in Canada, all of which resulted in increased money laundering threats. The significant findings described how organized crime is infiltrating various government and private organizations. The agency highlighted threats to the public sector, including transportation and construction, healthcare and pharmaceuticals, waste management, law enforcement, defence, and foreign affairs.

The agency indicated that thirty-one of the assessed organized crime groups (OCGs) have access via jobs within Canadian public sector agencies or departments. The report said:

- Of these, 26 percent are Mafia groups, 10 percent are outlaw motorcycle gangs and 6 percent are street gangs.
- While infiltration of the public sector seems to occur mostly at the local/regional levels, [OCG] may be using the benefits for interprovincial or international criminal activities.
- Public sector infiltration leads to rising costs of goods and services, misallocation of public resources, weakened policymaking, and damage to public confidence in government and law enforcement.
- Familial or romantic relationships and monetary benefits appear to be principal factors motivating corruption and infiltration of Canada's public sector. (Mackin 2022)

History of Proceeds of Crime Enforcement in Canada

Money laundering has co-existed with major criminals for decades. Several examples illuminate the dark history of dirty money in Canada. First, in the 1920s and 1930s, Rocco Perri, a Hamilton mobster used the name of his mistress, Bessie Starkman, to open bank accounts. It is alleged that a prominent businessman, Peter Larkin, allegedly established secret nest-egg accounts for former Prime Minister MacKenzie King. In the 1930s during prohibition, the Bronfman family illegally exported liquor to the United States and concealed the funds under false fronts to obscure ownership of the bank accounts.

The Québec Crime Commission study in 1977 revealed that Willie Obront, a Montréal-based money launderer, allegedly laundered $84.5 million which came in the form of cheques and was deposited in numerous bank accounts. Obront was one of only two non-Italian individuals who was accepted by the Bonanno and Controni organized crime families. He was deemed the Meyer Lansky of Canada. In a study undertaken by Dr. Stephen Schneider he wrote: "Obie also served as Cotroni chief banker and financial adviser, responsible for laundering money. For Montreal's Expo 67, Obie also helped the Cotronis land the meat and vending machine supply contract – most of which was tainted meat. In 1973, Obie was charged with tax fraud, sentenced to 20 months in jail, and ordered to pay $683,046 in back taxes (Schneider 2009).

Tax havens, which were heavily embrace by organized crime groups, emerged following the efforts of rich Canadians who wanted to escape Canada's tax regime. We all recall that it was tax evasion that resulted in the conviction of Al Capone; however, it cannot be understated that what worked for tax was of even more value for illicit proceeds. Quasi-respectable individuals such as Sir Harry Oakes, a gold miner from Northern Ontario, E. P. Taylor, the famed horse breeder, and Michael Degroot, founder of a waste management corporation all sought refuge in the Bahamas as secrecy laws had been enacted thanks to a former cabinet minister, Donald Fleming. In the 1960s, Fleming helped draft Bahama's financial secrecy laws.

In the 1980s a former Toronto lawyer, Donovan Blakeman laundered money for an international criminal organization. Between 1982 and 1987 it is estimated more than $100 million was managed. Blakeman established eleven shell companies in the Channel Islands; fifteen other shell companies in Liberia, the Virgin Islands, the Cayman Islands, the Netherlands Antilles, and Switzerland; fourteen secret bank accounts in the Channel Islands, Liberia, and other jurisdictions; and major real estate developments in West Palm Beach, Florida, Kitchener, Ontario, and Barrie, Ontario. Blakeman obscured the transactions by moving the money through the various accounts and jurisdictions which he dubbed the "Spaghetti Jungle." He repatriated the money for real estate investments using the loan-back technique.

In October 1992, the United States Financial Crimes Enforcement Network stated: "Of particular interest to investigators is the ease with which U.S. currency can ...be smuggled across the Canadian border and used to purchase Canadian bank drafts." Cases cited in support of this statement highlighted that Issac Kattan, a money launderer for a Columbian cartel, used bank accounts in Canada to help launder over $400 million in US cash. Members of the Cuntrera Sicilian crime family used bank accounts in Montréal to launder approximately US$36 million in heroin profits earned in the United States.

Canada's Response

The first real attempt by the Government of Canada to investigate the illicit profits obtained by organized crime came in 1972, when Revenue Canada, in conjunction with the solicitor general through the Royal Canadian Mounted Police (RCMP), was directed to conduct investigations using the Income Tax Act. It was taking a page from the Al Capone and Meyer Lansky investigations in the US. The overarching goal was to identify and attack the accumulation of unreported wealth to disrupt organized crime and reduce criminal activities. Although marginally successful, only taxes owing on illicit income was targeted, and the time it took for prosecution and the restriction imposed by Section 241 of the Tax Act lessened the effect.

241(1) Except as authorized by this section, no official or other representative of a government entity shall
(a) knowingly provide, or knowingly allow to be provided, to any person any taxpayer information.

(b) knowingly allow any person to have access to any taxpayer information; or

(c) knowingly use any taxpayer information otherwise than in the course of the administration or enforcement of this Act, the *Canada Pension Plan*, the Unemployment Insurance Act or the *Employment Insurance Act* or for the purpose for which it was provided under this section.

Marginal note: Evidence relating to taxpayer information
(2) Notwithstanding any other Act of Parliament or other law, no official or other representative of a government entity shall be required, in connection with any legal proceedings, to give or produce evidence relating to any taxpayer information.

Marginal note: Communication where proceedings have been commenced
(3) Subsections 241(1) and 241(2) do not apply in respect of
   (a) criminal proceedings, either by indictment or on summary conviction, that have been commenced by the laying of an information or the preferring of an indictment, under an Act of Parliament; or
   (b) any legal proceedings relating to the administration or enforcement of this Act, the *Canada Pension Plan*, the *Unemployment Insurance Act* or the *Employment Insurance Act* or any other Act of Parliament or law of a province that provides for the imposition or collection of a tax or duty.

This failure, and the fact that our US neighbours had instituted significant measures to attack proceeds of crime, pressured Canada to consider other avenues.

In 1982, under the direction of RCMP Assistant Commissioner Rod Stamler, the Anti-Drug Profiteering Units were created with the goal of examining the legislative regime of the day to determine its viability to attack proceeds of crime. The initial complement was fourteen investigators followed by an additional five in 1983. The early findings established that the legal framework of the day did not permit the seizing of intangibles (i.e., bank accounts and real estate). Notwithstanding this, there were a few successful cases in Alberta where the prowess of RCMP Sergeant Bob Preston resulted in the Court of Queen's Bench stretching the law to allow seizures in two cases, the Pakozdy case and Smith case but at the same time highlighted the need for legislative changes. Of interest, in the R. v. Smith case, His Honour quoted Exodus 21:28 to effect forfeiture of an automobile and rugs that were purchased with the proceeds of drug trafficking; "when an ox gores a man or woman to death, the ox shall be stoned, and its flesh may not be eaten." (Court of Queen's Bench, Alberta, *R v. Smith*) The ruling clearly evidenced that Canadian legislation needed to be expanded so that there was a recognition for the freezing and seizing of property, inclusive of bank accounts and real estate. In response, in 1989 to support the objective of seizing proceeds of crime leading to forfeiture, Parliament passed legislation to overcome some of the identified weaknesses under Bill C-61.

I began focusing on money laundering in 1983, at the National Program level. Previously I had been involved in undercover operations in Toronto in the mid-1970s and in Vancouver from late 1970 to 1980, where I successfully infiltrated some of the highest levels of organized crime that existed at that time. I formed an opinion that without attacking the profits and following the flow of money derived from criminal activity the criminal element continued to gain power.

As a neophyte at that time, I commenced studying and relying on subject matter experts in the United States and academics in Canada. It became obvious that to be a successful financial crime investigator it was necessary to enjoy working with financial files and be willing to rely on available certifications in the private sector. Additionally, it is essential that an investigator be committed for the long term since garnering the necessary skill set could be argued to be akin to an apprenticeship program.

In 1992 flowing from the fledgling anti-drug profiteering program and through the renewal of Canada's Drug Strategy, funding was made available over five years to create the Integrated Anti-Drug Proceeds of Crime Program (IADP). The units were in Vancouver, Toronto, and Montréal and were designed to bring together a linked system of enforcement-related resources, namely, the RCMP, Department of Justice (DOJ) counsel, forensic accountants, provincial and municipal police, and Revenue Canada – Customs Investigators. The overarching goal was to test the concept of investigating and prosecuting the upper echelons of money laundering and organized drug trafficking cases.

In 1993, legislation was enacted creating the offenses of laundering and possessing the proceeds of tobacco and alcohol smuggled in Canada.

This resulted in additional resources being provided to the Integrated Proceeds of Crime (IPOC) units.

During this period, a ski resort was seized in Québec and, as it was incumbent that the resort be managed prior to trial, it became apparent that there was a need for creating a management body to ensure assets under seizure were maintained. As a result, in 1993, the government passed the Seized Property Management Act under Public Works Canada.

A 1994 review of the adequacy and effectiveness of the IPOC Units found:

- IADP units demonstrated clearly that they have an impact on (criminal) organizations actively involved in money laundering within Canada. Unfortunately, their efforts are minuscule in comparison to the extent of the practice.
- Current proceeds of crime investigators are seizing only a small percentage of the estimated billions of dollars being laundered in Canada annually.
- At that time Canada has less than 200 trained POC investigators actively involved in money laundering investigations.
- Money laundering is associated with a wide variety of crimes in Canada, such as drug trafficking and importation but also alcohol and tobacco smuggling, fraud, and gambling just to name a few.
- In the view of the evaluators, Canadian resources to control money laundering are insufficient to make a significant impact in both the short term and long term. To promote greater involvement by other levels of government to fund POC investigations the current success and expertise of the IADP units must be used. (RCMP findings of which I was an author)

Two recommendations were forthcoming:

1. The IADP concept is expanded immediately to other centres across Canada.
2. A strategic plan is created to promote greater involvement by provincial and municipal law enforcement agencies in POC investigations.

This report resulted in the establishment of units in Edmonton, Calgary, Ottawa, London, Halifax, Fredericton, Winnipeg, Regina, Québec

City, and St. John's, as well as new funding and resources for all inte-grated partners, inclusive of municipal and provincial investigators. The funding model was designed so that all allotted funds had to be utilized by the integrated proceeds of crime units and in theory was not to be utilized in other investigative areas of the RCMP. The concept was in my view extremely sound; however, the RCMP senior management found ways to pull some of the funding for other areas of the organization. Suc-cess of the units depended on the manager. Many of the officers did not treat the personnel in partner agencies as equal colleagues, which resulted in rifts being created and, as you might expect, many of the officers kept in-house counsel off in a corner rather than making them a valuable part of the team.

Likely one of the biggest impediments to success was the constant turnover of resources stemming from the paramilitary promotion pro-cess. Instead of permitting skill-based pay, increases came solely through promotion and many of the investigators attached to the proceeds of crime units were highly skilled and therefore promotable in other areas of the Force. As such, members willingly accepted promotions outside of the units resulting in the IPOC units becoming an ongoing training ground with minimal expertise.

I can attest the model was appropriate, and with revisions to staffing policies and an acceptance that investigators from other police depart-ments were capable both as investigators and managers and that Justice lawyers needed to be an integral part of the team, investigative success was possible. In the Ottawa Unit we had a highly efficient team all treat-ed equally resulting in some highly laudable successes. Canada Revenue Agency was also made part of the team which added tremendous value.

One of the areas of legislation that from a practitioner's point of view has been the most helpful was the inclusion of the section under the Canada Drug Substances Act and the Criminal Code which defined offense-related property and enabled the seizure of both tangibles and intangibles subject to establishing a nexus to the criminal activity. Of-fence-related property has been a go-to solution for many law enforce-ment organizations since it is easier to establish a nexus to the criminal activity such as a vehicle used for transporting drugs, or a residence or building used as a grow op.

When examining the genesis of money laundering enforcement, it could be argued that Canada should be a leader; however, successive governments have failed to maintain a commitment to ensuring effective, efficient, and proactive enforcement.

Canada's Failures

Although this should have been effective, the IPOC program failed for several reasons. First the federal government failed to provide increased funding notwithstanding the fact that both wages and the cost of investigations increased due to various landmark decisions like Stinchcombe and Jordan. The RCMP's paramilitary system resulted in members seeking promotions in other units upon seeing that few promotions existed within. Over the years, many arguments for over-ranking positions and/or doing away with ranked positions and moving to skill-based pay were made, but RCMP leadership failed to accept the need, instead relying on their belief in a generalist investigator skill set. As a result, seeing as the investigators were highly skilled, they were also highly promotable; this resulted in ongoing movement of members and the inability to have the necessary talent retained within the units. In the mid-2000s when the units started showing significant vacancies, decisions were taken to eliminate the IPOC program thereby disadvantaging investigators aspiring to engage in financial investigations. This contributed to the current situation wherein Canada is seen as the weak link in combatting money laundering and transnational organized crime.

The attacks of 9/11 signalled the beginning of the end of the IPOC Units as RCMP resources were quickly hived off to undertake the terrorist files. This was followed by the introduction of Integrated Market Enforcement Teams which again hived off further IPOC resources, leaving units with massive vacancies.

Successive management endeavoured to hide the embarrassment of the vacancies since successive governments failed to shore up funding by eliminating specialized teams and creating multi-skilled teams. This resulted in generalized units that dealt with all manner of federal crimes and the reality was that valuable expertise was lost. Specialization started eroding in the mid-2000s, again leading to systemic failure to combat financial crime and money laundering. Canada came to be seen by transnational criminals as a weak link and a great place to launder funds through real estate, casinos, high-value purchases, and high-end vehicles.

As the legal profession won successive arguments against being brought under the money laundering regime, they were and continue to be duped by sophisticated organized criminals for purposes of establishing companies and having their trust accounts manipulated. A 2019 report in the *Edmonton Journal* explained: "For reasons of solicitor-client privilege, the accounts aren't subject to the same reporting requirements as other popular money laundering tools."(Wakefield 2019) A recent example is the transfer of funds to a lawyer's trust account for purposes of a large real estate investment; then, the investment allegedly does "not proceed" and thus the monies are sent out of a trust account to the criminal account which gives a surface appearance of legitimacy.

Recently, the United Kingdom-based Tax Justice Network's 2020 report concluded that, "Canada has a long history in the development of tax havens, but today it is becoming known as a destination for money laundering due to weak rules over corporate transparency and beneficial ownership. The country's weaker anti-money-laundering laws provide criminals with the anonymity to not get caught and likely not be prosecuted if they are caught." (Francis 2020)

Transparency International has ranked Canada at the bottom of all the G20 countries, due to its failure to meet G20 anti-money-laundering commitments (Transparency International 2018). Based on my work over the years, I would argue that much of this failure rests on the fact that governments at all levels have not taken financial crime seriously and, if anything, have contributed to the problem that exists today. For example, the federal government continually has failed to provide the necessary financing to ensure sustainable and effective investigative units. Many political leaders have sided with China resulting in a continuous flow of flight capital and ineffective controls further resulting in precursor chemicals and other chemical drugs flowing into Canada. Provincial governments have largely looked the other way when it comes to casinos and money laundering, knowing full well money is flowing from criminal elements. Municipal governments are failing to vet construction companies appropriately and approve development proposals without consideration for the genesis of the funding.

I have witnessed first-hand construction companies with strong links to organized crime entrenching themselves in municipal contracts. I also witnessed, during his tenure as chief of police in Cobourg, small communities having their main street stores renovated by unknown companies who paid cash to their contractors. The political leaders argued that it was good for the economy.

Due to its positive international image, Canada is seen by some of the more discerning crooks as their money-laundering venue of choice. This says much about how Canada's reputation among the international community could be tarnished if the "snow washing" problem continues through inaction at all levels of government (BNN Bloomberg 2020).

In the twenty-first century, where cyber-crime is increasing exponentially, it is time to look at a federal model, possibly like either the FBI or DEA. Those systems include probationary agents, agents, and senior field agents. For agents to remain in their field of expertise and gain further salary increases through the demonstration of further expertise is key. Although there is no perfect promotional system, success can be clearly linked to the retention and nurturing of experience-based expertise. Their focus relies significantly on the ability of its agents and investigators to locate the various criminal activities they are assigned. This component provides an understanding that investing in personnel's development can benefit the organization by improving the quality of work and customer satisfaction. The general and behavioural trends of the organization present an understanding that there is a need for a cohesive system that embraces the development of expertise.

Having had the opportunity to work with various US enforcement organizations during my policing career I witnessed first-hand the value of ensuring investigators remain in a specific area of enforcement, thereby developing a high degree of expertise. Most investigators I spoke with, unlike my former policing colleagues, were not looking for a promotion into another area but were content to stay in their chosen lane of expertise.

If we are to achieve any modicum of positive outcomes, we must accept that we are failing regarding anti-money laundering protections. First, we must acknowledge that we are getting it wrong with regards to our anti-money-laundering policies. Canada, clearly evidenced through the Cullen Commission's findings and various Transparency International reports, is falling farther behind, and in my opinion, becoming a weak partner to the Five Eyes network. (The Five Eyes is an intelligence alliance composed of Australia, Canada, New Zealand, the United Kingdom, and the United States. These partner countries share a broad range of intelligence with one another in one of the world's most unified multilateral arrangements.)

Canada must also embrace the fact that financial crime has now become extremely complex due to the likelihood of offshore jurisdictions being involved; also the use of shell and shelf companies are dominant amongst the criminal element and with the advent of crypto currencies, the internet plays a larger role. To criminal organizations, international borders are solely a hindrance which can be circumvented through legal frameworks and embracing a multitude of foreign jurisdictions.

If we accept that the internet provides a borderless environment for criminals of all stripes, then it can be understood that criminals are adaptive and use whatever tools are provided within society to protect their criminal enterprises. The world ensures there are no shortage of concealment methods from straw owners (i.e., individuals who act as beneficial owners who conceal the real owners), and to underground dark web offerings that serve to enhance criminal activity. These factors alone, demand that Canada embrace the need to have high-level investigative skills, skills that are continually expanded through both in-house and external training opportunities. This would provide an opportunity for law enforcement to be a viable threat to transnational criminals.

David Lewis the former executive secretary of the Financial Action Task Force (FATF), estimated only 1 percent of laundered funds are seized globally. Seen another way, this is a 99 percent failure rate which should not be ignored. Thus, the biggest threat in the fight against money laundering and the harm caused by money laundering is to tolerate the failing status quo of our anti-money-laundering policies, procedures, and practices.

The consequences of Canada's current failure were clearly highlighted in the testimony provided to the Cullen Commission. It concluded that transnational organized crime (TOC) poses a significant and growing threat to national and international security, with dire implications for public safety, public health, democratic institutions, and economic stability across the globe. To illustrate the impact on society of TOC, we refer to the 2011 White House Strategy to Combat Transnational Organized Crime which defined TOCs as "self-perpetuating associations who operate transnationally for the purpose of obtaining power, influence, monetary and/or commercial gains, wholly or in part by illegal means, while protecting their activities through a pattern of corruption and/or violence, or while protecting their illegal activities through a transnational organizational structure and the exploitation of transnational commerce or communication mechanisms." This serves to underscore why it is imperative Canada adopt appropriate measures. It is important to accept that TOC harms citizen safety, subverts government institutions, and can destabilize nations.

How, then, do we overcome what can only be described as systemic failures? We should be looking at the establishment of a National Financial Crime committee to look at gaps and make recommendations that will sustain investigations for the foreseeable future. We need to look at what skills are required and ensure units are formed with the identified skills in mind, whether from law enforcement, the public sector, or academia.

Global losses associated with financial crimes continue to climb year over year. Managing the investigative requirements associated with money laundering, fraud, and cyber incursions has never been a timelier imperative for provinces and Canada to protect society and thwart transnational organized crime while enhancing Canada's reputation on the world stage by demonstrating our financial system is not open for business to criminals.

Creating an effective enforcement response necessitates a whole-of-government approach and, beyond that, vibrant relationships with partner nations based on trust. These are essential if Canada is to be viable partner amongst groups such as the Five Eyes.

Due to the sophistication of transnational organized crime, all levels of government in Canada need to recognize that a failure to demonstrate a resolve to combating organized crime activities will result in Canada remaining the weak link in the global enforcement chain. This will require that Canada demonstrate an ability to:

- Disrupt, dismantle, and effectively prosecute criminal networks across the globe with a goal of minimizing their impacts to levels that can be handled by local law enforcement organizations.
- Promote a transnational, cross-organizational response, and development of strategic security partnerships.
- Ensure the ongoing coordination of intelligence and show leadership within the law enforcement community to ensure all actions serve the overall strategic goal of combatting organized crime activities.
- Recognize that money laundering cases require expert investigative resources and an integrated approach to be successful. There must be a recognition that financial crime investigators need to remain specialized and attached to their respective units for the long term. These units need to be able to recruit both sworn law enforcement from other departments and civilian members where expertise gaps exist (this was the case with the Integrated Proceeds of Crime model which today has been lost).
- Accept that prosecutors need, like financial crime investigators, to be assigned to specialized units for the long term to garner the necessary expertise to be able to deal with the complexities of the cases.
- Legislatively, it is time to either deal with the issues arising from Jordan, disclosure requirements, or create new legislation inclusive of a RICO-type statute; (South Africa created a federal/civil forfeiture system that took into consideration charter of rights issues).
- Acceptance by the government that it is to blame for the current situation in which Canada finds itself. Money laundering and financial crime cases are expensive to investigate and prosecute and therefore need ongoing funding commensurate with the size of the units; this funding needs to be solely dedicated to the units and not available for all other policing mandates.
- The legal profession needs to be brought into the PCMLTFA. The profession needs to understand that the amendments now refer

to "recklessness" which I would opine could easily be attached to many lawyers in their dealing with the "criminal element."

- Training needs to be a priority for understanding trans-national organized crime groups like Asian-based organized crime so that effective enforcement can be undertaken.

- FINTRAC, the oversight regulator, needs to play a more important role in administering regulation penalties to entities that continue to demonstrate a disregard for thwarting money laundering, including our Big Five institutions; i.e., Bank of Montreal, Bank of Nova Scotia, Canadian Imperial Bank of Commerce, Royal Bank of Canada and Toronto-Dominion Bank.

- That other provinces recognize that British Columbia is not alone in being a major conduit for transnational organized crime and money-laundering activities and that they, too, need to examine their enforcement gaps.

- Embrace a whole-of-government approach in support of law enforcement agencies to foster a cooperative partnership of networks to counter transnational organized crime

- Create trans-agency teams that would integrate legal experts, forensic accountants, civilian specialists, Canada Revenue Agency, Canada Border Services Agency, municipal and provincial partners, and property management experts, all of whom would be tasked with establishing the authority, legitimacy, and effectiveness of financial crime/proceeds of crime enforcement in Canada

- Establish a multi-jurisdictional government committee to examine legislative reforms which provide for more effective enforcement and prosecution of financial crime, relying on such reports as the 2011 *Report on Disclosure in Criminal Cases,* issued by the Steering Committee on Justice Efficiencies and Access to Justice.

This report clearly articulates the issues facing law enforcement and prosecution:

Effectively and efficiently gathering, managing, digesting and disclosing large quantities of information is an onerous task for the police and prosecution. Receiving, managing, and digesting large quantities of information is also an onerous task for defence counsel and judges. Resources committed to disclosure activities cannot be deployed elsewhere to address other pressing needs. Disclosure disagreements between the prosecution and defence frequently arise. The absence of statutory procedure to obtain early judicial resolution of disclosure disputes is particularly problematic. Failure to meet the demands of full disclosure leads to delayed and stayed trials. Irrespective of who is to 'blame', public confidence in the administration of justice suffers when serious cases, or a spate of less serious ones, are not determined on their merits.

Such challenges have benefited trans-national organized crime time and time again.

Canada should, at a federal level, adopt legislation such as the Racketeer Influenced and Corrupt Organizations Act (RICO) statute that was undertaken in the United States. A federal law designed to combat organized crime, it allows prosecution and civil penalties for racketeering activity performed as part of an ongoing criminal enterprise.

Under RICO, a person who has committed "at least two acts of racketeering activity" drawn from a list of thirty-five crimes (twenty-seven federal and eight state crimes) within a ten-year period can be charged with racketeering if such acts are related in one of four specified ways to an "enterprise." Those found guilty of racketeering can be fined up to $25,000 and sentenced to twenty years in prison per racketeering count.

Upon deciding to indict someone under RICO, the U.S. Attorney has the option of seeking a pre-trial restraining order or injunction to temporarily seize a defendant's assets and prevent the transfer of potentially forfeitable property, as well as require the defendant to put up a performance bond. This provision was placed in the law because the owners of Mafia-related shell corporations often absconded with the assets. An injunction or performance bond ensures there is something left to seize in the event of a guilty verdict.

In many cases, the threat of a RICO indictment can force defendants to plead guilty to lesser charges, in part because the seizure of assets would make it difficult to pay a defence attorney. Despite its harsh provisions, a RICO-related charge is considered easy to prove in court since it focuses on patterns of behaviour as opposed to criminal acts.

Additionally, one unique approach being adopted by Britain is the application of a levy on banks and other firms for anti-money laundering. The goal is to raise approximately $130 million to tackle dirty money. US regulators are now studying the value of what Britain has adopted as highlighted by New York's top financial regulator who stated that banks and governments have allowed money laundering to "metastasize" inside the banking system and wrap itself "within the guts of financial institutions" (Hudson 2020).

To highlight the essential need for a Federal RCMP response, we need only examine the latest organized crime prosecution failure which occurred in York Region of Ontario. York Regional Police say they are "extremely disappointed" that the Crown has decided to stay charges in a major organized crime investigation following allegations that police listened in on phone calls that were protected by solicitor-client privilege.

The 18-month-long investigation, dubbed "Project Sindacato," was launched in response to a spike in shootings and arsons in Vaughan and the surrounding area in 2017.

The investigation, which targeted a group accused of operating illegal backroom gambling dens, culminated in July 2019 with the arrest of fifteen people, including Angelo Figliomeni, who investigators allege to be the head of the Figliomeni crime family. At the time, police said $35 million worth of homes, sports cars, and cash were seized as part of the probe, all of which has been ordered returned.

This is not to be considered a criticism of municipal law enforcement; taking on organized crime requires a sophisticated integrated approach wherein all aspects of the investigative action are scrutinized by in-house counsel and the investigative team has proven to have the necessary expertise required for high-level organized crime investigations.

An examination of the RCMP's new financial crime investigative program would indicate the establishment of an "IPOC 2.0." What the report shows is that they have created investigative teams for all aspects of financial crime, the total complement of which is less than the initial IPOC unit formed in the 1990s. What has not been addressed is how the RCMP is able to ensure qualified resources are maintained within the units for extended periods of time and that promotions will not result in the constant in and out of units which results in the units being in a perpetual training mode.

The integrated concept also begs that outside resources are entrenched in the units and the oversight comes from a management team involving all participating agencies. Based on the sophistication of transnational organized crime groups, it should be evident to the reader that there is a need for an integration of diverse skill sets. This can be accomplished through the engagement of civilian members for such skills as forensic accounting, intelligence analysts, and major case computer experts. Due to the complexity of these cases, experienced in-house counsel must be supported and their role needs to be embraced.

Unless we begin to take financial crime seriously, we will fail because we lack focus, leadership, training, and the courage to admit to our failings. It is time to turn the page and implement strategies that are supported with the goal of being recognized as a leader in financial crime enforcement strategies.

To quote from a *Maclean*'s article on November 21, 2020, Supreme Court Justice Michel Bastarache stated that "The Mounties must be forced to reform: The time has come for an in-depth, external, and independent review of the organization and future of the RCMP as a federal organization. The Commission will have noted that an announcement was made in February of this year that a Security committee of MPs, senators are going to review RCMP's federal policing activities. The work of the Commission should be significant to this review.

References

Francis, Diane. 2020. "Canada's Embarrassing Money Laundering Problem." *Financial Post*. https://financialpost.com/diane-francis/diane-francis-canadas-embarrassing-money-laundering-problem.

Hudson, Michael. 2020. "Dirty Money Has 'Metastasized' Within Global Banking System, Top Regulator Says." *International Council of Investigative Journalists*. https://www.icij.org/investigations/fincen-files/dirty-money-has-metastasized-within-global-banking-system-top-regulator-says.

Mackin, Bob. 2022. "Organized Crime Has Infiltrated City Halls, Says National Crime Intelligence Agency." *The Breaker*. https://thebreaker.news/business/city-halls-infiltrated.

Schneider, Stephen. 2009. *Iced: The Story of Organized Crime in Canada*. Wiley.

BNN Bloomberg. 2020. "'Snow Washing,' SNC Fallout Push Canada Out of 10 Least Corrupt Countries Rankings." https://www.bnnbloomberg.ca/real-estate/video/snow-washing-snc-fallout-push-canada-out-of-10-least-corrupt-countries-rankings~1883477.

Transparency International. 2018. *G20 Countries Moving Too Slowly to Combat Financial Crime*. https://www.transparency.org/en/press/g20-countries-moving-too-slowly-to-combat-financial-crime.

Wakefield, Johnny. 2019. "Lawyers Launch New Trust Account Rules Over Money Laundering Concerns." *Edmonton Journal*. https://edmontonjournal.com/news/local-news/alberta-lawyers-bringing-in-new-trust-account-rules-over-money-laundering-concerns/.

8

The Powers, Operation, and Limits of the Financial Transactions and Reports Analysis Centre of Canada (FINTRAC)

Katarzyna McNaughton

Introduction[1]

Canada struggles with the efficacy of its anti-money laundering (AML) regime. Flaws were identified by the Financial Action Task Force (FATF) Mutual Evaluation Report (MER) in 2016, which emphasized the following issue: the Canadian Financial Intelligence Unit (FIU), called the Financial Transactions and Reports Analysis Centre of Canada (FINTRAC), is more responsive to law enforcement priorities as opposed to proactive (identifying new cases unknown to law enforcement) when it comes to the analysis of financial intelligence gathered from the private sector (FATF 2016, 35, 36, 42, 43). In addition, the 2019 Cullen Commission was established to investigate the scope and causes of the vast amounts of illicit drug money from China that were laundered through casinos and the real estate market in British Columbia (Cockfield 2019).[2] Cullen looked into the issue of FINTRAC's efficacy, and its findings are that FINTRAC suffers from the inability to produce reliable, actionable intelligence about money laundering activities that law-enforcement authorities could use for their investigative purposes.[3] Also, legal scholarship points to the fact that FINTRAC faces several challenges, including non-compliance with the Proceeds of Crime (Money Laundering) and Terrorist Financing Act (PCMLTFA) of 2000, impediments to information sharing, non-reporting by lawyers, and too much oversight by outside bodies (Pyrick 2021, 106).

These findings about FINTRAC's low capacity to produce quality intelligence are quite striking, considering a broader legal, political, and economic Canadian context. Canada has been an important international player in the anti-money laundering framework, and it also has a great economic potential to set up a fully functioning financial intelligence unit that cooperates with law-enforcement agencies. Furthermore, from an international perspective, several examples of effective national FIUs exist, and as such can be used as models of best practice.[4] Considering that Canada has resources and the availability to learn from other countries' best standards of practice, the emerging issues ask in what sense is FINTRAC different from other national FIUs, and what are the underlying factors preventing FINTRAC from producing top quality intelligence that can be effectively shared with law enforcement?

To address these issues, an in-depth inquiry into FINTRAC's statutory duties and their enforcement on the ground will be presented. This chapter offers a new perspective, where the focus of the examination of FINTRAC's functions is on "input-output" dynamics taking place among FINTRAC and law enforcement and the financial sector. It applies several research methods: legal and content analysis of publicly available sources, and data obtained from semi-structured interviews conducted with FINTRAC's representatives.[5]

Clearly, the Canadian AML framework and especially its enforcement must be reformed. So far, the response of the Canadian government has been to fund two additional AML task forces: the Anti-Money Laundering Action, Coordination, and Enforcement (ACE) Team and the Trade Fraud and Trade-Based Money Laundering Centre of Expertise. Additionally, following years of working in collaboration through a memorandum of understanding with the Office of the Superintendent of Financial Institutions (OSFI), and despite FINTRAC's authority to supervise financial entities, FINTRAC has taken over the full supervisory mandate over the banking sector to eliminate the overlapping jurisdiction with the OSFI. Legislative amendments were introduced into the Proceeds of Crime (Money Laundering) and Terrorist Financing Act of 2000 (PCMLTFA) requiring FINTRAC to make public all monetary penalties imposed upon the obliged entities. Lastly, recent amendments to the Canada Business Corporations Act[6] established the Canadian version of the Ultimate Beneficiary Owners (UBOs) register. A new AML requirement has been placed upon private corporations, which must establish a register containing up-to-date information on "individuals with significant control of such corporations (ISC)."[7] Despite the FATF's recommendations, the Canadian UBOs register was originally designed not to be accessible to FINTRAC, however legislative changes yet to come into force will provide FINTRAC access to a corporation's UBO.

Framing the Problem

In the context of the above reforms and critical evaluations by the FATF and the Cullen Commission, several questions arise. Firstly, how accurate are these evaluations of FINTRAC? In what sense is FINTRAC different from other national FIUs and how do these differences translate to its operational powers? Finally, how likely is it that the recent changes in the Canadian AML regime will strengthen FINTRAC's powers? This chapter examines these issues by introducing two main perspectives; i.e., legal, and socio-legal because both are helpful in explaining the nature and limited capacity of FINTRAC to produce quality intelligence. The legal perspective considers that FINTRAC was set up as an administrative authority that gathers a broad scope of reports about financial transactions from the obliged entities. However, due to constitutional constraints of protecting the privacy of citizens, FINTRAC does not have certain rights that other national FIUs have. For example, it cannot exchange intelligence directly with law enforcement, it does not have direct access to law enforcement and tax authorities' databases, nor can it approach directly an obliged entity for additional financial information. FINTRAC's setup is unique by comparison, and that has tangible implications for the quality, quantity, type, effectiveness, adequacy, timeliness, etc. of the financial intelligence it generates.

According to the second perspective, which takes the form of semi-structured interviews conducted with current and former representatives of FINTRAC, the main reason why FINTRAC is prevented from delivering more quality and quantity intelligence is linked with the phenomenon of limited system capacity of law enforcement to make use of the current level of intelligence being delivered. In other words, even if FINTRAC started producing more actionable intelligence, law-enforcement agencies are unable to make use of it because their system capacity is already overwhelmed.

It must be emphasized at the outset that, in terms of international AML standards established in 1990 by the FATF in the form of 40 Recommendations, FIUs are addressed in Recommendation 29 which allows each country to determine its own model. These standards do not suggest or impose any institutional design. Similarly, the European Union anti-money laundering directives require member states to establish FIUs; however, they fall short of suggesting a specific model. Therefore, FIUs worldwide are non-homogenous, meaning that they have diverse structure and modus operandi, and this may impede the international efforts in tackling money laundering.[8] The findings of this chapter are that FINTRAC is an administrative type of FIU that can be characterized by the following characteristics: it receives a high volume of financial transactions from the obliged entities, e.g., 31 million in 2019–20,[9] it delivers a low number of proactive disclosures to law-enforcement, and these outputs are of low quality and use to these authorities,[10] and most of its intelligence is disseminated to law enforcement in response to voluntary information records. As already mentioned, FINTRAC has a unique setup as an administrative authority that has enormous insight into the world of financial transactions (both legal and suspicious) that occur in Canada, but due to constitutional principles of privacy, FINTRAC is prohibited from pursuing certain functions, and as such, from making full use of its unique financial database. In addition, there are other reasons that contribute to FINTRAC's exceptionally low output of its huge intelligence data. According to interviewed representatives, the Canadian intelligence system does not have the capacity to make use of more data coming from FINTRAC. That is why FINTRAC tailors its dissemination to law-enforcement requests. In other words, the problem is not FINTRAC's intel but the capacity of law-enforcement authorities to use this intelligence.

The Role of FIUs in the Fight Against Money Laundering

FIUs and Financial Intelligence

Since the 1980s, international society has witnessed a substantial evolution of a new branch of public international law called anti-money laundering law (AML; Gilmore 199; Mitsilegas 2003; Paoli 2014). AML was originally set up to address the problem of illegal drug production and trafficking. The foregoing activity generates illegal profits which represent personal gain for the perpetrators and/or are used by criminals to finance future criminal acts. A broad spectrum of predicate crimes, i.e., drug crimes, human trafficking, weapons proliferation, embezzlement, tax evasion, etc., can generate financial value that is criminal per se, because it was obtained through illegal means. Criminals create complex chains of cross-border financial transactions, often involving shell companies and jurisdictions with strict banking secrecy (Cockfield 2017). The focus of international AML law is on money-laundering financial transactions, because they can be detected based on evidence left in the financial system, i.e., a "paper trail." The entire rationale of AML law is that, if law-enforcement agencies (LEAs) could have access to data consisting of conducted financial transactions, called financial intelligence, then they would be able to "follow dirty money to their origins." Hence, by relying on financial intelligence, LEAs could capture perpetrators of both the predicate crimes and the main offence of money laundering. At the core of AML framework, two functions are required to be established: the FIU with the analytical role for financial intelligence and the second one is the supervisory/regulatory role to enforce national legislation implementing the FATF 40 Recommendations. Therefore, in the AML regime, two actors play a main role. The first is the financial sector (FS) that is legally obliged to submit Suspicious Transaction Reports (STRs) to the Financial Intelligence Units (FIUs).[11] The second actor is the FIU established at the national level as the main intelligence centre. This second actor collects and analyzes received financial information. FIUs are also obliged to provide the results of their work in the form of financial intelligence to LEAs, as part of their dissemination function. While STR reporting is an FATF standard (Recommendation 20) for the financial sector, large cash transactions and more recently large virtual currency transactions are "staple" reports to be provided to the FIU for analysis from the obliged entities in many countries.[12]

FIUs' International Regulatory Framework

The origin of FIUs is linked with the evolution of international AML framework that from the very outset, emphasized the value of financial intelligence, and established a legal duty upon the financial sector to gather financial information about suspicious transactions. In this context, FIUs emerged as new policing bodies responsible for managing the surveillance of money movements at the national level (Levi and Maguire 2012) since tracing money launderers requires knowledge and skills covering national laws, regulations, investigations, analysis, criminology, finance, accounting, audit, etc. Thus, FIUs were developed as a link between countries' criminal law-enforcement authorities, administrative bodies, and the financial sector.

The general framework governing FIUs can be found in the 40 Recommendations (referred to as the FATF standards) issued by the FATF.[13] The Egmont Group[14] provides a forum for FIUs to discuss best practices, enhance member training through technical assistance, facilitate the exchange of intelligence and support its members in the fight against money laundering. According to the FATF standards, FIUs have three mandatory functions: to gather and analyze financial information and disseminate financial intelligence to various LEAs and other intelligence bodies.

Other facultative functions can also be granted to FIUs in the domestic laws of countries. For example, FIUs can have legislative powers, super-visory duties over the banking and non-banking sectors within the AML requirements, rights to freeze and/or suspend given financial transactions and/or banking accounts, and rights to prohibit certain banks and corre-spondent banks to operate within given market. Finally, FIUs can have investigative functions, meaning that their tactical analysis, focused on a particular target, i.e., individual or entity, is a result not only of their own analysis of gathered information. Instead, these FIUs carry out investiga-tions independently and/or together with other LEAs for the purpose of gathering additional financial intelligence. Often, in countries where FIUs are granted such investigative powers, the enactment of legal frameworks called public-public and public-private partnerships (PPPs), which enable FIUs to exchange tactical information directly with the financial sector and law enforcement, often occurs.[15] FIUs also cooperate domestically with LEAs, tax authorities, supervisory bodies, and internationally with foreign FIUs. During such cooperation tactical and/or strategic intelli-gence can be exchanged.

In terms of guidelines to be followed when designing an FIU, so far, no formal best practices were established. There is no single model of FIU that can fit into the AML regime of all countries. The FATF's 40 Recom-mendations constitute only a basic framework governing FIUs, meaning that countries are sovereign in their decisions as to how to fit FIUs into their domestic AML regime. Even though FIUs have been operating since the mid 1990s, they are not homogenous, and they differ in terms of their structures, resources, and powers. Typically, countries establish one of two main models: the administrative or the law enforcement FIU. In the latter model, the FIU's functions are granted to a special police unit which possesses usually strong investigative skills and powers, such as sharing tactical intelligence with law-enforcement and private sector, and the right to seize assets. It rarely has any oversight functions regarding compliance with AML regulations. In the administrative model, the FIU is established within the public administration structures, typically under the Ministry of Finance. In this case, the FIU does not have investigative powers, has a duty to provide tactical intelligence to law enforcement, and often has the role of supervisor/regulator to ensure AML compliance by reporting entities (FIs and Designated Non-Financial Business and Professions). Several countries have established a third type of FIU – a judicial FIU – which is often set up as a special unit within the General Prosecutor's Office. This particular model of FIU will combine features of law enforcement and administrative FIU. However, the reality of FIUs non-homogeneity is much more complex than the above description. Indeed, while illegal money flows are international, FIUs are national and shaped primarily by the local socio-political, historical, and economical processes.[16]

Financial intelligence is the outcome of the analytical work done by FIUs and should not be equated with criminal evidence. Once such intelligence is disseminated to LEAs, they conduct investigations aiming to produce evidence of committed and/or attempted predicate crimes and money laundering.

FIUs' Knowledge Gap and Functioning Challenges

While a complex, international regulatory regime that addresses illicit financial flows has been established, there are significant gaps in knowledge about FIUs, their diversity, and the legal and practical obstacles that FIUs encounter in their domestic and transnational cooperation. Fighting against money laundering is a difficult endeavour for several reasons. Firstly, criminals continuously invent new techniques of money laundering, and the scheme often depends on the type of crime that generated illicit money, and the likelihood of detection by a given country. Secondly, information asymmetry and structural problems in the financial sector–FIUs/law-enforcement relationship can be characterized as main factors affecting efficacy of any national AML framework. Information asymmetry that exists between criminals and law enforcement comes from the fact that adding more complexity to the chain of financial transactions is an easy task for criminals but disproportionately increases the effort needed for law enforcement to follow the chain. In theory, each link in the chain is detectable, because the movement of criminal value creates data that is visible to financial sector personnel, who are obliged to report the data to the financial intelligence units (FIUs) in the form of suspicious transaction reports. However, there is a substantial gap between policy/ theory and its enforcement because several dysfunctionalities that exist affect the efficacy of this entire framework. Although the financial sector has a theoretical capacity to detect illicit financial flows, often it lacks knowledge, and/or resources, and/or incentives to do so. Hence, the FIUs and law-enforcement agencies are confronted with a structural problem in their relationship with the financial sector. FIUs receive only the suspicious transactions that the financial sector submits to them. However, fighting illicit financial flows, to a large extent, depends on the quality of reports received by the FIUs and other agencies, and the quality of the financial analysis performed by the FIU. The best way to address these issues is by designing an institutional framework that has two functions: to provide the best quality of financial reports and other intelligence in a timely manner to FIUs, intelligence, law enforcement, and supervisory bodies, and to enable sharing of tactical intelligence among these bodies and in a transnational cooperation.

The Role of FINTRAC in the AML Framework of Canada

As previously mentioned, the international AML regulatory framework governing FIUs should be understood only as a starting point for a further legal analysis of any given national model of an FIU. In the case of Canada's FIU, FINTRAC, the key to understanding the scope of its proactive intelligence gathering, analysis and dissemination, lies in FINTRAC's narrow domestic AML mandate.[17] Namely, FINTRAC was set up in a particular domestic legal order, where its power to gather a large scope of financial intelligence (i.e., STRs and other threshold reports), has been considered a paradigm of "mass-surveillance without a warrant." In other words, FINTRAC's investigative capacity, the right to request any additional financial information directly from the reporting entities, and the right to freeze suspicious transactions was necessary to ensure that FINTRAC did not engage in unlawful searches and seizures.

Hence, FINTRAC from the very outset was established as an administrative type of FIU because of the above constitutional restraints. However, when the FATF published its 2016 evaluation report on Canada, it did not take into consideration Canadian domestic *common law* legal perspective within which FINTRAC was established. Therefore, the FATF's perspective, although attempts to evaluate and compare national models of FIUs, should be considered with caution as missing a relevant aspect in its analysis.

According to the FATF, FINTRAC is "more narrowly focused on LEA priorities" and investing less resources in "identifying through pro-active disclosures cases that LEA may not be aware of," hence, it mostly produces reactive disclosures that are linked to Voluntary Information Records (VIRs) submitted by law enforcement.[18] However, as several representatives of FINTRAC explained, and despite the fact that FINTRAC was not established as a query-type of FIU, where LEAs submit a question and FINTRAC responds, FINTRAC's model of operation should not be compared to an administrative "Mail-Box," with limited proactive analytical and dissemination capacity.

In the context of FINTRAC's evaluation by the FATF, several representatives of FINTRAC offered an insight into its *modus operandi.* For example, they confirmed that FINTRAC does not work on a query-response basis, because it focuses on its analysis of cases submitted by LEAs called VIRs. These cases are FINTRAC's highest priority, so it seldom analyzes other cases that were generated by other triggers. Furthermore, it was explained that FINTRAC does proactive disclosures (unknown individuals, organizations, or entities unknown to police, and these constitute about 10 percent of its disclosures) and the remaining disclosures are linked to VIRs submitted by law enforcement. One of FINTRAC's former employees acknowledged, although there is a need to produce proactive cases, there is a structural problem related to law-enforcement capacity to handle cases related to VIRs. Namely, FINTRAC produces thousands of disclosures to law enforcement annually, but law enforcement authorities find it difficult to deal with the influx. LEAs are "submerged with cases already, including the cases they provide as part

Figure 8.1: Designing the FIU Model to Fit into the Legal Framework of a Given Country

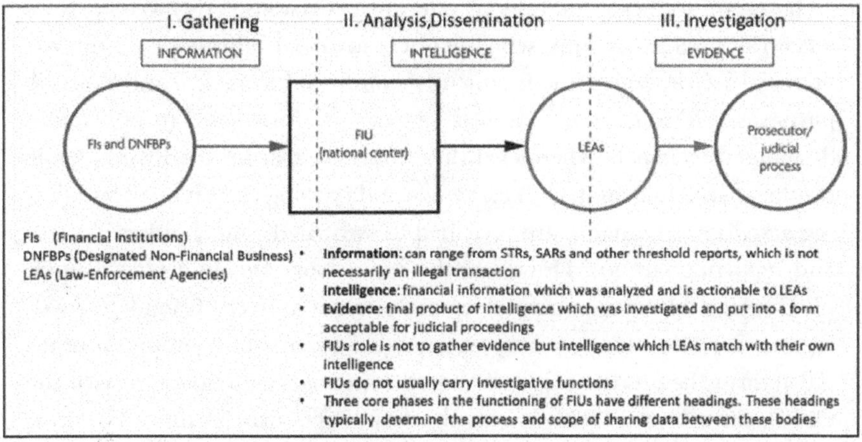

I. Gathering   II. Analysis,Dissemination   III. Investigation

INFORMATION   INTELLIGENCE   EVIDENCE

FIs and DNFBPs → FIU (national center) → LEAs → Prosecutor/judicial process

FIs   (Financial Institutions)
DNFBPs (Designated Non-Financial Business)
LEAs (Law-Enforcement Agencies)

- **Information**: can range from STRs, SARs and other threshold reports, which is not necessarily an illegal transaction
- **Intelligence**: financial information which was analyzed and is actionable to LEAs
- **Evidence**: final product of intelligence which was investigated and put into a form acceptable for judicial proceedings
- FIUs role is not to gather evidence but intelligence which LEAs match with their own intelligence
- FIUs do not usually carry investigative functions
- Three core phases in the functioning of FIUs have different headings. These headings typically determine the process and scope of sharing data between these bodies

Source: Author's own conceptualization.

of their VIRs. They are so overwhelmed that they tend to set aside the new cases (proactive disclosures) produced by FINTRAC." Therefore, the issue is lack of resources by LEAs to investigate what FINTRAC disseminates to them. Based on this comprehensive feedback, it appears FINTRAC is more administrative in nature than a law enforcement type of FIU. However, the picture is more complex than the narrative of the FATF.

FINTRAC's Statutory Functions

FINTRAC's legal status is governed by the Proceeds of Crime (Money Laundering) and Terrorist Financing Act (PCMLTFA) of 2000. FIN-TRAC employs 355 people, and its budget is CAD$60.2 million (FIN-TRAC 2019, 33–35). Its primary duties are prescribed in Section 40 of the PCMLTFA, which must be read in connection with several other provisions, namely, Section 54 and 58(1). Together, these provisions regulate a broad spectrum of FINTRAC's functions, which are divided into mandatory and optional.

Based on the legal analysis of relevant provisions, FINTRAC acts as a central intelligence hub, which gathers financial information from the financial sector, which is subsequently examined for tactical and strategic purposes.[19] Results of the tactical analysis are forwarded to police and designated recipients when legal thresholds are met for disclosure, while results of strategic analysis, i.e., trends and typologies of money laundering activities in Canada, are provided to two AML stakeholders: society and reporting entities. However, the supervisory function placed upon FINTRAC adds to the complexity of its role within the Canadian AML regime. Because its supervisory function is currently undergoing substantial reform (i.e., termination of shared supervisory jurisdiction with the OSFI), the role of FINTRAC, as the main supervisor in the AML area, will be examined in a separate part of this analysis. For this section, just a brief summary of FINTRAC's supervisory duties is offered.

FINTRAC ensures compliance with Parts 1 and 1.1 of the PCMLTFA. This means that it acts as a supervisory body monitoring the AML compliance of the banking sector, consisting of domestic and foreign banks and a broad range of non-banking financial entities such as cooperative credit societies, savings and credit unions,[20] life companies or foreign life companies, trust companies,[21] and loan companies.[22] It also acts as a supervisory body for federal trust and loan companies, securities dealing, investment services, and other domestic and foreign entities that provide money services, foreign exchange, electronic payments, virtual currency dealings, and other Designated Non-Financial Business and Professions (DNFBPs) like casinos, accountants, British Columbia notaries, etc.

FINTRAC cooperates with another federal authority called the Office of the Superintendent of Financial Institutions (OSFI 2022), which exercises prudential supervision of more than 400 federally regulated financial institutions. The main rationale behind FIUs' tendency to share the results of conducted supervision and financial intelligence with prudential supervisory bodies like OSFI in Canada is because detected AML violations and imposed penalties affect the financial stability and reputation of a given entity.

When FINTRAC fulfills its statutory duties as the central intelligence hub and the supervisory body, it receives substantial input from the financial sector. This input is two-fold: it encompasses financial transaction reports such as STRs and other reports, and based on conducted inspections of reporting entities, it also consists of specific knowledge about their implementation of the AML internal control systems and their adequacy to ML risks. Clearly, FINTRAC, as the main AML gatekeeper, is in possession of important intelligence and knowledge. However, FINTRAC's strength is determined by its two key functions: detection by intelligence production operations, and prevention activities and compliance enforcement by the compliance sector. These two functions are two of the several functions along the compliance continuum, where all parts need to be strong. In this analysis the emphasis is placed upon the intelligence function that is more common to all FIUs.

FINTRAC's Intelligence Analysis

Type of Input Provided to FINTRAC

The input received by FINTRAC is governed by Section 54(1) of the PCMLTFA, which stipulates the reporting entities must submit suspicious transaction reports (STRs) when they have reasonable grounds to suspect the transaction is related to money laundering or terrorist activity financing. However, information received by FINTRAC also consists of other financial transactions reports,[23] including the information from LEAs called voluntary information records (VIRs). According to the annual report of 2019:

> FINTRAC received 2,754 voluntary information records (VIRs) from Canada's police, law enforcement, and national security agencies, as well as from members of the public. The number of records that the Centre receives annually has nearly doubled in the past five years. Voluntary information records provide critical information on alleged criminals and

terrorists and are often the starting point for the Centre's analysis. These records are used by FINTRAC to establish connections between individuals and entities and to develop actionable financial intelligence for disclosure recipients. The significant increase in the number of voluntary information records received in recent years, particularly from police at all levels, is a clear indication of the value that is placed on the Centre's financial intelligence. (FINTRAC 2019, 10)

The total number of STRs received in 2019 was 235,661 (FINTRAC 2019, 37). This number is quite relevant, once we place it against the total number of cases disseminated to various LEAs in 2019, which was 2,276 so-called "unique disclosures of actionable financial intelligence" (FINTRACT 2019, 8). From these statistics, we can obtain basic insight[24] into the essence of the analytical work of FINTRAC. There are issues here that are unknown. For one, how many of the STRs received were subsequently used as part of financial disclosure cases, and how many of these cases were investigated by law enforcement? Second, what happens with STRs that are never used in a financial disclosure to law enforcement? Is there strategic feedback provided to reporting entities on STRs that are used/not used in subsequent financial disclosures to law enforcement? All that is provided in the annual report is the final result of FINTRAC's analytical job, that is, the number of disclosures of actionable intelligence.

FINTRAC's Access to Governmental Databases and the Analysis

FINTRAC has access to a broad spectrum of law-enforcement databases, including the Canadian Police Information Centre, the Royal Canadian Mounted Police's Security System, the Canadian Security Intelligence Service's database, and others (FATF 2016, 186). It does not seem that FINTRAC can automatically match its own STRs database against the targets identified in these law-enforcement databases. Also, there are problems with FINTRAC's direct access to the database of the Canada Revenue Agency (FATF 2016, 115). As previously mentioned, there were 2,276 disclosures to LEAs of actionable intelligence and the annual report points to several priorities of investigation (FINTRAC 2018,

11–13)[25]: trafficking of fentanyl, romance fraud, and human trafficking for sexual exploitation.

These themes of investigation resulted in tactical[26] and strategic intelligence. The former is described by FINTRAC as actionable intelligence and there were 148 disclosures to LEAs linked with illicit fentanyl, 100 disclosures linked with romance fraud, and 250 disclosures linked with human trafficking. The latter type of intelligence brought money laundering indicators of each illicit activity, which were subsequently published as FINTRAC's Operational Alerts, i.e., laundering of the proceeds of fentanyl trafficking, laundering of the proceeds of romance fraud. In addition to these statistics, FINTRAC provides a very general statement in terms of the efficacy of its tactical intelligence by saying:

> In 2018–19, FINTRAC's financial intelligence was used in a wide variety of money laundering investigations, where the origins of the suspected criminal proceeds were linked to fraud, drug trafficking, tax evasion, corruption, theft and other criminal offences. (FINTRAC, S.C. 2000, c. 17)

FINTRAC'S Analysis Results

Regarding the results of FINTRAC's strategic intelligence, the annual report states:

> In 2018–19, FINTRAC produced nine strategic financial intelligence assessments and reports and contributed its financial intelligence insight and expertise to numerous other regime partner projects. The majority of the Centre's strategic intelligence was focused on specific money laundering and terrorism financing issues, including a number of terrorism financing jurisdictions of concern. This intelligence was generated to support FINTRAC's own intelligence work as well as that of the Canadian security and intelligence community. The Centre also provided strategic financial intelligence to the Department of Finance Canada, as the lead of Canada's Anti-Money Laundering and Anti-Terrorist Financing Regime on a broad spectrum of policy issues, including the involvement of lawyers in money laundering, cryptocurrency and in relation to foreign beneficial ownership. (Proceeds of Crime Act 2000)

FINTRAC plans (as of 2021) to disclose actionable financial intelligence to members of the new Anti-Money Laundering Action, Coordination, and Enforcement (ACE) Team,[27] and to the new multi-disciplinary Trade Fraud and Trade-Based Money Laundering Centre of Expertise.[28] These two AML task forces are officially part of the broader efforts by Canada to remedy the most recently identified flaws in the AML framework.[29]

The Canadian model of the PPP was established in 2016, as the Canadian Major Reporters Forum Initiatives, within which strategic information on typologies of money laundering is shared among FINTRAC, LEAs, and the banking sector (Maxwell 2022, 83). The current AML framework in Canada does not allow the public and private sectors to exchange tactical information about customers or targets. Many experts emphasize that, even though the Canadian Criminal Code under Section 462.47 allows banks to reach out directly to law-enforcement agencies, including FINTRAC, many banks are reluctant to do so (Monroe 2020). Under the PPP framework, several projects were developed and indicators of human trafficking, fentanyl trafficking, and romance fraud were identified in the past few years.[30] However, for the purpose of expanding this PPP toward the tactical exchange of information, new legal provisions in the AML Act are needed.

As previously mentioned, the total number of received STRs in 2019 was 235,661 while the total number of cases disseminated to LEAs was 2,276 (1 percent). What can be said about FINTRAC's capacity to conduct tactical analysis, based upon this data? Very little, because to gain a deeper understanding about how FINTRAC's financial intelligence contributes to the work of LEAs, significant data to address the following questions is required:

1. How much and what kind of information from FINTRAC initiated investigations by LEAs?
2. What kind of information did FINTRAC provide to ongoing investigations?
3. What kind of information submitted by FINTRAC was crucial, meaning that it advanced ongoing investigations?

Unfortunately, publicly available sources do not provide a great level of detail and FINTRAC's own annual reports repeat the same conclusion: "FINTRAC's financial intelligence was used in a wide variety of money laundering investigations, where the origins of the suspected criminal proceeds were linked to fraud, drug trafficking, tax evasion, corruption, theft and other criminal offences" (FINTRAC, S.C. 2000, c. 17; FINTRAC 2018). It is difficult to determine whether FINTRAC or any other law-enforcement body in Canada conducts its own evaluation of the contribution of FINTRAC's disclosures to their investigative work. This is also a critical part of the present analysis, where information obtained from semi-structured interviews offers a deeper insight into the intelligence function of FINTRAC.[31]

FINTRAC interviewees explained the scope and the breadth of disclosures made by FINTRAC. In particular, disclosures may contain thousands of STRs. Thus, the relationship between intelligence received by FINTRAC and the disclosures made to LEAs is not "One-to-One, meaning that one STR received will be forwarded to LEAs as one disclosure." Disclosures should be understood as the result of FINTRAC's examination of its huge database which contains STRs, electronic fund transfers, large cash transactions, cross-border cash and seizure transactions, casino disbursements, etc.[32] One interviewee stated FINTRAC provides to its partners the results of tactical analysis, which means "Who the individuals involved are, what is the network of their connections, what kind of transactions, between which accounts did the money move, etc."

Furthermore, my interviewee described the FINTRAC analytical model, according to which, two types of analysis are carried out, i.e., strategic, and tactical, and there are two types of output provided to LEAs. The first output is called "VIR-related" actionable intelligence, meaning FINTRAC conducted an analysis of its intelligence, based upon a special disclosure made by LEAs called VIRs. The second type of output is proactive (usually unknown to law enforcement) actionable intelligence, which contains indicators of money laundering of the proceeds from specific predicate crimes.

When FINTRAC provides financial intelligence that is connected to VIRs, it means FINTRAC received details on targeted individuals and entities from LEAs, and subsequently examined its own databases, looking for relevant, matching financial transactions/information. As an agency representative explained,

> We would look into our database and see if there is a whole network associated with this targeted person. We would do the analysis on this network, and we would provide this intelligence to the LEAs. LEAs would be able to take that intelligence and get production orders and get back to the reporting entities, such as banks and ask to give them everything that is related to such a target, even the information that FINTRAC does not have on such targets, because banks did not have to submit it to us. Once banks get the production orders, they have to provide the requested information to LEAs. FINTRAC's role is to provide actionable intelligence to LEAs and it's for them to take this intelligence and investigate.

Regarding proactive actionable intelligence, FINTRAC conducts its own, independent strategic analysis, which aims to identify those targets which are not yet known to the police. An agency representative emphasized the huge role played by the Canadian PPP. Namely, once FINTRAC identifies specific indicators of money laundering, for example in its newest project called "Shadow,"[33] these will be provided to the private sector, which would subsequently insert these indicators into their transaction monitoring programs. The result is that the reporting entities would generate STRs related to these specific predicate crimes. In practice, the reporting entities would mark these STRs with a hashtag relating to the specific PPP program and subsequently, FINTRAC explores its own database to see if there are any other transactions related to these submitted STRs. The final product of this PPP cooperation is proactive disclosures from FINTRAC, which are submitted to LEAs as actionable intelligence. According to my interviewee, approximately 30 percent of FINTRAC's disclosures are proactive in nature.

Furthermore, when specifically asked about the FATF's conclusions of FINTRAC's "reactive" model of analysis (FATF 2016, 43), according to which "FINTRAC tailors its analysis to the law enforcement agencies' priorities" because it "focuses mainly on answering the VIRs and also discloses intelligence related to LEAs' priorities" (FATF 2016, 43). My interviewees rejected these findings. They argued FINTRAC was designed as an administrative type of FIU, which automatically excludes a "query-type" function, where LEAs submit a question and FINTRAC

Figure 8.2: FINTRAC's Dissemination of Intelligence (FINTRAC, S.C. 2000, c. 17)

DISCLOSURE PACKAGES BY RECIPIENT: 2018–19

Royal Canadian Mounted Police	Municipal Police	Canadian Security Intelligence Service	Provincial Police	Canada Border Services Agency
1,509	795	502	455	324

Foreign Financial Intelligence Units	Canada Revenue Agency	Provincial Securities Regulators	Communications Security Establishment	Canadian Armed Forces
253	252	74	20	8

Source: Proceeds of Crime Act 2001.

searches its database and responds. However, such an administrative nature of the FIU does not qualify it automatically as a mail-box type, because the police does not have direct access to FINTRAC's database. Furthermore, it was explained that the essence of communication between FINTRAC and LEAs can be described as "two, one-way process-es," where FINTRAC submits its disclosures and LEAs submit their own VIRs. However, these are two inputs, going back and forth, which, from the legal perspective are not a query-response type of communication per se. Moreover, my interviewees added that by designing such a model of FIU, where a clear distinction is made between the intelligence function of FIU and investigative functions of LEAs, there is no replication of the work between these agencies and the privacy of citizens is respected. Another benefit of such a model of FIU that receives a broader array of reports than only STRs (as prescribed by the FATF) is that FINTRAC actively (through legislation) gathers a huge amount of data on financial transactions (approximately 20 million transactional reports in 2022). According to FINTRAC's representatives, although FINTRAC aims to identify targets and networks which are not on the radar of LEAs, there are capacity issues on the side of law enforcement to investigate proac-tive cases disclosed by FINTRAC. In particular, it was explained that law-enforcement is under-resourced and unable to handle more financial intelligence from FINTRAC. It cannot handle even a 10 percent rate of proactive disclosures provided by FINTRAC.[34] Thus, if FINTRAC is submitting more proactive cases to LEAs, they will never be investigated, because LEAs are overwhelmed by their own investigations and not prioritizing new cases that might develop from proactive disclosures provided by FINTRAC.

FINTRAC's Communication with the Reporting Entities

In the context of FINTRAC's analytical powers, it must be emphasized that it does not have a right to demand from reporting entities any additional financial information. Instead of granting FINTRAC such a critical right, the PCMLFTA introduced an old-fashioned mechanism of orders, granted by a judge through a police or Canadian Security Intelligence Service, for disclosure of information (FINTRAC 2019).

FINTRAC's Supervisory Powers

Canada has a centralized FIU model, meaning FINTRAC not only acts as the main hub for gathering and assessing financial intelligence, but also as the main supervisory body ensuring the AML compliance of reporting entities (SC 2000 C 17 §40 e linked with part 3, §62–65). Such supervisory competence for FINTRAC was established in Section 40e of the PCMLTFA, which states that, as FIU, it is also responsible for ensuring compliance with the AML requirements; i.e., sufficient internal control mechanisms by reporting entities such as maintaining a compliance program, reporting STRs and other prescribed transactions, identifying and verifying the identity of clients, determining third parties in transactions and keeping records. However, such a leading supervisory mandate of FINTRAC must be interpreted from the broader perspective of the entire structure of the Canadian AML regime, which consists of various federal and provincial partners sharing the ultimate goal of preventing and detecting money laundering.

Also involved in the AML regime are thirteen federal departments and agencies[35] and other provincial and municipal law enforcement bodies and provincial regulators (including those with a supervisory mandate over the financial sector entities). What a complexity of such an AML regime translates into is that, when it comes to the supervision of compliance over the financial sector, there are areas of shared jurisdiction, exclusively federal jurisdiction, and sectors where only provincial supervisory authorities will act. For the purpose of this analysis, which is primarily concerned with the role of the Canadian FIU within the AML regime, the main focus will be placed upon FINTRAC's jurisdiction to supervise all reporting entities, both from the banking sector and non-banking sectors.

FINTRAC's supervisory mandate must be placed in a more specific context, that is, the structure and size of the Canadian banking sector. There are 36 domestic banks, 18 foreign banks, 28 foreign bank branches, 43 trusts, 15 loan companies, 63 life insurance and 149 insurance companies (OSFI 2014). Until recently FINTRAC shared its supervisory mandate with OSFI (FINTRAC 2019) and hence, the most critical question arising in the context of such an overlapping supervisory jurisdiction of two bodies is: who does what, and what does the cooperation look like on the ground?

According to FINTRAC's Annual Report of 2019, in 2018 it launched a

> pilot of a joint assessment approach to conducting compliance examinations of Federally Regulated Financial Institutions. Based on their assessment of the pilot, FINTRAC and OFSI are implementing a new approach to anti-money laundering and anti-terrorist financing supervision of these financial institutions.

Another important document providing some insight into the cooperation between these two bodies comes from the Cullen Report (Hoffman and Wray 2020) which acknowledged that such "joint supervisory mandate" constituted a weak feature in the Canadian AML framework and thus, supported granting FINTRAC an exclusive AML supervisory mandate. Another critical observation coming from this report is that it announces a major reformulation in the AML regime by assigning the Canadian FIU the exclusive supervisory mandate over the banking sector. Such an approach will also eliminate the overlapping supervisory jurisdiction of these two bodies. OSFI will remain the primary banking prudential supervisory body and as such "will be leveraging FINTRAC's work in assessing the strength of FRFIs' regulatory compliance and risk management practices" (FATF 2016, 16). FINTRAC's Annual Report of 2019, also describes this statutory change by saying that "FINTRAC will assume primary responsibility for conducting independent anti-money laundering and anti-terrorist financing assessments of the AML Act."

Having established that FINTRAC will become an exclusive supervisory body to monitor the compliance of the banking sector, one must consider very specific factors which determine the type of supervisory model enforced by FINTRAC. These factors can be grouped into three categories that are as follows:

1. FINTRAC's supervisory plan including inspection tools, publication of results and compliance guidance,
2. FINTRAC's operational definition of a "risk-based supervision,"[36] and
3. FINTRAC's sanctioning tools in cases of non-compliance.

Regarding the first two factors, it seems FINTRAC applies a "risk-based" approach to select financial entities that are going to be examined each year. The focus of attention is directed towards those entities that report a large number of STRs or are at higher risk of being abused for money laundering purposes, and larger businesses in higher-risk sectors. The data for the 2018–2019 reporting period reveals that FINTRAC conducted 497 compliance examinations. Inspections of the real estate sector (190), followed by money services businesses (112) and securities dealers (57). In its Annual Report of 2019, FINTRAC emphasizes the new funding announced in the 2019 Federal Budget will allow for expansion of its supervisory insight and, in 2019–20, especially towards the real estate and casino sectors, with a focus on the province of British Columbia. The question of how many banking and credit institutions were inspected in 2018–2019 remains problematic because there is not sufficient information to determine if any of the total number of (72) banking entities were among the inspected number (112) of money business services.[37]

Furthermore, regarding FINTRAC's sanctioning powers, the regulatory framework of the PCMLTFA 2000 is supplemented by the Proceeds of Crime (Money Laundering) and Terrorist Financing Administrative Mon-

Figure 8.3: FINTRAC's Model of Communication with LEAs Compared with a "Query-Type" FIU

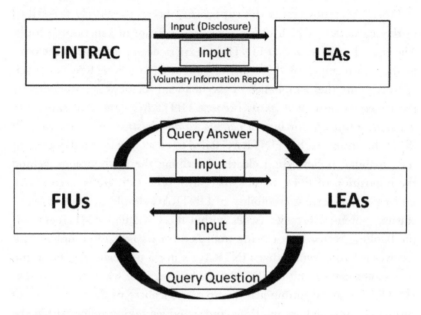

Source: Author's own conceptualization.

etary Penalties Regulations[38] (AMP Regulations). From the sanctioning perspective, the AMP Regulations are *lex specialis* while the AML Act is *lex generalis*. The AMP Regulations established a detailed classification of the violations triggered by the lack of compliance with the AML Act, especially, by grouping them into three classes of violations: minor, serious, and very serious. The maximum scope of monetary fines is set up in Section 73.1 (2) at the level of CAD$100,000 if the violation is committed by a person and $500,000 if applied toward a financial entity. There are two sanctioning tools utilized by FINTRAC. Non-financial notices of violation (AML Act §73.13) and financial penalties (AML Act §73.2). There is also a possibility for FINTRAC to propose a compliance agreement, and under such a scenario, a given entity is served with a notice of violation containing an offer to reduce the penalty proposed by half (AML Act §73.13). As of June 21, 2019, FINTRAC is obliged to publish decisions to punish non-compliant entities with monetary fines.

FINTRAC's powers as the supervisory body are clearly prescribed in the legislation, which offers a broad spectrum of sanctioning tools. The issue, however, is that FINTRAC experienced problems in the past, in the enforcement of these powers. Since 2016, FINTRAC's capacity to regulate the compliance of the financial sector was suspended by the Federal Court of Appeals because FINTRAC *"failed to supply an adequate rationale for how it calculated administrative policy fines."*[39] What this means is that FINTRAC failed to enact any internal document (i.e., manual, policy, etc.,) clearly describing the methodology behind the imposition of fines, so that the entire process is transparent. Such undermined deterrent credibility of FINTRAC should be considered as causing potential broader issues within the Canadian AML regime. If the banking sector is not being punished for its lack of compliance, it receives a strong signal that FINTRAC is not a powerful regulator and thus banks can submit to FINTRAC whatever they want. It means that FINTRAC may be getting just the tip of the iceberg of the total scope of suspicious financial transactions and activities taking place within the banking sector. In other words, FINTRAC's weak deterrent credibility may exaggerate the inherent weak point in any AML regime; i.e., banks get to decide when to file STRs, and only when applying supervisory tools toward them, can the real picture of legal and illegal financial flows which occurred, be seen.

FINTRAC corrected its error and issued its own AMP Policy (FINTRAC 2022b), which provides the financial sector with a comprehensive guideline of factors taken into consideration when assessing harm caused by the violations of various statutory requirements (i.e., compliance programs, large cash transactions, electronic funds transfer, suspicious transactions reports, Know Your Customer, etc.). Such AMP policy also established a detailed methodology to calculate monetary penalties.

According to FINTRAC's AMP policy, when "extensive non-compliance is observed, or little expectation of immediate or future compliance, FINTRAC may disclose such cases to LEAs" and more punitive imprisonment measures can be applied. In the context of FINTRAC's supervisory powers, FINTRAC is not legally obliged to notify LEAs about the results of its on-site and off-site supervisions of reporting entities, which may give reasons to suspect that money laundering might have occurred within the inspected entity. Such input from FINTRAC towards LEAs is voluntary, according to Section 65(1)[40] of the AML Act, which specifies "FINTRAC may notify appropriate LEAs about any information gathered as a result of conducted supervision that FINTRAC suspects on reasonable grounds may be relevant to investigation of the offense of lack of compliance." In 2018–19, FINTRAC disclosed seven such cases.[41]

Conclusions

In this chapter, the nature and modus operandi of FINTRAC was examined using a combination of research in legal analysis, content analysis of public sources, and data from semi-structured interviews. FINTRAC can be characterized as an administrative type of FIU. However, its intelligence gathering and analysis are limited compared to other administrative types of FIUs. In particular, the scope of financial information collected by FINTRAC is extraordinarily broad compared to most FIUs, but it does not have a right (contrary to most administrative types of FIUs) to go back to the reporting entity and request more information. Furthermore, nearly 80 percent of its analysis is triggered by VIRs (reactive disclosures), which means that, although FINTRAC has access to approximately 220 million financial transactions, due to law-enforcement capacity issues, FINTRAC's analytical resources for more proactive disclosures are not fully exercised. Furthermore, the administrative nature of FINTRAC results from its legal mandate, narrowly defined by the Canadian AML framework. This mandate translates into the following characteristics of FINTRAC: lack of investigative powers, lack of the right to freeze suspicious financial transactions, and lack of the right to request any additional financial information directly from a reporting entity.

The peculiarity of the Canadian AML framework that underlies FINTRAC's limited powers is linked to the definition of financial information defined by Canadian privacy legislation. Foremost, it is a category of private information that concerns the financial transactions of individuals who have not acted illegally. This is the initial legal assumption that creates the foundation for the Canadian FIU to operate as a national agency that gathers and disseminates a broad scope of financial information, i.e., suspicious financial transactions, threshold cash and virtual assets transactions, electronic funds transfers, and casino disbursements. Since FINTRAC is considered an authority that conducts "mass-surveillance" of Canadian society, its legal mandate must be narrowly defined, and proactive intelligence gathering, analysis, dissemination, and investigative powers are prohibited. Without such limitation, FINTRAC would violate the rule of law because such proactive powers would qualify as unlawful search and seizure. Following this line of reasoning, it also explains why FINTRAC does not have a right to freeze any financial transaction.

Regarding the FATF's evaluations of FINTRAC as a "passive "type of FIU, to the extent that it does not conduct its own analysis, the following must be emphasized. Data from semi-structured interviews did not confirm these FATF's findings. Although the majority of FINTRAC's analysis is triggered by law-enforcement requests called VIRs, this FIU has also developed its own indicators of money laundering and engages in proactive strategic analysis of intelligence that is based upon other than VIRs triggers. Although there is no formal public-public partnership under which FINTRAC and law-enforcement exchange tactical intelligence, FINTRAC responds to law-enforcement requests. However, this communication, during which VIRs are discussed, is also not a typical query-type exchange of information.

Furthermore, with reference to FINTRAC's new exclusive supervisory jurisdiction over the banking sector, this serious task must be accompanied by significant resources and tools. Based on publicly available sources, it is unclear how this task is going to be fulfilled by FINTRAC.[42] Furthermore, FINTRAC's supervisory mandate towards the banking sector triggers several other issues which are worth considering. Firstly, a "risk-based" supervision of any financial institution is a dynamic process that can be triggered by various factors: data from the financial sector, input from the FIU, input from LEAs, and input from whistle-blowers. Moreover, understanding money laundering risks of a given entity involves having on-going and/or frequent access to the financial data of the entity, different than STRs. Typically, supervisory bodies of various countries have established various mechanisms for regular data collection. This approach is often described as having a helicopter view of the entire private sector. That is, that statistical data (SD) in the form of intelligence of payments at the aggregated level are gathered, i.e., residents, non-residents, their turnover, inbound and outbound transactions, cross-border transactions. From the banking sector, even more complex data are obtained, for example, details on investment portfolios, correspondent banking, private banking relationships, trade-based products, etc. In addition to SD, other qualitative data are obtained (typically through questionnaires[43]) and a supervisory body that creates a switchboard assigning specific money laundering risks to entities within the financial market. Often, other innovative tools, i.e., API tools,[44] are enacted to gather data at the transaction level. Finally, it is a common international standard that supervisory bodies have direct access to all internal documents which evidence the quality of internal system controls, and the AML compliance communication channels inside the entity, i.e., protocols and minutes from the management meetings.

FINTRAC's deterrent power, as the main AML regulatory body, was undermined between 2016–2019, due to its problems in setting up a robust methodology to impose financial fines, including their proportionality with identified violations.[45] As a consequence, a strong signal was sent to the private sector that FINTRAC should not be taken seriously, because it lacks any deterrent power and does not fully comprehend the occurrences in the banking sector, i.e., types of violations and their causes, because of its failure to publish supervisory results. Making FINTRAC's supervisory work more transparent can be easily achieved by publishing more information on its website about conducted inspections and imposed sanctions. In fact, as of 2019, FINTRAC is legally authorized to disclose this information. Moreover, to become a truly knowledgeable supervisory body, FINTRAC should aim toward the most optimal model of supervision, i.e., balancing sample testing with thematic inspections. Through this combination of supervisory tools, FINTRAC can gain a deep and robust insight into the causes of the AML violations. From a broader, criminological perspective, FINTRAC's supervisory mandate would translate into an approach, which in addition to fostering compliance also secures deterrence[46] and prevention of reoffending by the reporting entities.[47]

FINTRAC, through its own supervisory work on the ground, gathers critical knowledge which should be shared with the financial sector to improve its compliance and prevent entities from recommitting the same errors. When such input is provided by FINTRAC to the financial sector, one could compare its function to a policymaker/regulator. The advantage of FINTRAC's leadership in proposing new measures in the AML framework, stems from the knowledge and understanding of lawbreaking in the AML area by reporting entities,[48] which FINTRAC has been accumulating through its supervisory work. Finally, if FINTRAC incorporates the knowledge gathered from conducted inspections into its supervisory model, it will follow the most optimal model of regulating business entities, as developed in Braithwaite's "Pyramid of Responsive Regulation."[49]

To conclude, the central question of which factors should be considered to evaluate FINTRAC's efficacy is a tricky one. One must acknowledge the AML model of any country can be depicted as an inverted triangle (Figure 8.4), often called the AML chain. Also, the entire AML model is built upon elusive criteria, i.e., questionable estimates of dirty money that went through the system and the unknown amount of illicit funds which were prevented from entering.

On the one hand, the ratio between the volume of information collected by FINTRAC and the number of proactive disclosures made to law enforcement[50] should be approached with great caution as an argument to reduce its funding. On the other hand, when comparing FINTRAC with other Western European law-enforcement-type FIUs that have extensive intelligence gathering and analysis powers, the emerging question

Figure 8.4: Schematic Conceptual Flow Chart Illustrating an Idealized Analysis and Comparison of the AML Regimes of Countries

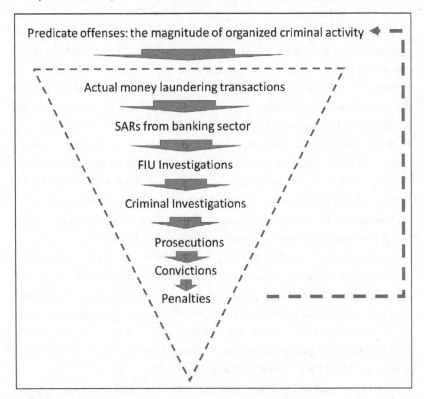

Legend: The effectiveness of the banking sector in reporting suspicious transactions is symbolized by arrow a; the effectiveness of the financial intelligence units by arrow b; the diligence and effectiveness of law enforcement by arrows c and d respectively, the effectiveness of the judiciary by arrow e and the strength of the deterrent punishment by f.

Ideally (a) requires knowledge that is unobtainable, but that can possibly be estimated by an assessment of the relative number of 'predicate' offences reported by law enforcement. Obviously, that would assume that the law enforcement effectiveness is equal across countries or some independent other means of assessing predicate offense volume. Data on SARs and FIUs investigation volumes and the remaining quantities are potentially available. The inverted triangle represents the expected huge deficit in convictions relative to the actual money laundering transactions; however, the relative magnitudes and *loci of attenuations* are the parameters of interest in the comparison between countries. Finally, the dashed arrow indicates the purpose of the AML regulations: reduction of predicate offenses.

is: what is needed to achieve an increase in the number of ML investigations, prosecutions, and convictions, and how can FINTRAC contribute to that strengthening?

Certainly, Canada's resources can match, if not exceed, what medium size European countries invest into their FIUs. If financial resources are not a source of national constraints, then what is? The answer is linked with two issues. The first is the constitutional restraints protecting the privacy of financial data of citizens. The second issue relates to the challenge of law enforcement's capacity to make use of FINTRAC's actionable intelligence. The first factor matters because an administrative agency like FINTRAC cannot operate on the ground as a law-enforcement-type FIU. Therefore, in Canada, changing the nature of FINTRAC would require reformation of the constitutional framework. Alternatively, Canada could set up a brand new, law-enforcement-type FIU, whose focus is re-directed from mass surveillance towards targeted surveillance. It would mean a Canadian FIU would pursue a more proactive analysis of financial intelligence, and actively exchange tactical intelligence with LEAs, intelligence bodies, tax authorities, and the private sector. However, as the findings of this chapter suggest, this solution still would not address the main problem in the functioning of FINTRAC, that is not about FINTRAC's intel per se but rather what happens at the law-enforcement level once FINTRAC's intel has been received.

The big question is whether Canadian society is ready to embrace such a change. Following the 2022 Russian invasion of Ukraine, it is a global policy priority to find levers that might help curb the conduct of Putin's political-criminal nexus, and other kleptocratic regimes. This is not a mere academic endeavour but is imperative to national security and the survival of democracy. Western democracies have been exploring a range of responses, including an array of sanctions, and financial data and financial intelligence are essential to sanction-enforcement and to combat the flow of dark money in general. Russian oligarchs have proven skilled and highly adaptive at bypassing control measures. Therefore, it is more important than ever to understand how money laundering typologies are evolving, and how the system can respond effectively. To do this, we need to strengthen and facilitate cooperation among FIUs, law enforcement, and the private sector domestically and transnationally. In March 2022, FINTRAC joined a newly established task force called Russia-Related Sanctions and Illicit Finance FIU Working Group and will be cooperating with nine other FIUs in this context (FINTRAC 2022c).

Notes

1 I would like to thank Professor Christian Leuprecht for his continuous support and comments on this chapter. Also, I would like to acknowledge the support from FINTRAC's Deputy Director, Barry MacKillop, whom I interviewed and who offered me an insightful perspective on the nature of FINTRAC. Finally, Denis Meunier's kind and detailed comments were extremely helpful and added to the value of this chapter.

2 On June 15, 2022, a full report by the Commission of Inquiry into Money Laundering in British Columbia was published (Hoffman and Wray 2020).

3 Supra note at 2. Also, while closing this chapter for the publication, Denis Meunier provided me with his critical evaluation of the accuracy of Cullen's Commission findings on FINTRAC. In particular, he argues that Cullen's report is not accurate when it comes to his conclusion of FINTRAC's lack of efficacy to produce timely and quality financial intelligence. The reason is because Cullen compared the millions of reports received by FINTRAC to the thousands of disclosures it makes to LEAs. In the light of the above Denis Meunier comments, two issues should be emphasized. Firstly, the conclusions of this chapter do not rely exclusively on Cullen's findings. It incorporates content analysis of other publicly available sources, and, most importantly, data from several semi-structured interviews with the representatives of FINTRAC. Secondly, on page 22, I have introduced relevant explanation from my interviewees that explained the common misconception of the scope and breadth of FINTRAC's disclosures. Thus, regardless of Cullen's findings, this chapter by itself raises the issue that production of financial intelligence is a complex process that cannot easily be described and quantified.

4 Especially, the UK and the Dutch models of FIUs. In the UK in 2015, the National Crime Agency launched the Joint Money Laundering Intelligence Task Force (JMLIT). This is a framework of cooperation in which the financial sector, law enforcement, and the FIU can exchange and analyze money laundering threats and typologies. Also, in the Netherlands, the FIU plays a major role in the production and dissemination of financial intelligence to LEAs, both proactively and upon request. It receives a significant amount of informa-

tion from obliged entities and the Dutch FIU's analytical products are of high quality and targeted to the needs of LEAs. In recent years, approximately 60 percent of law-enforcement investigations made use of STR information, and half of all terrorism financing investigations were triggered by the FIU's analytical products, according to FATF MER Report, 2022, The Netherlands, (8). https://www.fatf-gafi.org/media/fatf/documents/reports/mer4/Mutual-Evaluation-Report-Netherlands-2022.pdf.

5 Semi-structured interviews were conducted online in November and December 2020, with current and former pdf employees of FINTRAC, as part of my PhD dissertation research (McNaughton 2022).

6 S. 21.31 (2) of the Canada Business Corporations Act, identifies the Canada Revenue Agency (CRA) as an investigative body and FINTRAC under S.21.301 (not yet in force) may receive from the Director of Corporations Canada the register of UBOs the corporation has filed with Corporations Canada. As a result, the CRA currently is a potential recipient, and FINTRAC could be in a position, as soon as S 21.301 comes into force, to also become a recipient of UBO information. This is coming in 2023 with a publicly accessible BO registry.

7 This information is in addition to the current registers that corporations maintain for directors and shareholders. The Canadian UBOs Register is not a public database. The Director of Corporations Canada may request the information contained in the Register. Creditors and shareholders of a corporation or their personal representatives may, on application, require that the corporation or its agent allow them access to the Register. More details about the Canadian UBOs Register can be found at https://fintrac-canafe.canada.ca/guidance-directives/client-clientele/bor-eng.

8 It is beyond the scope of this chapter to elaborate in more detail about how non-homogeneity of FIUs impacts on their ability to exchange information among themselves. These difficulties are related to standardization of data and technical capacity to receive large data sets to be exchanged. In other words, although the FIUs' functions are generally the same at a broad level (gather STRs and analyze them, sends the result of analysis to LEAs and other intelligence authorities), at a national level, FIUs vary in terms of their modus operandi (McNaughton 2022).

9 Cullen Report at 1546.

10 Supra note at 1550. According to this report FINTRAC receives an enormous volume of reports from public- and private-sector reporting entities, but it produces only a modest number of intelligence packages that go to law enforcement. For example, in 2019–20, FINTRAC received over thirty-one million individual reports. In that same year, FINTRAC disclosed only 2,057 intelligence reports to law enforcement across Canada, and only 355 to law enforcement agencies in British Columbia.

11 For the purpose of this chapter, the term *financial sector* includes financial institutions (banks, insurance, securities, etc.) and designated non-financial business and professions (casinos, accountants, lawyers, etc.).

12 There are other reports that may or may not be provided to the FIU depending on each country's law. For example, in Canada, incoming and outgoing international electronic funds transfers (EFTs) over $10K are collected and analyzed, as are casino disbursement reports, large cash and large virtual currency transactions, terrorist property reports, cross-border currency reports and cross-border seizure reports.

13 The Financial Action Task Force was established in the '90s as the leading international body to regulate and coordinate the AML laws and policy. The 40 Recommendations are considered the FATF's principal set of the AML requirements which countries should implement into their domestic laws. These standards were modified several times, i.e., 1996, 2003, 2004, 2012. All texts can be downloaded at http://www.fatf-gafi.org/publications/fatfrecommendations/documents/the40recommendationspublishedoctober2004.html.

14 The Egmont Group is an international alliance of FIUs which, as of 2019, consisted of 164 FIUs worldwide. Its primary goal is ensuring that FIUs exchange financial intelligence effectively and in a secure manner. Membership of the Egmont Group is linked to an established set of requirements and legal conditions which guarantee the safe international sharing of financial intelligence. As mentioned, the FATF's 40 Recommendations in this area function as norms de minimis which must be detailed and implemented into the domestic framework of countries. See online: https://egmontgroup.org/en.

15 For comprehensive information about worldwide established PPPs, see especially Nick Maxwell, "Expanding the Capability of Financial Information-Sharing Partnerships" (March 2019) and other reports by Nick Maxwell from The Future of Financial Intelligence Sharing (FFIS) Programme and Royal United Services (RUSI). Reports are available online: https://www.future-fis.com/.

16 Findings of my PhD dissertation, which was an in-depth study of financial intelligence units (FIUs) from ten Western and Eastern (post-Soviet) countries and a critical assessment of the international anti-money laundering (AML) law approach. A crucial role is assigned to national FIUs, which is to gather, analyze, and disseminate financial intelligence. However, the AML regime does not seem to be working effectively, and I propose that this stems from a lack of appreciation, by international AML frameworks, that tackling financial crime is shaped by national legal and historical factors, which may impede international AML efforts. I show that FIUs are heterogeneous and cluster along a West-East dimension. The study does not evaluate FIU efficacy per se, but clarifies their modus operandi, which may lead to a better understanding of their efficacy in future studies. To make FIUs work effectively, identifica-

tion of their idiosyncratic problems is needed first, because issuing new global AML standards is not a solution (McNaughton 2022).

17 The following sections of the PCMLTFA regulate what FINTRAC can receive and collect as information, what FINTRAC can disclose, and establishes limitation on orders for disclosure of information. These are section 54(1), (2), 55(1), (2) and (3), 59(2), 60(1), (2). In contrast to other national FIUs, these sections narrow FINTRAC's legal mandate (Proceeds of Crime Act 2000).

18 According to the FATF MER Report of 2016, "FINTRAC tailors its analysis to the LEAs' operational priorities. It focuses mainly on answering the VIRs and also discloses intelligence related to LEAs' priorities" (43).

19 Such twofold classification of the analysis of financial intelligence obtained by FIUs is an internationally established standard. Sometimes, it is even prescribed in the domestic AML legislation.

20 Regulated by a provincial act.

21 Regulated by a provincial act.

22 Regulated by a provincial act.

23 Terrorist property reports (TPRs), casino disbursement reports, large cash transaction reports of $10,000 CAD or more (LCTRs) and threshold international electronic (incoming and outgoing) fund transactions of CAD$10,000 (EFTs) or more, cross-border currency reports, cross-border currency custom seizures (CBCRs) and movements (CBCRs), large virtual currency transactions (LVCTRs). According to FINTRAC's website, FINTRAC's database *receives* about 20 million transactional reports (FINTRAC 2022a).

24 An important assumption made for the purpose of this analysis is that it relies exclusively on the data contained in the annual report from the FINTRAC. To get a comprehensive view of the analysis, more data, especially through semi-structured interviews, should be gathered.

25 FINTRAC also produced strategic intelligence on the use of financial technology (fintech) for the purpose of terrorism financing. In 2018, FINTRAC published the *Terrorist Financing Assessment*.

26 FINTRAC used the term "actionable intelligence."

27 This new AML body will put together experts from the intelligence and law-enforcement forces to strengthen inter-agency coordination and cooperation and to identify and address significant money laundering and financial crime threats (Canadian Institute n.d.).

28 The budget proposes to invest $28.6 million over four years, beginning in 2020–21, with $10.5 million per year ongoing to create the multidisciplinary Centre of Expertise.

29 Among the most vulnerable sectors of the Canadian economy identified in recent years was the gambling and real estate market in British Columbia, where vast amounts of illicit drug money from China infiltrated casinos and luxury properties. As mentioned earlier, a special Governmental Commission of Inquiry into Money Laundering in British Columbia, i.e., the Cullen Commission,

was established in 2019, to examine the scope of the problem (Cullen Commission 2019). According to Transparency International (2016), the ownership of almost half of Vancouver's prime real estate, amounting to more than CAD\$1bn in anonymous wealth, was untraceable (Cribb and Oved 2017).

30 Projects Protect, Chameleon, Guardians (FINTRAC, S.C. 2000, c. 17).

31 FINTRAC's 2020–2021 Departmental Results Report at page 27 may provide some additional insight into LEA's assessment of actionable financial intelligence disclosures of FINTRAC disclosures, by year. See https://fintrac-canafe. canada.ca/publications/drr-rrm/2021-2022/2021-2022-drr-rrm-eng.pdf.

32 According to my interviewee, FINTRAC has more than 260 million financial transactions in its database annually.

33 The 2020 PPP project was devoted to child sexual abuse over the internet.

34 This according to Denis Meunier, who shared his perspective and experience of working for FINTRAC.

35 Department of Finance Canada, Department of Justice Canada, Public Prosecution Service of Canada (PPSC), Financial Transactions and Reports Analysis Centre (FINTRAC), Canada Border Services Agency (CBSA), Canada Revenue Agency (CRA), Royal Canadian Mounted Police (RCMP), Canadian Security Intelligence Service (CSIS), Public Safety Canada, Office of the Superintendent of Financial Institutions (OSFI), Global Affairs Canada, Innovation, Science and Economic Development Canada (ISED), Public Services and Procurement Canada (PSPC).

36 The risk-based approach is fundamental to anti-money laundering compliance and requires all stakeholders in the fight against money laundering, including law enforcement, government authorities, regulators, and industry, to identify, assess, manage, and mitigate risks linked with money laundering based on variables such as country or geographic risk, customer risk, and product or service risk. The central assumption behind the risk-based approach is that it does not have a legal definition and that the financial sector and other authorities can measure it. In the case of supervisory bodies, the risk-based approach means that they have the flexibility to decide the scope of the information they want to gather about the obliged entities, i.e., types of products and services offered, turnover, incoming and outgoing transfers, deposits, risk-appetite, number of non-residents, etc. Once such knowledge is obtained, supervisory bodies conduct their own calculation of ML risks associated with the activities of certain entity. Subsequently, supervisory authorities would compare the results of their risk assessment with the evaluation done by the entity itself. As a result of such analysis, supervisory bodies in any given country have a fairly solid insight into financial activities and the vulnerability of any given financial entity. Based on this knowledge, supervisory bodies decide the frequency and the scope of supervisory inspections within specific entities. See Luxembourg, FATF, *Guidance for a Risk-Based Approach: The Banking Sector*, 2014 and FATF, *Specific Risk Factors in Laundering the Proceeds of Corruption*, June 2012.

37 OSFI's Annual Report for 2019 does not contain any data about the number and results of the AML supervision of the banking sector.

38 The AMP Regulations are available at the FINTRAC website: https://laws-lois.justice.gc.ca/PDF/SOR-2007-292.pdf.

39 Three cases were examined by the Court: *Max Realty Solutions v. Attorney General of Canada*, 2014 FC 656; *Kabul Farms Inc. v. Canada*, 2016 FCA 143; *Contrevenant No. 10 v. Attorney General of Canada*, 2016 FCA 42. The same conclusion was reached: "[a]s part of procedural fairness, a party potentially liable for an administrative monetary penalty, such as the respondent, needs to know about any formula, guideline or supporting analysis the Director will rely upon in his assessment of penalties."

40 Similar regulation was established to govern voluntary transmission of information from FINTRAC towards the Canada Revenue Agency in the AML Act; see §65.02(1) and 65.01 (1).

41 In 2017–18, five cases were disclosed, while in 2016–17, one case was submitted (FINTRAC, Proceeds of Crime Act 2000, 23).

42 Under sections 62(1) and 62(2) of the Act FINTRAC can ask for any relevant information to be produced by a reporting entity for the purpose of ensuring compliance with Part 1 or 1.1. Sections 63.1 (1) and 63.1 (2) also oblige the reporting entity to provide any document requested by FINTRAC. See online: https://laws-lois.justice.gc.ca/eng/acts/P-24.501/page-11.html - h-399408.

43 Source: Author's own conceptualization. These include examination of the obliged entities of their understanding of various AML requirements, i.e., Know Your Customer, Customer Due Diligence, Politically Exposed Individuals, etc.

44 These new tools are introduced so that supervisory bodies can automatically receive detailed preliminary (operational) data and analyze them in various aspects, while financial market participants would no longer need to worry whether precise and detailed data, which complies with legal requirements, is submitted in a timely manner. This tool is often called "Corridor of Entry" because when the entity installs an extra API module, it will automatically collect the needed data from the entity's databases and submit them to the data reception module of the supervisory authority. Such a pilot tool was established for example, in Lithuania in 2020 (Bank of Lithuania 2020).

45 One of the comments made by my interviewee was that FINTRAC's lack of enactment of internal documents detailing the methodology of imposing financial fines seems like a major oversight. This includes its ability to establish meaningful fines, because when we are dealing with billion-dollar entities, imposing a $100,000 fine is not adequate.

46 Deterrence is a key concept in the classical school of criminology, which developed a theory of punishment. According to this theory, an individual makes a rational choice when it comes to deciding whether or not to engage in criminal behaviour. Thus, the classical approach designs penal policies based upon the assumption that criminals weigh the cost-benefit–trade-off rationally when

contemplating committing a crime. This concept of the "economics of crime" was first mentioned by Beccaria and Bentham, and later modernized by Becker, who suggested that government should develop a policy system wherein "crime does not pay." In other words, the cost of committing a crime (the severity, certainty, and celerity of punishment) must be higher than benefits (McNaughton 2022).

47 Through thematic inspections addressing root causes of violations.

48 Examples of such an active, quasi-legislative cooperation between the FIU and supervisory bodies can be found in several European countries. For example, in Estonia and Denmark, where the supervisory bodies identified that a lack of communication between managerial structures within a given financial entity and a lack of group-wide rules of procedure and internal AML control rules were among the key factors for non-compliance. Thus, new provisions were incorporated into the AML legislation of these countries to address identified flaws within the banking sector. The bottom line is that the input to improve the AML legislation, in the form of specific measures, did not start at the parliamentary level. Instead, it has been a "bottom-up" process, where the draft legislation was designed as a result of cooperation among FIUs, supervisory bodies and the private sector.

49 According to Braithwaite's (2002) framework, the most effective regulation entails escalating the regulatory response, depending on the scale of violations.

50 No federal agency collects data on money laundering convictions. FINTRAC's Annual Report also does not provide this data. According to the investigative project by Global News in 2019, between 2000 and 2016, there were 321 convictions, which places Canada's conviction rate at 27 percent. Countries like the UK have approximately a 50 percent conviction rate, while the US Department of Justice shows a rate of 85 percent. See more details on data gathered by Global News online: https://globalnews.ca/news/4939801/provinces-canada-fail-to-convict-money-laundering/.

References

Bank of Lithuania. 2020. "Bank of Lithuania Presents Solution to Streamline Reporting Procedures." https://www.lb.lt/en/news/bank-of-lithuania-presents-solution-to-streamline-reporting-procedures.

Braithwaite, John. 2002. *Restorative Justice and Responsive Regulation*. New York: Oxford University Press. http://johnbraithwaite.com/wp-content/uploads/2019/02/Restorative-Justice-and-Responsive-regulation-book.pdf.

Canada Business Corporations Act, R.S.C. 1985, C. C-44. https://laws-lois.justice.gc.ca/PDF/C-44.pdf.

Cockfield, Arthur J. 2017. "Examining Canadian Offshore Tax Evasion." *Canadian Tax Journal* 65 (3): 651–680. https://ssrn.com/abstract=3089864

———. 2019. "The High Price of Chinese Money Laundering in Canada." *Globe and Mail*. https://www.theglobeandmail.com/opinion/article-the-high-price-of-chinese-money-laundering-in-canada/.

Canadian Institute. n.d. "Carrie Hagerman." https://www.canadianinstitute.com/anti-money-laundering-financial-crime/speakers/carrie-hagerman/.

Cribb, Robert, and Marco Chwon Oved. 2017. "Lessons for Canada." *Toronto Star*. https://projects.thestar.com/panama-papers/lessons-for-canada/.

Cullen Commission. 2019. *Commission of Inquiry into Money Laundering in British Columbia*. https://cullencommission.ca.

FATF (Financial Action Task Force). 2016. *Mutual Evaluation Report*. Canada: FATF.

FINTRAC (Financial Transactions and Reports Analysis Centre of Canada). n.d. "About FINTRAC." https://www.fintrac-canafe.gc.ca/intro-eng.

———. 2018. *Annual Report*. Canada: FINTRAC. https://publications.gc.ca/collections/collection_2020/canafe-fintrac/FD1-2019-eng.pdf.

———. 2019. *Annual Report*. Canada: FINTRAC. https://fintrac-canafe.canada.ca/publications/ar/2022/1-eng.

———. 2022a. "FINTRAC, Law Enforcement and Intelligence Partners: Sharing Intelligence, Making the Links." https://fintrac-canafe.canada.ca/intel/general/1-eng.

———. 2022b. "Penalties for Non-Compliance." https://www.fintrac-canafe.gc.ca/pen/1-eng.

———. 2022c. "Russia-Related Sanctions and Illicit Finance FIU Working Group Statement of Intent." https://fintrac-canafe.canada.ca/new-neuf/nr/2022-03-16-eng.

Gilmore, William. 1999. *Dirty Money: The Evolution of Money Laundering Countermeasures*, 2nd ed. Strasbourg: Council of Europe Publishing.

Hoffman, Judith, and B. J. Wray. 2020. *Opening Statement of the Government of Canada*. Vancouver, BC: Department of Justice. https://cullencommission.ca/files/OpeningStatement-GovernmentOfCanada.pdf.

Levi, Michael, and Mike Maguire. 2012. "Something Old, Something New; Something Not Entirely Blue: Uneven and Shifting Modes of Crime Control." In *Policing: Politics, Culture and Control*, edited by Tim Newburn and Jill Peay. Oxford: Hart Publishing.

Maxwell, Nick. 2019. "Expanding the Capability of Financial Information-Sharing Partnerships." London: FFIS (Future of Financial Information Sharing). https://www.future-fis.com/uploads/3/7/9/4/3794525/pr%C3%A9cis_of_ffis_paper_-_expanding_the_role_of_fisps_-_march_2020.pdf.

———. 2022. *A Survey and Policy Discussion Paper: Lessons in Private-Private Financial Information Sharing to Detect and Disrupt Crime*. London: FFIS (Future of Financial Information Sharing). https://www.future-fis.com/uploads/3/7/9/4/3794525/rusi_ffis_survey_and_policy_discussion_paper_-_lessons_in_private-private_financial_information_sharing_to_detect_crime.pdf.

McNaughton, Katarzyna J. 2022. "The Role of Financial Intelligence Units (FIUs) in Shaping an Effective International Anti-Money Laundering Law and Policy." (PhD diss., Queen's University, 2022).

Mitsilegas, Valsamis. 2003. *Money Laundering Counter-Measures in the European Union, A New Paradigm of Security Governance versus Fundamental Legal Principles*. Alphen aan den Rijn, Netherlands: Kluwer Law International.

Monroe, Brian. 2020. "Regional Report: Canada Has Done 'Amazing Things' to Fight Crime through Public-Private Partnerships, but Still Hampered by Stringent Privacy Rules, Lack of AML Safe Harbors." Association of Certified Financial Crime Specialists. https://www.acfcs.org/regional-report-canada-has-done-amazing-things-to-fight-crime-through-public-private-partnerships-but-still-hampered-by-stringent-privacy-rules-lack-of-aml-safe-harbors/.

OSFI (Office of the Superintendent of Financial Institutions). 2014. "Who We Regulate." https://www.osfi-bsif.gc.ca/Eng/wt-ow/Pages/wwr-er.aspx?sc=1&gc=1#WWRLink11.

———. 2022. "About Us." https://www.osfi-bsif.gc.ca/Eng/osfi-bsif/Pages/default.aspx.

Paoli, Letizia. 2014. *The Oxford Book of Organized Crime*. Oxford: Oxford University Press.

Proceeds of Crime (Money Laundering) and Terrorist Financing Act, S.C. 2000, c 17. https://laws-lois.justice.gc.ca/eng/acts/P-24.501/page-10.html#h-398899.

Pyrick, John. 2021. "The Financial Transactions and Reports Analysis Centre of Canada (FINTRAC)." In *Top Secret Canada: Understanding the Canadian Intelligence National Community*, edited by Stephanie Carvin, Thomas Juneau, and Craig Forcese. University of Toronto Press. https://doi.org/10.3138/9781487536657-008.

Emerging Issues in Financial Crime: Challenges in Multilevel Governance

9

Underground Banking in Canada

Caroline Dugas, Pierre-Luc Pomerleau, and
David Maimon

Introduction

In reviewing the 2019 E-Pirate project and Project Collector,[1] the Royal
Canadian Mounted Police (RCMP) estimated that CAD$500 million had
been laundered by criminals (Schneider 2020) while CAD$32.8 million
of assets were frozen by Canadian authorities (Government of Canada 2019). In addition, the cities of Toronto and Vancouver have seen
a multiplication of underground currency exchange bureaus being used
to transfer funds, often from countries under sanctions (Cooper 2021).
Considering these trends, the 2020 Cullen Commission in British Columbia brought to light the difficulty of detecting illegal underground
banking systems and measuring their impacts on the Canadian economy.
For example, through the Athena Project,[2] the Financial Transactions and
Reports Analysis Centre of Canada (FINTRAC) provided a set of indicators for casinos and financial institutions (FINTRAC 2019) to detect
underground banking activities, such as deposits of a high volume of
bank drafts or regular clients who appear on casino premises with an individual that the casino had previously banned. Still, additional solutions
are needed to reduce the expansion of these networks.

In what follows, the concept of underground banking is explored, followed by descriptions of how underground banking in Canada poten-

tially facilitates money laundering and terrorist financing, some of the criminal networks that use them to launder funds, newer methods of money laundering involving casinos and real estate transactions (Schneider 2020), and what is referred to as fei-chien (i.e., transfer of funds through underground channels). Additionally, we provide best practices for reducing the use of underground banking for criminal activities based on recommendations from both scholars and practitioners.

Underground Banking

Underground banking is defined as a parallel system that operates outside a formal banking structure (FINTRAC 2019). According to the Financial Action Task Force (FATF), the modus operandi of underground banking involves the movement of funds without using official economic structures or instruments such as cash, cheques, or other valuable items. Instead, the funds are transferred by other means of communication between the parties, often through numerous intermediaries (FATF 2016, 2018). Historically, the primary purpose of moving money through informal means has been to legitimately assist family members (FATF 2013) or to meet various legitimate business needs (Zhao 2012). Indeed, in some countries, the banking structure is significantly underdeveloped, so underground mechanisms are in place to help the population transfer money to pay for various goods and services. For example, in Nepal, some regions are so mountainous that the official banking structure is non-existent (FATF 2013).

Today, underground banking is known by several names such as informal value transfer services/systems (IVTS), money or value transfer services (MVTS), informal fund transfer systems (IFTS), or by specific names from regional mechanisms like fei-chien, hawalas, hundi, poey kuan, and "the chop" (FATF 2016, 2018; Passas 1999; Zhao 2012).

Although many *underground banking systems* are used for legitimate purposes, criminal organizations have found ways to leverage these techniques to launder money or hide terrorist-financing activities (Cassara

Figure 9.1: One of the Modus Operandi of the Hawala Process

Country A

Country B

Hawaladar	→*Remittance code* →	Hawaladar

Cash   Cash

Sender	*Remittance code* →	Receiver

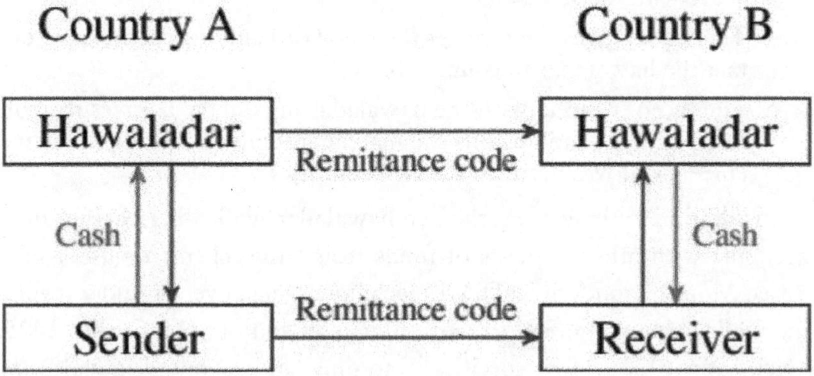

Source: Gräbner, Elsner, and Lascaux (2020).

2016). Passas (1999) and Zhao (2012) suggest that funds can be moved and laundered through casinos (chips), real estate transactions, currency exchange offices, or money remittance shops. Genesis (2018) adds that these money remittance shops can be hidden in jewellers, car rental agencies, grocery stores, travel agencies, phone shops, and import or shipping companies. Makhani (2018) simplifies the explanation by stating that informal transfer operations are not registered and are thus unlicensed by authorities.

For example, Figure 9.1 above shows one of the modus operandi of the hawala process.

1. An individual (the sender) from country A wants to send funds to another individual (the receiver) in country B.
2. The individual in country A (the sender) finds a hawaladar (an underground banker), pays the amount they want to transfer, and asks them to share it with the individual in country B.
3. The hawaladar in country A will contact a hawaladar from their network in country B and tell them how much the sender wants to

transfer. They also assign a password to the transaction, which they share with the sender.

4. The sender gives the receiver the password and instructions to contact the hawaladar in country B.

5. The receiver meets with the hawaladar in country B, gives the correct password, and claims the matching funds. However, no actual currency moves between the two countries.

In addition to these steps, the two hawaladars will either balance their accounts with other requests of funds from other clients or use Trade-Based Money Laundering (TBML) techniques (e.g., over or under invoicing while shipping goods) to move money in and out (McCusker 2005; Teichmann 2020). More specifically, to move money out, criminals may import goods at inflated prices or export goods at deflated prices. To move money in, they may import goods at deflated prices or export goods at inflated prices (Cassara 2016). This way, the fund transfers look like legitimate business activities.

Another tool criminals use is wire transfers between several bank accounts worldwide, involving correspondent banks (Chau and Van Dijck Nemcsik 2021). For international money transfers between correspondent banks from various countries, information sent from one institution to another is minimal (e.g., amount, originator, recipient of the funds). Thus, it may be very difficult to detect potential money laundering when the first bank does not perform adequate customer due diligence and strictly follows proper know-your-client (KYC) rules, such as verifying the person or entity sending the money (Chau and Van Dijck Nemcsik 2021). However, another way for financial institutions to detect these patterns is based on the detection of anomalies in transactional data. The improvement of the management of the data is an essential aspect of anti-money laundering that will be discussed later in this chapter.

Typical Hawalas are still used today, such as in the black market peso exchange and China's flying money (i.e., fei-chien). In the black market peso exchange, drug dealers give a currency broker US funds collected from drug sales in the United States. The broker would give the equivalent funds back to the drug dealer in pesos in Colombia without moving the cash across borders (German 2018). For example, the broker will find ways to launder the US dollars through other activities of import and export of goods this modus operandi has evolved; today, the use of TBML techniques is much more frequent. For instance, the drug dealer will buy goods in a given country, export them to another country (i.e., Columbia and Mexico), and sell the goods to obtain pesos (Teichmann and Falker 2020; Brecher 2018). During the Covid-19 pandemic, drug cartels considerably increase the investment of their funds in US real estate, as they could not export goods due to the closure of borders (Austin 2021).

Foreigners also brought back old techniques, such as fei-chien, to use underground banking networks to invest in real estate. Cassara (2016) provides an example of fei-chien:

> Let's say Wang in Guangdong province wants to send 1 million Chinese yuan of illicit proceeds to his brother in New York City. Wang gives the Guangdong "flying money" broker the yuan and in turn receives a code number. He trusts the broker as they have a familial relationship. The "flying money" broker in Guangdong directs his counterpart (perhaps a member of the same family) to pay the equivalent in U.S. dollars (approximately $152,000) upon presentation of the code. The code could be an expression in a telephone call, or a message contained in an e-mail. At times, a playing card or a portion of a currency note with a specific chop, marking, seal, or other physical sign must be presented to the broker as a sign of authentication. Upon receipt of the code, the New York "flying money" broker pays Wang's brother in New York City. (Cassara 2016)

Similar to the other types of underground banking techniques, the main reason behind the popularity of fei-chien is that the transaction commissions are lower than those charged by banks or traditional money remitters, but still profitable to the brokers at both ends of a transaction (Cassara 2016). Also, the brokers often use legitimate businesses as fronts, such as restaurants, "China shops," and trading companies (Cassara 2016). In addition to other market conditions (i.e., lower real estate prices, stability of the economy of the country, etc.), because it is easier and cheaper to transfer funds by fei-chien, the volume of funds received in Canada (among other places) to invest in real estate significantly impacts the increasing property values around the country (Cullen Commission 2020).

Underground Banking in Canada

In the last decade, major police investigations have shed light on the problem of underground banking in Canada. Underground banking techniques have always existed in Canada, but they have evolved to use casinos and real estate transactions (Passas 1999). Also, following the money laundering scandal in British Columbia, German (2019) coined the *Vancouver Model*. Unlike other underground banking structures, in the Vancouver Model, organized crime syndicates control both the initiation of transfers and the reception of funds in the IVTS. Accordingly, the criminal underground banker profits from commissions at both the initiation and the reception phases of each operation (Simser 2020; German 2019). In addition to the typical transfer of funds operation, criminals in this model use casinos to clean the cash received in Canada: (a) they bring the money to a casino to exchange it for casino chips, (b) they ask for the chips to be refunded (in the form of a cheque) by the casino so that gambling winnings can explain the funds, then (c) the cheques are used to pay for purchases of real estate.

This modus operandi was discovered through the 2015 RCMP E-Pirate project. This project investigated the financial activities of Paul "King" Jin, along with his company Silver International and its network, going back to 2011 (Schneider 2020). The E-Pirate project started in February 2015 following a complaint by the British Columbia Lottery Corporation (BCLC). The BCLC hired the company MNP to audit its Richmond River Rock Casino after it noticed that the casino accepted approximately CAD$13.5 million in $20 bills. At that time, Jin was suspected of running a multi-million dollar money laundering scheme through an underground money services business. As a consequence, Jin was banned from all BCLC casinos (Schneider 2020).

Furthermore, through his company, Jin was supporting Chinese individuals by bringing funds from China. In China, individuals are bound by the country's currency protection measures, which forbid them from transferring more than USD$50,000 out of the country (Sen 2020; Schneider 2020). Thus, they may use the services provided by professional money launderers like Jin to get their funds out of the country. Besides, Jin also helped drug dealers launder funds through casinos and real estate. He used the money collected through drug trafficking activities to fund the cash transfers from Chinese citizens to Canadian recipients. As a result of this investigation, a police raid was conducted in 2015, and two years later, nine other people were arrested (The Combined Forces Special Enforcement Unit 2017). In total, it is estimated that Paul Jin's network laundered CAD\$500 million (Cooper 2017).

In addition to the above case, the RCMP began Project Collector in 2016. This project was set up after the RCMP received information from the United States Drug Enforcement Administration (DEA) about regular exchanges of cash drops (i.e., bags full of cash; Cooper and Bell 2019). One of the main characters of the investigation was the underground banker, Farzam Mehdizadeh. Through this investigation, it was discovered that Mehdizadeh had been laundering money (since 2013) through an informal transfer system for drug traffickers. This system involved moving funds from their activities in Toronto and Montréal to numerous countries in Asia, the Middle East, and South America (RCMP 2019; Schneider 2020). According to the investigation, Mehdizadeh used wire transfers, bank drafts, and hidden currency services to move and launder funds from drug trafficking. As a result, the RCMP seized assets worth CAD\$32 million and arrested seventeen people, and the network was dismantled in 2019 (Cooper and Bell 2019; Schneider 2020). However, as Cooper and Bell (2019) argue, this network was part of the much more comprehensive network of Altaf Khanani, an individual with alleged links to Hezbollah, other terrorist groups, and drug cartels.

These two cases do not provide a complete assessment of the situation in the country, but they do offer a high-level overview of the underground banking problem in Canada. Unfortunately, as mentioned by Todd (2020) and Smart (2020), it is relatively easy for foreigners to transfer large sums of money from their country to the Canadian real estate market (e.g., Vancouver and Toronto) using various underground banking mechanisms. Furthermore, the E-Pirate project demonstrated that the underground banking network brought criminal activities to Canada. As Schneider (2020) stipulates, this is not an isolated situation as the port of Vancouver is often exploited for drug smuggling.

Moreover, the use of underground banking in Canada goes further given the new and used luxury car market in the country: exporters use third parties to buy cars and export them to countries worldwide. Underground banking was used to cover the payments for some of these purchases (Young 2019). Also, Cooper (2021) exposed a much broader problem of underground banking in the region of Toronto with the multiplication of hidden currency exchange shops. As these elements expose only the tip of the iceberg, additional solutions are required to discourage or even prevent the use of underground banking for criminal activities.

Best Practices and Recommendations

The problems surrounding underground banking activities are challenging to solve as these transactions are difficult to detect. Still, scholars and anti-money laundering specialists have identified several solutions over the years. For instance, Genesis (2018) proposes three main areas of focus to solve this issue. First, she recommends performing more research on the hawala modus operandi. Secondly, she claims that law enforcement needs more training to investigate these financial crime schemes. Third, she states that other red-flag typologies are required to assist financial institutions in monitoring potential suspicious activities.

Money Laundering Typologies

Along with the third recommendation of Genesis (2018), the FATF (2018) has provided documentation with examples of situations covering Canada's typologies. Other solutions, like the requirement for licensing (McCusker 2005) and the implementation of the FATF recommendations in businesses that operate some of the underground banking services (FATF 2013), were also proposed. Hawala might be the best-known method in underground banking, but the Canadian approach (the Vancouver Model) complicates detection and enforcement efforts (German 2019). On this front, it may be beneficial for financial institutions to have specific indicators and red flags to detect high-risk transactions (e.g., unregulated money transfer providers) orchestrated through their banking infrastructure. (See Indicators to Detect Suspicious Hawala and Other Similar Service Providers, FATF 2013). However, these indicators are often associated with high-level money laundering schemes that are difficult to translate into money laundering rules and scenarios among a vast quantity of banking transactions. Instead, government and law enforcement may want to consider providing more specific threat actor information, so analysts can swiftly identify perpetrators (i.e., professional money launderers) using shell companies and money mules to orchestrate their underground banking transactions using the banking system.

Improving Intelligence Capabilities Through Information-Sharing

The solutions identified above might help, but one central issue remains: none of the parties involved in investigating and detecting underground banking money laundering schemes have a complete view of the situation. The banking sector provides suspicious transaction reports to FINTRAC, for instance, and FINTRAC provides intelligence to the RCMP to conduct investigations and arrest professional money launderers in Canada and overseas. However, there are currently no formal communication channels to securely share anti-money laundering information and intelligence among banks (private to private information sharing), or similar channels among public to private (FINTRAC to banks) stakeholders or private to public partners (banks to RCMP). This situation creates intelligence silos and intelligence gaps (Shepticky 2004), where information flows from financial institutions to FINTRAC, then to law enforcement through suspicious transaction reports, and where every party develops suspicions based on the small portion of intelligence they have. Without a connection between everyone's information, no one sees the *bigger picture* of what is going on and the potentially significant economic ramifications of criminal networks. In addition, intelligence silos happen when a party involved in the investigation keeps information for itself, rather than sharing it with a trusted consortium of partners.

The lack of information sharing is a significant issue among financial institutions, law enforcement, and the government in Canada (Pomerleau 2019a; Pomerleau and Lowery 2020). In cases where financial institutions are involved in the flow of funds, they can only file suspicious transaction reports (STRs) and make risk management decisions (i.e., demarketing high-risk customers, companies, or correspondent banks) regarding the accounts. Regrettably, by demarketing a relationship at one bank without also enforcing sanctions on the criminal actors, the problem is only transferred from one bank to another. This situation only applies to money laundering involving the banking system. It does not apply to underground banking schemes conducted outside the banking system, which may be even more problematic as anti-money laundering specialists, intelligence officers, and law enforcement professionals do not have any visibility of these transactions.

The Importance of Public-Private Partnerships

In 2018, the report of the Canadian House of Commons Standing Committee on Finance recommended information-sharing mechanisms within the different government divisions and participants. In addition, it raised the need to share information between them and FINTRAC (Report to the Standing Committee on Finance 2018). Specifically, the Committee recommended implementing a public-private partnership in Canada similar to the Joint Money Laundering Intelligence Taskforce (JMLIT) in the United Kingdom.

The Joint Money Laundering Intelligence Taskforce (JMLIT)

JMLIT was launched in 2015 and is an integral part of the UK National Economic Crime Center (NECC). Members of this public-private partnership come from law enforcement, Her Majesty's Government (HMG), regulators, more than forty financial institutions, the Financial Conduct Authority, Cifas,[3] and five law enforcement agencies (National Crime Agency n.d.). It was created in response to economic crimes, ranging from organized crime threats to terrorist financing, and to identify long-term strategic vulnerabilities (Maxwell 2021). This partnership is an innovative model for information-sharing and has had positive results since its inception. It is internationally recognized as an example of best practices (National Crime Agency n.d.).

The JMLIT has four priority areas of focus, seeking to reduce or eliminate (1) the laundering of the proceeds of bribery and corruption, especially illicit finance from collapsed regimes (or those close to collapse); (2) trade-based money laundering, which includes a focus on illicit money flows hidden behind opaque corporate structures and beneficial ownership; (3) the laundering of the proceeds of human trafficking and organized immigration crime; and (4) terrorist financing, which includes a focus on foreign terrorist fighters and international money flows that support terrorist funding (JMLIT, n.d).

The Fintel Alliance

In 2017, the Australian Transaction Reports and Analysis Centre (AUSTRAC) launched the Fintel Alliance, the world's first public-private partnership that brings together government, industry, academia, and international partners to harness a new and collaborative approach to combating and disrupting money laundering and terrorism financing. Fintel Alliance members span government bodies, police forces, financial institutions, and academic and research institutions. Membership in the Fintel Alliance is by invitation from the AUSTRAC CEO and reflects the Alliance's operational and strategic objectives (AUSTRAC 2021). Currently, twenty-eight partners are working together to combat money laundering and tax evasion (AUSTRAC 2021).

Fintel Alliance partners foster a cooperative and trusting environment, working together to achieve the common objectives of combating and disrupting serious financial crime (Chadderton and Norton 2019). As a partnership, the Alliance does not create legally binding obligations on members. There are two information-sharing hubs where partners collaborate. First, the operation hub is a physical space where partners exchange and analyze financial intelligence face-to-face in close to real time, combining data with tracking tools and best practice methodologies from their organizations. Likewise, in the innovation hub, partners have an opportunity to co-design and test new technology solutions that assist in gathering and analyzing financial intelligence at an operational level. They also assess the impact of emerging technologies (Chadderton and Norton 2019).

Anti-Money Laundering Initiatives in Canada

Sharing information between such partners – who otherwise generally work separately with limited information – would improve investigation effectiveness and efficiency. In the case of the E-Pirate and Project Collector, it could have helped authorities understand the criminal strategies earlier. By implementing a partnership between private and public parties, Canada could leverage the other countries' experience. For example, the latest statistics obtained for JMLIT (as of June 2020) demonstrate that this partnership "led to closures of 3,400 accounts, £56 million in assets being seized or restrained, and 210 arrests" (U.K. Finance 2022). As Maxwell (2019) mentioned, the partnership should not be limited to major financial institutions, which means that members of a potential partnership, such as casinos among other strategic partners, should also be included.

In Canada, the sharing of information between authorities and financial institutions to detect money laundering started primarily in 2015 with Project Protect (i.e., a project to combat human trafficking), where financial institutions were invited to work with FINTRAC to develop typologies (Maxwell 2019). However, participants in the fight against money laundering in financial institutions still have concerns about financial institutions' capacity to manage more typologies (RUSI 2019). In fact, in 2017, there were 278 indicators provided by FINTRAC to help detect money laundering (Amicelle and Lafolla 2017). Therefore, in line with the work of Chadderton and Norton (2019), Canada could benefit from moving from a typology partnership to a formal information-sharing structure, similar to JMLIT or Australia's Fintel Alliance initiative.

Moreover, public-private partnerships will likely continue to develop. Indeed, in December 2020, the Royal Canadian Mounted Police (2020) announced additional financing dedicated to aiding in the fight against money laundering. With that, a taskforce called the Integrated Money Laundering Investigative Team (IMLIT) was established. However, following the money laundering scandal in British Columbia, this province acted and announced the creation of its own public-private partnership between thirty-eight different parties. The new network is named the Counter Illicit Finance Alliance of British Columbia (CIFA-BC) and the operations are led by the RCMP (2020).

Public-private partnerships around the world have shown numerous benefits, but some concerns remain when it comes to detecting underground banking activities. Among others, the use of data analytics through machine learning and artificial intelligence (AI) and the security and privacy of the information shared between partners are critical. These elements are discussed further with the solutions proposed by Pomerleau and Auger-Perreault (2020) and Pomerleau (2019a).

Leveraging Data Analytics and Machine Learning

The use of data is paramount for the detection of money laundering activities (e.g., underground banking). Hence, various data analytic strategies and machine learning techniques can be used to detect potential money laundering transactions. Unfortunately, this type of strategy is far from being a perfect science to detect money laundering, as such criminal threats are incredibly challenging to prevent. Nevertheless, organizations should use data analytics, machine learning, and intelligence sharing within their organization and external partners (Pomerleau 2019b).

Machine learning models have also been used to prevent and detect fraud, most notably in credit card fraud management (Pomerleau and

Auger-Perreault 2020). There are three categories of machine learning models: supervised, unsupervised, and reinforcement, with supervised and unsupervised learning the most prevalent in fraud risk management (Pomerleau and Auger-Perreault 2020). Similar to current efforts in fraud risk management, supervised learning algorithms such as decision trees, logistic regression, and support vector machines could more frequently be relied upon to detect money laundering schemes. On the other hand, unsupervised learning, such as clustering, does not use labelled data, and it could be helpful in money laundering investigations as it facilitates the detection of anomalies (Pomerleau and Auger-Perreault 2020).

Privacy-Enhancing Tools

Peer-to-peer intelligence sharing mechanisms such as key exchanges and hash validation (public-private key encryption sharing to allow participants to decentralize the data) and various forms of encryption such as homomorphic encryption – securing data in use, data at rest, and data in transit – should be used to share data securely (Pomerleau 2019a). These techniques enable data owners or data stewards to provide analysts (or processors) with an opportunity to undertake limited computations and provide guarantees that the analysts and investigators will not have access to raw data (Maxwell 2021).

Using a sophisticated level of encryption through an information-sharing platform would secure the information (e.g., confirmed cases of underground banking activities transactional data shared among banks) and better protect the entity sharing it with other members. Using the proper level of encryption is also vital to protect, transfer, and store confidential information. Dixon (2019) notes that new tools and platforms using technology such as homomorphic encryption is needed. Such tools will help protect victims' organizations and enable global investigations while also respecting the right to privacy. More specifically, advanced analytics, privacy-preserving capabilities, and machine-learning capabilities over combined data should be explored further (San Juan Menacho and Martin 2018).

Conclusion

As seen previously, underground banking allows individuals to move funds without going through official banking channels, and it has been used for a long time. However, only recently has Canada started to see major criminal cases that leverage underground banking. The money laundering schemes revealed by these investigations are not necessarily new, as the cases were rarely prioritized until recently. However, they do have real world economic and social effects. With the evolution of their modus operandi, numerous criminal networks are investing in real estate, and cities like Vancouver and Toronto have seen skyrocketing real estate prices. Following these events, the Cullen Commission was set up, through which journalists, experts from government authorities, and scholars have proposed different solutions. One solution that could allow Canada to be a leader in the fight against money laundering, and limiting the illicit underground banking system, would be to implement a countrywide public-private partnership involving financial institutions, FINTRAC, the RCMP, and other strategic stakeholders in the fight against money laundering to support information-sharing between the relevant participants. Some initiatives are ongoing with the investment of the RCMP in money laundering in British Columbia with the new CIFA-BC. However, it is still limited and more needs to be done to improve the efficacy of anti-money laundering measures in Canada. Machine-learning capabilities and privacy enhancement tools should be utilized to analyze money laundering patterns more accurately and to share information securely among anti-money laundering professionals, government, and law enforcement. Public-private information-sharing partnerships are relatively new worldwide. They still need to improve their structure and processes, but several benefits are already identifiable in preventing and detecting crimes such as money laundering, tax evasion, and human trafficking (Chadderton and Norton 2019; Maxwell 2019; RUSI 2019). Through such partnerships, operating at both the provincial and federal levels, the Canadian anti-money laundering regime would immensely gain by significantly reducing underground banking money laundering schemes and deterring professional money launderers from laundering funds in Canada.

Notes

1 https://www.rcmp-grc.gc.ca/en/news/2019/collecteur-project-a-vast-money-laundering-network-dismantled.
2 https://www.fintrac-canafe.gc.ca/intel/operation/casino-eng.
3 A UK fraud prevention service.

References

Amicelle, A. and V. Lafolla. 2017. "Reporting Suspicion in Canada: Insights from the Fight Against Money Laundering and Terrorist Financing." Working Paper, TSAS Canadian Network for Research on Terrorism, Security, and Society.

Austin, A. 2021. "Black Market Peso Exchange Evolving in the United States." *Insight Crime,* 26 January 2021. https://insightcrime.org/news/analysis/black-market-peso-exchange-us/.

AUSTRAC. 2021. "Fintel Alliance." https://www.austrac.gov.au/about-us/fintel-alliance.

Brecher, A. 2018. "Money Laundering Through the Black Market Peso Exchange." Target Letter. Development in Compliance & Enforcement, 12 June 2018. https://www.targetletterlaw.com/2018/06/12/money-laundering-through-the-black-market-peso-exchange/.

Cassara, J. 2016. "'Flying Money' May Land in U.S.: Is Chinese Money Laundering 'Flying' into Real Estate?" Banking Exchange, 21 February 2016. https://www.bankingexchange.com/news-feed/item/6079-flying-money-may-land-in-u-.

Chadderton, P. and S. Norton. 2019. "Public-Private Partnerships to Disrupt Financial Crime: An Exploratory Study of Australia's FINTEL Alliance." Swift Institute Working Paper No. 2017-003.

Chau, D., and M. Van Dijck Nemcsik. 2021. *Anti-Money Laundering Transaction Monitoring Systems Implementation: Finding Anomalies.* Hoboken, NJ: John Wiley & Sons, Inc.

Cooper, S. 2017. "Exclusive: How B.C. Casinos Are Used to Launder Millions in Drug Cash." https://vancouversun.com/news/national/exclusive-how-b-c-casinos-are-used-to-launder-millions-in-drug-cash.

———. 2021. "Ottawa Must Crack Down on Toronto Underground Banks, Community Leaders Say." *Global News,* January 27, 2021. https://globalnews.ca/news/7593255/ottawa-must-crack-down-on-toronto-underground-banks-community-leaders-say/.

Cooper, S., and S. Bell. 2019. "Toronto Man Arrested with $1M in Cash May Have Ties to International Money Launderer. Now, He's Allegedly Fled Canada." *Global News,* February 28, 2019. https://globalnews.ca/news/4949475/toronto-man-arrested-1m-cash-international-money-launderer-fled-canada/.

Cullen Commission, A. 2020. "Commission of Inquiry into Money Laundering in British Columbia. Interim Report." https://cullencommission.ca/com-rep/.

Dixon, W. 2019. "Fighting Cybercrime – What Happens to the Law When the Law Cannot Be Enforced?" https://www.weforum.org/agenda/2019/02/fightingcybercrime-what-happens-to-the-law-when-the-law-cannot-be-enforced/.

Financial Action Task Force (FATF). 2013. "The Role of Hawala and Other Similar Service Providers in Money Laundering and Terrorist Financing." FATF, Paris. https://www.fatf-gafi.org/media/fatf/documents/reports/Role-of-hawala-and-similar-in-ml-tf.pdf.

———. 2016. "Money or Value Transfer Services." FATF, Paris. https://www.fatf-gafi.org/media/fatf/documents/reports/guidance-rba-money-value-transfer-services.pdf.

———. 2018. "Professional Money Laundering." FATF, Paris. https://www.fatf-gafi.org/media/fatf/documents/Professional-Money-Laundering.pdf.

Financial Transactions and Reports Analysis Centre of Canada (FINTRAC). 2019. "Operational Alert: Laundering the Proceeds of Crime Through a Casino-Related Underground Banking Scheme." FINTRAC, Ottawa. https://fintrac-canafe.canada.ca/intel/operation/casino-eng.pdf.

Genesis, M. 2018. "A Guidance to Understand Hawala and to Establish the Nexus with Terrorist Financing." ACAMS, Miami. https://www.acams.org/en/resources/aml-white-papers/white-papers#alternative-remitters-d009653b.

German, P. 2018. "Dirty Money: An Independent Review of Money Laundering in Lower Mainland Casinos Conducted for the Attorney General of British Columbia." Peter German & Associates Inc. https://cullencommission.ca/files/Gaming_Final_Report.pdf.

———. 2019. "Dirty Money – Part 2: Turning the Tide - An Independent Review of Money Laundering in B.C. Real Estate, Luxury Vehicle Sales & Horse Racing." Peter German & Associates Inc. https://icclr.org/wp-content/uploads/2019/06/Dirty_Money_Report_Part_2.pdf?x94276.

Government of Canada. 2019. "Money Laundering Scheme: Enforcement Measures Taken by the Canada Revenue Agency in a Joint Investigation with the Royal Canadian Mounted Police." February 12, 2019. Montreal. https://www.canada.ca/en/revenue-agency/news/newsroom/20190212-money-laundering-scheme-enforcement-measures-cra-joint-investigation-rcmp.html.

Gräbner, C., W. Elsner, and A. Lascaux. 2020. *Trust and Social Control: Sources of Cooperation, Performance, and Stability in Information Value Transfer Systems*. Springer. https://doi.org/10.1007/s1061 4-020-09994-0.

Joint Money Laundering Intelligence Taskforce (JMLIT). n.d. "Public-Private Information-Sharing Partnerships to Tackle Money Laundering in the Finance Sector." https://thecommonwealth.org/sites/default/files/inline/4%20UK%20approach%20to%20public-private%20partnerships.pdf.

Makhani, R. 2018. "Informal Value Transfer Systems, Money Laundering, and the Financing of Terrorism: Canada's Response to The Threat." University of The Fraser Valley. https://core.ac.uk/download/pdf/236976995.pdf.

Maxwell, N. 2019. "Expanding the Capability of Financial Information-Sharing Partnership." Royal United Services Institute for Defence and Security Studies. https://rusi.org/sites/default/files/20190320_expanding_the_capability_of_financial_information-sharing_partnerships_web.pdf.

———. 2021. "Case Studies of the Use of Privacy-Preserving Analysis to Tackle Financial Crime." Future of Financial Intelligence Sharing (FFIS) Research Program. https://ag-pssg-sharedservices-ex.objectstore.gov.bc.ca/ag-pssg-cc-exh-prod-bkt-ex/413%20-%20FFIS%20Case%20Studies%20of%20the%20Use%20of%20Privacy%20Preserving%20Analysis%20-%20January%208%202021.pdf.

McCusker, R. 2005. "Underground Banking: Legitimate Remittance Network or Money Laundering System?" *Trends & Issues in Crime & Criminal Justice* 300: 1–6.

National Crime Agency. n.d. "Improving the U.K.'s Response to Economic Crime." https://www.nationalcrimeagency.gov.uk/what-we-do/national-economic-crime-centre.

Passas, N. 1999. "Informal Value Transfer Systems and Criminal Organizations: A Study into So-called Underground Banking Networks." https://papers.ssrn.com/sol3/papers.cfm?abstract_id=1327756.

Pomerleau, P.L. 2019a. *Countering the Cyber Threats Against Financial Institutions in Canada: A Qualitative Study of a Private and Public Partnership Approach to Critical Infrastructure Protection.* ProQuest Dissertations & Theses Global (2320957957).

———. 2019b. "Public-Private Partnerships: Port Security." In *Encyclopedia of Security and Emergency Management*, edited by L. Shapiro, and M.-H. Maras. Cham: Springer.

Pomerleau, P. L. and D. Lowery. 2020. *Countering the Cyber-Threats to Financial Institutions.* New York: Palgrave Macmillan.

Pomerleau P. L. and M. Auger-Perreault. 2020. "Fraud Risk Management: Using Fraud Analytics to Combat External and Insider Threats." In *Encyclopedia of Security and Emergency Management*, edited by L. Shapiro, and M. H. Maras. Cham: Springer.

Report to the Standing Committee on Finance. 2018. "Confronting Money Laundering and Terrorist Financing: Moving Canada Forward." 42nd Parliament, 1st Session. Ottawa: House of Commons. https://www.ourcommons.ca/DocumentViewer/en/42-1/FINA/report-24/.

Royal Canadian Mounted Police (RCMP). 2019. "Collecteur Project: A Vast Money Laundering Network Dismantled." February 12, 2019. Montreal. https://www.rcmp-grc.gc.ca/en/news/2019/collecteur-project-a-vast-money-laundering-network-dismantled.

———. 2020. "New Public-Private Partnership to Combat Money Laundering in British Columbia." December 16, 2020. British Columbia.https://www.grc-rcmp.gc.ca/en/news/2019/royal-canadian-mounted-police-announces-public-private-sector-partnership-fight-money

Royal United Services Institute Centre for Financial Crime and Security Studies (RUSI). 2019. "The Future of Financial Intelligence Sharing (FFIS)." Conference of Partnerships RUSI, October 11. Amsterdam. https://www.future-fis.com/uploads/3/7/9/4/3794525/ffis_2019_conference_of_partnerships_-_conference_report.pdf.

San Juan Menacho, V., and A. Martin. 2018. "Cyber Governance and the Financial Services Sector: The Role of Public-Private Partnerships." https://osf.io/preprints/socarxiv/ybqgm/.

Schneider, S. 2020. "Money Laundering in British Columbia: A Review of the Literature." https://ag-pssg-sharedservices-ex.objectstore.gov.bc.ca/ag-pssg-cc-exh-prod-bkt-ex/6%20-%20Money%20Laundering%20in%20BC%20-%20A%20Review%20of%20the%20Literature.pdf.

Sen, A. 2020. "Pulling the Plug on Money Laundering in British Columbia, Canada: Lessons Learned and Action Required." http://www.roycullen.com/Amartya_Sen_Essay_Contest_2020_final.pdf.

Sheptycki, J (2004). Organizational Pathologies in Police Intelligence Systems-Some Contributions to the Lexicon of Intelligence-led Policing in the European Journal of Criminology issue.

Simser, J. 2020. "Canada's Financial Intelligence Unit: FINTRAC." *Journal of Money Laundering Control* 23, no. 2: 297–307.

Smart, A. 2020. "Canada's Vulnerable to Money Laundering on Par with Similar Countries: Expert." *National Post*, May 28, 2020. https://nationalpost.com/pmn/news-pmn/canada-news-pmn/canadas-vulnerable-to-money-laundering-on-par-with-similar-countries-expert.

Teichmann, F. 2020. "Weaknesses of Underground Banking Systems." Springer Nature Switzerland AG 2020. https://link.springer.com/chapter/10.1007/978-3-030-39319-9_55.

Teichmann, F., and M. Falker. 2020. "Money Laundering via Underground Currency Exchange Networks." *Journal of Financial Regulation and Compliance* 29, no. 1: 1–14.

The Combined Forces Special Enforcement Unit. 2017. "Multiple Arrests Stemming from a Nearly Year-Long CFSEU-BC JIGIT Investigation into Organized Crime." https://cfseu.bc.ca/multiple-arrests-stemming-from-a-nearly-year-long-cfseu-bc-jigit-investigation-into-organized-crime/

Todd, D. 2020. Douglas Todd: Underground banking impacts us all. Vancouver Sun, September 24, 2020. https://vancouversun.com/opinion/columnists/douglas-todd-underground-banking-is-global-and-it-affects-us-all

U.K. Finance. (2022). Information Fusion in the Fight Against Financial Crime. https://www.ukfinance.org.uk/news-and-insight/blogs/information-fusion-fight-against-financial-crime.

Young, I. 2019. "Chinese Cash Fuels Vast Luxury Car Money Laundering in Canada, Involving Thousands of Fake Buyers." *South China Morning Post*, May 8, 2019. https://www.scmp.com/news/china/money-wealth/article/3009330/chinese-cash-fuels-vast-luxury-car-laundering-scheme-canada.

Zhao, L. S. 2012. "Chinese Underground Banks and Their Connections with Crime: A Review and an Appraisal." *International Criminal Justice Review* 22, no. 1: 5–23.

10

Trade-Based Money Laundering: Vulnerabilities in British Columbia and Canada

John A. Cassara

Introduction

The Financial Action Task Force (FATF) has declared that there are three broad categories of hiding illicit funds and introducing them into the formal economy. The first is via the use of financial institutions; the second is to physically smuggle bulk cash from one country or jurisdiction to another; and the third is the transfer of value via trade, also known as trade-based money laundering (TBML; FATF 2006).[1] The international community has devoted attention, countermeasures, and resources to the first two categories. Over the last thirty years, the anti-money laundering/counter-terror financing (AML/CTF) community has concentrated countermeasures almost exclusively on money laundering through financial institutions. However, for the most part, TBML has been largely ignored by practitioners and academics alike. TBML could be the world's largest money laundering methodology. It is also the least understood, recognized, and enforced.

Historically, the United States and Canadian governments and the international community have not focused attention or resources on the misuse of international trade to launder money, transfer value, avoid taxes, commit commercial fraud, and finance terror. Common adversaries – terrorists, criminals, kleptocrats, and fraudsters – have been operating in these areas with almost total impunity. The trade-based methodologies almost completely avoided detection by our traditional FATF-centric AML/CTF countermeasures. And unfortunately, to this day, considering the tremendous expenditure of resources to counter illicit finance, TBML and value transfer still receive little recognition. Perhaps it is because the subterfuges are hiding in plain sight.

Because of its diversity and sometimes complexity, the magnitude of TBML is difficult to quantify. It has never been systematically examined. According to the U.S. State Department, TBML has reached "staggering" proportions in recent years. It is found in every country. In its primary form, TBML revolves around invoice fraud and associated manipulation of supporting documents.

The rapid expansion of worldwide trade increases the possibilities for TBML. Today, total annual global merchandise trade is in the tens of trillions of dollars. The large volume of trade masks the occasional suspect transfer.

TBML encompasses customs fraud, tax evasion, export incentive fraud, VAT fraud, capital flight or the transfer of wealth offshore, evading capital controls, barter trade, underground financial systems such as hawala and the fei-chien – the Chinese "flying money" system, black market exchanges, and commercial trade-based money laundering such as transfer pricing and abusive trade-mis-invoicing.

Many of the above affect British Columbia and Canada. There are tremendous losses of applicable taxes and duties. To this end, this chapter will define TBML, briefly discuss the magnitude of the problem, and give numerous examples of the challenges this "hidden in plain sight" money laundering methodology poses for customs and law enforcement. Effective enforcement is virtually nil. Countermeasures do exist. Yet there is reason for optimism. With a recent explosion of publicly available data and advanced analytics, trade transparency is theoretically achievable.

Definition of TBML

The FATF defines TBML as "the process of disguising the proceeds of crime and moving *value* through the use of trade transactions in an attempt to legitimize their illicit origins." (FATF 2006) The key word in the definition is *value*. Instead of following the money trail via bulk cash or the electronic bits and bytes of a bank-to-bank wire transfer, with TBML, the shipments of commodities and trade goods are the central foci. Their sale and transfer – real and fictitious – can launder money, evade taxes and tariffs, and transfer value between cooperating parties in the transaction(s).

Magnitude of the Problem

There are no known official estimates of the global or country-specific magnitude of TBML. Since the issue impacts national security, the integrity of the global financial system, law enforcement, and the collection of national revenue, it is remarkable that TBML has never been systematically examined. As a result, there are few available metrics. And as with other topics involving money laundering, the magnitude of TBML depends on what is included in the count.

According to the World Trade Organization (WTO), the amount of global merchandise trade varies annually but averages approximately $20 trillion (2016). The U.S. Department of the Treasury notes that TBML is one of the most challenging forms of money laundering to investigate because of the sheer volume of international trade and the complexities of trade transactions (Department of the Treasury 2015). In "traditional" money laundering, money launderers mix or "co-mingle" illicit funds with the by far overwhelming percentage of legitimate money moving around and through the world's financial institutions. The same holds true with international trade. It is very easy to hide the occasional suspect, illicit, or fraudulent trade transaction in the tens of trillions of dollars of annual global merchandise trade.

According to Raymond Baker, a worldwide authority on financial crime and founding president of Global Financial Integrity (GFI), "Trade mis-invoicing – a prevalent form of TBML – accounts for nearly 80 per cent of all illicit financial outflows [...] that can be measured by using available data." (GFI 2014).

A GFI report notes that global traders "deliberately falsify the stated prices on invoices for goods they are importing and exporting as a way to illicitly transfer value across international borders." This falsification may be done to evade taxes, launder money, avoid currency controls, or hide profits offshore. GFI estimates a total of $8.7 trillion has disappeared via trade between 135 developing and 36 developed countries between the years 2008–2017. Approximately $818 billion occurred in 2017 with trends currently approaching $1 trillion a year (GFI 2020b).

Examining 2021 data, John Zdanowicz (2022), one of the few scholars who analyzes trade data for potential trade mis-invoicing, found that approximately $784 billion was moved into the US via over-valued exports and under-valued imports. Approximately $640 billion was moved out of the US via undervalued exports and over-valued imports. He then compared those numbers to the overall value of US imports and exports. He found (depending on import or export) approximately 14 to 17 percent of US trade could well be tainted by customs fraud and perhaps TBML.[2]

The above has serious fiscal ramifications. Zdanowicz estimates that the U.S. Treasury could have lost about $640 billion of taxable profits due to trade-based tax evasion and TBML (SEK Strategies 2022). The same type of revenue loss occurs in Canada. Using a fair estimate that 10 percent of worldwide trade is infected with customs fraud (in some countries it is many multiples of that), using the above WTO estimate that means there is about $2 trillion in trade fraud annually. And that number is only based on customs fraud. TBML is much more than that.

A Variety of TBML Threats

TBML is found in every country in the world – both developed and developing. But the massive transfer of wealth offshore through abusive trade mis-invoicing is particularly harmful to countries with weak economies, high levels of corruption, and little adherence to the rule of law. The developmental, human, and societal costs are staggering.

One major component of trade-based value transfer that is garnering increased attention is illicit financial flows (IFFs). IFFs are defined by the World Bank as the "cross-border movement of capital associated with illegal activity or more explicitly, money that is illegally earned, transferred or used that crosses borders." (The World Bank 2017). In economics, IFFs are generally considered a form of illegal capital flight. Capital flight occurs when money (and value) leaves primarily developing countries. Traditional thought places the onus to solve the problem on the developing country or the country exporting the capital. The study of IFFs makes the case that the country that receives or imports the capital is also involved and bears responsibility. Trade mis-invoicing is the major component of IFFs (Cassara 2020).

IFFs have a destabilizing impact on governments and society. Individuals suffer. IFFs nurture corruption, undermine governance, and reduce tax revenues. Some of the crimes behind the illicit flows of cash undermine economies, destroy the environment, and jeopardize the health and well-being of the public. Other negative consequences of IFFs include

- delayed development,
- promoted unemployment,
- diversion of scarce resources,
- fostering unfair competition,
- abrogating the rule of law,
- catalyzing social and political instability and unrest, and
- exacerbating societal rivalries and competition states.

Another threat associated with TBML that is receiving increased attention is trade's use in underground financial systems, particularly "alternative remittance systems." This methodology has been with us for hundreds of years. Trade-based value transfer has existed long before the advent of modern "Western" banking. In some areas of the world, trade-based value transfer is part of a way of life. It is part of the culture; a way of doing business. Historically and culturally trade-based value transfer is also used in "counter-valuation" between brokers such as hawaladars. Hawala has figured prominently post September 11 as it has been linked to terror finance, the Afghan Transit Trade, Iran/Dubai commercial connections, the Tri-Border region in South America, suspect international Lebanese/Hezbollah trading syndicates, non-banked lawless regimes such as those in Somalia and Libya, contested territory in parts of Syria and Iraq, and Iranian sanctions busting. "Counter-valuation" is discussed in more detail in the chapter during a discussion of the Chinese-centric alternative remittance systems known as "flying money."

By examining other forms of TBML, the magnitude of the problem increases further. For example, TBML is also involved with customs fraud, tax evasion, export incentive fraud, VAT/carousel fraud, capital flight or the transfer of wealth offshore, evading capital controls, barter trade, underground financial systems such hawala and fei-chien, the black market peso exchange (BMPE), and even "commercial" TBML such as transfer pricing and abusive trade-mis-invoicing.

Including all its varied forms, the argument can be made that TBML and value transfer is the largest and most pervasive money laundering methodology in the world. Conversely, it is also the least understood, recognized, and enforced. In comparison to the trillions of dollars in international general merchandise trade, successful TBML enforcement efforts are practically nil.

How Does TBML Work?

In its primary form, TBML revolves around invoice fraud and the associated manipulation of supporting documents. When a buyer and seller work together, the price of goods (or services) can be whatever the parties want it to be: There is no invoice police. As Raymond Baker succinctly notes, "Anything that can be priced can be mispriced. False pricing is done every day, in every country, on a large percentage of import and export transactions. This is the most commonly used technique for generating and transferring dirty money" (Baker 2005).

TBML often involves varied and sometimes elaborate schemes employed by fraudsters and criminal organizations to ensure their trades appear legitimate or unsuspicious. It is important to understand that the primary techniques involve invoice fraud and manipulation. They include

- over-and-under invoicing of goods and services,
- multiple invoicing of goods and services, and
- falsely described goods and services.

Other common techniques related to the above include:

- Short shipping: this occurs when the exporter ships fewer goods than the invoiced quantity of goods thus misrepresenting the true value of the goods in the documentation. The effect of this technique is similar to over-invoicing.

- Over shipping: the exporter ships more goods than what is invoiced thus misrepresenting the true value of the goods in the documentation. The effect is similar to under invoicing.

- Phantom shipping: No goods are actually shipped. The fraudulent documentation generated is used to justify payment abroad.

Invoice Fraud

Money laundering and value transfer through the over- and under-invoicing of goods and services is a common practice around the world. The key element of this technique is the misrepresentation of trade goods to transfer value between the importer and exporter or settle debts/balance accounts between the trading parties. The shipment (real or fictitious) of goods and the accompanying documentation provide cover for the transfer of money. Or sometimes the goods themselves are the transfer of value. Invoice fraud is generally considered customs fraud. Customs fraud is a specified unlawful activity (SUA) or predicate offense to charge money laundering. At the same time, TBML is sometimes a money-laundering methodology for SUAs.

One of the most common methods of invoice fraud is under-invoicing. By under-invoicing goods below their fair market price, an exporter is able to transfer value to an importer while avoiding the scrutiny associated with more direct forms of money transfer. The value the importer receives when selling (directly or indirectly) the goods on the open market is considerably greater than the amount he or she paid the exporter. Evasion of taxes and duties can also be a factor. Depending on the country or jurisdiction involved, tax evasion is also a SUA for money laundering.

For example, Company A located in Canada ships one million widgets worth $2 each to Company B based in Mexico. On the invoice, however, Company A lists the widgets at a price of only $1 each, and the Mexican importer pays the Canadian exporter only $1 million for them. Thus, extra value has been transferred to Mexico, where the importer can sell (directly or indirectly) the widgets on the open market for a total of $2 million. The Mexican company then has several options: it can keep the profits, transfer some of them to a bank account outside the country where the proceeds can be further laundered via layering and integration, share the proceeds with the Canadian exporter (depending on the nature of their relationship), or even transfer them to a criminal organization that may be the hidden actor behind the business transactions.

To transfer value in the opposite direction, an exporter can over-invoice goods above their fair market price. In this manner, the exporter receives value from the importer because the latter's payment is higher than the goods' actual value on the open market.

Invoice Manipulation Made Simple

To move money/value out:

- Import goods at overvalued prices or export goods at undervalued prices.
- To move money/value in:
- Import goods at undervalued prices or export goods at over-valued prices.

For example, Figure 10.1 below shows the fluctuating value associated with thousands of refrigerators exported from Country A to Country B via a series of shipments. The darker shade represents the declared value of the refrigerators upon export from Country A, and the light shade represents their declared value upon arrival in Country B. The horizontal line represents the time period over which these shipments occurred. The vertical line represents the value expressed in dollars. In this case the refrigerators

Figure 10.1: Fluctuating Value Associated with Thousands of Refrigerators Exported from Country A to Country B Via a Series of Shipments

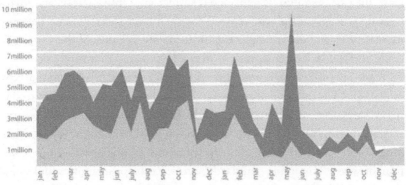

Note: At the end of the graph the shaded colors start to converge. The colors or values between imports and exports begin to match because data was compared, anomalies noted, and joint enforcement action taken by the two countries involved. Trade transparency was achieved. The comparative stability at the end of the chart reflects true market conditions.

were over-invoiced. The export data came from the "shippers export decla-ration" (SED) that accompanies the shipments. The import data came from the importing country's customs service. The declared export price should match the declared import price, taking into account there are some recog-nized but comparatively small pricing variables. In addition, the quantity and quality of refrigerators should also match – which occurred in this case. The difference in price between the dark and light shades represents the transfer of value from the importer to the exporter. In this case, the transfer represented the proceeds of narcotics trafficking.

There are incredible examples of trade mispricing. For example, Zdanowicz (2022) conducted a study analyzing US trade data. He found plastic buckets from the Czech Republic imported with the declared price of $972 per bucket. Toilet tissue from China is imported at the price of over $4,000 per kilogram. Bulldozers are being shipped to Colombia at $1.74 each. Of course, there are various reasons why the prices could be abnormal. For example, there could simply be data input or classifica-tion errors. However, recalling the above explanation of over-and-under invoicing, the abnormal prices could also represent attempts to transfer value in or out of the United States in the form of trade goods. At the very least, the prices should be considered suspicious. Only analysis and investigation will reveal the true reasons for such large discrepancies between market price and declared price. Unfortunately, because of the volume of trade and the lack of customs enforcement capacity that rarely occurs.

Trade mis-invoicing is widespread. According to GFI's Raymond Baker (2018): "The practice of trade mis-invoicing has become normalized in many categories of international trade. It is a major contributor to poverty, inequality, and insecurity in emerging market and developing economies. The social cost attendant to trade mis-invoicing undermines sustainable growth in living standards and exacerbates inequities and social divisions." TBML should be a tremendous global concern. Until there is a systematic focus on TBML overall AML/CTF efforts will continue to fail.

Service-Based Money Laundering (SBML)

Service-based money laundering is almost unknown in anti-money laundering enforcement. Like TBML, SBML revolves around invoice fraud and manipulation. But instead of laundering money or transferring value through trade goods, services are used. Common service-based laundering scams include accounting, legal, marketing, and natural resource exploration fees. Fraudulent construction costs, such as the mafia uses in Italy or those uncovered in Brazil's "Operation Car Wash" that spotlighted official corruption, is a common tactic (Cassara 2016). Software development, marketing surveys, professional fees, consulting, product promotion, etc. are other common "service" ruses.

The State Department's global anti-money laundering review (the annual INCSR report) cites one example of SBML where "offshore companies send fictitious bills to a Montenegrin company (for market research, consulting, software, leasing, etc.) for the purpose of extracting money from the company's account in Montenegro so funds can be sent abroad." (U.S. Department of State 2015). Fraudulent invoices generated from supposed concert promotions or other services that are difficult to quantify can be used to move illicit funds. Technical fees, such as writing computer code, add complexity to SBML schemes, and require investigators with specialized expertise.

Stopping SBML is no easy task. When investigating TBML, authorities can often track an item or a commodity, following a physical trail. For example, when a product is manufactured and sent from country A to country B, import and export data exist. Through analytics, authorities can discover anomalies that indicate customs fraud. The world-price norm of the trade good or commodity in question can be obtained. SBML, by contrast, leaves no physical commodity trail, and the value of the service on the invoice is almost always subjective.

Capital Flight and Underground Finance

According to a former Canadian Ambassador to Beijing, "China is the number one exporter of hot money to the world." (O'Brien n.d.) The exodus of capital has fueled worries about the Chinese economic outlook. Issues of concern include a China/US trade war, the plummeting Chinese stock market, fears of a real estate bubble, suspect loans and balance sheets by Chinese banks, fear of a currency devaluation, increasing debt, the theft of state funds by Chinese officials, paltry returns on savings accounts, the Covid-19 pandemic, the deteriorating situation in Hong Kong, and social unrest. Furthermore, as the Chinese government clamps down on corruption, savvy Chinese are transferring wealth out of the country (Cassara 2020).

From approximately 2006–2016, an estimated USD\$3.8 trillion in capital left China. Net foreign direct investment over the same period of time amounted to USD\$1.3 trillion, leaving the country with a net loss (Gunter 2017). In 2019, before the Covid-19 pandemic, China's hidden capital flight surged to a record high, suggesting that residents wanting to move money abroad are using unrecorded transactions to evade tight capital controls (*Bloomberg News* 2019).

Over recent years, the Chinese government/CCP has imposed capital controls on corporations and businesses, as well as its citizens. The

CCP has recently begun penalizing severe violators with jail time. Chinese citizens are restricted to sending the equivalent of approximately CAD$67,000 per person out of the country per year. So how does capital flee China? There are a number of methods by which capital can flee China, including

- tapping political and personal connections,
- using the transfer quotas of friends and family members to get money out of the country,
- channeling funds through gaming and junkets, particularly via Macau,
- using the special relationship with Hong Kong that serves as a financial conduit to the rest of the world,
- obtaining special financial services offered to the elites,
- trade-based value transfer, and
- underground financial systems.

Capital flight poses a few important questions and issues regarding illicit financial flows and money laundering:

1. Massive amounts of capital leave China. Is illicit money co-mingled with legitimate money?
2. Does China consider capital flight over the reporting threshold money laundering? If so, is that designation reciprocal in the receiving country?
3. For the US, Canada, and most other countries, receiving foreign capital is legal. In fact, it is often encouraged. However, money laundering could occur if the foreign capital includes the proceeds of crime or if it is used to further criminal activity in the destination country.
4. While the influx of capital can be helpful, it can also distort local markets, cause inflationary pressure, act as the catalyst for social disruption, distort local markets, create undue influence, etc.

Similar to Canada, locales in the United States have received an influx of foreign cash that has been channeled into the purchase of real estate. A report by the U.S. National Association of Realtors found that almost 60 percent of purchases by international clients are made in cash (Transparency International 2017). The average purchase price of residential housing by Chinese in the United States is $1 million (National Association of Realtors 2022). According to the Association, Chinese buyers have been the top foreign buyers in the United States both in units and dollar volume of residential housing for six years straight. There is also an increasing amount of investment interest by middle-class Chinese buyers. California is a favourite market for Chinese buyers as are Texas, Georgia, and Florida (Olick 2019). In the United States, there is little, if any, customer due diligence by real estate agents. US real estate agents are exempted from reporting suspicious transactions. It is not a coincidence that in 2019, the real estate lobby in the United States spent nearly USD$90 million dollars. There are nearly 600 registered real estate lobbyists (Open Secrets 2019).

Turning to Canada, the "Vancouver Model" of money laundering, was coined to capture when large amounts of money are taken out of China through informal value transfer systems and other means to avoid China's limits on money leaving the country. Once in British Columbia, the funds are sometimes mixed with cash from the drug trade and perhaps other illicit proceeds of crime, and then the cash is cleaned through BC casinos and private mortgages. The Vancouver Model thus involves capital flight, TBML, underground financial systems such as "flying money," and money laundering via real estate and other means.[3]

According to the 2008 FATF Mutual Evaluation Report (MER) on China, there are four primary means of laundering money: (1) via banks, (2) via bulk cash smuggling, (3) TBML and (4) the underground banking system. (FATF 2007). Points 3 and 4 are intertwined because invoice manipulation and trade fraud are commonly used in underground finance. Of note, the above was not discussed in the recent 2019 FATF MER on China nor was China's role as the major player in various forms of transnational crime, undermining the most recent MER's credibility (Cassara 2020).

Alternative Remittance Systems (ARS)

ARS are sometimes also called "underground banking," "parallel banking," or "informal value transfer systems." Occasionally everything is erroneously labelled "hawala" – an ARS found throughout the world with origins in the Middle East and South Asia. These informal channels operate outside of the ironically labelled "traditional" channels. It's ironic because for most of the migrants involved, the alternatives to Western-style or formal remittances are very traditional for them.

The following is a partial list of worldwide underground remittance systems. The names vary based on a number of factors including geographical locations and ethnic groups:

- Hawala – India, Afghanistan, Africa, the Middle East, Gulf, parts of the Americas
- Hundi – Pakistan, Bangladesh
- Undiyal – Sri Lanka
- Havaleh – Iran
- Door-to-door/padala – the Philippines
- Black market currency exchanges – Nigeria, South America, Iran
- Stash houses/casas de cambio – Latin America
- Phoei kuan – Thailand (Teochew Chinese)
- Hui kuan – China – (Mandarin Chinese)
- Fei-chien – "flying money," China
- Ch'iao hui – overseas remittances – (Mandarin Chinese)
- Chop shop – foreigners sometimes use this term to describe a Chinese system
- Chiti-banking – refers to the "chit" used for receipt or proof of claim in transactions; introduced by the British in China.

The two largest ARS are hawala (and its various sister systems such as hundi and undiyal) and the Chinese fei-chien or flying money (and related schemes). They are both global in scope. While there are no reliable estimates as to the magnitude of these two ARS, both are likely responsible for hundreds of billions of dollars in unregulated (and non-taxed) money transfers a year.[4] All of these systems operate in the same general way (described below). Another common denominator is that historically and culturally most of these underground financial systems or ARS use trade-based value transfer as a mechanism to settle accounts or balance the books between brokers.

Chinese underground financial methods or alternative remittance systems are primarily used to remit wages from the Chinese diaspora back to the homeland. Of course, authorities have no wish to interfere with hard-working immigrants sending money back to their home country to help support family. On the other hand, unfortunately, these low-cost and efficient financial systems and networks are also abused by criminals to move, transfer, and launder illicit proceeds. They are attractive because by their very nature they are opaque. Underground financial systems avoid government scrutiny, taxes, and countermeasures such as the filing of financial intelligence.

It is believed that fei-chien, i.e., flying money, was invented during the T'ang Dynasty (618–907 AD). At the time, there was a growing commodity trade within China. Some historians believe it was the rice and tea trades that were the catalysts for the new financial system (Trigler 2022). Ironically, as opposed to modern-day practice, the transfer schemes were not invented as an underground method of evading the grasp of authorities but rather as a tool by the government to facilitate taxation.

Over the centuries, the system continued to evolve. Chinese workers increasingly began to migrate to other provinces and then overseas. Their families at home needed financial support. Expatriate Chinese businesses began to develop side businesses of remitting money back to China. The international Chinese diaspora spread the indigenous financial system further still. Today, modern Chinese businesses as well as "Chinatowns" and "China shops" are found around the world. So is flying money.

Strong Chinese family bonds are incorporated into "guanxi," which is an overarching social system of rules that govern relationships and social behaviour. Guanxi is the guarantor of both secrecy and the integrity of the parties to the transaction. Those who violate its prescriptions find themselves a social outcast, essentially shunned in all circles. Guanxi is an integral component of fei-chien. In other words, similar to hawala and other indigenous informal value transfer systems, an essential element of fei-chien is trust.

The following is a hypothetical example to illustrate how flying money and TBML overlap and how it impacts British Columbia: Wang in Guangdong province wants to send 500,000 Chinese yuan renminbi (RMB) to his brother in Victoria, BC. (We will assume in this example that the money is from legitimate sources. The funds just as easily could be from the proceeds of criminal activity). Wang wants to protect his hard-earned money by investing in Canadian dollars and Canada. It is capital flight. Wang gives a Guangdong flying money broker the RMB and in turn, receives a code number. He trusts the broker as they have a familial relationship. The flying money broker in Guangdong directs his counterpart in Victoria (perhaps a member of the same family) to pay the equivalent in Canadian dollars (approximately $94,500) – less small commissions at both ends – upon presentation of the code. The code could be transferred via a telephone call or a message contained in an email or, for example, the Chinese messaging system, WeChat. Upon receipt, the Victoria flying money broker pays Wang's brother. The money did not physically leave China. The money paid was Canadian dollars controlled by the Victoria flying money broker.

Money and value are also sent back to China. Like all immigrant groups, Chinese citizens send money back home to help support their families. The same brokers are involved. Even though flying money largely operates on trust, family, clan, and community ties, the brokers are in business to make money. Occasionally they must settle accounts. Transactions go both directions. Using the above example, the Victoria broker might be running a deficit or a surplus with his counterpart in Guangdong. Various methods are used to settle accounts including banks, cash couriers, online payment services, and trade-based value transfers.

Surplus credits could also be used by a client unrelated to the original transaction/s. For example, credits could be used for the purchase of real estate in Victoria. For a fee, the client that wants money outside China pays RMB in China to a flying money broker and receives credit in the desired foreign location in local currency.

Another popular method of getting RMB out of China involves finding a foreign contact who would like to set up a private exchange for Chinese yuan. Flying money networks are sometimes used but so are informal personal networks and business associates. For instance, a person in Victoria puts their dollars into an account in Hong Kong belonging to the Chinese individual that wants money out of the country. The Chinese individual in China puts the equivalent in Chinese yuan into an account in China that is connected with the Victoria-based investor who wants the money in China.

What is often overlooked is that trade continues to be involved with the settling of accounts. This little understood concept was identified in the FATF mutual evaluation of China quoted above. Most flying money brokers are directly involved or associated with trading companies. As described earlier, invoice fraud and manipulation are employed – particularly over-and-under invoicing.

For example, a Chinese criminal gang based in British Columbia wants to send illicit proceeds back to China. Working with an intermediary, Chinese manufactured goods are sent to British Columbia. The goods are over-invoiced. Payment is made for the trade goods and the extra funds (over-invoiced) represent illicit proceeds laundered. Customs and law enforcement officials are hard pressed to recognize or counter this type of scheme.

Although commissions are paid to the brokers at both ends of the transaction, the commissions are less than banks or traditional money remitters such as Western Union charge. In comparison to large brick-and-mortar banks and money transfer chains, expenses are small. The brokers use legitimate businesses as fronts such as restaurants, "China shops," and trading companies. Of course, in the underground remittance segment of their business, they skirt regulations and taxes. In the United States, flying money brokers are technically classified as a money service business for the purposes of registration, licensing, and reporting financial intelligence. They do not comply, and it is rarely enforced.

Trade Finance

The physical shipment of trade goods involves a purchaser and a seller but can also include many more parties to the transaction, including shipping companies, insurance companies, port and terminal operators, freight forwarders, and customs agents in both the exporting and importing countries. The financial component involves the purchaser and seller and their respective financial institutions, and the payment for the transaction is settled on agreed-upon terms. This component is generally called "trade finance" (The Wolfsberg Group 2019).

Transactions whereby a bank provides some form of financing to a party in the transaction, such as a letter of credit, are referred to as "documentary transactions." In these transactions, banks generally process documentation involved in the trade transaction, such as the bill of lading, invoice, or packing list. The trade finance officer in the bank reviews the information underlying the transaction for soundness. The document review is undertaken to verify the trustworthiness of the transaction and also to see if there are any red flags or indicators of money laundering. If something suspicious is uncovered, the concerned financial institution may forward a Suspicious Transaction Report (STR) to the Financial Transactions and Reports Analysis Centre of Canada (FINTRAC).

It appears FINTRAC has not released the number of TBML-related STRs. However, there is a gaping hole in US Suspicious Activity Report (SAR) reporting covering TBML. The United States Financial Crimes Enforcement Network (FinCEN) found financial institutions had filed 7,044 SARs related to TBML from 2014 to 2018, including 1,673 in 2018. While that is a substantial number, FinCEN officials also noted that the number of TBML-related trade finance SARs is a very small portion of the total of 9.6 million SARs it received over the same period (General Accountability Office 2020). Combating TBML via the filing of STRs involving trade finance is not the panacea that many believe.

One of the primary vulnerabilities of financial and trade systems is "open account trade," in which the transaction is not financed by a bank. In open-account trade, the financial transaction between the buyer and seller – which underpins the trade transaction – is usually processed through a bank's automatic payment systems. There is no human review or intervention. As a result, the financial institution has limited visibility into the underlying reason for the payment.

According to The Wolfsberg Group, 80 percent of international trade that is processed through financial institutions is open-account trade (2019). Banks generally do not review documentation such as invoices, bills of lading, or customs. Financial institutions generally apply standard automated AML compliance processes and procedures, including sanctions screening, when processing payments for open account trade transactions. Thus, a bank's ability to recognize indications of possible TBML is limited for open-account transactions.

Countermeasures and US Approach to Fighting TBML

After 9/11, the US government spent an incredible amount of resources looking in many of the wrong places for terrorist assets while almost ignoring indigenous methods terrorists and their facilitators used to launder money, transfer value, and finance terror. Many of these revolved around trade. Trade analysis could be a "back door" into some of the underground financial networks.

In 2004, the United States government, specifically Homeland Security Investigations (HSI), created the world's first trade transparency unit (TTU).[5] The initiative seeks to identify global TBML trends and conduct ongoing analysis of trade data provided through partnerships with other countries. One of the most effective ways to identify instances and patterns of TBML is through the exchange and subsequent analysis of trade data. Anomalies can often be spotted by examining both sides of a trade transaction – resulting in "trade transparency."

A TTU is formed when HSI and a United States trading partner agree to formalize the exchange of trade data for the purpose of data identification, comparison, and analysis. The goal is trade transparency. The prerequisite for the TTU agreement is a "customs-to-customs" agreement, treaty, or memorandum of understanding.

The benefit of the TTU initiative is that the data already exists. There is no need for vast new expenditures or to struggle through labyrinths of bureaucratic hoops and approvals. Every country in the world has a customs service and already collects import and export data and associated information. Moreover, there has been an explosion of commercially available trade data over the last few years (see below). To help analyze the data, HSI has developed specialized software called the Data Analysis and Research for Trade Transparency System (DARTTS). Analysts and agents use DARTTS to examine trade and other data to generate leads for HSI investigations. DARTTS incorporates trade data (US imports and exports) reported to Customs and Border Protection (CBP) and financial data (such as SARs and CTRs) reported to FinCEN. The TTU also receives and disseminates targeted import and export data from its counterparts in partner countries. The system allows users to see both sides of a trade transaction or a series of trade transactions at a macro level, making it transparent to both countries. The concept is illustrated in Figure 10.1 previously explained above. Added value is created by overlaying financial intelligence, travel data, business registrations, and other data sets. As a result, TTUs can easily identify trade anomalies that could be indicative of customs fraud, TBML, contraband smuggling, tax evasion, and even underground finance. Once the macro anomalies have been identified, customs and law enforcement can drill down further to the micro level and identify the individual parties involved. Of course, investigations at the street and port levels are generally still required.

The TTU investigative tool has proven to be effective. As of 2015, the small TTU network seized well over $1 billion of assets.[6] In 2020, the U.S. General Services Administration conducted a Congressionally mandated review of the program (GAO 2020). While all agree the TTU concept is good, there have been numerous issues with its management and implementation (GAO 2020). The primary obstacle is that the TTU program has not been a priority for HSI.

Many countries are not interested in TBML; they are interested in combating trade fraud because it results in revenue. Governments around the world are increasingly cash-strapped and looking for new revenue streams. In the United States before the 1913 ratification of the 16th amendment to the United States Constitution that established Congress' right to establish a national income tax, the US government depended on customs duties for the majority of its national revenue. The same holds true today in many countries. Income tax systems can be rife with abuse, evasion, and corruption. Hence countries are examining ways to increase customs duties and taxes. Countries express interest in trade transparency and TTUs not necessarily to combat TBML but to crack down on trade fraud and enhance revenue. In the process of identifying customs fraud and increasing revenue, authorities also gain intelligence into TBML schemes and networks. It is a win/win.

As of 2020 there were seventeen operational TTUs in the international network. Most are in the Western hemisphere. Canada is not a member. There is a 1987 memorandum of understanding between the United States and Canada governing the exchange of primarily import data between the two countries. The data exchange occurs at the macro level. While helpful for monitoring trade, the information being exchanged does not have the necessary specificity or the requisite export information that is needed to combat TBML and value transfer. In the "next frontier of international money laundering enforcement," a global TTU network should be created that is somewhat analogous to the Egmont Group of Financial Intelligence Units.[7] (There are approximately 167 FIUs in the Egmont Group network).

Data and Technology

There is still ample room for applying data, analytics, and technological advances to combat TBML. By using state-of-the-art data and technology, international trade transparency is theoretically achievable or certainly possible at a factor many times over what exists today.

For example, in the above discussion of TTUs, it is apparent that monitoring trade data and associated international information such as travel, finance, shipping, logistics, insurance, and more generate tremendous amounts of data that can be applied to promote trade transparency. Web analytics and web crawling alone can search shipping companies and customs websites to review shipment details and compare them against their corresponding documentation. Advanced analytics can also be deployed to develop unit price analysis, unit weight analysis, shipment and route analysis, international trade and country profile analysis, and relationship analysis of trade partners and ports (PwC 2015).[8] And, of course, there is also classified data that could be better exploited to examine certain questionable aspects of trade and nefarious actors.

Each country has its own unique customs and other government services that track myriad trade, import, and export data at both the macro and micro levels. This data is generally considered law enforcement/ customs sensitive. It is generally not in the public domain. However, over recent years, more and more trade data are being released. Trade information is developed and circulated. Public and private sources of material have resulted in an explosion of trade data that is available – often for a fee. Much of the data is macro-oriented. It is often not possible to obtain granular information such as the identifiers of individual traders and shippers. Yet sometimes through analysis, that very information can be extrapolated.

Some publicly available trade data sources are the United Nations Comtrade database, Datamyne, PIERS, Import Genius, Panjiva, Tradessparq, WiserTrade, Infodrive India, and SICEX. In addition, Dr. John Zdanowicz offers International Trade Alert, and GFI offers GFTrade for trade price anomaly detection based on world norm trade price analysis and related information.

Many experts believe that distributed ledger technology (DLT) such as blockchain represents great promise in detecting and preventing trade mis-invoicing – the biggest component of TBML. There are three possible techniques: (1) comparing invoices against each other, (2) comparing invoices against the generally accepted market price/s, and (3) comparing values declared to customs with the values in the financial transactions (Peters 2020).

In the first option, customs authorities and other relevant "smart" partners could use the information available on a DLT platform to compare the invoice submitted by the exporter to the invoice submitted by the importer. The analytic platform could compare the two documents, adjusting for "cost, insurance and freight" (CIF) and "free on board" (FOB) differences. Most countries report imports on a CIF basis, whereas most exports are reported using the FOB valuation. This CIF/FOB conversion is one of the many challenges in analyzing trade data, along with transshipment and re-export complexities. The import and export invoice comparison would allow customs on both sides to identify mis-invoicing and charge the correct export or import duties. However, this comparison would not identify "same-invoice faking" where trading partners agree to report the same false value on invoices. Hence the need for the second comparison option.

The next option would be for customs authorities and smart partners to compare invoices against the generally accepted market price/s for that product. GFI's GFTrade already uses this technique to compare the invoice value with what that same product is trading for, based on updated official government data from forty-three countries.[9] This allows customs authorities to identify possible trade mis-invoicing even while the shipment is still in port. Correct duties can then be levied.

A third option, if applicable, is to have DLT compare the invoices presented to customs with the values sent to the financial institutions involved in the letter of credit process. This option means that customs authorities and other partners participating in the DLT platform, such as customs and tax authorities, could compare the letter of credit and the invoices to verify that they match. If not, payment of the correct customs duties would be required for release.

There are already prototypes for some of the above. In 2018, the United States CBP piloted a proof-of-concept assessment to evaluate the application of blockchain technology to the process of submitting documents for cargo entry. As noted, blockchain allows different users to make transactions and then creates an unchangeable, secure record of those transactions. DLT, including blockchain, share and verify information across many or multiple devices to increase transparency, reduce the risk of tampering, and remove the need for a trusted third party. The goal of the CBP assessment is to prove that a standards-based, fully digital system could be created to replace the existing paper-based system. Manual document handling is insecure, facilitates fraud, and slows logistics. Hopefully, the new technology will improve auditability, increase transparency, and more clearly identify suppliers and manufacturers, which could help better identify fraudulent documentation and assist with trade transparency (GAO 2019).

In 2018, Maersk and IBM announced the creation of a new platform – TradeLens – to provide more efficient and secure methods for conducting global trade that also uses blockchain technology. The platform is intended to provide timely end-to-end supply-chain visibility for businesses and authorities along the supply chain. It will enable regulatory and customs authorities to closely monitor the flow of goods, carry out risk assessments, and perform regulatory processing in an efficient manner, thereby reducing the risk of illicit activity, including TBML. TradeLens is an interconnected ecosystem of supply chain partners – cargo owners, ocean and inland carriers, freight forwarders and logistics providers, ports and terminals, customs authorities, regulators, and more. TradeLens runs on a permission matrix and blockchain, ensuring every party to a shipment has access only to their information and a secure audit trail of all transactions (GAO 2019).[10]

The newest generation of "smart" shipping containers also hold promise in combatting TBML. Studies show that a single shipping transaction involves an average of twenty-eight different entities including ports, forwarders, carriers and customs agencies (Sok 2017). Smart containers offer real-time monitoring anywhere in the world of a container's location, its internal conditions, and physical integrity. The new technology features access controls so each container remains sealed until the shipper authorizes the opening of each container. The data generated for each container can also provide customs agencies with an additional tool to identify safe containers that qualify for expedited clearance.

While an international TTU network, increased data, robust analytics, blockchain technology, smart containers, and other countermeasures are certainly not going to solve the diversity of TBML challenges, widespread use will definitely assist law enforcement and customs. The larger question is whether or not policymakers want to move in the direction of international trade transparency.

TBML Vulnerabilities in Canada and British Columbia

Canada is not immune to current threats from TBML. As discussed, there are many different typologies related to TBML. A study of customs fraud and related invoice manipulation would show that the problem is serious, widespread, and results in substantial revenue loss for Canada and its provinces. Likewise, while little data or case examples (see below on why this needs to be resolved) are available, Chinese capital flight to Canada linked to trade-based value transfer merits scrutiny as does Chinese underground financial systems such as flying money.

A further TBML methodology that should concern Canadian authorities is the black market peso exchange (BMPE). The BMPE is one of the largest money laundering methodologies in the Western Hemisphere (FinCEN Advisory 1997). In the "traditional" BMPE model, narcotics traffickers sell at a discount the dollar proceeds of US drug sales within the United States to black market peso brokers based in Mexico and Colombia. In turn, the brokers "place" the illicit proceeds into the US financial system and use the funds to purchase trade goods that are sent to Colombia or Mexico.[11] No money crosses borders. Only the ownership of the currencies involved changes hands. In years past, US drug dollars were used by black market brokers to purchase Marlboro cigarettes, Bell helicopters, US manufactured electronics, and so on. The company representatives or trade brokers did not know or were "willfully blind" regarding the origin of the funds used to purchase the merchandise. The same type of BMPE takes place in Europe. Illicit proceeds are used to purchase European manufactured products that are shipped to Mexico, Colombia, and other drug-producing countries.

Increasingly, the purchasers, logistics, foreign exchange specialists, and trade intermediaries are Chinese and Chinese organized crime groups.

They arrange for drug dollar purchases of Chinese merchandise (much of it counterfeit) to be sent to Central and South America including Colombia, Mexico, the Tri-Border area, and the Colón Free Trade Zone.

Another Chinese money laundering innovation that stymies criminal investigators is the growing use of "mirror accounts" or "mirror swaps." (Dalby 2021) Once again, the challenge for the cartels is how to move the drug cash in the US and Canada back to the cartels in Mexico and other countries. With mirror accounts, sometimes simply called "swaps," Chinese brokers often working with Chinese organized crime groups and the cartels identify Chinese/American businesses that are willing to cooperate. The businessman receives the drug cash from the broker. The generally cash-intensive business later "places" the proceeds of crime into the financial system. Meanwhile, these complicit businesses are asked to transfer a designated amount of drug money through Chinese banking apps to accounts based in China. Using a currency converter app on a smartphone, the participants agree on the exchange rate. The broker then gives the routing information of a bank account in China to the Chinese/American businessperson. The bank data is provided by the cartels. The mirror transaction or swap occurs when the participating businessperson takes possession of the drug cash, while simultaneously transferring the equivalent in Chinese RMB from their own account in China to the bank account number provided by broker. The Chinese/American businessperson also receives a commission. Once the money is offshore in China, the value can be further re-routed to Mexico or elsewhere per the instructions of the cartels. No money is wired directly from the US or Canada to China or elsewhere.

The challenge for law enforcement is that the foreign transfers of funds are made without involving financial institutions. Mirror accounts avoid a primary AML/CFT countermeasure – financial intelligence reporting requirements. It is a very effective modern spin-off of the ancient flying money system.

Furthering the laundering process, sometimes a follow-up swap is accomplished in Mexico. Transaction/s are completed to make the illegal drug proceeds look like a legitimate business transaction, for example, the purchase of Chinese manufactured goods. Or Chinese/Mexican businesses are identified that have access to pesos and that are willing to exchange them for the yuan in China. The laundered drug dollars that started in the US or Canada, then swapped for yuan, are finally in the form of clean laundered pesos in Mexico controlled by the cartels or their business representatives. In this context, there is similarity to the BMPE described above.

Discussing the BMPE, FINTRAC notes "brokers send suspected illicit funds held in Latin America or the U.S. to Canadian trading companies, wholesalers, dealers and brokers via electronic funds transfer and, to a limited extent, cash courier. These entities subsequently send the funds to entities in multiple jurisdictions, including China, Hong Kong and the U.S., to pay for goods." Further, according to FINTRAC, "Brokers send suspected illicit funds held in Latin America to U.S.-based entities of varying types, as well as to China or Hong Kong-based trading companies, through electronic funds transfer via a Canadian financial institution acting as a correspondent bank." (FINTRAC 2018).

FINTRAC analysis does not address the BMPE laundering of Canadian drug dollars in Canada. While there are few if any investigations, there is a very good probability that Canadian drug dollars are used to directly or indirectly purchase Canadian manufactured goods, commodities, and raw materials. It would also be very easy for narco-trafficking organizations to use Canadian brokers or trading companies to set up a network of anonymous shell companies in various domestic and foreign locations that assist in BMPE or BMPE-like operations. Canada does not have a central registry of beneficial ownership information. In addition to the traditional BMPE destinations such as Columbia and Mexico, authorities should examine the origin of funds used to purchase Canadian products shipped to or routed through Venezuela and Cuba.

Another TBML methodology is the misuse of the international gold, precious metals, diamonds, and gems industries. These represent large sectors of the Canadian economy – including British Columbia. Over the last thirty years, the misuse of gold, gems, and precious metals have consistently been used in countries around the world to launder staggering amounts of money. In that timeframe, some of the largest money laundering cases in history have involved gold.

Depending on its form, gold is both a commodity and a monetary instrument. Gold is a readily accepted medium of exchange accepted anywhere in the world. In times of uncertainty, gold offers stability. Gold offers easy anonymity to money launderers. Depending on the need, the form of gold can be easily altered. There is a worldwide market and cultural demand. Gold transactions can be easily layered or hidden. Gold, in its varied forms, can easily be smuggled and by weight represents much more value than cash. Gold is often used in fraudulent TBML schemes; for example, importing gold scrap at prices higher than gold bullion represents TBML methodology. In parts of the world, gold is the favoured commodity to use in underground financial systems such as hawala when brokers "counter-value" or balance the books in over-and-under invoicing schemes.

While there have been major investigations around the world involving the misuse of gold, precious metals, diamonds, and gems it is not clear if cases have been made in Canada. Certainly, Canada is vulnerable. Canada has all the factors that would enable gold and precious gems to be used as a money laundering mechanism. Countermeasures are known. Gold in all its many forms should be an automatic red flag for customs, law enforcement, intelligence agencies, and bank compliance officers – particularly when the sourcing, destination, or routing is problematic. Trade data for gold in almost all its forms should be collected and analyzed. Anomalies should be identified, and the results disseminated. Money laundering via the misuse of the international gold trade should be prioritized simply because gold represents one of the prime risks for laundering large amounts of money or transferring large amounts of value. Also, gold manufacturers and dealers should set up AML/CFT compliance programs. The challenge is that these common-sense countermeasures are not sufficiently implemented (Cassara 2020).

Recommendations

To combat the insidious practice of TBML, there are a number of recommendations that can be offered:

1. Transparency in AML case statistics: To determine an effective strategy against TBML, it is absolutely necessary to have straightforward and transparent investigative and case statistics at both

federal and provincial levels. According to data provided by BC's Ministry of the Attorney General, fifty money-laundering cases were submitted to the BC Prosecution Service between 2002 and 2018. Only ten individuals were found guilty. Of course, others may have been found guilty of other offences (Russel 2019). As noted earlier, federal money laundering conviction statistics are also disappointing. In addition to the above statistics, authorities should determine specifically how many TBML cases have ever been worked in British Columbia and Canada as a whole. How many resulted in successful convictions? How many TBML-related assets were seized and ultimately forfeited? How many law enforcement and other personnel have been devoted to combating TBML?

2. How many TBML STRs have been filed? The US FinCEN released the annual compilation of TBML SAR data. FINTRAC should do the same for Canada and each of the provinces. The suspicious transaction report (STR) data will help determine if TBML compliance regarding trade finance is effective.

3. Create a specialized unit within the RCMP to investigate money laundering including TBML: According to a 2019 press report, no single RCMP member was dedicated to money laundering investigations in British Columbia (St. Denis 2019). If accurate, that is the crux of the problem. AML success comes down to enforcement as measured by convictions and forfeitures. In order to be more effective in recognizing and investigating TBML in all its varied forms, the RCMP and others involved will have to change the culture of the bureaucracies.

4. It is an often overlooked truism that criminal organizations engage in crime for the money. Yet law enforcement does not like to emphasize following the money because it is difficult and time consuming. Following the money and value trails should be prioritized. For that to happen, incentives for the investigators must change. Training will be required. Expertise must be developed. Agencies and departments should develop short- and long-range implementation plans and be held accountable.

5. Create a Canadian Trade Transparency Unit (TTU): The Canada Border Services Agency (CBSA) might explore establishing a TTU. The CBSA already collects trade data and intelligence. It conducts operational targeting. Incorporating the mission of trade transparency easily fits into its mission. The ideal would be for represen-

tatives of the CBSA, the RCMP, the Canada Revenue Agency, and FINTRAC to be co-located within the TTU. The TTU will develop investigative leads that can then be forwarded to the specialized money laundering investigative unit briefly discussed in recommendation #3 above. The establishment of a TTU will be a net revenue gain for the government. As discussed, a systematic crackdown on trade fraud should result in fines, penalties, taxes, duties, and forfeitures. The proposed TTU could explore joining the established TTU network, but it isn't essential. The important thing is to form a specialized Canadian unit that focuses on trade fraud that may be indicative of TBML and value transfer.

6. Explore the viability of technical solutions: Canadian authorities should examine advanced analytic solutions, distributed ledger technology, the use of smart containers and other technical innovations. Some of these have been briefly described in this statement.

7. Establish a national registry of beneficial ownership information: The BC Ministry of Finance has delayed the transparency register requirements under the Business Corporations Act. Because TBML and money laundering, in general, is transnational in scope, Canada as a whole should have a central/national beneficial ownership registry.

8. Examine Service-Based Money Laundering (SBML): Victoria, BC, is a thriving centre for business development and economic investment and offers an incredible array of domestic and international commercial and professional services. Authorities should keep SBML in mind when examining money laundering vulnerabilities in Victoria and British Columbia.

9. Create a specific FATF recommendation to counter TBML. Within the AML/CFT community, it is the FATF that makes things happen. For many reasons, the FATF has dragged its feet regarding the creation of a separate FATF recommendation on TBML. Canada and other concerned nations should have their FATF delegations introduce and push for the adoption of FATF Recommendation #41, Countering TBML.

Notes

1 Some of the material in this paper comes from: John Cassara, *Trade-Based Money Laundering: The Next Frontier in International Money Laundering Enforcement* (Hoboken, New Jersey: Wiley, 2015). Also, see the author's written statement for the hearing on "Trading with the Enemy: Trade-Based Money Laundering is the Growth Industry in Terror Finance" before the Task Force to Investigate Terrorism Financing of the House Financial Services Committee, February 3, 2016. https://financialservices.house.gov/uploadedfiles/hhrg-114-ba00-wstate-jcassara-20160203.pdf.

2 Data and analysis given to the author by Dr. John Zdanowicz.

3 For further information on money laundering via real estate please see John A. Cassara, "Money Laundering and Illicit Financial Flows: Following the Money and Value Trails," Chapter 8 on *Real Estate*, 2020, Amazon Kindle.

4 According to the World Bank, official global remittances totaled approximately $625 billion in 2018. Because unofficial remittances are hidden, there are no reliable numbers regarding the magnitude of the problem. However, the IMF believes, "Unrecorded flows through informal channels are believed to be at least 50 percent larger than recorded flows." Thus, using the above World Bank and IMF estimates, unofficial remittances are enormous.

5 For further information see the TTU website at https://www.dhs.gov/trade-transparency.

6 March 26, 2015: email exchange between the author and Hector X. Colon, who was unit chief/director of the TTU.

7 "The Next Frontier in International Money Laundering Enforcement" is the subtitle of my book on TBML.

8 Summarized in John Cassara, *Trade Based Money Laundering – The Next Frontier in International Money Laundering*, 164. 2020. Hoboken, New Jersey: Wiley.

9 For more information on GFTrade see https://gfintegrity.org/gftrade/.

10 See also https://www.tradelens.com.

11 "Placing, layering, and integration" are the three stages of money laundering. There are a variety of ways to place illicit funds into the financial system. The primary method is structuring transactions under the financial intelligence reporting threshold.

References

Baker, Raymond. 2005. *Capitalism's Achilles Heel*. Hoboken, New Jersey: John Wiley & Sons.

———. 2018. "Global Financial Integrity Releases New Study on Trade Misinvoicing in Nigeria." GFI Press Release. https://gfintegrity.org/press-release/

global-financial-integrity-releases-new-study-on-trade-misinvoicing-in-nige-ria/.

Cassara, John. 2016. "Service-Based Money Laundering: The Next Illicit Finance Frontier." *Foundation for the Defense of Democracies.* https://www.fdd.org/analysis/2016/05/19/service-based-money-laundering-the-next-illicit-finance-frontier/.

———. 2020. *Money Laundering and Illicit Financial Flows: Following the Money and Value Trail.* Amazon KDP.

Bloomberg News. 2019. China's Hidden Capital Flight Surges to Record High. https://www.bloomberg.com/news/articles/2019-10-11/china-hidden-capital-flight-at-a-record-in-2019-iif-says.

Dalby, Chris. 2021. "How Chinese Criminals Secretly Move Millions for Mexico Cartels." Insight Crime. https://insightcrime.org/news/chinese-money-launderers-mexico-cartels-move-millions-secret/.

Department of the Treasury. 2015. "National Money Laundering Risk Assessment." https://home.treasury.gov/system/files/246/National-Money-Laundering-Risk-Assessment-06-12-2015.pdf

Financial Action Task Force (FATF). 2006. *Trade Based Money Laundering.* https://www.fatf-gafi.org/media/fatf/documents/reports/Trade%20Based%20Money%20Laundering.pdf.

———. 2007. *Mutual Evaluation of China.* https://www.fatf-gafi.org/countries/a-c/china/documents/mutualevaluationofchina.html.

FinCEN Advisory. 1997. *Colombian Black Market Peso Exchange.* https://www.fincen.gov/sites/default/files/shared/advisu9.pdf.

FINTRAC. 2018. *Operational Alert: Professional Money Laundering through Trade and Money Services Businesses.* https://fintrac-canafe.canada.ca/intel/operation/oai-ml-eng.

General Accountability Office (GAO). 2019. *Countering Illicit Finance and Trade: U.S. Efforts to Combat Trade-Based Money Laundering.* https://www.gao.gov/products/gao-20-314r.

———. 2020. *Trade-Based Money Laundering - U.S. Government Has Worked with Partners to Combat the Threat, but Could Strengthen Its Efforts.* https://www.gao.gov/assets/gao-20-333.pdf.

Global Financial Integrity. 2014. *The Economist Highlights the Scourge of Trade Mis-invoicing.* https://financialtransparency.org/the-economist-highlights-the-scourge-of-trade-misinvoicing/

———. 2020a. *Why a Public-Private Partnership is Urgently Needed to Combat Trade-Based Money Laundering.* https://gfintegrity.org/why-a-public-private-partnership-is-urgently-needed-to-combat-trade-based-money-laundering.

———. 2020b. *Trade-Related Illicit Financial Flows in 135 Developing Countries: 2008-2017.* https://gfintegrity.org/report/trade-related-illicit-financial-flows-in-135-developing-countries-2008-2017/.

Gunter, Frank. 2017. "Why China Lost About $3.8 Trillion To Capital Flight In The Last Decade". *Forbes*. https://www.forbes.com/sites/insideasia/2017/02/22/china-capital-flight-migration/?sh=a7ec16f4a37c.

National Association of Realtors. 2022. "In the Past Year, Chinese Investors Purchased $6.1 Billion Worth of Property in the US After Being Banned by Other Countries for Pushing Up House Prices." *Gateway Pundit*, July 28. https://www.thegatewaypundit.com/2022/07/past-year-chinese-investors-purchased-6-1-billion-worth-property-us-banned-countries-pushing-house-prices/.

O'Brien, Frank. n.d. "Property Sales Spike Money Laundering." *Compliance Alert*. https://www.calert.info/details.php?id=105.

Olick, Diane. 2019. "Chinese Buyers Expand Their Reach in the U.S. Housing Market as the Middle Class Gets in on the Act". *CNBC*. https://www.cnbc.com/2019/01/08/chinese-middle-class-buying-up-american-residential-real-estate.html.

Open Secrets. 2019. *Real Estate Lobbying*. https://www.opensecrets.org/industries/lobbying.php?ind=F10++.

Peters, Andrew. 2020. "A Link in the Chain: Harnessing Blockchain for Trade Integrity". Global Financial Integrity. https://gfintegrity.org/a-link-in-the-chain-harnessing-blockchain-for-trade-integrity/.

PricewaterhouseCoopers (PwC). 2015. *Goods Gone Bad: Addressing Money Laundering Risk in the Trade Finance System*. https://silo.tips/download/january-goods-gone-bad-addressing-money-laundering-risk-in-the-trade-finance-sys.

Russel, Andrew. 2019. "Not Just B.C.: Most Provinces in Canada Fail to Secure Convictions in Money-Laundering Cases." *Global News*. https://globalnews.ca/news/4939801/provinces-canada-fail-to-convict-money-laundering/.

SEK Strategies. 2022. *U.S. Tax Coffers Lose $640 billion of Taxable Profits due to TBML Evasion and Money Laundering in 2021*. https://www.prnewswire.com/news-releases/us-tax-coffers-lose-640-billion-of-taxable-profits-due-to-trade-based-tax-evasion-and-money-laundering-in-2021-says-sk-strategies-301539461.html.

Sok, Haylee. 2017. "Smart Shipping Container Technology Comes to North America". *Global Trade*. https://www.globaltrademag.com/smart-shipping-container-technology-comes-north-america/.

St. Denis, Jen. 2019. "Not a Single Federal Police Officer Is Working to Bust Money Launderers in B.C." *The Star Vancouver*. https://www.thestar.com/vancouver/2019/04/08/bc-money-laundering-report-finds-no-federal-officers-dedicated-to-case.html.

Transparency International. 2017. *Doors Wide Open*. https://www.transparency.org/en/publications/doors-wide-open-corruption-and-real-estate-in-four-key-markets#.

The Wolfsberg Group. 2019. *Trade Finance Principles*. https://iccwbo.org/publication/wolfsberg-trade-finance-principles/.

The World Bank. 2017. *Illicit Financial Flows*. https://www.worldbank.org/en/topic/financialsector/brief/illicit-financial-flows-iffs.

Trigler, Jacob. 2022. "Indicators of Informal Funds Transfer Systems; A Comparison of Traditional and Modern Systems." (Monterrey Naval Post Graduate School Thesis). https://apps.dtic.mil/dtic/tr/fulltext/u2/a494175.pdf.

U.S. Department of State. 2015. *International Narcotics Control Strategy Report, Volume II Money Laundering. Montenegro Country Report.*

World Trade Organization. 2016. World Trade Statistical Review. https://www.wto.org/english/res_e/statis_e/wts2016_e/wts2016_e.pdf.

Zdanowicz, John. 2022. *Trade-Based Money Laundering and Terrorist Financing.* https://ag-pssg-sharedservices-ex.objectstore.gov.bc.ca/ag-pssg-cc-exh-prod-bkt-ex/361%20-%203%20Zdanowicz%20Article%20Trade%20Based%20Money%20Laundering.pdf.

11

Organized Crime, Trade-Based Money Laundering, and the Canada–United States Trade Stream

Todd Hataley and Jamie Ferrill

Introduction

Transnational organized crime is big business; it is estimated to generate US$870 billion globally each year (Barker 2013). Given that most of these funds are at some point dirty money, it is widely accepted that a significant amount is laundered (Levi and Soudjin 2020). Typically, money is laundered through banks, money-transfer systems, currency exchange systems, hawala, and more recently crypto-currency exchanges (Shelley 2018). One of the often-overlooked methods of the money laundering process is trade-based money laundering (TBML), ergo, the intersection of transnational organized crime and TBML. There are TBML schemes that stand out clearly as transnational organized crime initiatives, such as the black-market peso exchange. In reality, though, TBML schemes are inherently transnational in nature, and they generally rely on the complicity of actors on both sides of international trade transactions. What's more, organized crime is underpinned by money laundering in its various forms. The extent, however, to which transnational organized crime participates in TBML is not well understood, either on a global scale or, as in the case of this chapter, between Canada and the United States.

TBML, in simple terms, is a money laundering technique that exploits international trade streams as a means of laundering the proceeds of criminal activity. As a practice, TBML can include several different strategies, employed by different groups of criminal actors, including more traditional organized crime groups (OCGs). The main strategies known to be employed include over and under-invoicing shipments of goods and services, multiple invoicing of goods and services, and falsely described goods and services (Cassara 2016). Short-shipping, over-shipping, and phantom shipping are other common techniques (Cassara 2016).

The purpose of this chapter is to evaluate the *potential* for the Canada–United States trade stream to be exploited by organized crime groups for the purpose of TBML. The word *potential* is used intentionally for a number of reasons. First, to the best of our knowledge, no organized crime group in Canada has been convicted of money laundering using this methodology, as either a substantive offence or as a secondary offence tied to the proceeds of criminal activity. There are several reasons for this, which will be discussed. Second, using global estimates of TBML it is possible to make some extrapolations of the potential for TBML activity within the Canada–United States trade stream. Finally, by deconstructing the trade process between Canada and the United States we can identify points vulnerable to exploitation by organized crime groups.

This chapter will begin with an overview of TBML and its various techniques; we will look at those different techniques and examine some of the common elements that have been observed in money laundering schemes. The second part will explore trade flow between Canada and the United States, drawing some conclusions about the potential for the trade stream to be exploited by organized crime. The third part will look specifically at the Canada–US trade process and identify points within that process that are vulnerable to exploitation by organized crime groups.

What Is TBML?

The standard definition for TBML comes from the Financial Action Task Force (FATF), which defines TBML as "the process of disguising proceeds of crime and moving value through trade transactions to legitimize their illicit origin" (FATF 2006). In 2008 FATF expanded their definition of TBML to include at the end "or to finance their activities" (FATF 2008). Although the definition has evolved from its original definition, Soudijn (2014) maintains that the definition assumes a focus on the fraudulent trade of legal goods in the legal trade stream. As a result, there is a dependency on documentation from banks, shippers, and customs agencies to help recognize TBML. Under this definition, he claims, enforcement agencies often look the wrong way for evidence of TBML. The focus of enforcement agencies is generally on the misrepresentation of price, quality, or quantity.

However, 80 percent of trade transactions is completed via open account trade. That is, they take place without intermediaries, instead with agreements directly between buyer and seller (Soudijn 2014). Thus, these transactions may not result in the documentation traditionally relied on by banks for identifying TBML. Moreover, the focus on price, quality, and quantity assumes that TBML cannot occur on shipments of true value, which Soudijn demonstrates by way of a case study to be false. Using linkages between terrorism financing and TBML, Delston and Walls (2009) have argued that the techniques for combatting this money laundering strategy should include those involved in the supply chain. This would include trucking and shipping companies, customs agencies, and customs brokers. This argument is further developed by Liao and Acharya (2011), who maintain that international customs cooperation and the standardization of customs controls would go a long way to combatting TBML.

To better understand the vulnerabilities associated with TBML, Cassella (2019) argues that what is most important is not the schemes that are perpetrated, but rather the elements that are common to all these schemes. He goes on to identify six: the use of shell companies in jurisdictions with strong privacy laws, poor compliance by financial institutions, the lack of cooperation between financial institutions, corruption and poor enforcement, the use and acceptance of third parties to purchase goods on behalf of others, and the inability of governments to recover criminal proceeds.

How It's Done

There are several documents involved in any international shipping transaction. These documents are a must for a number of different actors involved in the trade process. For the purchaser and the seller, these documents represent the terms of the financial transaction – what is bought and sold and what the terms of the sale are. For the transportation companies, these provide a description of what is being transported, its weight, and any special terms the cargo may need for handling. For customs agencies, documentation provides vital information about what is being transported, from where, to whom, and the value of the product for taxation purposes. Finally, since not all buyers want to pay for goods before they arrive, these documents provide information for banks who may act as intermediaries, brokering the transaction with a promise of payment – generally known as a letter of credit. The role of banks is an interesting one and will be returned to later in the chapter. Here, the key methods of TBML (over/under invoicing, multiple invoicing, falsely described goods) are explored with their potential links to OCGs.

The following is a list of some of the paperwork that may accompany an international trade transaction. Further down in the chapter we will look specifically at Canadian and United States' requirements in terms of documents for import and export of goods across the Canada–US border.

- Commercial invoice – information on weight and description of goods.
- Transport document – details of goods for transportation and transportation arrangements.

- Insurance documents – insurance for goods in transit.
- Certificate of origin – details of where the product is made.
- Certificate of inspection – second opinion if goods are as described.
- Packing list – used for shipments divided into smaller packages.
- Weight certificate – used when goods are sold by weight. (Naheem 2016)

The falsification of any of these documents, referred to by some authors as the falsification of trade documents, is generally the first part of the TBML process.

Over- and under-invoicing is, as it sounds, overvaluing or undervaluing a product on an invoice in order to move value from one jurisdiction to another. By invoicing a product at a value less than it is worth, an exporter can shift value to the importer. For example, if an exporter ships one million plastic buckets with a value of $2/unit to Canada from the United States, but on the invoice the exporter only bills the importer $1/unit, the importer only pays $1 million dollars for a shipment worth $2 million. The exporter has effectively sent an additional value of $1 million to Canada. This process can also be done in reverse.

So, why would someone want to under- or over-invoice a product? Simply, they want to transfer value from one jurisdiction to another to avoid taxation, reduce taxation, or in the case of transnational organized crime, hide, or wash, illicit funds. As an example, a cocaine dealer in the United States may sell $1 million worth of cocaine to an OCG in Canada. The cocaine travels to Canada using traditional smuggling routes and ends up in the hands of the OCG in Canada. Now the problem becomes transferring the $1 million to pay for the cocaine back to the United States. The Canadian OCG has a few options. They can bulk smuggle the cash; however, they are still left with the problem of having to launder this money in the United States. Or they can conduct a number of small banking transactions below reporting thresholds and then move that money using a similar process through the international banking system. Or finally, they can engage in TBML.

Should the option of TBML be chosen, the Canadian OCG, through an import/export company would import products from or via the United

States from a company controlled by the American group. For example, the Canadian importer may purchase paper products from the American group for a real value of $10,000, but have a declared value of $1 million (over invoiced). Upon delivery to Canada, the Canadian group pays the American group the declared value, effectively transferring $1 million to the American group, laundered at a cost of 1 percent. In this example, the Americans have over-invoiced on a paper products shipment to repatriate $1 million originally owed for the cocaine deal. Moreover, the money was sent through the legitimate trade stream, meaning upon landing in the United States the money has been cleaned.

Turning to multiple invoicing, this involves the repeated invoicing of the same international shipment or service. Unlike the previous technique of over- or under-invoicing, in a multiple invoicing scheme there is no need to misrepresent the cost of any product being shipped. This type of TBML may be more frequently seen in the provision of services, for two reasons. First, it is difficult to put a value on services provided – or in some cases not provided. Services, unlike trade in products, do not have a tangible good that can be "objectively" valued. The unique nature of service provision makes it difficult to compare against other service products. Consider for example, an OCG in Canada that wants to repatriate money owing to a different OCG in the United States. Through an associated company, the US group bills an associated Canadian OCG for "entertainment" or "consulting" services. The Canadian OCG pays for the service as a means of repatriating the money owing. What constitutes a service and how to measure the value of services that are provided, represents a significant future challenge to combatting TBML.

Another challenge is that it is equally difficult to determine the number of times a service was provided. Thus, multiple invoicing for services and goods becomes rather difficult to detect. Using the previous example of a Canadian OCG repatriating money owing to an American criminal group, the invoicing can be broken down into multiple smaller amounts totalling the amount owed. This has the added benefits of reducing liability by spreading out the risk across multiple invoices should the invoicing practice be investigated. In addition, invoicing for smaller amounts is less likely to raise enforcement flags.

Finally, as the name states, goods and services can be falsely declared as a means of reducing or increasing their value in the transshipment process. This may also include the process of phantom shipping, in which no good or service is actually provided, but is still invoiced. In terms of the former, for example, to move a shipment of copper from Country A to Country B, the importer declares the copper to be a product of lesser value, such as painted paving stones. In this scheme, by mislabelling the export product, the exporter is able to transfer value out of Country A to Country B. This scheme is frequently used to move raw materials out of countries with less developed export controls, thus depriving these countries of desperately needed tax revenues. An investigation described by Delston and Walls (2012) illustrates a customs fraud scheme in operation for at least five years in Ireland, in which the owner of the largest fruit and vegetable distributor falsely declared imports. The end result was a prison term of six years for the distributor.

TBML is a general term that can apply to a number of different schemes that can be better suited to different groups and for different purposes, as illustrated above. White-collar criminals are generally more interested in moving value to lower taxation zones, hiding profits, or paying bribes to corrupt state officials. This adds to the already complex landscape of TBML as tax evasion and capital flight may mirror the processes involved in TBML. The core difference is, however, that TBML must require efforts to disguise the proceeds of crime (FATF 2006). In other words, it requires dirty money.

Canada/United States Cross-Border Organized Crime

The United Nations Convention against Transnational Organized Crime defines organized crime as "a structured group of three or more persons, existing for a period of time and acting in concert with the aim of committing one or more serious crimes or offenses, in order to obtain, directly or indirectly, a financial of other benefit" (quoted in Kleemans and van Koppen 2020, 387). Kleemans and Koppen (2020, 388) further state that organized crime groups are generally transnational in character. Transnational, or cross-border organized crime activity between Canada and the United States, frequently takes a back seat to similar linkages between the United States and Mexico. This has to do with the volume of contraband transiting the border, including, but not limited to drugs and illegal migrants (Albanese 2013). Canada, however, is not without its own criminal ties to the United States. Goods smuggling (drugs, counterfeits, alcohol, tobacco, firearms), money laundering, and illegal immigration have all been identified as OCG-specific threats to the Canada–US border (Drug Enforcement Administration, Federal Bureau of Investigations, Royal Canadian Mounted Police 2006).

Fuelling these threats even further, the legalization of marijuana in Canada has been followed by unprecedented seizures of marijuana destined for the United States from Canada. According to the United States Customs and Border Protection (CBP) seizures of marijuana are up by over 1,000 percent since 2018, the year Canada legalized marijuana, with methamphetamine and cocaine also seeing small year-over-year increases (USCBP 2021). Canada Border Services Agency (CBSA), the agency responsible for all ports of entry (POE) into Canada, has seen a consistent number of firearms and prohibited weapons seized at POE over the last three years (CBSA 2021a). In 2021, 1,000 firearms and firearms parts were confiscated in 409 different seizure actions: 233 were in Ontario, 88 in British Columbia, and 21 in Québec (House of Commons 2022). According to the Toronto City Police, 85 percent of handguns seized in Toronto are traced back to the United States (Howorun 2021).

Human smuggling and human trafficking also have linkages between Canadian and American OCGs. According to Statistics Canada, 32 percent of the human trafficking cases prosecuted in Canada between 2009 and 2018 included individuals who were trafficked across the international border (StatsCan 2020). Finally, links between traditional OCGs are also well documented between Canada and the United States. The Rizzuto crime family in Montréal was long known for its ties to the New

York mafia (United States Department of Justice 2014). More recently the death of a Hamilton-based crime figure suggested a return to links between the Hamilton and the Buffalo mafia (Taekema 2020). According to the Royal Canadian Mounted Police (RCMP), in 2020 there were over 2,000 OCGs operating in Canada, with over half characterized as international, and 29 percent suspected of being involved in money laundering (Northcott 2021). Suffice to say, that although the Canada–United States crime linkages do not receive the attention that the United States–Mexico crime linkages receive, they are clearly established and active in the movement of illicit commodities across the Canada–United States border.

Trade and the Threat of TBML

OCGs generate dirty money from the activities outlined in the above sections. To disguise their ill-gotten gains, they need to launder them. According to the United Nations, the value of money laundering on a global scale is estimated to be between 2–5 percent of global GDP, or between $800 billion and $2 trillion US dollars (estimates by the International Monetary Fund [IMF] go as high as US$4 trillion). Of that total, it is believed that only 1 percent is successfully confiscated (Raza, Zhan, and Rubab 2020, 911). Cassara (2020, 77) argues that the most pervasive method of money laundering is through the trade system or TBML. As we have explored, we also ascertain that TBML is a major method of money laundering; ergo, the efforts to understand vulnerabilities in the trade system and cross-examine those with the OCG modus operandi.

To estimate the *potential* for TBML across the Canada–US border, we can extrapolate from known trade data and approximations of the value of money laundered on a global scale. According to the World Trade Organization (WTO), in 2019, global trade in merchandise was estimated at approximately US$19 trillion, not including almost US$6 trillion in services (WTO 2020). Using the 2–5 percent range estimated by the United Nations, this suggests that money laundering through the global trade stream is estimated to range between US$380 billion to US$950 billion in 2019. We can apply a similar extrapolation to the Canada–

Table 11.1: Potential for TBML

	Value of trade	Potential value for TBML 2–5 percent
Canada exports to the United States 2020	$270,000,000,000	US$5.4–13.5 billion
United States exports to Canada 2020	$255,000,000,000	US$5.1–12.75 billion

United States trade stream. Using 2020 data, exports from Canada in 2020 to the United States were valued at US$270 billion, and imports from the United States to Canada were valued at US$255 billion (United States Census Bureau 2021).

These estimates require some clarity. First, as noted by the FATF, money laundering is a clandestine process, and as such it is impossible to know exactly the levels to which it occurs on a global scale (Cassara 2020, 8). Thus, we speak in terms of *potential* and not exact numbers or case studies. Second, both Canada and the United States have highly developed and professional customs services, which may suggest a greater level of enforcement. However, at the same time, trade between Canada and the United States is largely risk managed and based on self-compliance between importers and exporters. This suggests that the system is open to potential exploitation by managing out risk and accounting for the relatively low level of random inspections on commercial goods crossing the border. Third, these numbers represent a total *potential* for TBML between the two countries of all forms of TBML. This total would include companies that falsely invoice to transfer value between the two countries. The total value linked to traditional organized crime groups would likely be a smaller percentage of these numbers – but significant, nonetheless. Finally, it is important to note that money laundering is one of those processes that is dynamic and constantly changing (Cassella 2019, 394), and that OCGs will expand their skill set as required to move their "dirty" money into the legitimate money stream. Moreover, if there are positive gains to be made, OCGs are known to learn and adapt, professionalizing their capacity to meet new enforcement challenges.

Importing into Canada

As noted above, the process of importing into any country requires a number of different actors and documentation. This section will describe the import process from the United States (or any country for that matter) into Canada and evaluate points of vulnerability in this trade process. The following is adapted from the processes outlined by the CBSA website, *Importing Commercial Goods into Canada,* where they draw out a six-step process for importing into Canada (CBSA 2021b).

Step 1: Preparing to Import

Amongst other steps, the individual/organization will have to obtain a business number (BN). This number is the link to the Canada Revenue Agency, which will track all imports, taxes and duties paid. This first step is also the gateway to fraudulent importation. BNs are frequently held by numbered corporations that intentionally attempt to distance the company from the beneficial owner. In addition, a BN may also be associated with the use of nominees in place of the beneficial owner, providing even further distance between the beneficial owner and the import business.

This is also the step where CBSA suggests that individuals/organizations determine whether or not transactions will require the services of a customs broker. Customs brokers in Canada act as agents on behalf of the importer, completing all the necessary documentation, collecting and remitting taxes and duties, and any number of other tasks as required. In Canada, customs brokers are licenced by CBSA, which provides a level of professionalism, screening, and accountability for those becoming customs brokers. However, it is also a system that has the potential for exploitation by OCGs. As the keeper of record, the information that ultimately is forwarded to the shipper and to CBSA, is only as good as what is provided by the customs broker. Customs brokers can be lied to, bribed, threatened, or any number of other actions to incentivize them to act in a certain way, creating a further level of vulnerability.

If a customs broker is used to facilitate the movement of product into Canada, they are generally responsible for the following documentation:

- Commercial invoice or a Canada Customs Invoice (CCI). The commercial invoice, one of the documents that is susceptible to fraud, must contain certain information, including the name and contact information of both the exporter and the importer, a specific description of the goods being imported, the weight, the price, the terms of delivery, purchase order numbers, insurance, and date on which the items began their journey to Canada. A simple review of the required information illustrates the number of areas where the information on an import into Canada can be in some way deceptive. An importer who is the non-beneficial owner, the description of goods, and the description of price and point of origin can all be easily manipulated at this point.

- Bill of lading (BOL). The BOL is issued by the exporter to the carrier and describes the goods to be shipped and the terms of the shipment. A copy is also forwarded to the importer, or the broker acting on the behalf of the importer. At this level there is the potential for the exporter to be party to the money laundering scheme. The exporter has the capacity, within the BOL, to misrepresent the cargo, or to ship no cargo at all (i.e., phantom shipping).

- Manifest or Cargo Control Document (CCD). The CCD is prepared by the shipper and lists all the items being shipped, based on information provided by the exporter. Based on the information provided by the shipper to CBSA, the cargo is assessed a cargo control number, which is used to monitor the shipment, as well as to assess duties and taxes. At this level, it is possible either or both the shipper and the exporter have the capacity to fraudulently enter or not the items being shipped. With consolidated shipments (a cargo load with items from multiple exporters), the search for items fraudulently in the system becomes much like searching for a needle in a haystack.

- Shipper's Export Declaration (SED). The SED is completed by the exporter but does not travel with the goods and remains in the United States. It serves two purposes. First, it provides statistical data on exports from the United States. Second, it has a regulatory function in that any goods over a certain value ($2,500 for cargo; $500 for postal) requires a SED.

Step 2: The Classification of Goods

At this stage, goods are assigned a tariff classification number. Every good entering Canada is assigned a tariff classification number, which determines how those goods are treated by customs. The tariff classification number is assigned based on the declaration of goods being exported. Thus, inaccuracies in the declaration stage will be carried on to the tariff classification and ultimately how the goods are treated at the border and the amount of duty and/or tax collected on the cargo. As explored, false declarations are one of the common means by which TBML is executed, and a major way in which duties and taxes are either reduced or avoided at the border.

Step 3: Determining Duties and Taxes

Duties and taxes on goods entering Canada are assessed in two ways. For goods entering from the United States, duties will be determined by the United States–Mexico–Canada Trade Agreement (USMCA). Second, most goods being imported into Canada are subject to Canadian Goods and Services Tax (GST). Duties and taxes are generally worked out by the customs broker, paid by the broker and reclaimed from the importer. Although not a stage that can be directly exploited, indeed it is probably best to hide in plain sight in this case, any costs associated with duties and taxes need to be worked into the cost of laundering the money.

Step 4: Shipping and Reporting Your Goods

The shipping stage is another vulnerable point in a TBML scheme. Shipping companies, (trucks, air, or sea) have a long history of being used to smuggle contraband into Canadian territory, but in a TBML scheme, their role is different. Most goods are going to enter Canada from the United States by land, or rather, by truck. In 2016 almost 72 percent of all imports from the United States entered Canada by truck (BCTA 2017). Trucks moving cargo into Canada from the United States must register for and receive a carrier code from CBSA to further register for

ACI eManifests. ACI eManifest (Advanced Commercial Information) gives (and requires) commercial carriers the ability to provide information on the cargo they are carrying before arrival in Canada. The cargo is then subject to the Pre-Arrival Review System (PARS), for clearance before arriving at the international border. PARS is the default system for the clearance of cargo entering Canada. It is in providing the information in advance of arriving at the POE that a cargo carrier may or may not be complicit in TBML. Within the carrier stream, there are several points of vulnerability. From bonded warehouses to pre-clearance, the system can be exploited at a number of points of entry, but this analysis is beyond the scope of this chapter. What is important at this stage is that the manifest presented by a cargo carrier needs to be consistent with that submitted to CBSA by the customs broker; inconsistencies could signal a reason for secondary inspection. The manifest, however, could well differ from the Shipper's Export Declaration, since the SED is an export document, not an import document, and not part of the cargo declaration. In a suspected case of TBML, cross-referencing the two may provide valuable information.

Step 5: Getting Your Goods Released

Having cargo released by CBSA generally requires that all duties and taxes be paid before release. The B3-3, or the Canada Customs Coding form, is essentially an accounting document that determines taxes and duties to be paid on the import cargo. Like other documents that follow the cargo in the stream, this document must be consistent with all other documents, particularly the CCI, CCD, and BOL. Depending on how duties and taxes are paid (at the port, in advance, or after release) there may be as few as one copy of this document or as many as three.

Step 6: After Your Goods Are Released

Once goods are released both the importer and CBSA have the opportunity to re-assess the taxes and duties paid on the cargo and adjust as necessary. Importers are told to hold their paperwork for a six-year period, and CBSA has the right to re-assess or inspect at any point within four years. For investigators who suspect or are actively investigating a TBML scheme, this time period provides an opportunity to assess suspect importations after the completion of a substantive investigation.

The importation of cargo from the United States to Canada involves a number of actors who, may or may not, be complicit in any scheme to launder money through the Canada–US trade stream. Brokers, shippers, and customs agents all have a role in the movement of cargo across the border and corruption at any stage (although corruption is not even necessary) could signal a TBML scheme. Although customs brokers are encouraged to "know their clients," many of the transactions that they broker on a daily basis are done by phone, email, or both. If a client wants to import goods from the United States, they need only call up an approved customs broker from the CBSA website and engage their services. There is currently a list of 303 licenced customs brokers on the CBSA website (CBSA 2021c).

The good news is that the movement of cargo from the United States to Canada involves paperwork – and a lot of it. And while this provides for several entry points and vulnerabilities for exploitation by criminal groups, it also allows the potential for a great deal of oversight on the import process. Given the potential for oversight, why is there still a potential for TBML to occur within the Canada–United States trade stream? The answer has to do with rates of physical inspection. Goods entering Canada can be targeted for inspection for a number of reasons: A pre-arrival referral for examination based on an assessment from the National Targeting Center, a request by a participating national government agency, first port of arrival referral made by a Border Services officer, or random selection (Brock 2021). Although CBSA does not release statistics on the rates of inspections on goods moving from the United States and into Canada across a land border, those rates are estimated globally to be approximately 5 percent (Businesswire 2021). In the absence of verifying whether or not the goods being transported are actually those that are listed on the various import documents, TBML potential is high.

Conclusion

The purpose of this chapter was to explore the *potential* for OCGs to exploit the Canada–United States trade stream for the purpose of TBML. Just as the trade stream has access points to be exploited, OCGs have certain characteristics and tactics that would draw them towards TBML as a form of money laundering. That is, both concepts are inherently transnational, both require complicit networks on either side of the border, and both aim to ultimately avoid detection in terms of profiteering. Building on this, Miller and colleagues (2016) noted the importance of globalization, specifically the advances in communications, lower transportation costs, the creation of global value chains, and increases in urbanization which have come together to create linked national economies that simultaneously create new market opportunities for both TBML and organized crime.

What then, can this tell us about organized crime groups and the *potential* to exploit the Canada–United States trade stream? Importation from the United States into Canada is based on a system of risk-management and self-compliance, both of which have multiple entry points for exploitation by OCGs; especially as they commonly depend on transborder activities, corruption, and mixing illicit with licit businesses (UNODC 2002). CBSA, the agency responsible for the importation of goods into Canada, relies on information entered into the system by, in most cases, customs brokers, and in a small number of cases, by individuals. The information gathered by the broker comes from the client, a client with a business number that anyone can obtain with very little effort. Entering false information into the trade system at the starting point by hiding the beneficial owner and falsifying documents at the broker stage, starts the process of TBML between the United States to Canada. The documentation accompanying cargo is subject to analysis by CBSA agents and/or random checks to determine if the cargo will be inspected. But it is only upon physical inspection either at the POE or beyond, that the goods declared on the manifest, BOL, and the invoice can actually be confirmed. Even upon inspection, it may be difficult or impossible to determine the actual value of a product, beyond having an expert to provide analysis. Think for example of artwork, antiques, and other items that may carry a subjective value, not to mention the provision of services (which opens a whole new can of worms).

The purpose here is not to suggest that to stop or eliminate the potential for TBML across the Canada–United States border all cargo has to be inspected. Given the volume of trade crossing the border between Canada and the US, that would be an impossibility without shutting down the economy. Rather there must be better connections between those who investigate money laundering (police) and those responsible for controlling trade across the international border: customs agents, brokers, and shippers. Moreover, those public-private connections must be international insofar as information needs to be easily shared between Canadian officials and officials from other countries. Canadian and American investigators will need to develop knowledge of the trade system, identify vulnerable points, be aware of what types of indicators to look for during and after an investigation, and determine which judicial authorizations, including Mutual Legal Assistance Treaties (MLAT), if necessary, are required to access information. Given the obviously transnational theme of TBML, it has also been suggested that there is a need for the development of a risk-based customs audit as a way of combating the problem of TBML, given the limits of state-based resources.

Finally, advancing the study and investigation of money laundering (specifically TBML) needs to consider the evolution of criminal activity. Cassella (2018) has convincingly argued that both money laundering statutes and investigative techniques surrounding those statutes, are out of date. The money laundering model of "placement, layering and integration" most commonly learned by investigators, is obsolete, Cassella argues, for three reasons: the model is overly restrictive in directing how investigators look at money laundering, the investigative technique does not correspond with what information the prosecutor requires, and the model does not accurately reflect the vast range of money laundering techniques today. Coupled with this, as Naheem (2019) has observed, money laundering and TBML have become increasingly complex and will only become more so, enhanced by technological advances and virtual currency transactions. Looking to the future of the Canada–US trade stream and the potential for TBML, three observations can be made to conclude. First, OCGs will continue to evolve their tactics and methodologies as required to make money. This would include adopting TBML and future forms of it, to launder cash. Second, the Canada–United States trade stream is vulnerable to exploitation at several entry points. Moreover, investigative techniques and legislation seem to lag especially nimble OCGs. Finally, the challenges surrounding interdicting and even understanding TBML will only get more difficult as new technologies and cryptocurrencies emerge and become mainstream. TBML could very well become the methodology of choice for OCGs, and as a result, the incidents of, and groups incorporating TBML, will increase in the future. Ergo, adaptation by bodies with enforcement and investigative mandates, further analysis of customs processes and vulnerabilities, attendance to new affordances, and transnational public-private cooperation are going to be absolutely necessary for the fight against TBML.

References

Albanese, Jay. 2013. Organized Crime in North America. In *Transnational Organized Crime: An Overview from Six Continents* edited by Albanese and Reichel. Thousand Oaks: Sage Publications.

Barker, J. 2013. Transnational Organized Crime. https://www.aph.gov.au/About_Parliament/Parliamentary_Departments/Parliamentary_Library/pubs/Briefing-Book44p/TransnationalCrime

BC Trucking Association (BCTA). 2017. Canada – US Trade by Truck. https://www.bctrucking.com/industry/trade.

Brock, Jan. 2021. Why Was My Shipment Referred for Examination by CBSA? https://www.pcb.ca/post/the-cost-of-cbsa-examinations.

Businesswire. 2021. Cargo Inspection Market Report. https://www.businesswire.com/news/home/20210624005731/en/Cargo-Inspection-Market-Report---Global-Forecasts-from-2021-to-2026---ResearchAndMarkets.com Accessed 02/10/2021.

Canada Border Services Agency (CBSA). 2021a. Canada Border Services Agency Seizures. https://www.cbsa-asfc.gc.ca/security-securite/seizure-saisie-eng.html.

———. 2021b. Importing Commercial Goods into Canada. https://www.cbsa-asfc.gc.ca/import/guide-eng.html.

———. 2021c. List of Licensed Custom Brokers. https://www.cbsa-asfc.gc.ca/services/cb-cd/cb-cd-eng.html Accessed 02/10/2021.

Cassara, John A. 2016. *Trade Based Money Laundering: The Next Frontier in International Money Laundering Enforcement*. New Jersey: John Wiley and Sons, Inc.

———. 2020. *Money Laundering and Illicit Financial Flow*. Publisher unknown.

Cassella, Stefan. 2018. "Toward a New Model of Money Laundering." *Journal of Money Laundering Control* 21, no. 4: 494–497.

———. 2019. "Illicit Finance and Money Laundering Trends in Eurasia." *Journal of Money Laundering Control* 22, no. 2: 388–399.

Delston, Ross, and Stephen C. Walls. 2009. "Reaching Beyond Banks: How to Target Traded Based Money Laundering and Terrorist Financing Outside the Financial Sector." *Case Western Reserve Journal of International Law* 41, no. 1: 85–118.

———. 2012. "Strengthening Our Security: A New International Standard on Trade Based Money Laundering Is Needed Now." *Case Western Reserve Journal of International Law* 44, no. 3: 737–746.

Drug Enforcement Administration, Federal Bureau of Investigations, Royal Canadian Mounted Police. 2006. Canada/US Organized Crime Threat Assessment. https://www.publicsafety.gc.ca/lbrr/archives/cn27630-eng.pdf.

Financial Action Task Force (FATF). 2006. Trade Based Money Laundering. http://www.fatf-gafi.org/ dataoecd/60/25/37038272.pdf.

———. 2008. Best Practices on Trade Based Money Laundering. https://www.fatf-gafi.org/media/fatf/documents/recommendations/BPP%20Trade%20Based%20Money%20Laundering%202012%20COVER.pdf.

House of Commons. 2022. Standing Committee on Public Safety and National Security. Number 004, 1st Session, 44th Parliament. https://www.ourcommons.ca/DocumentViewer/en/44-1/SECU/meeting-4/evidence.

Howorun, Christina. 2021. "Run for the Border: Guns Smuggled from US Land on Toronto Streets." https://toronto.citynews.ca/2021/04/23/gun-chase-smuggled-guns-border-toronto/.

Kleemans, Edward, and Vere van Koppen. 2020. Organized Crime and Criminal Careers. *Crime and Justice* 49: 385–423.

Levi, Mike, and Soudjin, Melvin. 2020. "Understanding the Laundering of Organized Crime Money." *Crime and Justice* 49: 579-631.

Liao, Jasper, and Arabinda Acharya. 2011. "Transhipment and Trade Based Money Laundering." *Journal of Money Laundering Control* 14, no. 1: 79–92.

Miller, Rena, Liana W. Rosen, and James K. Jackson. 2016. Trade Based Money Laundering: Overview and Policy Issues. Congressional Research Service. https://sgp.fas.org/crs/misc/R44541.pdf Accessed 05/10/2021.

Naheem, Mohammed Ahmad. 2016. "Trade Based Money Laundering: A Primer for Banking Staff." *International Journal of Disclosure and Governance* 14, no. 2: 95–117.

———. 2019. "Anti-Money Laundering/Trade Based Money Laundering Risk

Assessment Strategies – Action or Re-Action Focused? *Journal of Money Laundering Control* 22, no. 4: 721–733.

Northcott, Paul. 2021. Just the Facts – Organized Crime. https://www.rcmp-grc.gc.ca/en/gazette/just-the-facts-organized-crime Accessed 26/09/2021.

Raza, Muhammad Subtain, Qi Zhan, and Sana Rubab. 2020. "Role of Money Mules in Money Laundering and Financial Crimes: A Discussion through Case Studies." *Journal of Financial Crime* 27, no. 3: 911–931.

Shelley, Louise I. 2018. *Dark Commerce: How a New Illicit Economy is Threatening Our Future.* Princeton: Princeton University Press.

Soudijn, Melvin R. J. 2014. "A Critical Approach to Trade Based Money Laundering." *Journal of Money Laundering Control* 17, no. 2: 230–242.

Statistics Canada (StatsCan). 2020. Trafficking in Persons in Canada, 2018. https://www150.statcan.gc.ca/n1/pub/85-002-x/2020001/article/00006-eng.htm Accessed 26/09/2021.

Taekema, Dan. 2020. "Dead Man Walking: Mobster Pat Musitano Has Been Shot and Killed. What Happens Now?" https://www.cbc.ca/news/canada/hamilton/musitano-death-mafia-mob-1.5646395.

United Nations Office of Drugs and Crime (UNODC). 2002. Results of a Pilot Survey of Forty Selected Organized Criminal Groups in Sixteen Countries. https://www.unodc.org/pdf/crime/publications/Pilot_survey.pdf Accessed 05/10/2021.

United States Census Bureau. 2021. Trade in Goods with Canada. https://www.census.gov/foreign-trade/balance/c1220.html Accessed 27/09/2021.

United States Customs and Border Protection (USCBP). 2021. Drug Seizure Statistics. https://www.cbp.gov/newsroom/stats/drug-seizure-statistics.

United States Department of Justice. 2014. "Alleged Rizzuto Crime Family Associate Sentenced to 10 Years Imprisonment." https://www.justice.gov/usao-edny/pr/alleged-rizzuto-organized-crime-family-associate-sentenced-10-years-imprisonment.

WTO. 2020. Highlights of World Trade in 2019. https://www.wto.org/english/res_e/statis_e/wts2020_e/wts2020chapter02_e.pdf Accessed 27/09/2021.

12

Task Specialization in Organized Crime Groups: Money Laundering and the Montréal Mafia

Stephen Schneider

Introduction

One of the many contentious debates in the study of organized crime is whether the offenders involved specialize in certain functions. This task specialization is said to be especially warranted in functions that may require a specific set of technical skills and knowledge. Money laundering has been described as one criminal function that necessitates a certain level of expertise, especially if large amounts of cash are involved and complex (transnational) methods, channels, and transactions are employed.

This chapter is concerned with exploring two interrelated fields within the study of organized crime. The first deals with the ongoing debate about the nature, scope, and existence of task specialization within organized crime groups (OCGs) and mafia-style criminal organizations specifically.[1] The second is related to the predominance of what has been variously called the "professional money launderer," the "money laundering specialist," or the "third-party money launderer."

Despite the abundant theoretical conjectures and a vigorous debate regarding task specialization within OCGs, there continues to be a paucity of empirical research and a lack of published case studies. Moreover, despite the attention dedicated to the issue of money laundering in the extant literature, not to mention the resources allocated to proceeds of crime enforcement globally, there is a limited number of studies examining the extent to which money laundering has become a specialized task and vocational calling.

In addressing these voids, the principal research questions explored in this chapter are as follows: Do (mafia-style) OCGs require a money laundering specialist? Do they have a sufficient division of labour that allows members to specialize in money laundering? If so, are these functions compartmentalized to the extent that the individuals performing them are excluded from carrying out the dominant revenue-generating functions of the OCGs? To what extent are specialized money laundering tasks confined to core members of mafia-style OCGs (or are they also delegated to external associates or other independent contractors)? Is there a certain threshold within an OCG, in terms of illicit revenues earned, that requires the services of an internal money laundering specialist or an external contractor?

An attempt is made to answer these questions by examining the case of the Montréal Mafia, in which members and associates appear to specialize in money laundering. Between the early 1960s and the 1990s, this function was served in succession, somewhat, by three individuals or groups: William Obront (1960s and 1970s), the Caruana-Cuntrera group (1970s, 1980s, 1990s), and Joseph Lagana (1990s). This money laundering function existed despite a change in the group's leadership over the years: Obront served under Vic Cotroni and Paoli Violi (while the Montréal Mafia was still a wing of New York's Bonanno Family), the Caruana-Cuntrera group was closely linked with the Sicilian faction of the Montréal Mafia under Nicolò Rizzuto (who briefly took over after a violent coup in the late 1970s), while Joseph Lagana served as a key lieutenant to Vito Rizzuto, who assumed the leadership from his father in the early 1980s.

The money laundering role was carried out not just by core members but by close associates who could not qualify as made members but were nonetheless powerful within the informal hierarchy of the Montréal Mafia. While these specialists were instrumental in laundering the vast illicit proceeds generated by this criminal group, they were also involved in handling related administrative financial duties, as well as revenue-generating crimes such as gambling, loansharking, market manipulation, and drug trafficking.

When generalized to answer the research questions, this case study suggests that while mafia-style OCG members and associates may be responsible for carrying out specific functions that require some degree of technical skills, they are also expected to carry out other important functions of the OCG, in particular revenue-generating crimes. Thus, the concept of task specialization is somewhat equivocal; there is some level of specialization, but it is performed within the parameters of a multi-functional generalist offender. To be of value to the OCG, all members and associates must be able to contribute directly to its raison d'être: generating revenue.

The case study also provides some insights into third-party money laundering. The specialist members and associates of the Montréal Mafia provided money laundering services to other OCGs and, on at least one occasion, the Rizzuto mafia family turned to a third-party contractor for such services (which turned out to be a police undercover operation). The fact that this atypical money laundering outsourcing was mistakenly delegated to police illustrates the dangers of using third-party contractors and may reinforce the necessity of delegating such criminal activities to trusted OCG members and associates.

Research into this case study entails both secondary sources as well as primary sources that include investigative files and court documents from the RCMP Anti-Drug Profiteering Units and Combined Forces Special Enforcement Units as well as unpublished intelligence reports produced by the RCMP.

Task Specialization in Organized Crime

The literature on organized crime indicates that some OCGs and criminal networks are characterized by task specialization whereby the participating offenders undertake one or more specific functions. Lyman and Potter (2014, 16) say this is especially true in "organized crime hierarchies" where there is a "division of labour" which consists of a "relatively clear allocation of tasks and 'job' descriptions." Vito and Maahs (2015, 333) cite "specialization and a division of labor" as important attributes of OCGs. Other sources identify the "specialization of work tasks" (Hagan 1983) or simply "specialization" as an attribute of OCGs (Albanese 2015). Lupsha (1983, 60–61) characterizes organized crime as "an activity, by a group of individuals, who consciously develop task roles and specializations." The Commission of the European Communities and EUROPOL (2001) state that criminal organizations are made up of multiple offenders, each with his or her own "appointed tasks." Like legitimate corporate organizations, in OCGs "attempts to reach the maximum division of labour and specialisation of its employees" is crucial for improving operations and maximizing profit" (Schloenhardt 1999, 216).

Criminal Intelligence Service Canada emphasizes how important an offender's skill sets are to modern criminal networks many of which are made up of

> ... temporary alliances of individual criminals who merge their *particular skills* to better achieve success in specific criminal enterprises. Once a specific criminal venture is completed, these individuals may continue to collaborate on further criminal activities, or the group may dissolve. Although the individuals may go their separate ways, they sometimes reform into new groups based upon the *skill requirements* of new criminal opportunities. The nature and success of such networks *are largely determined by individual characteristics and skills* among those who act as their component parts (Criminal Intelligence Service Canada 2006, 6, emphasis added).

The nature and extent of specialization have also been explored and debated within the context of mafia-style OCGs that restrict membership to a core group based on certain attributes but may also retain numerous "associates" who play both minor and key roles. The vocation of the specialist varies widely based on the needs of the criminal group and may include chemists, pilots, car thieves, dock workers, enforcers, accountants, or lawyers. The 1986 U.S. President's Commission on Organized Crime alludes to the need for specialized functions that may fall outside the limited skills and resources of the inducted core members of mafia-style OCGs. "Organized crime is the collective result of the commitment, knowledge, and action of three components: the criminal groups, each of which has at its core persons tied by racial, linguistic, ethnic, or other bonds; the protectors, persons who protect the group's interests; and specialist support, persons who knowingly render services on an ad hoc basis to enhance the group's interests" (President's Commission on Organized Crime 1986, 19). Siegel (2018, 515) adds, "transnational organized crime involves a continuous commitment by primary members, although individuals with specialized skills may be brought in as needed."

In contrast to the above arguments, Southerland and Potter (1993, 253) contend, "Tasks in criminal organizations are typically interchangeable and require little sophisticated skill or education" and that "specialization is usually unnecessary and counterproductive because it restricts the freedom of the enterprise to get work done on an efficient basis by using all available manpower in the process" (Southerland and Potter 1993, 254).

Albini (1971) says that OCGs can be made up of both specialized and nonspecialized offenders. For Beare (2003, xxii), "empirical research reveals a complex mix of organized criminal offenders ranging from sophisticated 'specialists' to 'opportunists' – all operating in the same crime field." Research into organized cyber-crimes shows that some require certain technical skills, such as coding and programming to hack into well-protected digital intranet systems or encrypted communications, while other cyber-crimes can be carried out by anyone with access to the internet, such as sending out mass phishing emails or trafficking goods online (Brush 2020; Lavorgna 2020). When online offenders lack technical knowledge, they seek third-party assistance through online sources (via the dark web, discussion boards, social media; Leukfeldt et al. 2019, 341).

In sum, some of the literature appears to support the notion that a division of labour and task specialization is present in both mafia-style hierarchical OCGs and flatter horizontally organized criminal networks (although there is no consensus as to which type of organizational structure is more in need of and conducive to task specialization). The literature also supports the arguments that organized crime groups and networks are made up of a mix of generalists and specialists and that within mafia-style OCGs, specialized tasks may be farmed out to close associates or independent contractors.

Money Laundering as a Task Specialization: A Conceptual and Empirical Overview

Law enforcement cases, criminal intelligence information, and scholarly literature suggest that money laundering has become a specialized function and has prompted the emergence of the so-called professional money launderer (PML). Offenders associated with an OCG and/or active in an illicit market may specialize in this function (or at least devote part of their responsibilities to this task) while independent "third-party" PMLs contract out their services. In their study examining the extent to which drug trafficking groups use third-party money laundering contractors, Malm and Bichler (2013, 372) describe a "professional launderer" as an "individual involved in money-laundering, but not involved in any other aspect of the drug market." A PML may also include criminalized professionals working in the licit economy who are fully cognizant of the illegality of their work and their role as a bridge to the legitimate economy. In an unpublished federal enforcement strategy document dated 2020, the RCMP characterizes "professional money launderers" as "sophisticated actors who engage in large-scale money laundering for TNOC [transnational organized crime]. Professional money launderers may be accountants, bankers, lawyers, import/export companies, realtors, and / or money service businesses" (RCMP 2020).

Based on these two sources, there appears to be some contradictions as to what falls under the label of a "professional money launderer." Levi (2021, 102) provides one way of reconciling this discrepancy: the former is made up of "full-time organized criminals" while the latter is involved in "organized crime facilitation via otherwise legitimate or semi-licit legal and accounting professionals." Regardless of this distinction, the one agreed-upon attribute of PMLs is "they are not involved in the predicate crime, often have no familial or friendship ties with the criminal but only come into play when the money has to be cleaned" (Soudijn 2014, 202).

Based on a survey of thirty-one investigations into large-scale cocaine importation conspiracies in Europe, Soudijn (2014, 207) argues that PMLs do not necessarily "have to be connected to formal occupations, but could also occur in a clandestine cash environment (e.g., underground banking)." He refers to these specialists more broadly as "financial facilitators." In criminogenic terms, a facilitator "is an outsider whose expertise is contracted by the criminal to solve logistic bottlenecks." Thus, a "facilitator is not just anyone who assists in the commission of a crime but somebody who delivers essential services." In Soudijn's study, "the focus is on financial facilitators" – those who assist "a criminal in some key way with money laundering. Such assistance can range from the activities carried out by a professionally trained accountant to an unschooled hawala banker" (Soudijn 2014, 202). These offenders are "not part of the network committing the predicate crimes but come into play when they are hired for their expertise" (2014, 203). This study found that "high-level drug dealers" made use of "financial facilitators" in about half the cases examined. About one-third of the facilitators could be described as underground bankers, sending money or value between countries through an informal value transfer system (IVTS). Another dominant financial service provided was "giving money a legal appearance in order to buy property with it or to invest in the legal economy" (Soudijn 2014, 207).

In its 1993 national drug intelligence report, the RCMP acknowledges that some criminal organizations have employed professionals who specialize in providing money laundering services. "Parallel money networks are established to channel payments and/or launder illicit funds. In such a compartmentalized structure, professional money launderers with no involvement in drug trafficking per se play a pivotal role in the planning and execution of many large-scale laundering operations" (RCMP 1993, 51). The RCMP also asserts that certain drug trafficking organizations channel illicit funds through money pipelines established by other crime groups. "Larger organizations sold their money laundering services to smaller ones and commingled proceeds as they were transferred into various accounts" (RCMP 1993, 52).

During the 1990s, the RCMP's Anti-Drug Profiteering units recognized the need for money laundering services by criminal entrepreneurs and how this niche could be filled by specialists. They did so through ambitious reverse sting operations in which undercover officers posed as PMLs to identify and collect intelligence and evidentiary information on large-scale drug-trafficking organizations by luring them to fake money service businesses with the promise of laundering drug money (*Montreal Gazette* 1994a, 1994c, *The Province* 1996; *Vancouver Sun* 1996; *Ottawa Citizen* 1998). More recently, the RCMP's *Federal Policing Strategic Plan, 2020-23,* indicates they will "prioritize a money laundering investigation when it targets a professional money launderer, international money controller network, or other major facilitator such as a complicit Money Service Business (MSB)" (RCMP 2020, 15).

In its 2015 report entitled *Assessment of Inherent Risks in Money Laundering and Terrorist Financing in Canada,* Finance Canada includes the following analysis of third-party money laundering.

> Large-scale and sophisticated money laundering operations in Canada, notably those connected to transnational OCGs, frequently involve third-party money launderers, namely professional money launderers, nominees or money mules. Of the three, professional money launderers pose the greatest threat both in terms of laundering domestically generated proceeds of crime as well as laundering foreign-generated proceeds through Canada (and through its financial institutions). Professional money launderers specialize in laundering proceeds of crime and generally offer their services to criminals for a fee. These individuals are in the business of laundering large sums of money and by their very nature have the sophistication and capability to support complex, sustainable and long-term ML operations. As a group, they use many different methods and techniques, sometimes within the same scheme, to launder money that is challenging to detect. The professional money launderers are of principal concern since they are often the masterminds behind large-scale money laundering schemes and are frequently used by the most powerful transnational OCGs in Canada. (Finance Canada 2015, 22)

A 2018 report by the Financial Action Task Force (FATF) characterizes a professional money launderer as those individuals, organizations and networks that are involved in "third-party" laundering for a fee or commission. They do not physically handle the cash, but instead "provide expertise to disguise the nature, source, location, ownership, control, origin and/or destination of funds to avoid detection. PMLs may provide the entire infrastructure for complex money laundering schemes (e.g., a "full service") or construct a unique scheme tailored to the specific needs of a client that wishes to launder the proceeds of crime." These PMLs may "provide a menu of generally applicable services, with the result that the same laundering techniques (and potentially the same financial channels and routes) may be used for the benefit of multiple organised crime groups" (FATF 2018, 6).

In its 2019 annual report on organized crime, the Criminal Intelligence Service Canada discusses specific "money laundering service provision networks" that "coordinate and move large sums of money to legitimize criminal proceeds on behalf of Canadian and international OCGs" including triads based in China and Mexican drug cartels (Criminal Intelligence Service Canada 2019, 4, 11). The following year, CISC published a report entitled *National Criminal Intelligence Estimate on the Canadian Marketplace: Money Laundering and Fraud,* which declares that some PMLs based in Canada launder hundreds of millions of dollars per year (Criminal Intelligence Service Canada 2020, 3). Among the cases obliquely referenced in these two reports, one concerns a money service business, based in the Vancouver suburb of Richmond, that may have laundered up to a billion dollars in illicit funds. The PML's clients were said to be Chinese nationals illegally transferring money out of China to Canada and criminal organizations involved in drug trafficking. This PML allegedly laundered the funds through underground banking networks, informal value transfer services, legal and illegal casinos, loans, mortgages, and real estate purchases. The PML benefited financially from this specialization through commissions on all transactions conducted, interest on loans and mortgages provided, as well as liens against properties that were provided financing (Langdale 2017; FATF 2018; German 2018; Schneider 2020).

Other police investigations appear to confirm that some PMLs offer their illicit services through legally incorporated money service businesses (see Dugas, Pomerleau, and Maimon in this volume). A 2016 investigation into a currency exchange firm in North York, Ontario allegedly uncovered a global underground banking network accused of laundering $100 million in just one year. It was reportedly part of a larger network of underground bankers in Toronto and Montréal believed to be connected to Middle Eastern organized crime and terrorism financing. The owner, who faces facing sixteen criminal charges, including laundering drug money, tax evasion, and possession of the proceeds of crime, was arrested after police discovered stacks of cash worth $1.3 million hidden in a hockey bag, a backpack, and a leather travel bag in the trunk of his car (Cooper 2021, 472; *Global News* 2019).

In contrast to studies and police evidence documenting third-party money laundering specialists, Malm and Bichler (2013) argue that most organized and entrepreneurial criminal offenders are involved in "self-laundering." Based on a sample of 129 OCGs drawn from a 2007 RCMP organized crime threat assessment for British Columbia, they found that 80 percent of the groups laundered their own illicit funds while 12 percent were involved in laundering because of kinship or friendship ties – which they characterize as "opportunistic" (not professional) money laundering. Only 8 percent of the cases involved money laundering by a "professional." In short, "the findings suggest that within the illicit drug market, most money laundering is conducted by individuals with other roles in the drug trade, these self-launders would be identifiable through predicate crimes" (Malm and Bichler 2013, 377). While they conclude that "individuals who engage in money-laundering occupy an important structural position relative to others in the drug market," this importance may be inflated because most of them are engaged in other illicit market activities such as drug trafficking or smuggling (Malm and Bichler 2013, 376–377).

Other research suggests that the extent of third-party PMLs is minimal compared to self-laundering by criminal offenders. A study by the Council of Europe (2006) found that only one-third of all money laundering cases in 2004 involved offenders in which money laundering was their primary criminal role (as cited in Malm and Bichler 2013, 367–368).

Reuter and Truman (2004, 112) report on the results of a 1997 survey of correctional inmates in the United States. Of those serving time in a federal institution for a money laundering conviction, most reported some involvement in a revenue-generating predicate offence as well. "Two-thirds of those had some drug involvement and another 18 percent reported fraud/forgery convictions."

It is not surprising that self-laundering may predominate as few offenders generate enough money to require the services of an outside specialist (Levitt and Venkatesh 2000; Levi and Reuter 2006; Soudijn 2014). For some researchers, the engagement of a money laundering specialist is dependent upon the amount of illicit revenue generated and the capacity of the offender behind the predicate crime to manage and disburse a large amount of cash (often in small denominations) without attracting suspicion. Levi (2021, 99) writes that once the offender "generates a volume of business too large to spend immediately and/or to store physically in a place he considers safe (including a bank account or real estate which may be in the name of others), the drug dealer or other illicit trader will need someone with other skills to launder the revenues, at least on an intermittent if not regular basis if he intends to continue a life of crime." Malm and Bichler (2013, 366) contend, "mid-to-upper level drug traffickers are likely to require money laundering services due to the large and consistent amounts of cash they receive." Soudijn (2012, 151) writes, "When extremely large sums of money are involved, as is the case with wholesale narcotics, then it pays to contract out the work of changing the money, instead of doing the job in-house." Notwithstanding the above, the literature is "unclear at what point money laundering is contracted out" (Soudijn 2014, 203) let alone the various other factors to be taken into consideration to ascertain when such third-party services are used. PMLs may also not be used extensively because the cost of their services is too great relative to the volume of profits generated from the predicate offence. "Setting up trusts and using offshore companies require registration and consultancy fees" while costly professional advisors may also be needed (Levi and Soudijn 2020, 580).

Case Study: Task Specialization, Money Laundering, and the Montréal Mafia

The label "Montréal Mafia" refers to an ongoing OCG that dates to the 1950s when New York's Bonanno mafia family made a concerted effort to consolidate many of Montréal's vice rackets, while also establishing the city's commercial marine ports as a conduit for heroin imported from Europe. In the process, they formed a wing of the Bonanno family in Québec that, by the end of the decade, was headed by Vincenzo (Vic) Cotroni. At the core of this *decina* were some twenty inducted "men of honour," including Paolo Violi who would eventually share the *Capo Decina* powers with Cotroni beginning in the mid-1960s. Full-fledged membership in the Montréal Mafia was available only to those of Italian descent. However, tensions between the traditional Calabrian and Sicilian rivals boiled over, culminating in a violent coup by the Sicilian faction headed by Nicolò (Nick) Rizzuto, who had Violi murdered in 1978. He then handed over the reins of Québec's Bonanno wing to his son, Vito, who turned it into an autonomous mafia family in its own right. As Lamothe and Humphreys (2006, 208) write, "few fully recognized the growing influence of the Sixth Family" – a title that alludes to the independence and power of the Montréal Mafia under the Rizzutos by equating it with the five New York mafia families. Vito Rizzuto evolved into what Nicaso and Lamothe (2005, 44) called the "epitome of the modern global gangster" who forged a vast international criminal conglomerate that eventually would surpass the reach, wealth, and power of any of the New York families. In 2007 Rizzuto pleaded guilty in a New York courtroom for his part in the murder of Bonanno mafia family members and was sentenced to an American penitentiary. In 2012, he was deported back to Canada and died of natural causes on December 23, 2013, in Montréal.

Over its many years of existence, the business of the Montréal Mafia entailed a diverse range of profit-oriented organized crimes, including gambling, liquor smuggling and bootlegging, loansharking, drug trafficking, prostitution, protection rackets (extortion), business racketeering, price-fixing, labour racketeering, the theft and fencing of stocks and bonds, mass-marketing fraud, stock market manipulation, and counterfeiting. Members and associates of the Montréal Mafia also controlled several legally incorporated businesses that were used to carry out both legitimate and illegitimate commerce and to launder the proceeds of crime. Indeed, the vast amounts of cash generated from its illegal activities made money laundering such an important tactical imperative for the Montréal Mafia that it became a major preoccupation of senior members and associates.

William Obront

During the 1970s, the Québec Police Commission Inquiry into organized crime in that province concentrated much of its work on the "Cotroni-Violi group." William (Obie) Obront was identified by the commission as a key figure in this criminal organization. Because he was not of Italian heritage, Obront could never have qualified as a "man of honour." Yet, according to the commission, he "appears to have been the individual charged with accomplishing various tasks for the Cotroni-Violi group, particularly in the corporate and financial spheres" (Québec Police Commission Inquiry on Organized Crime 1977a, 26). In his role as "chief financial consultant" to the criminal group, one of Obront's main tasks was to launder and re-invest illegal revenues into both licit and illicit business ventures. Over the course of 1974 and 1975 alone, it was estimated that Obront handled more than $80 million in cash for the Montréal Mafia and its associates (Québec Police Commission Inquiry on Organized Crime 1977b, 148).

According to the Québec Police Commission, during the early to mid-1970s, Obront maintained at least nine personal accounts at four banks. From 1974 to 1975, forty-six people and fourteen companies made cash deposits, ranging from $2,500 to $1.7 million. Over the course of these two years, the deposits, which included Obront's own revenue plus that laundered for other members and associates of the Cotroni-Violi group, totalled more than $18 million. He also incorporated several companies to hide, legitimize, and invest vast amounts of dirty money. Despite a lack of formal business training, Obront appeared to be well at ease in the legitimate world of commerce and, between 1950 and 1975, he was involved in thirty-eight companies as owner, shareholder, or director (Québec Police Commission Inquiry on Organized Crime 1977a, 69, 73, 84; *Toronto Star* 1977).

Obront was also involved in numerous revenue-generating crimes over the years, carried out independently and in close coordination with or under the protection of the Montréal Mafia. He played a key role in helping Paoli Violi take control of illegal bookmaking operations in the Ottawa-Hull area. Obront's predicate crimes overlapped with his "financial consultant" duties in that he was often called upon to find financing for drug trafficking and other capital-intensive entrepreneurial crimes carried out by local mafia members and associates. Project financing ranged from a few thousand dollars to millions of dollars. He incorporated companies such as Trans-world Investments Ltd., which provided capital to both legal and illegal business ventures but was nothing more than an elaborate loansharking operation given the usurious interest rates he charged his clients. The Québec Police Commission heard testimony that Mitchell Bronfman, heir to the Seagram's liquor empire, paid Obront over $1 million in interest on a loan (as cited in the *Globe and Mail* 1977).

By combining his revenue-generating crimes and his money laundering, Obront maximized his illicit profits and cleaned them at the same time. The money his companies lent out was often the proceeds of drug trafficking or extortion, while the resulting loan payments, interest, or investment returns would be claimed as legitimate revenue. He was also active in the stock market through which he laundered the proceeds of crimes committed by himself and others. Using accounts established at seven different brokerage firms, he boosted returns from the companies he invested in by manipulating share prices through heavy trading with mafia associates and company insiders. He was eventually charged with more than four hundred counts of fraudulently manipulating stock market shares over a fifteen-year period. In addition, he laundered money through companies, such as Obie's Meat Market, which served as a cover for his loansharks who posed as travelling salesmen for the business. The company was also a front for the Cotroni-Violi group's infiltration of

Montréal's Expo 67, to which it supplied tainted meat (Québec Police Commission Inquiry on Organized Crime 1977a, 65–66, 72–73, 116, 125–129, 149–154).

The Caruana-Cuntrera Group

On July 16, 1998, arrests were made as part of a series of pre-dawn raids throughout the Greater Toronto Area that targeted the leaders and members of the so-called Caruana-Cuntrera group, which police claimed was one of the world's largest importers and distributors of illegal drugs. Among those arrested in Project Omerta was Alfonso Caruana of Woodbridge, Ontario whom police claimed was the head of the group. Sworn testimony from police informant, Oreste Pagano – a member of the Camorra Mafia in Italy, and the middleman between Caruana and Colombian cocaine suppliers – revealed that between 1991 and 1998, he brokered one cocaine shipment of 4,526 kilograms smuggled into Canada and another 8,200 kilograms smuggled into Italy. Pagano estimated that each of these shipments netted the Caruana-Cuntrera group CDN$36 million (Bourque and Senechal 1988; Marini 2000; Nicaso and Lamothe 2000).

The patriarchs of the two clans, Pasquale Cuntrera and bothers Leonardo and Liborio Caruana, were born in Siciliana, a small village on the southern shores of Sicily, which was also the birthplace of Nick Rizzuto and his son Vito. Joined by blood and intermarriage, the three families were so intertwined that Italian authorities referred to them collectively as the Siciliana Mafia Family. According to the Combined Forces Special Enforcement Unit in Toronto, the Caruana-Cuntrera group also specialized in money laundering, not only handling the proceeds of its illegal activities but from other crime groups as well. When Nick Rizzuto gained control of the Montréal Mafia in the late 1970s, the Caruana-Cuntrera group became its principal drug trafficking and money laundering arm. As Edwards writes, the three families helped transform the Montréal Mafia from a neighbourhood-based group that "mediated community disputes" to a "multi-national drug trafficking conglomerate" (Edwards

1990, 177). The RCMP estimated that between 1978 and 1985, the Siculiana Family imported into Montréal more than 700 kilos of heroin, and between 1984 and 1987, 63,000 kilos of hashish. The sizes of their drug shipments were unprecedented; in 1984, British authorities seized a 58-kilo shipment of heroin hidden in furniture from Thailand that was destined for Montréal. The following year Gerlando Caruana, Alfonso's brother, was arrested, charged, and convicted in connection with the heroin (Bourque and Senechal 1988; Demont 1988; Marini 2000).

The drug bust prompted a larger investigation into the activities of the Caruana-Cuntrera group. While searching through the bank records of Gerlando Caruana, police discovered what they believe was a massive money laundering operation and international cash transport service for the Montréal Mafia and other crime groups. Much of it was overseen by Alfonso Caruana who played mostly a financial role in the group and used bank accounts, wire transfers, bank drafts, real estate transactions, cash smuggling, and shell companies to launder the proceeds of crime. The Caruana-Cuntrera group also relied heavily on professionals such as lawyers, bankers, financial advisors, and accountants, to facilitate their money laundering. They would expressly seek out the help of bank managers of Italian descent and then use bribery or intimidation (based on their connections with the mafia) to ensure compliance and loyalty.

Their earliest money laundering activity dates to 1978 when the three Caruana brothers (Alfonso, Gerlando, and Pasquale) returned to Montréal from Venezuela and established their first shell company "Les Importations Carvel." Each of the brothers also secured a $10,000 loan through Aldo Tucci, a manager at the City and District Savings Bank located on St.-Jean Blvd. With Tucci's help, the RCMP estimated that the Caruanas eventually laundered more than $10 million at this bank branch. Much of the cash deposited was in American funds and was so plentiful that it supplied all the other branches in the Metropolitan Montréal area with US currency, with enough left over to be sold to competitors. At a National Bank branch located on St. Michel Blvd., Giuseppe Cuffaro, a senior member of the Caruana-Cuntrera group and one of its main launderers, had co-opted the bank manager there and between

November 1981 and October 1982 he brought in $14 million in cash. In 1981 alone, Alfonso Caruana had made cash deposits of US$9 million. In total, between 1978 and 1984, it was estimated that the Caruana-Cuntrera had laundered US$33 million through personal and corporate bank accounts in Canada. Once the cash was deposited, it would be quickly withdrawn in the form of bank drafts sometimes in amounts of hundreds of thousands of American dollars (Bourque and Senechal 1988; Demont 1988; Marini 2000; Nicaso and Lamothe 2000).

Their international laundering operation also involved wire transferring drug money from bank accounts in Toronto and Montréal to Miami, Houston, and Mexico City, and then to numbered accounts in Lugano, Switzerland, and from there, to Columbia (to purchase cocaine). On December 20, 1980, Pasquale Cuntrera wire transferred US$1 million to an account at the Credit Swiss Bank branch in Bellinzona, Switzerland. The holder of the account was Leonardo Greco, boss of the Bagheria Mafia family, located in Palermo Sicily. In 1981, the RCMP detected $21.6 million that passed through Alfonso Caruana's bank accounts in the course of only a few months.

The international police investigation into the Caruana-Cuntrera group revealed they had set up and operated dozens of companies spread throughout numerous countries, including Canada, Venezuela, Switzerland, Thailand, Italy, and the Netherland Antilles, to launder their illicit revenues and to facilitate cash transfers and drug shipments. At the same time, they relied heavily on more rudimentary methods to launder money and to pay for drugs on the international market. Oreste Pagano told police that he and Alfonso Caruana preferred to make cash transactions from "hand to hand." Millions of dollars in cash were physically transported across the Canada–US border and to various other countries. Between 1978 and 1984, police estimated that Giuseppe Cuffaro moved more than US$20 million in cash from Montréal to Switzerland. On November 27, 1978, Alfonso Caruana and Cuffaro arrived in Zurich on a Swiss Air flight from Montréal and were fined for failing to declare US$600,000 in cash discovered in false-bottom suitcases. Caruana paid a small fine and was released. As part of his work in purchasing cocaine for the Caruana-Cuntrera group during the 1990s, Pagano admitted to transporting millions of dollars in cash by vehicle from Montréal to Miami to pay for the drugs (Nicaso and Lamothe 2000; *Toronto Star* 2000; KPMG 1999; Marini 2000).

Giuseppe Lagana

In 1995, a Montréal lawyer named Giuseppe (Joseph) Lagana was sentenced to thirteen years in prison after confessing to laundering at least $47 million. Two other lawyers, Richard Judd and Vincenzo Vecchio, both of whom worked in Lagana's law firm, also pleaded guilty and were sentenced to seven and a half years behind bars. Police accused Lagana, who faced 241 criminal charges, of being a close associate of Vito Rizzuto serving multiple roles for the Montréal Mafia including money laundering and drug trafficking. He was also an intermediary between Rizzuto and cocaine suppliers and other organized crime groups. Some RCMP sources speculated that he was a made member of the Rizzuto Mafia family.

The bust by the RCMP was the culmination of a three-year sting operation, called Project Compote, in which the Mounties set up a phony currency exchange business in downtown Montréal under the name of the Centre International Monétaire de Montréal (CIMM). They then had informants spread the word that it was established by underworld figures expressly to launder drug money. The fabrication was so successful that forty-two people were eventually arraigned on charges of laundering $98 million through CIMM. Lagana and his associates were accused of laundering at least $91 million.

Undercover officers who worked at CIMM did business directly with Lagana and the other lawyers. Lagana undertook numerous activities related to laundering the illicit funds: coordinating pick-ups of drug money; personally transporting the money to CIMM; giving instructions (to undercover officers) for the conversion of funds into larger denominations, other currency, or bank drafts; arranging for international wire transfers, and opening bank accounts and establishing companies in Switzerland to receive the money transfers. According to police, Lagana was personally responsible for delivering more than $15 million in Canadian funds to CIMM over four years and, as the police operatives gained his trust, the amounts steadily increased: $410,065 in 1991, $2,615,355 in 1992, $5,763,762 in 1993 and $6,593,165 in 1994. In addition to Vecchio and Judd, Lagana used other employees of his law firm to deliver cash to CIMM. This included a security guard at his law office building who couriered approximately $5.5 million to CIMM between 1991 and 1992.

The investigation also uncovered a plot to ship 558 kilograms of cocaine from Colombia to Britain on behalf of the Hells Angels. Jorge Luis Cantieri, who ran numerous import-export companies in Montréal, was handed a fifteen-year prison term for organizing the cocaine shipment. Lagana's role was to serve as a financial intermediary between the Hells Angels and Cantieri. In the last months of the investigation, police observed Lagana in regular contact with a high-ranking member of the Sherbrooke chapter of the Hells Angels, who was also responsible for financing the cocaine shipment destined overseas for the Hells Angels International. Police also intercepted communications that Lagana was laundering cash provided by Hells Angels members. The Sherbrooke chapter member reportedly collected the cash from other Québec Hells Angels chapters, which would then be turned over to Lagana or one of his junior lawyers.

In the charges filed against Lagana, Vito Rizzuto was identified as an unindicted co-conspirator in the drug shipment. Rizzuto was also listed on a police warrant as one of twenty-seven individuals and thirty-four companies whose bank, accounting, personal, sales, and financial records could be seized if found at Lagana's law office. Rizzuto was not charged; however, other high-ranking members of the Montréal Mafia, such as Vincenzo Di Maulo and Domenico Tozzi, were convicted of money laundering and drug trafficking offences. Tozzi also specialized in money laundering for the Rizzuto crime group and, from December 2, 1991, to July 28, 1994, he was accused of bringing in more than $27 million to CIMM. Police alleged the money was derived exclusively from the drug trafficking connected to the Rizzuto mafia family (RCMP Case File Number: 1991-SEEA-10744; KPMG 1999; Lamothe and Humphreys 2006; Cédilot and Noël 2011; *Montreal Gazette* 1994a, 1994b, 1994c, 1995, 1996a, 1996b, 1996c, 1997; *Globe and Mail* 1995; *National Post* 2001).

Discussion and Analysis

The case study indicates that a specialized money laundering function did exist within the Montréal Mafia during the time frame covered. However, it was not so specialized that those carrying it out avoided other functions, including the most important job of generating revenue for this OCG. The money laundering role was performed, not just by inducted members ("men of honour") of the local mafia but by non-member associates as well. The case study also provides some insights into the existence and use of third-party money launderers in at least two respects. First, while under the leadership of Vito Rizzuto, some money laundering functions were entrusted to a third party (which in this case turned out to be a police undercover operation). Second, the money laundering specialists who were members or associates of the Montréal Mafia also appeared to provide their services to other OCGs. Joseph Lagana was accused of providing financial intermediary services for the Hells Angels while William Obront and the Caruana-Cuntrera group were suspected of commissioning their financial services to OCGs other than the Montréal Mafia.

Drawing from this case study and the extant literature, those engaged in money laundering can be demarcated into three categories: "money laundering specialists," "professionals laundering money," or "professionals facilitating money laundering." What all three categories have in common is that they exclude any individual or organization that *unknowingly* facilitates money laundering and related crimes. In other words, for both conceptual and law enforcement purposes any discussion of the money laundering specialist or professional should be limited to those (offenders) who knowingly carry out this illegal function.

Money Laundering Specialists. This category includes criminal offenders who carry out money laundering duties as a core member or close associate of an OCG. They often lack legitimate professional training and accreditation; instead, much of their skills and expertise come from their experience working in the illegal economy, primarily through the commission of profit-oriented organized crimes. These experiences mean they often seek out laundering opportunities that capitalize on the underground economy (e.g., currency smuggling, covert money service businesses, informal value transfer systems, loansharking). At the same time, they have a basic or even an advanced understanding of legitimate commercial and financial sectors and transactions, which they exploit. They provide laundering services on an in-group basis (as part of the OCG) but may also act as independent third-party contractors to other criminal entrepreneurs.

Professionals Laundering Money. This category encompasses criminalized professionals operating in the legitimate economy who use their accreditation, expertise, and resources to orchestrate money laundering schemes. These services may be an aberration from or only a fraction of their overall legitimate work or they could consume a much larger share. The extant literature provides case studies or examines more generally corrupt lawyers who coordinate elaborate money laundering operations using their expertise and resources (such as legal trust accounts) or professional duties (e.g., facilitating real estate transactions, incorporating companies; Schneider 2004; 2006; Beare and Schneider 2007; Benson 2020; RCMP 2020; Criminal Intelligence Service Canada 2020). In addition to money laundering, these professionals may also be involved in other profit-oriented organized crimes that may or may not be connected to their training and occupation.

Professionals Facilitating Money Laundering. This category also includes professionals who work in the legitimate economy, but unlike the previous category they do not instigate or coordinate money laundering schemes. Instead, they use their position to knowingly undertake specific transactions that enable money laundering. They do not have direct connections to an OCG, but are at the service of, and may be corrupted by OCG members or those occupying the first two categories. They serve as an important conduit for the (cash) proceeds of crime entering the legitimate economy and will also use the legitimate services and assets available to their profession to help launder the funds once the illicit cash has been converted to other assets. In the case study covered by this research, the most notable professionals who populate this category are bankers who knowingly accept large amounts of cash and/or conduct highly suspicious transactions for a questionable client.

The last two categories can include entire organizations and corporations that have been chronically implicated in money laundering and other financial crimes due to institutionalized corruption and malfeasance, or at least blatant willful blindness, including, law firms (Bernstein 2017; Obermaier and Obermayer 2017; Benson 2020) and banks (U.S. Department of Justice 2012; United States Senate, Permanent Subcommittee on Investigations 2012).

These three categories are not necessarily mutually exclusive; their boundaries can be quite blurred and there are more similarities than differences, especially between the first two. For this case study, the "money laundering specialists" and the "professionals laundering money" both worked on an in-group basis with the Montréal Mafia, and both operated in the illicit and licit economies. Another common trait was that the work carried out for the Montréal Mafia was not confined to money laundering; it also involved revenue-generating activities. Obront was active running bookmaking, gambling, fraud, and loansharking operations for Vic Cotroni and Paolo Violi and also worked independently as a drug trafficker, the Caruana-Cuntrera group was involved in heroin and cocaine trafficking, while Lagana was implicated in a cocaine trafficking conspiracy. This evidence suggests that the money laundering task specialization for the Montréal Mafia is not absolute; its members and associates also operated as generalists that handled multiple tasks.

Thus, the findings from the case study appear to support the conclusions of Malm and Bichler (2013): self-laundering was the norm for Montréal Mafia as it was mostly carried out "in-house" by those who also perpetrated revenue-producing organized crimes. Combining revenue-generating predicate crimes with money laundering (e.g., Obront's loansharking that used cash generated from drug trafficking and extortion as its principal source of financing) provides another rationale for arguments that offenders involved in predicate crimes are self-laundering. There is one notable exception, however: Joseph Lagana relied on a third-party money launderer (CIMM), which may have been necessary due to the sheer amount of cash required to be laundered (more than $90 million). Given the large sums involved and the dangers of using a largely unknown third party, approval would most likely have come directly from Vito Rizzuto. The fact that Lagana fell victim to a police undercover operation illuminates the dangers of using third-party contractors and reinforces the need to delegate such criminal activities "in-house" to trusted OCG members and associates.

The question of whether there is a certain financial threshold to necessitate the services of a third-party money laundering specialist is difficult to answer based solely on this case study. What is known is that during the period covered, the Montréal Mafia earned hundreds of millions of dollars from a vast array of criminal enterprises and semi-legitimate businesses which appear to have necessitated the need for all three of the above-mentioned categories. As Soudijn (2014, 203) notes, "It is likely that financial facilitators come into play when large sums of money are involved, but it is unknown where the demarcation line, if any, lies. Criminals might differ from one another very much where their need for assistance is concerned."

The amount of money to be laundered may not be the sole criterion that influences when an OCG turns to an external money laundering specialist. The Caruana-Cuntrera group laundered as much, if not more, drug trafficking proceeds (as specialists within the Montréal Mafia who sometimes relied on professionals facilitating money laundering, in particular bankers) as Lagana did through CIMM (the third-party money laundering specialists). As such, an equally important criterion for determining when a third-party money laundering specialist is used may be the capacity of the OCG to launder large volumes of illicit cash through its internal expertise and resources. The Caruana-Cuntrera wing of the Montréal Mafia appears to have had these qualities and resources while Lagana may have lacked them (and therefore had to turn to CIMM).

This case study may help inform the other analytical framework applicable to this research; that is, whether key functions within Mafia-style

OCGs are performed exclusively by core members. As the findings show, important tasks such as capital financing, producing revenue, and laundering that revenue were carried by both made members and associates closely tied to the Montréal Mafia. Insight into how the same functions are carried out by both members and associates can be gleaned through an understanding of the two kinds of ranks and degrees of power in the Cotroni-Violi *decina*: (1) a formal hierarchy, consisting of a well-defined line of command and in which positions were dictated by ethnicity, kinship, and seniority, and (2) an informal power structure that ranked each member, and even external associates, at a different level of authority and importance based on the individual's personal and business relationships with the mafia's leaders and/or their ability to produce revenue (Québec Police Commission Inquiry on Organized Crime 1977a). The formal hierarchy of the Cotroni-Violi organization had a *Capo Decina* at the top, followed by an underboss, and then several lieutenants, each of which was responsible for a crew of around five soldiers (*picciottis*) assigned to a particular geographic region of Montréal. Not all members of the same formal rank were necessarily equal, however. A *picciotti* who had unique skills or made the *decina* a lot of money had more stature than his official rank indicated (Québec Police Commission Inquiry on Organized Crime 1977a, 51). While he could never be a made member, William Obront was exceptionally powerful in the Montréal Mafia (and reported directly to Cotroni and Violi) because of his financial and business skills, his capacity to raise capital to fund large deals, and his ability to generate revenue and to launder money. What this suggests is that the most important criterion for power within the Montréal Mafia was not necessarily one's status as a "man of honour," but one's ability to make money for the *decina* (indeed, every member or associate was expected to contribute directly or indirectly to the revenue-generating goals of the organization).

Conclusion

This case appears to support the contention that OCGs producing a large amount of illicit (cash) revenue require and can accommodate a money laundering specialist function and that individuals and groups both internal and external to an OCG have emerged to assume this work. Thus, this case study straddles the line between those who argue that OCGs and other criminal entrepreneurs are mostly engaged in self-laundering versus those who contend this function may be farmed out to external third-party money laundering specialists. With respect to the former, the OCG members or close associates carry out the self-laundering function as generalists responsible for multiple functions (most importantly, those that generate revenue for the OCG). These findings call into question the assertions that a defining characteristic of PMLs is that they are not involved in predicate offences, such as drug trafficking. In contrast, OCG members or associates tasked with money laundering may contract out their services to third-party money laundering specialists.

These findings are tempered by a scarcity of data that would provide a more robust accounting of the nature and scope of the different roles played by the money laundering specialists (not to mention the professionals laundering money and the professionals facilitating money laundering) or the overall complexion of money laundering by the Montréal Mafia. The extent to which this OCG relied on internal money laundering specialists versus third parties beyond those identified by research or police evidence is largely unknown. These empirical shortcomings are emblematic of the inherent challenges in conducting rigorous and generalizable research into money laundering and organized crime generally.

While these findings confirm that some level of task specialization and a division of labour exists within the Montréal Mafia, this conclusion cannot be generalized past the money laundering function. More research is needed to examine historical and contemporary OCGs, in all their various forms, to discern their organizational structures and whether a discernable division of labour and task specialization exists.

Regardless of the limitations of this research, given that the time frame covered by this case study dates to at least the early 1960s, these money laundering specialists are not a new phenomenon. Whatever they are called, or the specific role played, they can perform a critical support function for an OCG, or what Klerks (2000) calls "defensive counter-strategies." Money laundering is not an inherently revenue-generating function; instead, it is part of the ostensible objective of any successful OCG: maximizing opportunities while minimizing risks (Vander Beken 2004, 476).

Note

1   For an overview of what constitutes a mafia organization, see Paoli (2020) and Reuter and Paoli (2020).

References

Albanese, Jay S. 2015. *Organized Crime in America: From the Mob to Transnational Crime*. New York: Routledge.

Albini, Joseph L. 1971. *The American Mafia; Genesis of a Legend*. New York: Appleton-Century-Crofts.

Benson, K. (2020). *Lawyers and the Proceeds of Crime: The Facilitation of Money Laundering and its Control*. New York: Routledge.

Beare, Margaret E. 2003. *Critical Reflections on Transnational Organized Crime, Money Laundering, and Corruption*. Toronto: University of Toronto Press.

Beare, Margaret E. and Stephen Schneider. 2007. *Money Laundering in Canada: Chasing Dirty and Dangerous Dollars*. Toronto: University of Toronto Press.

Bernstein, Jake. 2017. *Secrecy World*. New York: Henry Holt and Co.

Bourque, M. J., and C. Senechal. 1988. *Project Pilgrim*. Montreal: RCMP Montreal Anti-Drug Profiteering Unit Intelligence Report (Unpublished).

Brush, Kate. 2020. "What is Cybercrime? Effects, Examples and Prevention." *SearchSecurity*. https://searchsecurity.techtarget.com/definition/cybercrime.

Cédilot, Andre, and Andre Noël. 2011. *Mafia Inc.: The Long, Bloody Reign of Canada's Sicilian Clan*. Toronto: Random House Canada.

Commission of the European Communities, and EUROPOL. 2001. *General Conclusions of the Forum on Organised Crime Prevention, the Hague, 4th and 5th November 1999*. The Hague, Netherlands: Commission of the European Communities and EUROPOL.

Cooper, Sam. 2021. *Wilful Blindness: How a Criminal Network of Narcos, Tycoons and CCP Agents Infiltrated the West*. Montréal, Toronto: Optimum Publishing International.

Council of Europe. 2006. *Organised Crime Situation Report, 2005*. Strasbourg: Council of Europe.

Criminal Intelligence Service Canada. 2006. *Annual Report on Organized Crime in Canada*. Ottawa: Criminal Intelligence Service Canada.

———. 2019. *Public Report on Organized Crime in Canada*. Ottawa: CISC.

———. 2020. *National Criminal Intelligence Estimate on the Canadian Criminal Marketplace: Money Laundering and Fraud 2020*. Ottawa: CISC.

Demont, John. 1988. "A Dangerous Trail: Police Pursue the Profits from Drug Sales." *Maclean's*, October 31: 40–42.

Edwards, Peter. 1990. *Blood Brothers: How Canada's Most Powerful Mafia Family Runs Its Business*. Toronto: Key Porter Books.

Finance Canada. 2015. *Assessment of Inherent Risks in Money Laundering and Terrorist Financing in Canada*. Ottawa: Department of Finance Canada.

Financial Action Task Force (FATF). 2018. *Professional Money Laundering*. Paris: FATF.

German, Peter. 2018. *Dirty Money, Part I. An Independent Review of Money Laundering in Lower Mainland Casinos Conducted for the Attorney General of British Columbia*. Vancouver: Peter German and Associates.

Global News. Feb. 28, 2019. "Toronto Man Arrested with $1M in Cash May Have Ties to International Money Launderer."

Globe and Mail. Feb 4, 1977. "Mitch Bronfman Paid Obront $1 Million Interest, Probe Told."

———. June 30, 1995. "Lawyer Jailed for 13 Years."

Hagan, Frank E. 1983. "The Organized Crime Continuum: A Further Specification of a New Conceptual Model." *Criminal Justice Review (Atlanta, Ga.)* 8, no. 2: 52–57.

Klerks, Peter. 2000. "Groot in De Hasj: Theorie En Praktijk De Georganiseerde Criminaliteit. (Big in Hash: Theory and Practice of Organised Crime)." Doctoral Dissertation, Eramus University.

KPMG. 1999. *1998/99 Performance and Accountability Review of the Anti-Smuggling Initiative Volume I. Technical Report*: Report submitted to the Department of the Solicitor General.

Lamothe, Lee, and Adrian Humphreys. 2006. *The Sixth Family: The Collapse of the New York Mafia and the Rise of Vito Rizzuto*. Toronto: Wiley & Sons Canada.

Langdale, J. 2017, November 2. Impact of Chinese Transnational Crime on Australia: Intelligence Perspectives [lecture]. New South Wales Police Force's Intelligence Conference.

Lavorgna, Anita. 2020. "Organized Crime and Cybercrime." In *The Palgrave Handbook of International Cybercrime and Cyberdeviance*, edited by T. J. Holt and A. M. Bossler, 117–134. Champlain: Palgrave Macmillan.

———. 2021. "Making Sense of Professional Enablers' Involvement in Laundering Organized Crime Proceeds and of their Regulation." *Trends in Organized Crime* 24, no. 1: 96–110.

Levi, Michael, and Peter Reuter. 2006. *Money Laundering*. Chicago: University of Chicago Press.

Levi, Michael, and Melvin Soudijn. 2020. "Understanding the Laundering of Organized Crime Money." *Crime and Justice* 49, no. 1: 579–631.

Levitt, Steven D., and Sudhir Alladi Venkatesh. 2000. "An Economic Analysis of a Drug-Selling Gang's Finances." *The Quarterly Journal of Economics* 115, no. 3: 755–789.

Lupsha, Peter A. 1983. "Networks Versus Networking: Analysis of an Organized Crime Group," In *Career Criminals*, edited by G. P. Waldo, 59–87. Beverly Hills, CA: Sage.

Lyman, Michael D., and Gary Potter. 2014. *Organized Crime*, 6th ed. Upper Saddle River, NJ: Pearson.

Leukfeldt, E. Rutger, Edward R. Kleemans, Edwin W. Kruisbergen, and Robert A. Roks. 2019. "Criminal Networks in a Digitised World: On the Nexus of Borderless Opportunities and Local Embeddedness." *Trends in Organized Crime* 22, no. 3: 324–45.

Malm, Aili, and Gisela Bichler. 2013. "Using Friends for Money: The Positional Importance of Money-Launderers in Organized Crime." *Trends in Organized Crime* 16, no. 4: 365–381.

Marini, Regina. 2000. *Italian Organized Crime. Money Laundering Techniques.* Toronto: RCMP Toronto Integrated Proceeds of Crime Unit (unpublished).

Montreal Gazette. 1994a. Money-Laundering Ring Smashed; Lawyers Arrested, Assets Frozen, Cocaine Seized in Raids." Aug 31.

———. 1994b. "Many Fish Caught in Mounties' Net; But Biggest Got Away, They Say." Sept. 1.

———. 1994c. "RCMP Traces Cash in Huge Money-Laundering Case." Oct. 16.

———. 1995. "Lawyer Handed 13-Year Prison Sentence for Overseeing Money-Laundering Scheme." June 30.

———. 1996a. "Di Maulo Pleads Guilty." Mar. 14.

———. 1996b. "Tozzi Gets 10-Year Term." Mar. 21.

———. 1996c. "Man Sentenced to Four Years for Money Laundering." Oct. 2.

———. 1997. "Two Friends of Mobster Found Guilty." May 23.

Morselli, Carlo, Thomas Gabor, and John Kiedrowski. 2010. *The Factors that Shape Organized Crime.* Public Safety Canada.

National Post. 2001. "The Man They Call the Canadian Godfather." Feb. 26.

Nicaso, Antonio, and Lee Lamothe. 2000. *Bloodlines: The Rise and Fall of Mafia's Royal Family.* Toronto: HarperCollins.

———. 2005. *Angels, Mobsters, and Narco-Terrorists: The Rising Menace of Global Criminal Enterprises.* Toronto: John Wiley & Sons.

Ottawa Citizen. 1998. "RCMP's Sting Aided Drug Lords." June 11.

President's Commission on Organized Crime. 1986. *America's Habit: Drug Abuse, Drug Trafficking, and Organized Crime.* Washington, DC: Government Printing Office.

Paoli, L. 2020. "What Makes Mafias Different?" *Crime and Justice* 49, no. 1: 141–222.

Québec Police Commission Inquiry on Organized Crime. 1977a. *Organized Crime and the World of Business.* Québec: Editeur officiel du Québec.

———. 1977b. *The Fight Against Organized Crime in Quebec: Report of the*

Commission on Organized Crime and Recommendations. Québec: Editeur officiel du Québec.

Reuter, Peter, and Edwin Truman. 2004. *Chasing Dirty Money: The Fight Against Money Laundering*. Washington, DC: Institute for International Economics.

Reuter, P., and L. Paoli. 2020. "How Similar are Modern Criminal Syndicates to Traditional Mafias?" *Crime and Justice* 49, no. 1: 223–287.

Royal Canadian Mounted Police (RCMP). 1993. *RCMP National Drug Intelligence Estimate 1992/93*. Ottawa: RCMP.

———. 2020. *RCMP Federal Policing Strategic Plan 2020-2023*. Ottawa: Royal Canadian Mounted Police.

Schloenhardt, Andreas. 1999. "Organized Crime and the Business of Migrant Trafficking: An Economic Analysis." *Crime, Law and Social Change* 32, no. 3: 203–233.

Schneider, Stephen. 2004. "Money Laundering in Canada: A Quantitative Analysis of Royal Canadian Mounted Police Cases." *Journal of Financial Crime* 11, no. 3: 282–291.

———. 2006. "Testing the Limits of Solicitor-Client Privilege: Lawyers, Money Laundering, and Suspicious Transaction Reporting." *Journal of Money Laundering Control* 9, no. 1: 27–47.

———. 2020. *Money Laundering in British Columbia: A Review of the Literature*: Submitted to The Commission of Inquiry into Money Laundering in British Columbia.

Siegel, Larry. 2018. *Criminology: The Core*, 7th edition. Belmont, CA: Wadsworth Publishing Company.

Soudijn, Melvin. 2012. "Removing Excuses in Money Laundering." *Trends in Organized Crime* 15, no. 2: 146–163.

———. 2014. "Using Strangers for Money: A Discussion on Money-Launderers in Organized Crime." *Trends in Organized Crime* 17, no. 3: 199–217.

Southerland, Mittie D., and Gary W. Potter. 1993. "Applying Organization Theory to Organized Crime." *Journal of Contemporary Criminal Justice* 9, no. 3: 251–267.

The Province. 1996. "Police Spring Trap in Massive Drug Haul." Jan. 25.

Toronto Star. 1977. "Banker Moved $84 Million for Underworld." Jan. 21.

———. 2000. "The Bust That Almost Wasn't. Two-Year Probe of Caruanas Cost $8.8 Million." May 4.

United States Senate, Permanent Subcommittee on Investigations, Committee on Homeland Security and Government Affairs. 2012. *Permanent Subcommittee on Investigations, United States Senate. U.S. Vulnerabilities to Money Laundering, Drugs, and Terrorist Financing: HSBC Case History*. Washington, DC: United States Government Printing Office.

U.S. Department, of Justice. 2012. "HSBC Holdings PLC. and HSBC Bank USA N.A. Admit to Anti-Money Laundering and Sanctions Violations, Forfeit $1.256 Billion in Deferred Prosecution Agreement." *Department of Justice Press Release*, December 11.

Vancouver Sun. 1996. "Business People Laundered Cash." Jan. 26.

Vander Beken, Tom. 2004. "Risky Business: A Risk-Based Methodology to Measure Organized Crime." *Crime, Law and Social Change* 41, no. 5: 471–516.

Vito, Gennaro F., and Jeffrey Maahs. 2015. *Criminology: Theory, Research, and Policy*, 4th edition. Burlington, MA: Jones & Bartlett Learning.

Containing Financial Crime: Innovations in Multilevel Governance

13

Canadian Cryptocurrency Conundrums: A Socio-Technical Systems Analysis of Crypto Laundering in Canada

Caitlyn Jenkins, Rhianna Hamilton, and Christian Leuprecht

Introduction

In 2022, experts identified US$20.6 billion in illicit cryptocurrency transactions, an all-time high (Chainalysis 2023, 5). While an estimated three quarters of cryptocurrency payments are legal, illicit payments are pervasive, accounting for a quarter of cryptocurrency activity (Foley, Karlsen, and Putniņš 2019). Cryptocurrency is a digital asset used for purchase, trade, investment, and other financial needs and takes place on a virtual public ledger referred to as a "blockchain." The term "cryptocurrency" is often used interchangeably with "crypto," "virtual currency," "crypto coin," and "digital currency" (Clements 2022, 3; Leuprecht, Jenkins and Hamilton 2022); throughout the chapter we refer to this type of asset as "cryptocurrency." Similarly, "crypto laundering" is a term that refers to money laundering that takes place using cryptocurrency either in part or holistically. This encompasses any criminal scheme engaging in money laundering, the process of turning "dirty money" into "clean money" usable in the financial system (Leuprecht et al. 2022).

Crypto laundering differs from traditional money laundering in that it focuses on the illicit trade of crypto coins in addition to traditional state-backed funds. Crypto laundering thus encompasses schemes using crypto coins, like Bitcoin, and schemes using non-fungible tokens (NFTs), a blockchain-based image or entity that has a unique ID and corresponding metadata, for example an image or painting (Clements 2022, 43). Cryptocurrency entered the market in 2009 through the creation of Bitcoin by an anonymous individual referred to as "Satoshi Nakamoto." The backdrop of the 2008 financial crisis and its associated distrust in traditional finance garnered Bitcoin significant support in its infancy (Redshaw 2017, 46). To this day, Bitcoin is the most popular form of cryptocurrency with 42.42 percent of the market capitalized by Bitcoin as of February 2022 (CoinMarketCap 2022). This is also reflected in the illicit market where Leuprecht, Jenkins, and Hamilton's sample suggests that Bitcoin is the most popular cryptocurrency used in criminal schemes, in three quarters of their cases (2022).

The creation of Bitcoin, and subsequently cryptocurrency payments, has changed the global financial system by enabling the use of virtual assets untethered to any single country. This has assisted criminals with circumvention of traditional financial system, and, by extension, traditional anti-money laundering (AML), know your customer (KYC), and combatting the financing of terrorism (CFT) procedures. The relative novelty, constant changes in the crypto market, and lack of base knowledge of crypto laundering patterns have all impacted Canada's regulatory response to crypto laundering, and cryptocurrency generally. Canada's regime has been described as a "robust and wide-ranging regulatory governance framework" (Clements 2022, 55). While Canada's cryptocurrency regime may be evolved and quite regulated, this is not necessarily true for its crypto laundering mitigation regime. For example, Canada currently has no measures in place to regulate the buying or selling of NFTs, despite estimates that more than US$8 million in illicit funds have been laundered through NFTs and US$100 million worth of NFTs being reported stolen between 2021 and 2022 (Elliptic Connect 2022, 4). In comparison, the European Union requires that anyone purchasing or selling a work of art, including virtual art such as NFTs, carry out customer due diligence through their agreement on the *EU Markets in Crypto-Assets.*

As such, this chapter takes specific concern with crypto laundering regulations within Canada, and abroad as they specifically pertain to crypto laundering and will explore the current regulatory landscape of Canadian crypto laundering responses.

Most cryptocurrency transactions operate nearly independently from any traditional state-backed financial system, which makes government oversight difficult. This attribute has raised both praise and concern. Bitcoin and other forms of decentralized cryptocurrencies, such as Ethereum and Monero, are notoriously difficult to track due to their pseudo-anonymous nature. Services such as "mixers," "cross chain bridges" and "tumblers" disburse the transactions and further hide the origins of funds by distorting and layering cryptocurrency transactions, a technique that appeals to criminals who are laundering money (Clements 2022, 29). The Ethereum-based cryptocurrency mixer Tornado Cash was used as a designated ML tool for 52 percent of NFT scam proceeds before it was hit with United States' Office of Foreign Assets Control (OFAC) sanctions in 2022 (Clements 2022, 4). Similarly, RenBridge has facilitated the laundering of the equivalent of at least US$540 million, which included the proceeds of ransomware attacks by North Korea (Elliptic Connect 2022). It is complexities like these that Canada's crypto laundering regime remains unequipped to address.

Canada has taken an active, though not leading, role in the emerging world of cryptocurrency regulation. The Canada Securities Administration (CSA), Bank of Canada, Payments Canada, and the Canadian Imperial Bank of Commerce have all integrated blockchain technology into their respective systems (Ducas and Wilner 2017, 540; Clements 2022, 6). The Canada Revenue Agency (CRA 2022) is working within a framework set by the Organisation for Economic Co-operation and Development (OECD) that builds on existing reporting standards. Within Canada, provinces have also put forward regulations, with the Ontario Securities Commission (OSC) providing the Toronto-based TokenGX with exemptive relief from dealer registration requirements among other privileges (Dewan and Samra 2017; Ontario Securities Commission 2017). Following this in 2022, Alberta passed the Financial Innovation Act (FIA; Alberta

Government 2022). The first of its kind in Canada, this FIA allows financial technology (fintech) companies to develop and test new services, for example a new crypto coin (Clements 2022, 20), within the province and provides them with a "regulatory sandbox" to do so (Alberta Government 2022). Like many other regulatory changes in the Canadian cryptocurrency sphere, the impact of recent changes is hard to gauge. The speed with which cryptocurrency-based crime evolves is far faster than the Canadian policy development addressing it. This means that Canada is limited in its address of complex ML schemes like crypto laundering.

Scholarship on cryptocurrency has generally focused on critical analyses of regulation as well as empirical or practical studies on the transfer and prevention of crypto laundering. One preoccupation has been the efficacy of existing regulatory frameworks as they relate to domestic institutions (Pocher and Veneris 2021; Gamble 2017; Ponsford 2015; Niji Oni 2021; Bergström 2019). Scholars are studying the practical mechanisms that launderers have used to move money and suggest either technological or investigative solutions to these issues (Kethineni and Cao 2020; Sanchez 2017; Custers, Oerlemans, and Pool 2020). Other crypto laundering scholarship applies different theoretical approaches to crypto more broadly. For example, Desmond, Lacey, and Salmon (2019) apply a socio-technical systems approach to their overview of crypto laundering literature. The theory advocates for a combined institutional analysis of human, social, and technological factors (Locke and Sommerville 2010). That socio-technical approach examines the human, technological, and political features of crypto laundering.

This chapter applies systems thinking to evaluate Canada and its capacity to address crypto laundering. Specifically, we analyze the effectiveness of Canadian institutions that address crypto-laundering and assess the mitigation measures in place. We identify the actors who are regulating and investigating cryptocurrency in Canada and how responsive Canada's regulatory framework is to the socio-technical system in which crypto laundering operates. To tackle crypto laundering, our systems analysis identifies a need for Canada to (1) centralize the dissemination of information, and (2) develop transboundary relationships and approaches that address crypto laundering on a global rather than merely on a domestic scale. First, this chapter contextualizes cryptocurrency within financial crime in Canada. Second, it draws on data on the Royal Canadian Mounted Police (RCMP) to review relevant investigative and prosecuting agencies. Third, it provides an overview and analysis of regulations set out by the Canadian government and the Financial Action Task Force (FATF). The conclusion makes recommendations about shifting to a systems approach in response to emerging crypto-laundering trends in Canada.

Materials and Methods

The Cryptocurrency Landscape

Cryptocurrency is becoming ever more popular, despite frequent market volatility such as the May 2022 crypto crash and the November 2022 FTX crash (Clements 2022, 46; Browne 2022). Bitcoin's service launch in 2009 was premised on removing financial reliance from banks and state-tied finance following the 2008 banking crisis (Redshaw 2017, 46). In December 2022 there were at least 21,844 cryptocurrencies with about half of those inactive (McGovern 2022). Many of the cryptocurrencies that have emerged since 2009 are also based on resisting traditional finance; however, there has been an evolution in purpose for many coins (Redshaw 2017, 46). Central bank currencies have emerged as a government response with some governments' state-owned cryptocurrencies tied to their respective financial systems (Clements 2022, 9). This is done to encourage crypto users to operate within government confines and increase regulatory oversight. For example, in 2018 Venezuela introduced "Petro," or PTR, a state-tied crypto coin backed by the oil and gas industry (Chohan 2018, 1). Similarly, the Bank of Canada has begun exploring different models of implementation for a state-backed Canadian cryptocurrency based on the potential decline in useage of traditional currency (Bank of Canada 2022). The rise and subsequent use of state-backed coins have raised concerns about government surveillance, privacy, cyber security risks, and operational efficacy (Clements 2022, 9). Other coins have been put forward as investment opportunities; some of these coins are referred to as "stable coins" as their value is pegged to a stable security, for example the United States Dollar or gold (Clements 2022, 9). Stable coins are the most prominent type of coin, representing 90.37 percent of the total cryptocurrency market as of February 2023 (CoinMarketCap 2023). Other investment coins are fad coins meant to garner investment support, many of these are legal opportunities for interested opportunists. These coins are of particular risk to the public if they are fraudulent, because of the lack of public understanding regarding this technology. Losses from cryptocurrency investment scams reached C$163.9 million in 2021 alone. The Canadian Anti-Fraud Centre observed that most of these schemes offered higher-than-standard monetary returns which consistently resulted in largescale losses or total losses to investors (Canadian Anti-Fraud Centre 2022).

Akin to traditional finance, many actors operating within the cryptocurrency industry are guilty of engaging in financial crime practices such as fraud, insider trading, and money laundering (Félez-Viñas, Johnson, and Putniņš 2022). For example, OneCoin, a crypto coin based in Bulgaria, turned out to be a pyramid scheme that defrauded investors of about $4 billion worldwide (Qadir and Ahmad 2021, 275). In April 2022 Coinbase, the United States' largest cryptocurrency trading platform, saw its manager and two associates prosecuted for facilitating insider trading and wire fraud, an issue that is appearing systemic within the company (Félez-Viñas, Johnson, and Putniņš 2022, 1).

Other coins have pushed beyond the goals of Bitcoin, further separating finance from state entities. These coins are referred to as altcoins and are often developed to further anonymize cryptocurrency. Monero is an example of a coin aimed at increasing privacy for those who sue people and is intent on distancing itself from the financial system (Monero 2022; Clements 2022, 29). While many of the transactions that take place on these anonymous blockchains are legal, they have caught the attention of criminals and have become a popular mode of laundering money. These coins are not only useful for hiding funds and anonymizing actors, but they also operate in spaces that lack regulatory oversight. Decentralized finance lacks procedures to address money laundering, have little to no KYC procedures, and regulation for virtual trading platforms (Clements 2022, 29). These private coins are thus disproportionately vulnerable to exploitation by money laundering schemes.

The most popular types of cryptocurrencies are decentralized and use peer-to-peer blockchains: Bitcoin, Litecoin, Ethereum, and Monero are all examples of decentralized cryptocurrency (FATF 2014). The blockchain functions as a digital ledger that records details of each transaction. Cryptocurrency is transferred between digital "wallets," each with its own cryptographic signature. Each transaction also has a unique signature, known as a "hash." Most blockchains are public, but only collect details associated with each hash, without identifying the sender or receiver. Other blockchains are private, which allows some cryptocurrency transactions to remain more elusive, for example, Monero. The blockchain operates simultaneously as a mode of exchange, a record of asset ownership, and a mode of investment, making it a complex and layered form of technology.

Centralized cryptocurrencies, which have largely fallen by the wayside, have a central administrator to control the currency and monitor transactions that occur on the blockchain. Examples of centralized currencies include WebMoney and PerfectMoney, as well as Liberty Reserve and E-Gold, both of which are now defunct. Centralized currencies align more closely with how the global financial system has traditionally operated due to their central authority and administration. That makes centralized forms of cryptocurrency less popular than decentralized ones.

The pseudo-anonymous nature of blockchain technology has allowed criminals to hide their identity, circumvent banks, increase intermediary points made in illicit transactions, make tracing of illicit funds more difficult for law enforcement, raise questions about jurisdictional responsibility, and increase criminal activity in the virtual domain. This has all happened with little to no increase in overhead costs for criminal actors. In summary, cryptocurrency can provide an easier, less resource-intensive, and more subtle way to move value illegally. To address cryptocurrency-based money laundering, law enforcement and regulatory bodies must become equipped to address the virtualization and internationalization of money laundering. The advent of crypto laundering highlights issues within a lagging anti-money laundering system that benefits criminals.

A Socio-Technical Systems Approach

This chapter uses a socio-technical systems approach, originally grounded in mathematics, but with significant application to social-scientific analysis of technological forces such as cryptocurrency. A socio-technical systems lens stresses the operational system that shapes individual institutions, actors, technology, or social attitudes. In the case of crypto-laundering, a socio-technical systems approach postulates technology, such as blockchain, as an intervening variable within a greater system, comprising political variables such as government regulation, economic variables such as trends in the global financial system, and social variables such as human behaviour in the form of criminal activity and emergent technological innovation (Baxter and Sommerville 2011). That is, crypto laundering must be understood within the socio-technical system of which it is part (Desmond et al. 2019). In applying empirical research, this chapter builds on the approach of Desmond, Lacey, and Salmon (2019), using their initial assumption that crypto laundering is best understood in the context of a socio-technical systems approach. This approach to crypto-laundering stresses technological variables such as tumblers, human variables, criminal networks, alongside institutional variables such as investigative agency capacity. Crypto laundering operates in a complex system that is neither centralized nor stagnant, which is why we are positing a systems approach to study this problem (Desmond et al. 2019, 427).

Canadian Agencies Addressing Crypto Laundering

Due to the asymmetric and constitutional characteristics of the Canadian federation, one of the hallmarks of Canadian law enforcement is its decentralization (Hataley and Leuprecht 2019). That is reflected in the way Canada approaches cryptocurrency: multiple organizations and agencies

Table 13.1: Frequency of Canadian Agencies in ML/TF

Agency	Frequency
Royal Canadian Mounted Police	7
Public Safety Canada	1
Public Prosecution Service of Canada	1
Integrated National Enforcement Team	2
Le Directeur des poursuites criminelles et pénales	1
Canadian Security Intelligence Service	2
Canada Revenue Agency	1
BC Securities Commission	1

with a crypto laundering mandate, yet limited jurisdictional oversight and clarity on deconflicting responsibilities. Rather than creating specialized investigative capacity for cryptocurrency, Canada has redundant resources and roles among various organizations (Leuprecht et al. 2022). There is no central organization equipped to harness synergies in investigative capacity, consistency regulation, and dissemination of up-to-date research and information on crypto laundering. This generates redundancy, poor information sharing, and limited options to build specialized skills. This section draws on the RCMP as a critical case study in addressing crypto laundering: where the organization excels and where it falls short.

Data in this chapter draws from a larger sample of data on money laundering and terrorist financing. Individual money laundering, terrorist financing, and crypto laundering cases were collected from law databases, such as West Law and CanLii, and then coded using our own instrument. Relevant to this chapter are data points on the agency that investigated and prosecuted the schemes in question. When a branch of an organization was listed in a legal document, we coded the specific sub-agency used. For example, the Integrated National Enforcement Team (INSET) is led by the RCMP but was coded as an individual organization because of their level of investigative involvement. When data was unavailable in legal documents, this information was coded using secondary source research from newspapers, press releases, or policy briefs. This data was intended to uncover which organizations are interacting with Canadian money laundering and terrorist financing, and whether they are adequately equipped to do so. While the following analysis is focused on investigative agencies, we also coded the main groups prosecuting the crime in question. The data was analyzed using a simple frequency-table approach.

In our sample, the RCMP deals with the most money laundering cases of any agency in Canada; consequently, for the purposes of this chapter it serves as a critical case study to evaluate Canada's investigative capacity for crypto laundering. Other notable organizations and suborganizations that came up frequently include INSET and the Canadian Security Intelligence Service (CSIS).

Institutions differ in how they operate, the jurisdictions they cover, and their respective mandates. The number of RCMP occurrences may be a function of it being more specific about cryptocurrency than other agencies, such as the CRA. While on the surface the RCMP appears to be the most prepared of the agencies in our sample to investigate or work with investigators to address money laundering, even the RCMP lacks central jurisdiction, consistent resources, and community engagement of organizations, such as the CRA.

RCMP Capacity to Address Crypto Laundering

The RCMP is Canada's lead agency in addressing money laundering and terrorist financing, as reflected in our sample. However, it has plenty of room to grow in addressing these issues, especially crypto laundering. It suffers from a lack of expertise, lack of resources, and the persistent difficulty in addressing transnational cases (which tends to characterize crypto laundering generally) that require multi-jurisdictional cooperation. Still, the RCMP has noteworthy initiatives including a national cryptocurrency coordinator and guidelines for the investigation and seizure of virtual assets; training on all levels through professional development courses on national financial crime, proceeds of crime, financial integrity, and cybersecurity; collaboration with partners to improve their awareness of cryptocurrency and its role in financial crime, including the

National Cybercrime Coordination Centre (NC3; RCMP 2022) and an incipient Financial Crime Coordination Centre (FC3). To improve the monitoring and investigation of the illicit use of Bitcoin, police departments across Canada have acquired software tracing tools to track the flow of digital funds (Cullen 2020, 48).

NC3 has software to track ransomware. Since the beginning of the 2022 fiscal year, 55 percent of NC3's Canadian cases have involved ransomware attacks (RCMP 2022). The visibility of these attacks does not necessarily represent the nature of cybercrime, or by extension, crypto laundering. Addressing crypto laundering will require a focus on the financial and human drivers of cybercrime, not just technological ones. As a result, cyber units can play a supporting role but are no silver bullet for systemic change in investigative operations.

At the same time, law enforcement is overwhelmed by the sheer volume of crypto crime. In the first quarter of 2022 alone, the Richmond detachment of British Columbia's RCMP Division received twenty-two reports of cryptocurrency fraud with economic losses totalling $2.6 million (Canadian Press 2022). Between 2017 and 2021, the RCMP documented a 400 percent increase in cryptocurrency fraud, including fraudulent investment opportunities and extortion (Matassa-Fung 2021). Similarly, in 2022 Saskatchewan saw a major uptick in cryptocurrency fraud with the Swift Current RCMP reporting CD$361,000 in losses and Maidstone RCMP seeing CD$570,000 in losses (Kiedrowski 2023). While police are getting better at tracking Bitcoin and prosecuting related cyber-enabled crime, the exponential growth in crypto crime, combined with the development of altcoins, tumblers, and mixers makes it difficult for law enforcement to keep up.

Implementing a Socio-Technical Approach in the RCMP

Many law enforcement officers have no idea what a "blockchain" is, nor would they understand money laundering patterns if they came across them. A better understanding of how cryptocurrency operates and how crypto-laundering works financially is indispensable (Leuprecht et al.

2022). To minimize crypto laundering, the RCMP needs more resources and training opportunities, and the organization needs to expand beyond ransomware to discern and uncover "tumbler functions," minimize fraudulent cryptocurrency investment schemes, and unpack the role of NFTs in concealing funds. Those involve collaboration with other organizations and regulatory agencies, as will be discussed in the next section. The RCMP would benefit from looking at tumblers and mixers as integral to money laundering schemes, analyzing and investigating them as they do banks in traditional financial crime schemes. Increasing jurisdiction and oversight over these emerging technologies will not only help the RCMP in understanding the structure and schemes of crypto laundering but could be a potential vehicle in uncovering cases. Furthermore, the RCMP must appreciate why a criminal would choose one cryptocurrency over another (for example the use of Bitcoin vs. Monero) and provide better links between the financial system's traditional AML approaches (as discussed in this volume in the chapter by Simpson and Field) for banking and crypto laundering.

Beyond the expansion of investigative capacity and resources, the RCMP has difficulty investigating transnational crimes (Cullen 2022). This issue plagues just about every domestic intelligence agency, but the inherently global nature of crypto laundering makes it a particularly difficult crime for domestic institutions to investigate, let alone prosecute. That leaves the RCMP with two options to address transnational crypto laundering and its jurisdictional complexities: Either transnational cases are passed off to organizations with ready capacity to work with other countries and investigative agencies, such as CSIS or Interpol. This option neither fosters better knowledge of crypto laundering within the RCMP, nor does it decrease the burden on domestic agencies. However, it could be an opportunity to foster RCMP crypto-laundering connections and create information sharing agreements. Or the RCMP builds out its capacity to work with agencies in other jurisdictions to increase capacity to investigate crypto laundering. While the RCMP does currently have liaison officers in various countries to support their investigations, this is an insufficient model to address cryptocurrency. Rather than having individuals representing the RCMP abroad, the RCMP could increase its information sharing mechanisms with relevant parties, for example police organizations in other states or with agencies such as Interpol. This option involves the development of long-term plans through international agreements and partnerships, a long-term initiative that would improve the RCMP's capacity to dedicate time and resources to crypto laundering.

The RCMP's ability to perform investigations, have jurisdictional access, and authorize warrants is reliant on federal and provincial legislation and regulations. These regulations will be further discussed in the next section. For now, we observe that the development of regulations should include provisions that support investigative work into crypto laundering. For example, current regulatory standards in Canada provide oversight to businesses in the crypto currency trade but lack oversight for individuals engaging in cryptocurrency (Clements 2022, 21). This makes it more difficult for the RCMP to authorize investigations into individuals independent from businesses in the cryptocurrency sector who are engaged in crypto laundering. This is indicative of a need for comprehensive legislation that allows the RCMP the necessary resources and jurisdiction to conduct their investigations.

Canada's 2022 Federal Budget Report proposed C\$17.1 million over five years to conduct a review of the "digitalization of money" (Government of Canada 2022). This largescale investment is based on concerns about the use of cryptocurrency as a tool to evade sanctions, specifically regarding Iranian entities (Clements 2022, 30). This five-year period of funding provides Canada with a significant opportunity to enhance current regulatory measures to combat money laundering but, more importantly, to investigate how crypto laundering is operating within Canada to inform investigative practices. At this point, effective prevention of crypto laundering entering Canada is impossible, because it is so prevalent. However, there is an opportunity to remove some crypto laundering players from the Canadian economy and leverage that to prevent Canada from becoming a crypto laundering destination.

Many of the shortfalls the RCMP are facing are emblematic of issues with Canada's crypto laundering regime broadly. For example, the

CRA lacks many mechanisms to cooperate with foreign partners and faces slow bureaucratic processes to developing up-to-date training on crypto laundering, particularly as it pertains to tax evasion (Government of Canada 2022). Some standards are being set by organizations such as the OECD, which outlines how tax law and administration can be put to effective use, and opportunities to standardize tax law and tax investigation as it pertains to cryptocurrency (OECD 2022). These organizations would all benefit from a central authority, for example FATF on the international level, or the CRA on the domestic level, creating clear guidelines and support systems for investigative agencies trying to broaden their knowledge of cryptocurrency. The mounting number of victims of crypto-fraud also suggests a need for greater public awareness (Matassa-Fung 2022). Mitigation could take the form of public education to recognize theft disguised as an investment opportunity and false cryptocurrency requests from individuals impersonating government or law enforcement.

Regulation of Crypto Laundering in Canada

The Proceeds of Crime (Money Laundering) and Terrorist Financing Act (PCMLTFA) is the most notable piece of legislation regulating financial crime, including crypto laundering, in Canada. In 2019, "virtual assets" were added to the Act. The amendments stipulate that anyone "dealing in virtual currencies," be it virtual currency exchanges, digital wallet providers, or similar businesses must register with the financial Transactions and Reports Analysis Centre of Canada (FINTRAC). They must also implement a compliance program that is in accordance with FINTRAC standards. As of June 2021, a reporting entity has mandated reporting "the receipt from a person or entity of an amount of $10,000 or more in virtual currency in a single transaction" to FINTRAC as well as the receipt of $100,000 or more in virtual currency from a Politically Exposed Person (PEP), Head of an International Organization (HIO), their family members or close associates (Government of Canada, 2019). In response to the federal government invoking the Emergency Measures Act as a response to Canadian convoy protests, additional changes were also made to the Act in 2022 to cover crowdfunding through virtual currencies (Justice Laws 2022). The 2022 changes to the Act now require crowdfunding platforms, which use virtual currency record-keeping, obligations, and subjects them to oversight by FINTRAC (Clements 2022, 22).

Most changes to the Act pertaining to ML resulted from a 2016 report from the FATF, which subsequently rates member countries on their compliance with its recommendations.

FATF originally rated Canada as non-compliant with Recommendation 15 – New Technologies and has since changed its rating to "mostly compliant," due to the 2019 amendments to the Act. With the amendments, Canada has

> [E]stablished an obligation for reporting entities to include the assessment and documentation of ML/TF risks, taking into consideration their products, services and delivery channels, the geographic location of their activities and any other relevant factor in their compliance programs. If a person/ entity intends to carry out a new development or introduce a new technology that may have an impact on clients, business relationships, products, services or delivery channels or the geographic location of their activities, they shall assess and document the risk before doing so. (FATF 2021)

These amendments reflect systems thinking on virtual currencies and their socio-technical nature. The current PCMLTFA requires diverse regulations that consider the kind of businesses dealing with cryptocurrencies, a way to counter the pseudo-anonymity of blockchain technology with in-depth reporting, and record keeping requirements and differentiating standards that match the behaviour of potentially illicit transactions. For example, while every entity that deals in virtual currency must report transactions over $10,000 to FINTRAC, record keeping differs by the nature of the agent. Financial entities, money service businesses, and foreign money service businesses are required to keep records of any virtual currency transaction over $1,000 dollars (Government of Canada 2019). To launder stolen or illicit cryptocurrency through these businesses, criminals often break transactions into many smaller sums to avoid detection. This regulation contributes to the prevention of small-sum transaction techniques. However, security dealers, casinos, life insurance companies, companies, or accountants, only have to keep records of virtual currency transactions over $10,000 (Government of Canada 2019). These types of businesses often deal in larger sums, and any attempt to clean illicit virtual currency in this fashion is more likely to involve larger amounts.

Risk assessment is an important contributing factor to the success of such socio-technical systems. Similarly, a risk-based approach has also been flagged as integral to AML efforts. The virtual currency amendments to the Act have marked a shift to risk-based thinking in crypto-laundering regulation. However, more is needed to implement a comprehensive systems approach in the investigation and regulation of crypto laundering, which we will explore in the following section.

Moving Toward a Systems Approach in Canada

Central to socio-technical systems thinking is the organizational structure of an entity as a point of analysis. Crypto laundering has an organizational structure comprised of interdependent licit and illicit actors within the broader global economy. It contains a complex network of relationships across actors, software, and hardware. Any attempt to understand and ultimately contain the proliferation of cryptocurrency in money laundering requires an understanding of these actors. It requires an approach that deals with crypto networks as a whole, rather than in discreet parts. To do so, investigation and regulation of crypto laundering must situate both knowledge and practice within this systems approach.

Knowledge

One of the main barriers to the prevention and prosecution of crypto laundering is a lack of understanding of cryptocurrencies per se. On the hardware and software side of crypto networks, investigators must be aware of how the technology functions, what is required to use cryptocurrencies, and be able to differentiate between different cryptocurrencies and their functions. In 2021, there were more than 7,000 different crypto coins in use, now in 2023 that number is up to 9,314 active coins (CoinMarketCap 2023). Governing actors' lack of knowledge about hardware

Figure 13.1: Modelling a Typical Money Laundering Scheme

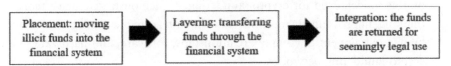

and software complicate prevention. While those laundering cryptocurrency may not completely understand the technology either, their use of the cryptocurrency nonetheless manipulates the government's dearth of knowledge to commit financial crime. You need to have a certain level of understanding of cryptocurrencies to leverage them in the commission of financial crime. A potential solution is the creation of a dedicated cybersecurity team within all investigating and governing agencies dealing with the abuse of cryptocurrencies or a cybersecurity expert group that can work with relevant entities as consultants. The team could evaluate potential crypto-laundering cases through a technical lens and explore potential vulnerabilities for abuse within blockchains, which in turn can be used in preventative measures for regulatory and investigative initiatives.

On the human side of crypto networks, government agencies must adapt their understanding of money laundering broadly. The standard model of money laundering – placement, layering, and integration – has been largely taken for granted as to how money laundering functions in the real world. However, the introduction of cryptocurrency has disrupted this understanding insofar as cryptocurrencies complicate this simple three-step process (Figure 13.1; Leuprecht et al. 2022). For example, we have documented crypto-laundering schemes that bypass the placement stage in this model altogether. Others created a pre-layering stage in which funds acquired were completely legitimate (that is, absent a precursor crime). Another was found to have mirroring layering and integration stages from multiple actors within one scheme. Yet another created a completely self-sustained and self-contained money laundering model as an offshoot for illicit funds derived from other sources (Leuprecht et al. 2022). In short, these cases did not conform to expectations based on the conventional model. However, institutions still largely rely on this model, even for crypto laundering. To demonstrate true systems thinking, improvements must be made that integrate the behaviour of the human component in complex relationships, software, and hardware in crypto-laundering networks.

Practices

From a socio-technical systems perspective, investigating agencies and regulatory bodies that address crypto-laundering affect the decisions of criminal networks through their own informational relationships. How authorities change and relate to one another affects how they relate to financial crime. For example, the RCMP's improved ability to trace the illicit use of Bitcoin with private sector tools correlates with a rise in illicit use of altcoins such as Monero. These coins have ledger technology that is more private and more difficult to track than Bitcoin (Monero 2022). If we treat investigative and regulatory agencies as interdependent within networks of crypto laundering, the opposite should also be true: how government agencies relate to these illicit networks and with one another should be a function of changes in crypto laundering.

The prosecution and regulation of crypto laundering has been diffuse: several agencies on multiple levels of government, each with their discreet mandate. Breaking up authority on these crimes makes it difficult to see the larger organizational structure of networks and relationships that is central to systems thinking. Much of Canada's AML regime has been built in pieces as new issues have arisen. As new tools and behaviours of money laundering are introduced, such as cryptocurrency, institutions play catch-up to fit them within the regime, which precipitates gaps and vulnerabilities. However, if we shifted this perspective to understand Canada's AML regime as interdependent with the crimes they prosecute, these institutions become more flexible and adaptable to evolve within the money laundering process. Within the actual practices of the AML regime, this may look like a streamlined system of information sharing or increased collaboration among agencies. For crypto-laundering in particular, Canada's AML regime would benefit from a central authority that treats crypto-laundering as a socio-technical system within its mandate and provides clear guidance to other agencies in the crypto-laundering ecosystem.

Yet, there is little evidence of a systems approach within the knowledge or practices of Canada's AML regime. It is difficult to visualize, therefore, how exactly this approach might function. However, the Cullen Commission (2022) demonstrates the possibility of systems thinking within state initiatives. Its *Final Report* had a section on virtual assets and associated recommendations. Akin to propositions in this chapter, Recommendation 86 identifies the need for a "dedicated provincial money laundering intelligence and investigation unit, ensure that law enforcement, regulators, and Crown counsel with relevant duties are trained to recognize indicators and typologies of money laundering through virtual assets" (Cullen 2022, 1383). This recommendation highlights the importance of adequate knowledge about crypto-laundering and practices that can withstand evolution within the law and crimes themselves.

Throughout the section, the Cullen Commission emphasizes the importance for law enforcement and government agencies to develop capabilities to deal with the technological and human elements of virtual assets to prevent their abuse. Cullen embodies the spirit of systems thinking by acknowledging the complexity of the problem as a whole while analyzing its constituent parts. The result is a series of recommendations that are meant to deal with the system of crypto laundering by evaluating the provincial AML regime in British Columbia.

Due to the transnational nature of crypto laundering, however, a systems approach on a provincial scale is an inchoate application of the theory. Future legal or regulatory attempts to deal with crypto-laundering need to be cognizant of the socio-technical nature of cryptocurrency networks as well as the role of the state in influencing and being influenced by evolving dynamics of these networks.

Conclusion

In this chapter, we applied a socio-technical systems theory approach as discussed by Desmond et al. (2019) to the Canadian context. Specifically, we identified elements of this socio-technical systems approach that already exist within Canada's capacity to address crypto-laundering and additional steps to be taken. First, the chapter established laundering of cryptocurrency as part of a greater socio-technical system, and for it to be approached as such. Using the RCMP as a case study, the chapter explored how investigative agencies currently tackle crypto-laundering and how to implement a socio-technical systems approach. The chapter also discussed the role of the PCMLTFA in regulating crypto-laundering and how new amendments to the Act may align with socio-technical systems thinking. Finally, the chapter gauged options to apply socio-technical systems thinking to Canada's AML regime. The recommended changes will better equip investigative and regulatory agencies at containing and prosecuting crypto laundering. Two of the biggest issues in tackling crypto laundering are confusion concerning approaches to stop these types of crimes and confusion about jurisdictional responsibility for cryptocurrency. This hampers investigation and prosecution. The socio-technical systems approach described in this chapter seeks to mitigate both problems.

Future areas of research in crypto laundering would benefit from a comprehensive analysis of investment schemes, altcoins, tumbler websites, and NFTs. While these mechanisms proliferate in financial crime, there is little scholarly research. Crypto-laundering research would also benefit from a broader understanding of the technology itself and how it operates, as researchers and officers alike struggle to comprehend the complex technology used to commit these crimes. Minimizing crypto laundering will require higher technological literacy in this regard.

References

Alberta Government. 2022. "Financial Innovation Act." July 1, *Government of Alberta Publications*. https://open.alberta.ca/publications/f13p2.

Bank of Canada. 2022. "Central Bank Digital Currency." Digital Currencies and Fintech: Projects.

Baxter, Gordon, and Ian Sommerville. 2011. "Socio-Technical Systems: From Design Methods to Systems Engineering." *Interacting with Computers* 23, no. 1: 4–17. doi: 10.1016/j.intcom.2010.07.003.

Bergström, Maria. 2019. "Legal Perspectives on Money Laundering." In *Research Handbook on Transnational Crime*, edited by Valsamis Mitsilegas, S. Hufnagel, and A. Moiseienko, 98–111. Cheltenham: Edward Elgar Publishing. https://doi.org/10.4337/9781784719449.00014.

Browne, Ryan. 2022. "Binance Deploys $1 Billion to Keep Crypto Industry Afloat After FTX Collapse." *CNBC*, November 24. https://www.cnbc.com/2022/11/24/binance-creates-1-billion-crypto-industry-fund-after-ftx-collapse.html.

Canadian Anti-Fraud Centre. 2022. "Canadian Anti-Fraud Centre Bulletin: Crypto Investments." News & Alerts, March 8. https://fcnb.ca/en/news-alerts/canadian-anti-fraud-centre-bulletin-crypto-investments.

Canadian Press. 2022. "More Than $2.6M Lost to Cryptocurrency Frauds in Less Than Four Months: RCMP." *CTV News*, April 13. https://www.ctvnews.ca/sci-tech/more-than-2-6m-lost-to-cryptocurrency-frauds-in-less-than-four-months-rcmp-1.5860778.

Canada Revenue Agency (CRA). 2022. "Section 3 – Introduction to the Canada Revenue Agency (CRA)." Government of Canada. 2022. https://www.canada.ca/en/revenue-agency/corporate/about-canada-revenue-agency-cra/canada-revenue-agency-ministerial-transition-documents-november-2015/section-3-introduction-canada-revenue-agency-cra-1.html.

Clements, Ryan. 2022. "*Commissioned Paper: Cryptocurrency: Challenges to Conventional Governance of Financial Transactions.*" Ottawa: Public Order Emergency Commission. https://publicorderemergencycommission.ca/files/documents/Policy-Papers/Cryptocurrency-Challenges-to-Conventional-Governance-of-Financial-Transactions-Clements.pdf.

Chainalysis. 2023. "The 2023 Crypto Crime Report: Everything you need to know about cryptocurrency-based crime." Chainalysis. February. The Chainalysis 2023 Crypto Crime Report

Chohan, Usman W. 2018. "Cryptocurrencies as Asset-Backed Instruments: The Venezuelan Petro." *SSRN*. February 7. https://ssrn.com/abstract=3119606.

CoinMarketCap. 2022. "Today's Cryptocurrency Prices by Market Cap." CoinMarketCap. February. Cryptocurrency Prices, Charts And Market Capitalizations | CoinMarketCap

Cullen, Austen. 2020. "Proceedings at Hearing of November 23, 2020." In *The Commission of Inquiry into Money Laundering*.

———. 2022. "*Commission of Inquiry into Money Laundering in British Columbia.*" Final Report. Vancouver, Cullen Commission. https://cullencommission.ca/files/reports/CullenCommission-FinalReport-Full.pdf.

Custers, Bart, Jan-Jaap Oerlemans, and Ronald Pool. 2020. "Laundering the Profits of Ransomware; Money Laundering Methods for Vouchers and Cryptocurrencies." *European Journal of Crime Criminal Law and Criminal Justice*, 28, no. 2: 121–152. doi: 10.1163/15718174-02802002.

Desmond, Dennis B., David Lacey, and Paul Salmon. 2019. "Evaluating Cryptocurrency Laundering as a Complex Socio-Technical System: A Systematic Literature Review." *Journal of Money Laundering Control* 22, no. 3: 480–97. https://www.emerald.com/insight/content/doi/10.1108/JMLC-10-2018-0063/full/html.

Dewan, Rajeev and Valenteena Samra. 2017. "*OSC Grants Exemptive Relief to Token Funder Inc.*" Vancouver: McMillan. https://mcmillan.ca/insights/publications/osc-grants-exemptive-relief-to-token-funder-inc/.

Ducas, Evangeline, and Alex Wilner. 2017. "The Security and Financial Implications of Blockchain Technologies: Regulating Emerging Technologies in Canada." *International Journal: Canada's Journal of Global Policy Analysis* 72, no. 4: 538–562. doi:10.1177/0020702017741909.

Elliptic Connect. 2022 "Cross-Chain Crime: More Than Half a Billion Dollars Has Been Laundered Through a Cross-chain Bridge." *Elliptic Connect*, October 2022: https://hub.elliptic.co/analysis/cross-chain-crime-more-than-half-a-billion-dollars-has-been-laundered-through-a-cross-chain-bridge/.

Félez-Viñas, Ester, Luke Johnson, and Talis J. Putniņš. 2022. "Insider Trading in Cryptocurrency Markets." *Social Science Research Network* 1, no. 20. SSRN: https://ssrn.com/abstract=4184367 or http://dx.doi.org/10.2139/ssrn.4184367.

Financial Action Task Force (FATF). 2014. "*Virtual Currencies: Key Definitions and Potential AML/CFT Risks.*" Paris: FATF. https://www.fatf-gafi.org/media/fatf/documents/reports/virtual-currency-key-definitions-and-potential-aml-cft-risks.pdf.

———. 2021. "*Anti-Money Laundering and Counter-Terrorist Financing Measures: Canada.*" Research Report No. 4. Enhanced Follow-up Report & Technical Compliance Re-Rating, Paris: FATF. https://www.fatf-gafi.org/en/publications/Mutualevaluations/Fur-canada-2021.html.

Foley, Sean, Jonathan R. Karlsen, and Tālis J. Putniņš. 2019. "Sex, Drugs, and Bitcoin: How Much Illegal Activity Is Financed through Cryptocurrencies?" *The Review of Financial Studies*, no. 32: 5. doi: 10.1093/ rfs/hhz015.

Gamble, Connor. 2017. "The Legality and Regulatory Challenges of Decentralised Crypto-Currency: A Western Perspective." *International Trade and Business Law Review* no. 20: 346–361.

Grauer, Kim, Will Kueshner, and Henry Updegrave. 2022. "Introduction." In "*The 2022 Crypto Crime Report.*" Chainalysis, 2–8. https://go.chainalysis.com/2022-crypto-crime-report-demo.html.

Government of Canada. 2019. "Proceeds of Crime (Money Laundering) and Terrorist Financing Act." *Justice Law*. https://laws-lois.justice.gc.ca/eng/acts/P-24.501/FullText.html.

———. 2022. "Tax Fairness and Effective Government." In *Federal Budget*, April 7, 2022. https://budget.gc.ca/2022/report-rapport/chap9-en.html.

Hataley, Todd, and Christian Leuprecht. 2019. "Canada." In *Public Security in Federal Politics*, edited by Christian Leuprecht and Todd Hataley, 53–77. Toronto: University of Toronto Press.

Kethineni, Sesha, and Ying Cao. 2020. "The Rise in Popularity of Cryptocurrency and Associated Criminal Activity." *International Criminal Justice Review* 30, no. 3: 325–344. https://doi.org/10.1177/1057567719827051.

Kiedrowski, Ryan. "Crypto Crime up across Saskatchewan." *SaskToday*. Jan 24. Crypto crime up across Saskatchewan - SaskToday.ca

Justice Laws. 2022. "Emergency Economic Measures Order." February 15, *Government of Canada*. https://laws-lois.justice.gc.ca/eng/regulations/SOR-2022-22/FullText.html.

Leuprecht, Christian, Caitlyn Jenkins, and Rhianna Hamilton. 2022. "Virtual Money Laundering: Policy Implications of the Proliferation in the Illicit Use of Cryptocurrency." *Journal of Financial Crime*, 19 September 2022. https://www.emerald.com/insight/content/doi/10.1108/JFC-07-2022-0161/full/html.

Lock, Russell, and Ian Sommerville. 2010. "Modelling and Analysis of Socio-Technical System of Systems." *IEEE*, March. https://ieeexplore.ieee.org/document/5628610/authors#authors.

Matassa-Fung, Darrian. 2021. "Cryptocurrency Fraud Grew 400% in Canada, RCMP Says." *Global News*, March 23. https://globalnews.ca/news/7713786/cryptocurrency-fraud-grew-400-in-canada-rcmp-says/.

McGovern, Thomas. 2022. "How Many Cryptocurrencies Are There in The World in 2022?" *Earthweb*, December 3. https://earthweb.com/how-ma-ny-cryptocurrencies-are-there/.

Monero. 2022. "What is Monero (XMR)?" Monero. October 4, 2022. https://www.getmonero.org/get-started/what-is-monero/.

Niji Oni & Co Legal Practitioners. 2021. "Regulation of Cryptocurrency in Various Jurisdiction across the World." *SSRN Electronic Journal*, May. https://papers.ssrn.com/sol3/papers.cfm?abstract_id=3841589.

OECD. 2022. "Forum on Tax Administration." OECD. November 2022. https://www.oecd.org/tax/forum-on-tax-administration/.

Ontario Securities Commission. 2017. "Token Funder Inc Decision." October 17. https://www.osc.ca/en/securities-law/orders-rulings-decisions/token-funder-inc.

Pocher, Nadia, and Andreas Veneris. 2021. "Privacy and Transparency in CBDCs: A Regulation-by-Design AML/CFT Scheme." *IEEE International Conference on Blockchain and Cryptocurrency*, ICBC 2021: 1–9. https://ieeexplore.ieee.org/document/9461090.

Ponsford, Matthew P. 2015. "A Comparative Analysis of Bitcoin and Other Decentralized Virtual Currencies: Legal Regulation in the Peoples Republic of China, Canada, and the United States." *Hong Kong Journal of Legal Studies* no. 9: 29–50. https://www.academia.edu/10291465/A_Comparative_Analysis_of_Bitcoin_and_Other_Decentralised_Virtual_Currencies_Legal_Regulation_in_the_Peoples_Republic_of_China_Canada_and_the_United_States.

Qadir, Aram Mohammed Amin, and Rebwar Mohammed Ahmad. 2021. "One Coin – Scam Cryptocurrency Impact on Financial Market." *Technium Social Sciences Journal* no. 16: 27–282.

RCMP. 2022. "The National Cybercrime Coordination Unit (NC3)." Royal Canadian Mounted Police. https://www.rcmp-grc.gc.ca/en/nc3#a1.

Redshaw, Tom. 2017. "Bitcoin Beyond Ambivalence: Popular Rationalization and Feenberg's Technical Politics." Thesis Eleven, 138, no. 1: 46–64. https://journals.sagepub.com/doi/10.1177/0725513616689390.

Sanchez, Edgar G. 2017. "Crypto-Currencies: The 21st Century's Money Laundering and Tax Havens." *University of Florida Journal of Law and Public Policy* 28, no. 1: 167–192. https://scholarship.law.ufl.edu/jlpp/vol28/iss1/6.

14

Private-Public Partnership Opportunities in the Canadian AML and Regulatory Landscape

Pamela E. Simpson and Cameron Field

> I have concluded that more must be done to explore constitutionally permissible ways of developing actionable intelligence that is responsive to the needs of law enforcement agencies. (Cullen 2022)

Public-private partnerships (PPP) between private financial institutions and other reporting entities, financial intelligence units (FIUs), and law enforcement agencies are celebrated for their ability to aid each other in the unified fight against financial crime in Canada. However, each entity would benefit from improvements to information-sharing frameworks within PPPs to increase enforcement capabilities against perpetrators of financial crime. As federally regulated entities, each Canadian financial institution has obligations under Canada's anti-money laundering and terrorist financing legislation, i.e., the Proceeds of Crime Money-Laundering and Terrorist Financing Act (PCMLTFA), to implement robust anti-money laundering (AML) programs. The purpose of these programs is to detect, report, and mitigate any money laundering or terrorist financing activity identified within an organization's operating environment. This is achieved through reporting entities, like financial institutions, to share information with the Financial Transactions and Reports Analysis Centre of Canada (FINTRAC), Canada's Financial Intelligence Unit (FIU), which then provides relevant information to Canadian law enforcement to reduce financial crime in Canada. Public and private entities alike benefit from understanding the illicit flow of money within Canada. Reporting entities' mandatory compliance with AML regulations safeguards them from exorbitant fines, reputational impairment, and financial loss. Accurate and timely intelligence sharing between partners within AML PPPs would enable reporting entities to improve detection capabilities and provide more actionable intelligence to FINTRAC and subsequently law enforcement, ultimately reducing the illicit flow of money within Canada.

PPPs provide enhanced oversight, detection, and prevention of Canada's myriad financial and other criminal issues. Specifically, PPPs have been lauded by industry professionals for "[coming] together under a single banner, to marshal their forces against money laundering, romance scams and other frauds, child exploitation and human trafficking" (Monroe 2021). Recent PPPs continue to show improvement in strengthening Canada's fight against money laundering, in contrast to 2016 when Canada received a dismal evaluation in tackling money laundering from the Financial Action Task Force (FATF) Mutual Evaluation Report (MER). The 2021 follow-up report from the FATF shows some improvement, with Canada overturning six of the recommendations from "non-compliant" to at least partially compliant (FATF 2021). Canada should continue its upward trajectory in improving its AML regime by focusing on actionable information-sharing processes within PPPs.

Increasing the effectiveness surrounding AML PPPs between Canada's major financial institutions, other reporting entities, FIUs, and law enforcement rely on information-sharing agreements in place remaining compliant with privacy laws, the ability to optimize the type of information requested and shared between public and private entities and providing an efficient yet secure process for sharing such information. However, while PPPs contribute to holistic intelligence and data sharing between partners, the relationship can be hampered by stringent privacy controls, inefficient processes related to requesting information, and an incomplete feedback loop to improve AML modelling.

The first half of this chapter details the information-sharing frameworks within Canadian PPPs, and the strengths and weaknesses of the information-sharing processes within these groups. The second half of this chapter looks to the United States' Bank Secrecy Act (BSA) and PATRIOT Act Sections 314a and 314b as a framework for Canadian legislation to adopt and enhance information-sharing processes within PPPs. Finally, the chapter concludes with a case study of the Counter Illicit Finance Alliance of British Columbia (CIFA-BC), demonstrating the evolving advantages found within existing PPPs and recommendations to enhance the efficiency and quality of data shared within PPPs moving forward.

Overview of the Information-Sharing Landscape between Financial Intelligence Units, Financial Institutions, and Law Enforcement within Private-Public Partnerships

This section begins by describing the structure of, and initiatives undertaken by, Canadian AML PPPs. Next, it will outline information-sharing structures between PPP participants and identify current avenues for sharing within the intelligence continuum. Canada's intelligence continuum for information sharing within PPPs is shaped by the PCMLTF Act. Canada currently has a compliance-focused AML regime through the PCMLTFA, with subsequent guidance from FINTRAC and the Office of the Superintendent of Financial Institutions (OSFI). AML-focused PPPs within Canada identify and report specific types of criminal activity in addition to regulatory compliance reporting. Since the adoption of PPPs by FINTRAC, law enforcement, and reporting entities, the reciprocal flow of information has increased investigative and enforcement capabilities, dramatically improving community safety. Notably, Canada's top federally regulated banks participate in PPPs with the aforementioned groups to supplement the mandatory disclosure process of suspicious transactions to FINTRAC. This has resulted in the creation of various projects undertaken to combat specific crimes throughout Canada. Since 2016, "the public-private model has expanded out from identifying indicators of human trafficking (#project protect), to other types of crime such as romance fraud (project chameleon or #chameleon), [and] opioid and fentanyl trafficking (#project guardian or #fentanyl)" (ACFCS 2020). The results of these efforts can be seen through the disruption and dissipation of select human trafficking networks, illicit fentanyl networks, romance scams, money laundering in casinos, and online child exploitation rings notably, Project Protect, praised as being the "first of its kind in the world" (Public Safety Canada 2022). Project Protect exemplifies how increased collaboration between PPP participants can reduce crime in Canada. According to Public Safety's National Strategy to Combat Human Trafficking 2019-2024, FINTRAC was able to provide 500 disclosures of actionable intelligence to law enforcement across all levels of government in support of human trafficking investigations (Public Safety Canada 2022).

In this intelligence continuum, the three participating groups (i.e., FINTRAC, law enforcement, and reporting entities) within the PPP play an integral role in sharing intelligence through legally sanctioned channels. For example, it is common for law enforcement agencies to publish media and public notices when persons are arrested and charged with crimes. In many of these notices, police will provide the name, age, and city along with the related charges. Financial institutions deploy an array of powerful and diverse media tools that scan for adverse media posts and cross-reference them with current customer data. If matches are established between adverse media and customers, then financial institutions assess their clients' risk posture and determine if there is an obligation to file suspicious transaction reports (STRs) to FINTRAC. FINTRAC then assesses all incoming information, usable and workable intelligence, and makes disclosures to law enforcement agencies of potentially workable intelligence when feasible. Law enforcement can then engage FINTRAC with details of ongoing investigations through a voluntary disclosure. This provides a source of intelligence for FINTRAC as it seeks to assess and distill incoming information from more than 31,000 sources (FINTRAC 2016). Law enforcement is not able to access the raw data reported to FINTRAC by reporting entities. Instead, law enforcement sends FINTRAC a request for information, and FINTRAC conducts the analysis on the raw data, which it then sends back to law enforcement. This process can be time-consuming and adds a layer of analysis and filtering to the information.

Through coordination with the Canadian Bankers Association (CBA) and participating financial institutions, law enforcement and intelligence agencies can circulate information on persons of interest and suspects in ongoing criminal probes. Financial institutions then commence reviews of identified persons to whom they provide financial services on the premise that they are potentially involved in criminal activities. If financial institutions determine a reporting obligation is required, for instance, identifying suspicious activity on the identified person's account, then STRs are filed, and the financial institution's legal obligations are satisfied. FINTRAC then assesses all incoming information from institutions and discloses the financial intelligence to a law enforcement agency when warranted.

While FINTRAC remains a necessary middle node in the exchange of information from reporting entities to law enforcement, law enforcement agencies can disclose information directly to reporting entities. This method of information sharing is undertaken through a proactive disclosure. Law enforcement and intelligence agencies can provide direct disclosures to industries, such as financial institutions, through confidential bulletins or organized meetings and correspondence. While this may seem like a viable solution to obtaining and sending actionable intelligence directly between reporting entities and law enforcement, there are certain limitations which are explored further in the next section.

Canada's current information-sharing regime stipulates that law enforcement is entitled to conduct targeted or general disclosures related to ongoing public safety issues. Such authority can be found in such statutes across Canada by provincial legislatures. In a more targeted setting, law enforcement can provide information directly to various industries, for example, financial institutions, in the interests of community safety. Provided law enforcement documents the process and information shared and discloses all aspects of their investigative process for future court proceedings (*Regina v. Stinchcombe* refers [1991] 3 SCR 326), these steps are authorized by provincial statute.[1]

Within PPP meetings or exchanges, law enforcement can provide details of community safety risks and lists of persons of interest in their investigations to financial institutions. It is at this point the intelligence continuum described previously is engaged and information starts to move through legally sanctioned channels.

Issues with the Information-Sharing Framework in Canada

In practice, the intelligence continuum for intelligence sharing between PPPs are hindered by three overarching issues. The current intelligence-sharing process in place leads to unactionable, and inefficient intelligence dissemination for law enforcement. The restriction on types of data that can be shared lessens the reporting entity's ability to improve detection and reporting capabilities and disallows AML models to evolve with fully realized data sets. Finally, reporting entities are unable to conduct quality control and assurance on current AML models due to the lack of feedback from FINTRAC on reports and information submitted for assessment.

The first issue with information-sharing frameworks in Canada is the restricted quality and inefficiency of information sharing between law enforcement and financial institutions. The exchange of information offered by law enforcement through targeted disclosures is helpful for financial institutions and law enforcement, albeit the information being shared is limited. Through PPPs, law enforcement can provide general information about persons of interest and ongoing investigations. Reporting entities, such as financial institutions, then respond through an STR to FINTRAC, which provides analyzed information to law enforcement. Law enforcement is unable to access the raw data provided by reporting entities and cannot make targeted requests for information (RFIs) to financial institutions, instead making a general notice. The efficiency of the process is hindered by law enforcement having to request data from FINTRAC after it has published a broad notice and receive data that may have been so restricted that it will not aid in the investigation.

Secondly, information sharing between financial institutions is limited by an inadequate formal process for sharing personally identifiable information (PII). Currently, the process to share information between peer institutions "relies on an investigator and requires manual information gathering and sharing by all the involved institutions" (Chaudhary 2021) due to privacy constraints. The ability to synergize information to create nodes and networks of potential illicit activity through innovative technologies is missing critical information due to limits on information-sharing processes, as rarely are financial institutions provided feedback on STRs filed. PPPs are missing a framework to establish a mandatory sharing protocol that protects members when aiding in illicit financing operations. The mandate is essential to develop due to Canada's privacy and regulatory landscape. The Personal Information Protection and Electronic Documents Act (PIPEDA), Canada's privacy framework, details "how private-sector organizations collect, use, and disclose personal information in the course of for-profit, commercial activities in Canada" (Chaudhary 2021). From a private sector perspective, protecting customers' privacy is the top concern. Thus, privacy frameworks, such as PIPEDA, frame the culture of information sharing within the AML process and can restrict information sharing, such as PII, related to illicit financial networks.

Finally, the process of information sharing between financial institutions and FINTRAC is not reciprocal, with FINTRAC failing to provide timely feedback and updates to financial institutions of STRs that have been filed. The current information-sharing regime between financial institutions and FINTRAC rests on RFIs, as "information sharing is a careful balance between efficacy and protecting the rights of Canadians, and that they do perform outreach work with reporting entities to provide them with information on potentially suspicious transactions and indicators to identify money laundering trends" (Chaudhary 2021). To move from merely responding to incidents to creating effective long-term strategies, financial institutions need to be provided with notable updates to the information previously supplied to FINTRAC. This would enable financial institutions to help with the investigation appropriately should new information come to light and strategically refine their AML programs by utilizing the updated data and analyzing temporal patterns to create more robust internal controls and processes.

FINTRAC enforces the PCMLTFA for reporting entities and receives information related to suspicious financial activity. In terms of sharing information with the reporting entity, FINTRAC may "disclose information to another specified government institution if the information is relevant to the recipient institution's jurisdiction..." (House of Commons, Canada 2018). However, the process for providing valuable intelligence for forensic analysis to financial institutions is not widely utilized. For example, testimony from reporting entity witnesses to the House of Commons highlighted "the lack of feedback that FINTRAC provides to the reporting entities" (House of Commons 2018), indicate that reporting entities, such as financial institutions, often execute a check-the-box exercise when reporting, but are not provided additional information after submitting a STR. Thus, financial institutions very rarely gain any specific feedback from FINTRAC that is not already publicly available.

The intelligence continuum offered within existing PPPs and proactive disclosures provided by law enforcement enable some intelligence-sharing amongst private-public partners. The current information-sharing process should include more information earlier in investigations and allow for voluntary information sharing between peer institutions. As explored in the upcoming section, the US PATRIOT Act provides reporting entities with shared communication between financial intelligence units (such as FINTRAC), law enforcement, and peer organizations within an industry. Analyzing the US PATRIOT Act and relevant components are crucial to understand how to strengthen information sharing relevant to Canada's AML regime while complying with existing privacy legislation.

Identifying Advantages to the US AML Legislation through the Bank Secrecy Act (1970) and the PATRIOT Act (2001) Sections 314a and 314b

Information-Sharing Processes

The AML information-sharing landscape in the United States is shaped by a series of significant pieces of legislation. The two most impactful pieces of legislation to date are the Bank Secrecy Act (BSA) and the PATRIOT Act and will be the primary pieces of legislation analyzed for increasing actionable information sharing within Canadian AML PPPs. The BSA, passed by Congress in 1970, established requirements for financial institutions and banks to keep records on the "source, volume and movement of currency and other monetary instruments transported into or out of the United States or deposited in financial institutions" (FFIEC 2015). From 1970 to 1996 a series of legislation strengthened the BSA requirements to impose criminal liability on a person or financial institution knowingly laundering money, set a requirement for robust compliance programs within financial institutions, and developed mandatory Suspicious Activity Reporting (SAR; FFIEC 2015). The BSA's significance to AML is only second to the PATRIOT Act.

Post-September 11, 2001, the United States government enacted the PATRIOT Act (a statute titled Uniting and Strengthening America by Providing Appropriate Tools Required to Intercept and Obstruct Terrorism), "to deter and punish terrorist acts in the United States and around the world." (Office of the Director of National Intelligence 2021). Within it contained provisions about information sharing between financial institutions and federal enforcement agencies (314a), information sharing amongst peer financial institutions (314a), and a voluntary information-sharing framework amongst financial institutions (314b). This piece of legislation contributed to meaningful information sharing amongst public and private entities to identify and deter illicit financial flows in the US. Looking first to Section 314a, the objective is to "[establish] procedures for information sharing to deter money laundering and terrorist activity" and "allow state, local, and certain foreign law enforcement agencies access to the information-sharing program (FFIEC 2021) and achieves this aim through encouraging information sharing between PPP. FinCEN reported that "regulations under Section 314(a) enable federal, state, local, and foreign (European Union) law enforcement agencies, through FinCEN, to reach out to more than 34,000 points of contact at more than 14,000 financial institutions to locate accounts and transactions of persons that may be involved in terrorism or money laundering," with the result that FinCEN has processed 5,286 requests for significant criminal investigations, with 717 cases involving terrorism/terrorist financing, and 4,569 cases of money laundering (FinCEN 2022). Section 314a within the PATRIOT Act provides investigative bodies with the power to scrutinize financial accounts across all institutions participating in the sharing of information, enabling financial institutions to add the new data to enhance AML models (Wilejto-Rieken 2018). In addition, law enforcement agencies can "[investigate] terrorist activity or money laundering [and] may request that FinCEN solicit, on its behalf, certain information from a financial institution or a group of financial institutions" (FFIEC 2021). The operationalization of this two-way communication may be attributed to the resources afforded to FinCEN and law enforcement. With these resources, the process enables transparency as FinCEN reviews and processes requests from law enforcement bodies and notifies the financial institutions with conflicts of interest. FinCEN also makes a highly secured database available to financial institutions to aid in forensic investigations. As stated on FinCEN's website, "State and Local law enforcement agencies can access the Bank Secrecy Act data through a secure web connection after their agency has entered into a Memorandum of Understanding with FinCEN. FinCEN provides training, and monitors use to ensure that the BSA information is properly used, disseminated, and kept secure" (FinCEN 2022). The information is reciprocal, and financial institutions can create actionable objectives regarding the new information provided, aiding in securing the institution against individuals perpetuating financial crime.

The robust information-sharing framework in Section 314a is supplemented by 314b which aims to increase the voluntary passage of information between financial institutions. 314b allows information exchanges between peer financial institutions, and "promotes mutual understanding and trust among the entities. The institutions will have a united and strengthened level of scrutiny of suspicious money wiring, transactions, and accounts" (FinCEN 2022). While the information shared in this format is limited, the interconnected nature of financial transactions enables criminals to route money through various institutions to place, layer, and integrate the funds into criminal organizations or individuals. A system created with security by design enables institutions to move from a "need to know" to a "need to share" security perspective while complying with federal privacy policies.

The processes outlined above are subject to speculation, as Gordon (2012) writes: "millions of STRs have been forwarded to FIUs by financial institutions throughout the world, although how many have resulted in further investigation, prosecution, and conviction is not publicly available." While information on the STRs and SARs themselves remain obscured, some research containing data aggregation of SAR and STR filings resulting in law enforcement action has been released. Firstly, the number of STRs and SARs filed in Canada and the US, respectfully, remains public information and is subject to scrutiny. According to the FinCEN database containing SAR filing metric, 2,504,511 SARS were filed across all reporting entity groups in 2019, with 3,069,453 in 2020.[2] This data does not account for all transaction data reporting, only SARs. According to a study conducted by the Bank Policy Institute (BPI), regarding the most recent statistics on actions taken from SARs filed, in 2017 only 4 percent of SARs filed warranted follow-up inquiries from law enforcement, rendering more than 95 percent as precautionary filings (BPI 2018). By comparison, the Cullen Commission reported that, "in

2019–20, FINTRAC received over 31 million individual reports. In that same year, FINTRAC disclosed only 2,057 intelligence reports to law enforcement across Canada" (Cullen 2022, 3). This reporting data includes all transaction reports, extending beyond just STRs. However, whether it be an STR or transaction or transfer report, reporting entities must comply with reporting regulations to advance the goal of mitigating money laundering in Canada. The numbers above indicate a mere 0.000065 percent of suspicious reports filed provided actionable intelligence and warranted a follow-up inquiry by law enforcement in Canada. Increasing the number of suspicious reports to FIUs will not in itself result in tangible law enforcement action. Increasing the efficacy of information sharing within PPPs to analyze and share actionable intelligence will help drive actionable outcomes for reporting entities' AML models and law enforcement objectives, as seen with the US approach.

Given the goal of reporting STRs and SARs is to identify, detect, and respond to possible instances of money laundering, the US model shows more than marginal success compared to its Canadian counterpart. The BSA and PATRIOT Act both provide amnesty for private sector reporting of possible money laundering activity and provides beneficial intelligence to law enforcement respecting the privacy of consumers. By comparison, FINTRACs current information-sharing model hinders the analysis provided to both law enforcement and reporting entities due to its intermediary role in minimizing information shared in line with privacy regulations, resulting in the impediment of actionable intelligence provided and received by reporting entities and law enforcement. Adopting information-sharing amnesty, and specifically a secure channel for information sharing, outlined through the BSA and PATRIOT Act would provide an enhanced collaborative avenue for PPP to share information between law enforcement and reporting entities in Canada in conjunction with current privacy laws. For example, US financial institutions may use the information obtained under partner sharing in section 314(b) to determine whether to file a SAR, but the intention to file the SAR cannot be disclosed. This process ensures compliance with the BSA, and SARs are then filed through FinCEN's secure portal. FinCEN is then able to triage the SARs and proceeds to inform law enforcement if there is actionable intelligence. Additionally, and importantly, law enforcement including the FBI and DEA can access the secure FinCEN database to analyze raw data.

The BSA and PATRIOT Act provides a framework for Canadian law to strengthen AML information-sharing processes between private and public entities. That said, the PATRIOT Act has been criticized from a privacy perspective, as reporting entities and/or law enforcement "may end up exposing the private information of innocent individuals who have no connection to money laundering and terrorism whatsoever" (Wilejto-Rieken 2018). So, in this model, the Canadian legal regime should also maintain strict privacy laws to protect citizens' personal information from abuse of power. In implementing robust processes for information sharing displayed within the PATRIOT Act framework, privacy, and AML regulations should work in tandem to protect Canadian institutions and citizens.

No amicable platform for voluntary information sharing between financial institutions is commonly used within Canada. The report – *Confronting Money Laundering and Terrorist Financing: Moving Canada Forward* – of the Standing Committee on Finance (House of Commons 2018) states that "PIPEDA limits the information businesses collect to what is essential for the business transaction(s)," which severely limits the amount of information that can be shared between reporting entities to tackle broader money laundering/terrorist financing (ML/TF) networks. Hearing from witness testimony, the Canadian Health and Life Insurance Association supported adopting best practices from other regions, and changes to current privacy laws to allow for better information sharing within the privacy sector. The sentiment is echoed by the Canadian Bankers Association (CBA), highlighting that further information sharing is necessary given the amount of data collected by financial institutions (House of Commons 2018, 41). This is in direct contrast to the BSA and PATRIOT Act which includes formal processes for information sharing, enabling two-way communication for both peer-to-peer information sharing and to aid both public and private partners.

Privacy Frameworks and Information Sharing in PPPs

As discussed, optimizing the types of information shared among entities and persons in Canada is severely limited by the PIPEDA (Office of the Privacy Commissioner 2021). While law enforcement in Canada has interpreted this Act more broadly and liberally, financial institutions have interpreted it more conservatively in line with their customer privacy priorities and reputational risk. As with all legislation in jurisdictions with advanced legal systems, they are subject to repeated attempts at interpretation, case law, and generational reviews to ensure relevancy.

One such channel of bank-to-bank (B2B) cooperation is through an industry construct referred to as the bank crime prevention and investigation framework (BCPIF; Office of the Privacy Commissioner 2015). In this framework, B2B information exchanges are regulated through industry-accepted standards of information sharing with modest oversight by the CBA. This framework is in place for limited information sharing between BCPIF-trained bank employees investigating breaches of customer contracts, fraud, and other federal offences.

An example of this framework facilitating information sharing between peer financial institutions to detect and mitigate fraudulent transactions is observed through the Supreme Court case *Christine Ren, et al. v. Royal Bank of Canada*.[3] The appellants argued their rights were violated under PIPEDA due to the disclosure of information between financial institutions (Toronto-Dominion Bank and Royal Bank of Canada), however the exchange of information took place under the authority of PIPEDA, and the appeal was dismissed. Beyond this case from 2009, there are not many examples of this framework being utilized; however, the protection it affords peer-to-peer information sharing is beneficial to uncovering financial crime networks that expand beyond financial institutions.

Although this framework does not rival the US PATRIOT Act 314a and 314b legislation, it does allow for a nominal amount of information to be exchanged between Canadian banks intent on protecting sacrosanct customer information amidst federal guidance and legislation. Expanding on this framework to strengthen voluntary information sharing between financial institutions within a legal process and secure portal would aid

FIUs and law enforcement in their investigation and help strengthen the organization's internal data and controls.

Strengths in Existing PPPs: A Case Study of the Counter Illicit Finance Alliance of British Columbia

As a result of a series of money laundering scandals found operating within casinos in British Columbia (BC), a large PPP was established to better address a method of money laundering referred to as the Vancouver Model coined by Australian academic John Langdale. This form of money laundering gained notoriety for its success and was examined in detail by retired RCMP senior commander Peter German (2018) and eventually a BC provincial commission headed by Justice Austin Cullen (2022).

After extensive adverse media on the Vancouver Model, the BC government, the RCMP, financial institutions, FINTRAC, and other affected entities formed a working group. The objective of this group is to address the sharing of intelligence and add visibility to the AML steps being taken in a multi-disciplinary environment. After considerable work, this effort was dubbed Project Athena by the RCMP and eventually adopted by the PPP working group, formalized by a media release in December 2020. In addition, after industry and law enforcement engagement, FINTRAC published guidance for all reporting entities, including Canada's major financial institutions, to identify money laundering in casinos (FINTRAC 2019).

The RCMP then established the Counter Illicit Finance Alliance, British Columbia (CIFA-BC) with the members from Project Athena after further information gathering from industry and law enforcement. This newly formed alliance sought to increase the flow of information and intelligence amongst public and private partners to better enable the detection of financial crime and money laundering in Canada (RCMP 2019).

One of the hallmark features of the CIFA-BC framework is the strategic information sharing amongst partners. This framework document states in part:

> CIFA-BC's success depends on the exchange of timely, high quality strategic information to carry out its activities. This requires parameters to provide

clarity around what is permissible, and more specifically lawful, in a FISP setting. (RCMP 2019)

CIFA-BC's unique information-sharing framework attempts to bring critical stakeholders together to address financial crime and money laundering and ensure that critical intelligence gets to the proper entities. The recently released Cullen Report supports the importance of PPP collaboration with CIFA-BC, noting it is a "promising step" for how organizations such as the Chartered Professional Accountants-BC (CPA-BC) will involve itself in further money laundering efforts (Cullen 2022, 1305). The inclusion of groups such as CPA-BC helps ensure that the framework acknowledges the limits partners face when sharing proprietary information or information identified as being personally identifiable information protected in PIPEDA legislation and provides an avenue for peer information sharing within PIPEDA's privacy parameters. The Cullen Commission report does identify issues with the framework (Cullen 2022, 1513), such as strategic versus tactical information sharing; however, the following policy recommendations seek to build on the CIFA-BC PPP model, and PPP frameworks across Canada at the federal and provincial level, to strengthen the information shared between partners to combat ML/TF.

Conclusion and Policy Change Recommendations

Enhancing information-sharing processes within public-private partnerships will better equip FINTRAC, law enforcement, financial institutions, and other reporting entities to protect Canadian institutions and the public against money laundering in Canada. Moving forward, Canada is left with a plethora of information-sharing constructs created to deal with outdated privacy laws and cumbersome and competing institutional requirements and priorities. However, what has become clear is that financial institutions, law enforcement, and government agencies have created internationally recognized partnership frameworks that have successfully tackled some of Canada's most vexing community safety issues.

Seeking best practices for ensuring privacy while sharing pertinent AML information from existing legislation, such as the US BSA and

PATRIOT Act, would enhance information sharing in Canada. This would complement already developed information exchanges that artfully comply with strict privacy laws. We acknowledge that the Canadian federal government has sought to modernize privacy laws in an increasingly digital world through its Digital Charter (Government of Canada 2021). It is also anticipated that PIPEDA will be amended further as political channels clear for further modernization. Whether or not these laws allow for the modernization of information and intelligence exchanges between law enforcement, intelligence agencies, financial institutions, federal agencies, and other provincial regulators remain to be seen. Canada has already distinguished itself despite legal challenges and is well situated to be a global leader in financial crime and terrorist financing interdiction given it has the right resources and legal tools.

Further recommendations can be implemented to enhance the sharing of information related to money laundering activity in Canada and create a culture of voluntary disclosure. Within coded PPPs, law enforcement and financial institutions should have access to, and be free to talk about, raw data. The information within this context should be used to determine whether to file a STR, but the decision to file should not be shared with other partners. Next, law enforcement agencies should have access to raw data through a secure FINTRAC portal. This would help aid law enforcement in their investigations and provide law enforcement the ability to create targeted RFIs for specific financial institutions given the raw data. This also eliminates the need for law enforcement to craft broad notices that may not be applicable to all financial institutions. This streamlined process would increase efficiency and reduce the resources needed from FINTRAC.

Second, CIFA-BC should be considered a possible framework for future Canadian PPPs in AML. CIFA-BC provides a space for public and private members to share red flag typologies. Further, the participating entities are expected to share as much as they can/have. PIPEDA protects the voluntary aspect of information sharing, and if an entity feels it cannot share the information, that entity is protected by PIPEDA. However, a culture of sharing relies on the expectation for participating entities to consistently provide evolving analysis. This requirement should be embedded into the operating procedure. This will allow participating entities to share PII in a controlled and closed setting, enhancing independent reporting, and law enforcement RFIs and investigative capabilities.

Notes

1 *R. v. Stinchcombe*, [1991] 3 S.C.R. 326.
2 This data was collected from FinCEN's website (https://www.fincen.gov/reports/sar-stats/sar-filings-industry). Researchers aggregated the data by gathering and totaling SARs filed by each industry (casino/card club, depository information, housing, government sponsored enterprise, insurance companies, loan or finance companies, money service businesses, other, and securities/features) for 2019 and 2020.
3 *Christine Ren et al. vs. Royal Bank of Canada* [2009] SCC 33076. https://www.scc-csc.ca/case-dossier/info/sum-som-eng.aspx?cas=33076.

References

Association of Certified Financial Crime Specialists (ACFCS). 2020. Regional Report: Canada Has Done 'Amazing Things' to fight crime through public-private partnerships, but still hampered by stringent privacy rules, lack of AML Safe Harbors. https://www.acfcs.org/regional-report-canada-has-done-amazing-things-to-fight-crime-through-public-private-partnerships-but-still-hampered-by-stringent-privacy-rules-lack-of-aml-safe-harbors/.
Bank Policy Institute (BPI). 2018, 2. https://bpi.com/wp-content/uploads/2018/10/BPI_AML_Sanctions_Study_vF.pdf.
Chaudhary, Garima. 2021. "Next-Gen Information Sharing and Collaboration Framework Using Graphs." ACAMS Today, February 17, 2021. https://www.acamstoday.org/next-gen-information-sharing-and-collaboration-framework-using-graphs/.
Cullen, Austin F. 2022. "Commission of Inquiry into Money Laundering in British Columbia." Cullen Commission, June 15, 2022. https://cullencommission.ca/.
Financial Action Task Force (FATF). 2021. "Anti-Money Laundering and Counter-Terrorist Financing Measures Canada: 4th Enhanced Follow-up Report & Technical Compliance Re-Rating." FATF-GAFI, October 2021. https://www.fatf-gafi.org/media/fatf/documents/reports/fur/Follow-Up-Report-Canada-2021.pdf.
Financial Crimes Enforcement Network (FinCEN). 2021. "FinCEN's 314(A) Fact Sheet." FinCEN, December 28, 2021. https://www.fincen.gov/sites/default/files/shared/314afactsheet.pdf.

———. 2022. "Support of Law Enforcement." https://www.fincen.gov/resources/law-enforcement/support-law-enforcement.

Federal Financial Institutions Examination Council (FFIEC). 2015. "FFIEC BSA/AML Examination Manuel." February 27, 2015. https://bsaaml.ffiec.gov/manual.

———. 2021. "Assessing Compliance with BSA Regulatory Requirements." BSA/AML InfoBase. https://bsaaml.ffiec.gov/manual/AssessingComplianceWithBSARegulatoryRequirements/07.

Financial Transactions and Reports Analysis Centre of Canada (FINTRAC). 2016. "FINTRAC, Law Enforcement and Intelligence Partners: Sharing Intelligence, Making the Links." March 1, 2016. https://www.FINTRAC-canafe.gc.ca/intel/general/1-eng.

———. 2019. "Operational Alert: Laundering the Proceeds of Crime through a Casino-Related Underground Banking Scheme." December. https://www.FINTRAC-canafe.gc.ca/intel/operation/casino-eng.

German, Peter M. 2018. "Dirty Money: An Independent Review of Money Laundering in Lower Mainland Casinos Conducted for the Attorney General of British Columbia." March 31, 2018. https://news.gov.bc.ca/files/Gaming_Final_Report.pdf.

Government of Canada. 2021. "Canada's Digital Charter: Trust in a Digital World." Innovation, Science and Economic Development Canada, January 12, 2021. https://www.ic.gc.ca/eic/site/062.nsf/eng/h_00108.html.

House of Commons, Canada. 2018. "Confronting Money Laundering and Terrorist Financing: Moving Canada Forward." 42nd Parliament, 1st Session, November 2018. https://www.ourcommons.ca/Content/Committee/421/FINA/Reports/RP10170742/finarp24/finarp24-e.pdf.

Monroe, Brian. 2021. "Regional Report: Canada Has Done 'Amazing Things' to Fight Crime through Public-Private Partnerships, but Still Hampered by Stringent Privacy Rules, Lack of AML Safe Harbors - Cfcs: Association of Certified Financial Crime Specialists." ACFCS, May 6. https://www.acfcs.org/regional-report-canada-has-done-amazing-things-to-fight-crime-through-public-private-partnerships-but-still-hampered-by-stringent-privacy-rules-lack-of-aml-safe-harbors/.

Office of the Director of National Intelligence (ODNI). 2021. "USA Patriot Act." https://www.dni.gov/index.php/who-we-are/organizations/ise/ise-archive/ise-additional-resources/2116-usa-patriot-act.

Office of the Privacy Commissioner of Canada. 2015 "Due Diligence Must Be Exercised and Documented When Applying Exemptions to Disclosing Personal Information without Consent." July 29. https://www.priv.gc.ca/en/opc-actions-and-decisions/investigations/investigations-into-businesses/2014/pipeda-2014-018/.

———. 2021. "The Personal Information Protection and Electronic Documents Act (PIPEDA)." December 8. https://www.priv.gc.ca/en/privacy-topics/privacy-laws-in-canada/the-personal-information-protection-and-electronic-documents-act-pipeda.

Public Safety Canada. 2022. "National Strategy to Combat Human Trafficking 2019-2024," July 21. https://www.publicsafety.gc.ca/cnt/rsrcs/pblctns/2019-ntnl-strtgy-hmnn-trffc/index-en.aspx.

Royal Canadian Mounted Police (RCMP). 2019. "CIFA-BC Framework." April 9. https://ag-pssg-sharedservices-ex.objectstore.gov.bc.ca/ag-pssg-cc-exh-prod-bkt-ex/847%20-%20CIFA-BC%20Framework%20revised%20April%209%202021.pdf.

Wilejto-Rieken, Monika. 2018. "USA Patriot Act, Section 314(a) and 314(b) Information Sharing: Beneficial and Detrimental Effects of the Act." http://files.acams.org/pdfs/2018/USA_Patriot_Act_M_Wilejto-Rieken.pdf.

15

Taking Money Laundering Seriously: Some Provincial Pieces of a Global Strategy

Michelle Gallant

Introduction

It is a little unusual for provincial or territorial law to intersect with a global criminal interdiction strategy. While the bulk of Canadian integration of the transnational money laundering strategy happens through national regulation, there are important contributions made by, or that could be made by, the provinces and territories – many of which are mentioned by Jeffrey Simser (this volume). This chapter surveys three contributions that these local, as opposed to federal, laws make, or could make, toward the realization of transnational aspirations. These consist of provincial civil forfeiture regimes, provincial piercings of corporate opacity, and the regulation of lawyers. Each of these inputs converge with, although they are not necessarily ordained by, the global strategy. They undergird its strength or otherwise help break the bonds between finance and transnational criminal phenomenon.

The Global Money-Laundering Strategy and the Federal Regime

Although not all domestic developments related to money laundering are necessarily driven by external imperatives, the global anti-money laundering strategy is the most significant influence. From the earliest inception of a financially focused approach to international criminal phenomenon through to the present, Canada's internal posture towards money laundering continues to be shaped by transnational anti-money laundering conventions and the need to align domestic regulation with precepts forged in international forums.

The global strategy connotes a control approach intended to mitigate the financial dimensions of crime. Its conceptual origins derive from a late twentieth century appreciation of the enormous financial yields associated with the trade in illegal drugs. Rather than shrink under the force of control efforts dating back to the opium wars of the nineteenth century, the global trade in illegal drugs had grown exponentially. The failure of global regulation was attributed to the money involved, and to financial tactics deployed to hide resources or "cleanse" drug monies of their criminal taint (Gilmore 2004). Moreover, while discrete national, predominantly American, money-laundering controls had begun to emerge, modern finance's fluid, mobile order was thought to sterilize any individual state-based initiatives. A new modern global model was needed.

The formal construction of a modern strategy began in 1988. With the conclusion of a drugs control convention, the international community sought to grapple with the financial undercurrents of the drugs trade by endorsing a control model centred on drug money and financial activity associated therewith (Convention Against Illicit Traffic in Narcotic Drugs and Psychotropic Substances 1988). This finance-centric model swiftly gained credence. In international circles, tackling anti-money laundering became a favourite weapon, an approach that could be leveraged against any crime. It gradually spread to corruption, organized crime, terrorism, and the proliferation and trade in weapons of mass destruction.[1]

The decisive architecture of the modern model consists of a set of international money laundering and terrorist financing standards largely distilled from international instruments (FATF 2012). Organized into forty standards, this architecture is loosely divided into three parts. The first part mandates the criminalization of money laundering and the implementation of forfeiture, or confiscation, regimes.[2] Criminalization connotes the universal recognition of money laundering as a criminal offence. Forfeiture, or confiscation, contemplates laws that permit the seizure and divestiture of resources connected to criminal activity. The second part commands the adoption of money-laundering prevention machinery.[3] Arguably a crucial lynchpin of the modern finance-centred model, this part imposes a series of requirements on financial institutions, financial actors, and other entities whose services or works are prone to exploitation by money launderers. This part decrees matters such as the reporting of suspicious financial activities, requirements to fully identity clients or users of financial and other services, and requirements to collect, and maintain, detailed records of financial activities. This prevention machinery also directs enhanced corporate transparency.[4] The third part of the global model comprises standards designed to coordinate international action against money laundering and facilitate the exchange of information.[5]

These international money laundering and terrorist finance standards principally dictate the content of Canadian anti-money laundering laws. For the most part, the anchoring of the standards occurs through federal law. Canadian criminal law criminalizes the act of money laundering and permits the forfeiture or confiscation of the proceeds of crime.[6] Federal law establishes comprehensive money laundering prevention machinery and creates a national financial intelligence agency.[7] Federal machinery imposes financial reporting, identity and record-keeping requirements on financial intermediaries and other actors. Consistent with the standards, national law establishes a capacious prevention and detection system that stretches from banking and wire transfers to casinos and charities, to real estate, and trading in high-value commodities. Nascent national regulation, as discussed latterly, has begun to abrogate corporate transparency.

Although federal law is the principal vehicle of anti-money laundering governance, there are at least three aspects of the global enterprise to which provincial or territorial law contributes or could contribute. First, provincial civil forfeiture regimes contribute to, or supplement, the global entreaty to confiscate, or forfeit, resources linked to criminal activity. Some provinces have begun to shred corporate opacity as it relates to provincially constituted corporations. Also, the provinces could deliver some substance to the global prevention and detection standards in connection with lawyers and money laundering.

Provincial Civil Forfeiture Law

Many provinces have enacted laws that enable the taking of assets linked to crime.[8] Typically prompted by concerns about the ravages of organized crime and drug trafficking, these enactments, while not identical, tend to share certain attributes and are usually identified as civil forfeiture law. The commonly shared features consist of the attaching of forfeiture to criminal offences;[9] the enabling of the forfeiture of the proceeds of crime, and sometimes the forfeiture of the instruments of crime;[10] and the specific incorporation of the civil standard of proof as the standard that governs the forfeiture process.[11] A further feature of provincial civil forfeiture is that the subject of the action, the respondent, is the money, the proceeds, rather than the owners of the property.

While federal criminal law implements the international standard related to confiscation or forfeiture, provincial law adds something different. Under the federal regime, the forfeiture of criminal or laundered assets applies post-conviction; resources only stand poised to federal forfeiture once a criminal conviction is obtained.[12] This particular arrangement – a conviction activating access to a forfeiture regime – is arguably sufficient, without more, to secure compliance with the international money laundering model.[13] Provincial law permits assets or proceeds linked to crime to be forfeited without a prior criminal conviction. This feature distinguishes the provincial devices from their federal counterparts. In specie, provincial law displaces a requirement to prove beyond a reasonable doubt that some offence, in relation to the property, has occurred. It is sufficient, to secure the taking, to prove in accordance with the civil legal standard that the property derives from, or relates to, some crime.

To global aspirations to capture assets linked to money laundering, provincial civil law is a remarkable contribution. The civil device strengthens the asset-centred strategy by effectively altering the rules of engagement. It is significantly easier to forfeit laundered resources through a civil legal process than a criminal process. The civil orientation, particularly the explicit incorporation of the civil standard as the governing standard for forfeiture, reinforces the global strategy.

Moreover, particularly relevant to a global pursuit, the provincial devices rely on the relatively unfamiliar concept of *in rem* jurisdiction. *In rem* jurisdiction connotes the liability of the *res*, the thing. Legal proceedings usually, whether civil or criminal, operate upon the basis of *in personam* jurisdiction or the liability of persons. Civil or criminal actions are levied against individuals or corporate entities. *In rem* jurisdiction, or the liability of the *res*, the thing, has its origins in admiralty law or the law of high seas.[14] In that context, it proves useful as means of asserting jurisdiction over ships allegedly involved in illegal activity on the seas. Seizing the *res* when it arrives at a domestic port helps secure some measure of domestic jurisdiction in relation to activities that, occurring on the high seas, would otherwise escape national reach. This curious feature of provincial law, the liability of the thing, or the assertion of *in rem* jurisdiction, proves eminently useful in the context of global money laundering. It suffices, for the purposes of provincial law, that merely the property linked to crime lands within a province. Provided the property, the *res*, settles on local terrain, it can be captured by the provincial regimes.

To the global strategy, the instrumental value of provincial civil forfeiture is obvious. By the same token, they elicit controversy. The nub of the controversy centres on the fusion of a civil process with allegations of criminal activity. This fusion invites constitutional tensions. One of these tensions was settled in 2009. Ontario's civil forfeiture venture triggered complaints that the regime exceeded provincial legislative competence. Arguably, civil forfeiture occupied criminal legal terrain, the exclusive reserve of the federal Parliament. In 2009, the Supreme Court of Canada found that civil forfeiture was not an exercise in criminal law but came within provincial legislative competence with respect to matters of civil rights.[15] No other constitutional inquiry – notably potential Charter of Rights violations – has yet made its way to the highest court.[16]

Importantly, the provincial approach, the coupling of a civil process with allegations of criminal activity, is not unique. Other jurisdictions –

the United States, the United Kingdom, Ireland, and Australia – have laws that permit resources linked to money laundering to be forfeited through civil processes or forfeited without a predicate criminal conviction.[17] For the most part, foreign constitutional, or rights-based, litigation suggests that most courts agree that civil devices adhere to the rule of law.[18]

Arguably, too, the full potential of civil devices has yet to be exercised. Civil forfeiture could be applied to any crime. Although the provincial devices feature most frequently in the context of drug offences, the devices could be used to forfeit the proceeds of corruption, tax evasion, or fraud. Even corporate crimes could be the subject of civil forfeiture actions.

Enhancing Corporate Transparency

Pervasive connections between money laundering, crime, and corporations are standard fare in contemporary transnational discourse.[19] A 2015 Canadian-based assessment of money laundering and terrorist finance repeatedly mentions "front," or "shell" companies as central money laundering devices.[20] The insertion of a corporation generally displaces critical connections between transactional activity and the human orchestrators, or beneficiaries. The corporate form acts as an opacity conduit. Lord Denning once eloquently described corporate entities as the puppets of sentient beings.[21] The metaphor aptly describes the function of corporations in contemporary money laundering: the corporation shields the identity of those who control, or orchestrate, activity from which they ultimately acquire some criminal financial benefit.

While mandatory financial reporting, client identification requirements, and the retention of financial records lend visibility to potential money laundering activity, the pervasive opacity conducted through corporations attracts explicit mention under the global strategy.[22] The global standards identify the "beneficial ownership" and control of corporations as problematic phenomena. A beneficial owner, in the language of the standards, "refers to the natural person(s) who ultimately owns or controls a customer and/or the natural person on whose behalf transaction is being conducted."[23] The standards mandate the provision of adequate, accurate and timely access to information about beneficial ownership and the control of legal persons, *qua*, corporations.

As the principal domestic participant in international matters, Canada has been a little slow in engendering corporate transparency. Repeat evaluations of domestic compliance with global standards chide Canada for not adequately attending to transparency (FATF 2008, 2016c). The Canadian federalism structure fetters the ability to attend to corporate "puppets" through national regulation alone since corporate governance is a federal and a provincial matter: federally incorporated entities come under federal regulation, whereas provincially incorporated corporations come under provincial governance (Canadian Constitution n.d.).

In response to repeat chidings, in 2017 the federal, provincial, and territorial governments agreed to strengthen beneficial ownership transparency with regard to corporations.[24] Diverse efforts have begun to sprout at the federal and provincial level. Amendments in 2018 to corporate law require that federally constituted, privately held entities collect and retain information related to beneficial ownership.[25] Rather than use the language of "beneficial ownership," the law requires that corporate entities establish a registry of "individuals with significant control." Significant control generally denotes a capacity to influence corporate affairs.[26] Additional changes in 2019 mandate the disclosure of information related to "individuals with significant control" upon request, to federal investigative bodies.[27] Early in 2020, the federal government-initiated conversations regarding the establishment of a Canadian public registry of beneficial ownership information in the context of privately held corporations (Government of Canada 2020).

At the provincial level, the only significant development has occurred in the province of British Columbia. In 2019 British Columbia introduced a transparency mechanism applicable to transactions related to real property.[28] The newly minted device requires the filing of transparency declarations and the maintenance of a registry. Applicable to land transfers and land ownership, the new law speaks broadly to transparency, rather than uniquely to corporate transparency. Moreover, while the BC transparency may relate to the 2017 pledge, it is more directly the product of the local impacts of money laundering.[29] Of all the provinces and territories, the BC experience with money laundering appears to be the most dire.

Although attending to corporate transparency may not, for most local jurisdictions, be a matter of local urgency, it is only through the machinations of local law that pan-Canadian transparency can be achieved. To the outside world, the world of the international, Canada is a cohesive whole. Global money laundering standards anticipate pan-Canadian compliance. Federal initiatives cannot stretch to provincially incorporated entities. Securing the global money laundering standards requires the active and willing participation of local orders of government.

Lawyers, Self-Governance and a Potential Role for the Provinces

A third aspect of the global strategy concerns a piece of anti-money laundering regulation in which a provincial role has yet to be asserted. In a lengthy story that began in 2001, the provinces have largely been content to watch debates unfold between the provincially regulated professions of law, and federal attempts to integrate lawyers into a federal anti-money laundering mechanism. International standards call for the inclusion of lawyers in money laundering prevention.[30] Under the international mechanism, lawyers form part of a collection of "designated" professions charged with anti-money laundering obligations. Canada has been faulted for failing to comply with international norms because of its failure to regulate lawyers.[31] The failed attempts are a source of some dispute. Through a series of legal challenges, provincial law societies have successfully repudiated incorporation into any federal scheme. Dissatisfaction with this state of affairs provides fodder for what a province might be prompted to do to counter money laundering. Most provinces have enacted civil forfeiture regimes. Many have begun to confront the problem of corporate transparency at the provincial level. None have reacted to collisions between global standards and the legal profession.

The story of lawyers and money laundering consists of repeated efforts by the federal government to build a seamless national anti-money laundering apparatus. In 2001, federal law sought to impose suspicious transaction reporting requirements – requirements successfully imposed upon a coterie of entities whose work touches upon financial transactions – onto lawyers. Provincial law societies alleged that the federal rules interfered with solicitor-client privilege or otherwise endangered the independence of lawyers (Gallant 2009). In the face of this series of challenges, the federal government retreated. A decade later, national law entertained the prospects of a more limited role for lawyers in money-laundering prevention. The proposed regime contemplated the collection of detailed information by lawyers about their clients and their clients' activities and potential access to that information by federal agencies.[32] Again, however, the provincial law societies intervened.

In 2015, the Supreme Court of Canada determined that the second national effort was unlawful.[33] The federal regime posed a significant risk of undermining a lawyer's commitment to their clients.[34] That commitment fell within the box of protections guaranteed by section 7 of the Charter. The federal regime interfered with section 7 protections, an interference which the Court determined was not justified in accordance with section 1.

The tensions that have unfolded over two decades relate to federal efforts to satisfy global mandates in relation to lawyers. Amidst this tension, the provincially regulated legal professions implemented their own anti-money laundering regimes. Model rules promulgated by the Federation of Law Societies, the collective voice of the Canadian legal profession, encourage the pan-Canadian adoption of lawyer-centric anti-money laundering regulation. The model rules, subsequently adopted by the provincial law societies, anticipate the refusal of lawyers to accept large cash transactions and requirements that lawyers fully and properly identify their clients including actively taking steps to verify the actual identity of clients.[35] Distinct and separate from the federal apparatus, the rules impose lawyer-centric anti-money laundering governance. The rules leave anti-money laundering governance, and the policing of compliance, in the hands of the provincial law societies. In this, the provincial regimes are separate from the national anti-money laundering regime.

It is pertinent to point out that opposition to any federally ordered regime does not derive from any arrogant assumption that lawyers, and the provision of legal services, are immune to money laundering penetration. Opposition is kindled by the particular part that lawyers occupy in the justice system. Lawyers, unlike bankers or other financial intermediaries subjected to federal regulation, are advocates and protectors of the rule of law. From the perspective of the legal profession, a perspective confirmed by the Supreme Court, proposed national regimes fail to adequately respect the essential independence of lawyers. A much-repeated refrain is the idea that the nationally ordered regimes risk converting lawyers into agents of the state. The national regimes fail to adequately accommodate the distinct role of lawyers or protect their independence. The preferred mechanism for anti-money laundering governance, from the perspective of the provincial legal regulators, is the mediation of governance through the provincially constituted law societies. This medium best protects the distinct identity and function of lawyers within the Canadian justice system.

The 2015 Supreme Court decision did not foreclose the possibility that some future regime, neatly and deftly crafted to preserve the special status of legal counsel, could survive constitutional muster.[36] Despite two abortive attempts, a third try could conceivably accommodate the concerns expressed by the legal profession and effectively, and lawfully, bring lawyers into some national regulatory regime. Obviously, accommodation within a national regime would secure compliance with the global standards.

These decades-long debates about effective money-laundering governance have yet to centre on a role that the provinces, and provincial law, could play. That potential role derives from the fact that provincial law confers onto the provincial professional legal regulators their very capacity of some degree of autonomous rule. Self-governance, the regulation of lawyers by law societies, is a creature of provincial law.[37] To a large extent, the provinces have been content to watch, rather than react, to concerns about money laundering and lawyers. Since provincial law accords governance, the provinces could rescind that governance.

There is nothing sacrosanct in the tradition of legal professional self-governance. The 2015 Supreme Court decision admonished the contents of the particular national instrument that sought to institute a federal money-laundering regime applicable to lawyers. Significantly, the decision determined that a lawyer's commitment to their client enjoyed a measure of constitutional protection.[38] The decision said nothing about the institution of legal professional governance. Lawyers could be governed differently.

Repeated efforts by the federal government to subject lawyers, particularly financial transactional work accomplished by, and through, lawyers, demonstrate the urgency of compliance with international standards. Such efforts may also evince a lack of trust in the sufficiency of money-laundering governance through provincial law society regulators. A 2016 review of Canadian compliance with global anti-money standards did not express confidence in the capacity of the provincial law societies to realize effective governance (FATF 2016b, ch. 5). Serious global money laundering scandals have involved law firms. Widely known money laundering episodes have centred on lawyers, on the complicity of lawyers in impropriety, although not specifically on Canadian-based law firms.[39] There is reason to be sceptical of the legal profession's capacity to effectively govern its own members in relation to money laundering.

Bromwich (2018) instructively, and compellingly, makes the salient point that "money laundering is sufficiently calamitous to justify state regulation under section 1 of the Charter." Short of federal regulation, there is scope for provincial reconsideration of deference to the governance of lawyers by lawyers. A "tradition," long and well-established, is conferred by provincial law. It may be that provincially prescribed governance ought to yield to the imperatives of suppressing money laundering. Such a yielding would be bold and dramatic. It would undoubtedly engender resistance. At the same time, it is certainly a path worthy of investigation. It could be a piece of the global money-laundering strategy that the provinces could supply.

Conclusion

While the bulk of the global money laundering strategy is orchestrated through federal law, there is ample room for provincial involvement. Civil forfeiture laws, although not mandated by the global framework, constitute a significant provincial piece. Work concerning corporate transparency in connection with provincially constituted corporations is a second essential piece. A retreat from the tradition of autonomous self-governance by the legal profession could be an important third provincial contribution to curbing global money laundering.

It is always inherently difficult to build a coherent national strategy within a constitutionally federated state. Different levels of government have unique competencies (i.e., federal criminal law) and similar competencies (i.e., federal and provincial corporate governance). Perennial bickering about responsibilities for the adequacies, or inadequacies, of anti-money laundering governance between the federal government and the provinces can impede the development of rigorous effective laws. Even amongst the provinces and territories, there can be disagreement – the discrete impacts of money laundering in one jurisdiction can trigger geographically centred anxieties not shared by other regions – the triggering of the Cullen Commission in British Columbia would be a case in point. And individually, the provinces are likely to be loath to disturb the statutory self-governance conferred onto the legal profession.

For a country within which different governmental actors have both distinct and shared powers, it may be that developing a resistance to money laundering requires more collaborative work. A national task force composed of a balance of federal, provincial, territories, and possibly, municipal, actors might hold more potential for helping to realize a seamless tapestry of anti-money laundering laws. Recommendations that flowed from a fully representative body would carry more weight and avoid nasty jurisdictional clashes. Participation in the very act of devising a coherent strategy generally engenders a healthier compliance ethic. Strategies that descend from above, with no real participation by the actors into whose constitutional competencies aspects of the strategy fall, tend to encounter more resistance. A national strategy, devised by representatives of all constituencies, warrants consideration. At the very least, it would demonstrate a clear Canadian commitment to effective anti-money laundering governance which, as Ahmed suggests, appears to be lacking (Ahmed, this volume).

Notes

1 There are four main treaties: Convention Against Illicit Traffic in Narcotic Drugs and Psychotropic Substances (1988), Convention for the Suppression of the Financing of Terrorism (1999), Convention Against Organized Crime (2000), Convention against Corruption (2003). Although a collection of United Nations Security Council resolutions speaks to the financial model, there are two principal resolutions: UNSC S/Res/1373, 2001 and UNSC S/Res/1540, 2006.

2 *FATF Standards*. Recommendations 3 and 4.

3 *FATF Standards*. Recommendations 9 to 25. Recommendations 26–35 cover supervision and institutional structures.

4 *FATF Standards*. Recommendations 24 and 25.

5 *FATF Standards*. Recommendations 36–40.

6 *Criminal Code*, RSC 1985, c C-46, s.462.31 and s.462.37-462.46.

7 Proceeds of Crime (Money Laundering) and Terrorist Finance Act, S.C 2000, c. 17.

8 See, for example, Civil Forfeiture Act, SBC 2005, c. 29; Criminal Property Forfeiture Act, CCSM c. C308; Civil Forfeiture Act, SNB 2010, c. C-4.5; Civil Forfeiture Act, 2007, c. 27.

9 For example, see Criminal Property Forfeiture Act, s. 1 and s.3(1). The law applies to proceeds of crime and the instruments of crime connected to unlawful activity. Unlawful activity is defined as acts and offences under Canadian law, Manitoba law, the law of other Canadian provinces and territories and unlawful property and acts outside of the jurisdiction which, had they occurred in Canada or Manitoba, would constitute offences.

10 For example, see Criminal Property Forfeiture Act, s.3(1).

11 For instance, section 17.12 of the Criminal Property Forfeiture Act (Manitoba) provides: "Except as otherwise provided under this Act, a finding of fact

or the discharge of a presumption in any proceedings under this Act is to be made on a balance of probabilities."

12 In certain instances, federal law permits the non-conviction-based taking and applies the criminal standard of proof: *Criminal Code*, s. 462.38.

13 FATF, Recommendation 4 provides that countries "...should consider adopting measures which allow such proceeds or instrumentalities to be confiscated without requiring a criminal conviction (non-conviction based confiscation) or which require an offender to demonstrate the lawful origins of property alleged to be liable to confiscation, to the extent that such a requirement is consistent with the principles of their domestic law."

14 See generally, *Martineau v. MNR*, [2004] 3 SCR 737.

15 *Chatterjee v. Ontario* (Attorney General) [2009] 1 SCR 624.

16 An interesting 2020 challenge, successful at the trial level, is that the "future" prong of provincial civil forfeiture law is ultra vires provincial jurisdiction: *British Columbia (Director of Civil Forfeiture) v. Angel Acres Recreation and Festival Property Ltd.*, 2020 BCSC 880 (CanLII).

17 See generally, Elgar (2009).

18 For example, see recent decisions of the European Court of Human Rights and the Court of Justice of the European Union: *G.I.E.M. and others v. Italy*, 28 June 2018, Strasbourg; Case C-234/18 ('Agro In 2001'), Judgement 18 March 2020, Luxembourg.

19 See Van der Does de Willebois et al. (2011); UN Security Council (n.d.).

20 See Department of Finance (2015).

21 *Wallensteiner v. Moir* [1974] 3 All E.R. 217 at 238.

22 FATF Recommendations 24 and 25.

23 FATF Recommendations Glossary, "Beneficial Owner."

24 www.canada.ca/en/department-finance/programs/agreements/strengthen-beneficial-ownership-transparency.html. In 2018 the creation of a pan-Canadian beneficial ownership registry system was recommended: See *Confronting Money Laundering and Terrorist Financing: Moving Canada Forward, Report of the Standing Committee on Finance* November 2018, Recommendation 1 (that the Government of Canada work with the provinces and territories to create a pan-Canadian beneficial ownership registry for all legal persons and entities).

25 Canada Business Corporations Act, RSC 1995, c. C-44, section 21.1.

26 Ibid. section 2.1. Significant control refers, in part, to individuals with any number of shares that carry more than 25 percent of voting rights.

27 An Act to Implement Certain Provisions of the Budget Tabled in Parliament on March 19, 2019, and other measure, SC 2019, chapter 29, section 98 (Strengthening Anti-Money Laundering and Anti-Terrorist Financing Regime).

28 Land Ownership Transparency Act, SBC 2019, chapter 23.

29 The situation regarding money laundering would have been extremely dire to have spawned four recent money laundering inquiries: Commissioner Austin

Cullen (2020); Peter German (2018, 2019), and Maloney, Somerville, and Unger (2019).

30 *FATF Standards* (2012), Recommendation 22.

31 FATF (2016a). A 2008 review had previously identified a problem with the Canadian regime and its application to legal counsel: FATF (2008).

32 While the regulatory regime was complex, a specific point of contention was the possibility that information collected by lawyers regarding what their clients could, not necessarily would, be shared with the federal money laundering regulator.

33 *Canada (Attorney General) v. Federation of Law Societies* [2015] 1 SCR 401.

34 Ibid.

35 See, for example, "Model Rules to Fight Money Laundering and Terrorist Finance." https://flsc.ca/national-initiatives/model-rules-to-fight-money-laundering-and-terrorist-financing/.

36 *Canada (Attorney General) v. Federation of Law Societies* [2015] 1 SCR 401.

37 For example, Legal Profession Act, CCSM (Manitoba) c L 107.

38 *Canada (Attorney General) v. Federation of Law Societies* [2015] 1 SCR 401.

39 For instance, the law firm of Mossack Fonseca is at the heart of the Panama Papers scandal. See Will Fitzgibbon (2018).

References

Bromwich, R. 2018. "Where is the Tipping Point for Governmental Regulation of Lawyers? Perhaps it is in Paradise: Critically Assessing Regulation of Lawyer Involvement with Money Laundering After Canada (Attorney General) v. Federation of Law Societies." *Manitoba Law Journal* 41, no. 1.

Canadian Constitution. n.d. "Agreement to Strengthen Beneficial Ownership Transparency," s 91(2) federal powers; s 92(11) provincial powers. www.canada.ca/en/department-finance/programs/agreements/strengthen-beneficial-ownership-transparency.html.

Cullen, Austin. 2020. "Commission of Inquiry into Money Laundering in British Columbia," May 2019, (interim report issued December 10, 2020).

Department of Finance. 2015. *Assessment of Inherent Risks of Money Laundering and Terrorist Financing in Canada.*

Financial Action Task Force. 2008. *Third Mutual Evaluation on Anti-Money Laundering and Combatting the Financing of Terrorism: Canada.* 29 February, 214–247.

———. 2012. *International Standards on Combatting Money Laundering and the Financing of Terrorism and Proliferation,* (updated to October 2020, [FATF Standards]).

———. 2016a. *Anti-Money Laundering and Counter-Terrorist Financing Measures: Canada Mutual Evaluation Report*, 77–78.

———. 2016b. "Chapter 5." In *Anti-Money Laundering and Counter-Terrorist Financing Measures: Canada, Mutual Evaluation Report*.

———. 2016c. "Chapter 7." In *Anti-Money Laundering and Counter-Terrorist Financing Measures, Canada, Mutual Evaluation Report*.

Fitzgibbon, Will. 2018. "New Panama Papers Scandal Leak Reveals Firm's Chaotic Scramble to Identify Clients, Save Business Amid Global Fallout." *International Consortium of Investigative Journalists*, June 20. https://www.icij.org/investigations/panama-papers/new-panama-papers-leak-reveals-mossack-fonsecas-chaotic-scramble/.

Gallant, M. 2009. "Uncertainties Collide: Lawers and Money Laundering, Terrorist Finance Regulation." *Journal of Financial Crime* 16, no 3: 201–219.

German, Peter. 2018. *Dirty Money: An Independent Review of Money Laundering in the Lower Mainland Casinos Conducted for the Attorney General of British Columbia*, March 31.

———. 2019. *Dirty Money – Part 2: Turning the Tide – An Independent Review of Money Laundering in B.C. Real Estate, Luxury Vehicle Sales and Horse Racing*, March 31.

Gilmore, W. 2004. *Dirty Money: The Evolution of International Measures to Counter Money Laundering and Financing of Terrorism*, 3rd ed. Strasbourg: Council of Europe Publishing.

Government of Canada. 2020. *Strengthening Corporate Beneficial Ownership Transparency in Canada*. https://www.ic.gc.ca/eic/site/142.nsf/eng/00001.html.

Maloney, Maureen, Tsur Somerville, and Brigitte Unger. 2019. "*Combatting Money Laundering in BC Real Estate*." Government of British Columbia. https://www2.gov.bc.ca/gov/content/housing-tenancy/real-estate-bc/consultations/money-laundering.

UN Security Council. n.d. Report of the Panel of Experts Established Pursuant to Resolution 1874. S/2018/171. Security Council, 59/292-77/292 (Finance).

Van der Does de Willebois, E. et al. 2011. "The Puppet Masters: How the Corrupt Use Legal Structures to Hide Stolen Assets and What to Do About It." Stolen Asset Recovery Initiative. Washington, DC: World Bank Group.

Young, S. N. M. 2009. *Civil Forfeiture of Criminal Property: Legal Measures for Targeting the Proceeds of Crime*. Cheltenham: Edward Elgar Publishing.

Financial Crime in Canadian Federalism: Federal and Provincial Policy Options

16

Responses to Money Laundering and Canadian Intergovernmental Affairs

Jeffrey Simser[1]

The world is made of that which demands to be observed. (Aichinger 2018)

Introduction

Money laundering observed is property legerdemain, an art of trickery that paints criminal gains with the patina of legitimacy. Criminal revenue disperses across a continuum of activities: some revenue flows immediately into lifestyle consumption, some revenue is reinvested in the enterprise, and sometimes the revenue is laundered. Laundering occurs for many reasons: laundering puts profit outside of the reach of predatory criminal rivals, properly laundered assets appear to the casual observer to be legitimate (and thus provide utility to the criminal), and it enables sophisticated criminals in concealing their control of significant assets (tax authorities can assess the net worth of an individual against their reported income). Like other crimes, not all laundering is carefully planned. Sometimes laundering is adventitious and just good enough (Levi 2013, 32): those arrangements work if no one is inquiring deeply into them. On the other hand, sophisticated arrangements can challenge the most competent financial investigator. This chapter examines Canada's intergovernmental policy response to money laundering. Information gateways are foundational to that response. One cannot prevent activities one does not understand. One cannot detect what one cannot see. One certainly cannot disrupt or investigate the unknown. Many of the policy options in this chapter cross intergovernmental boundaries, between provinces and the federal government; law enforcement agencies operate at the municipal, provincial, and federal level; all policy options call for improvements to the information gateways currently available to law enforcement. On June 3, 2022, Mr. Justice Cullen delivered his final report of the *Commission of Inquiry into Money Laundering in British Columbia* (the "Cullen Commission") which adds a sense of urgency to these policy options.

Canada has a federal political system: responsibilities are constitutionally distributed among a national government, ten provincial governments, three northern territorial governments, and municipal governments. Core anti-money laundering (AML) measures are federal responsibilities spread across thirteen departments and agencies (see citations in Cullen Commission 2022, 5). The Department of Finance has the lead for domestic and international responsibilities. The Department of Justice is responsible for criminal law and procedure and related Mutual Legal Assistance Treaty matters. Global Affairs Canada is responsible for the designation of terrorist groups and individuals. Public Safety Canada plays a role in national security and public safety. The Financial Transactions and Reports Analysis Centre of Canada (FINTRAC) is a federal agency that operates as our national financial intelligence unit (FIU). FINTRAC has a regulatory role, creating barriers to money laundering. FINTRAC is also an information gateway, collecting and analyzing information from regulated entities. If a statutory test is met, FINTRAC may disclose information to law enforcement and tax authorities. The FIU supports the national tax authority and security establishment.

Along with the federal departments and agencies, provincial governments have numerous responsibilities for AML activities in Canada including company incorporation, as a tax authority, and land registry systems. There are federal and provincial prosecutors. There are federal, provincial, and municipal police forces. Enforcement and disruption occur through prosecutions and asset forfeiture.

As the preceding chapters have demonstrated, the mysteries of financial crime and money laundering desperately need to be solved. This concluding chapter has four parts. Part one considers the vulnerabilities posed by money laundering. Part two looks at prevention and detection: prophylactic anti-money laundering (AML) policy devices. Part three considers remedial and enforcement mechanisms to investigate and disrupt laundering. Finally, part four examines policy options for the future. All four parts of this chapter consider information gateways and inter-governmental policy interactions. Information collected at a provincial or local level can be disclosed to the federal FIU and then distributed back through federal or provincial law enforcement officials. There is a constant interchange among all levels. Policy responses are only as strong as the system as a whole. At the time of writing, external events are driving change. Extraordinary cooperation among provinces and the federal government is underway in the fight against money laundering.

Money Laundering and the Vancouver Model

The province established the Cullen Commission in response to a report written by Peter German which examined, amongst other things, money laundering. That report included a typology, coined the "Vancouver Model." While parts of that typology are beyond the scope of this chapter (loan sharking, for example), the Vancouver Model explains how vast amounts of money have been laundered through an informal value transfer system (IVTS), a money services business with an underground banking network that matches supply and demand. The IVTS infrastructure helped Chinese nationals work around Communist government currency controls: regardless of their wealth, a citizen is limited to transmitting $50,000 a year outside China which they must transact through a state-sanctioned bank.[2] To avoid state oversight, a mainland Chinese citizen can transfer money to a local underground banker. The money may be legitimately earned (or not). Currency control evasion is not a crime in Canada. The underground banker notifies their Vancouver counterpart. When that Chinese citizen visits Canada, the Vancouver underground banker provides them with Canadian cash (less a fee). That cash did not physically move over the border. The Chinese underground banker brokers shipments to Canada of drugs or contraband; the recipients of those shipments do not pay the Chinese mainland broker. Rather, the recipients provide money to the Vancouver underground banker (drug sales in Canada create cash); the underground banker gives the cash to the visiting Chinese national; everything is then reconciled amongst the participants. The Chinese national in Vancouver can take the cash to a Canadian casino (often in a form consistent with street drug proceeds – a hockey bag of $20 bills). Many of the gamblers put their money at risk and lost all or most of it. Some gamblers, after a bit of gambling, might seek from the casino higher denomination bills (a technique known as refining – larger denominations of cash are less bulky) or a cashier's cheque. Some casinos use chips that are fungible in other locations (Macau, Las Vegas, and so on); those chips are then the modality of laundering. Laundering is about moving value and there are innumerable techniques to do so. For example, cuckoo smurfing enables laundering through access to the accounts of foreign students studying in Canada. They unwittingly agree to help a fellow citizen by accepting deposits into their account and allowing the money to be wired to other accounts. The student takes a small fee to supplement their studies. That money might be transferred to settle a casino patron account; winnings from that account are laundered. The casino payout offers an apparently legitimate provenance. Where did the money come from? "I had a good day at the tables."

FATF: Continuing AML Challenges for Canada

The Vancouver Model received considerable public attention when Dr. German's report was issued. Money laundering measures in Canada are evaluated periodically by an international body, the Financial Action Task Force (FATF). FATF routinely publishes typologies to assist stakeholders involved in AML. The Vancouver Model appears in one such typology, albeit thinly disguised. Using details from a specific investigation (E-Pirate), the typology chronicles a professional launderer who managed flows of roughly $1 billion per year for a fee of 5 percent per transaction. This launderer is connected to more than forty different organizations, including drug dealers (who were critical to the value-transfer and the procurement of cash). One final note: the underlying criminal prosecution for E-Pirate collapsed because of disclosure problems; related seized property is currently the subject of a civil asset forfeiture proceeding (FATF 2018).

Understanding Money Laundering: PLI

FINTRAC's website explains that there are "three recognized stages in the money laundering process," namely placement, layering, and integration (PLI). Some models add two steps: justification moves the assets beyond a mere intermingling and creates a credible legend for their provenance; extraction places cleansed assets in the hands of the operating mind of the enterprise. Within the PLI model, placement, the first step, occurs when illegally generated funds move into the legitimate economy. For example, cash is deposited in a bank account. Indeed, the focus of PLI is on cash which explains the illegal drug trade, where street-level transactions occur in cash. AML systems have corresponding cash-focused mitigation measures in Canada: mandatory reporting for larger cash transactions, reporting on suspicious transactions and client identification protocols. In the second stage, layering, money launderers run the placed funds through transactions, converting their lucre into different forms. Moving funds around disguises origin and obscures the audit trail. For example, back-to-back wire transfers make no economic sense (the launderer pays a fee for each transfer) but as a layering technique, the transfers make tracing difficult, particularly if they cross international borders. The money launderer knows that law enforcement must accomplish three things before assets are interdicted: first, they have to find the assets; second, they must trace the assets back to the source; finally, they have to connect those traced assets to unlawful activity (or in a prosecution, a specific criminal). Tracing is a resource-intensive task for law enforcement. Each step traced leads to another request to deduce the next historical step in the asset flow. Integration is the third and final stage in the PLI laundering process. Here the launderer takes assets with a sufficiently concealed provenance and "integrates" them into the apparently legitimate holdings of the criminal. Successfully laundered funds are free from the fear of interdiction. Unlike cash, which is at risk of theft by rival criminals, integrated assets are safer and more secure. The operating minds of a criminal enterprise can now purchase luxury homes, personal luxury items, send their children to private schools or invest in legitimate businesses. This model of the laundering process is of a circular design: funds are designed to go on a journey that obscures their origin but end up back in the control of the originator with the veneer of legitimacy.

There are some weaknesses with PLI as a theoretical model. Money laundering by tax evaders, insider traders, computer hackers and garden-variety fraudsters follows modalities limited only by the imagination; Bitcoin, stolen credit cards and purloined cheques do not require cash placement. White-collar criminals often do not need a placement step, but they often move their pilfered assets offshore, a process one expert describes as closer to displacement than placement (Levi 2013, 10). PLI is often premised on the notion that a criminal wants cleansed assets under their control. Some criminals want to disguise their relationship to any assets at all; tax authorities, for example, can use net-worth techniques to compare legitimate income against assets. PLI as a money laundering model is not likely to fall off the regulators' radar; PLI provides a tidy narrative for policymakers and an apparently simple explanation for complex activity (like FINTRAC). A more rigorous model might capture non-cash laundering activities better (fraud), pre-laundering activities (setting up trusts, accounts, and so on) and bring a different rigour to the layering activity (costly back-to-back wire transfers do not make economic sense). Rather than focusing on cash, AML systems could look at sectors and geographies more broadly to identify vulnerabilities and corresponding mitigation measures (Sterling 2015).

Money Laundering Techniques

The attention that PLI lavishes on cash creates some blind spots but has some virtues as a model. For some forms of unlawful activity, cash is king. Cocaine is sold to users on the street for cash; that cash, particularly if the denominations are small, is heavy and bulky (44 pounds of cocaine can translate into 220 pounds of $10 bills; Simser 2008, 15). What techniques are available to a launderer? As with any activity, there is a range of possibilities. One simple laundering technique uses a nominee, preferably someone close like a family member, and transfers assets into their name. Such an arrangement is reasonably susceptible to detection: the otherwise impecunious pensioner mother of the drug dealer probably did not pay for a mansion with her own money. There are innumerable ways of deploying intermediaries. The above-noted "cuckoo" technique can ensnare unwitting actors, students living abroad or businesspeople looking to avoid high currency exchange transaction fees.

Trade-based money laundering (TBML) schemes, like the black-market peso exchange, use drug proceeds in the United States to purchase goods locally and to settle the drug transaction when those goods are exported to a source country, like Columbia. Manipulating the value of imports or exports can also facilitate money laundering; overpaying for low-grade emeralds, for example, can move money from a narcotics consuming country, like the US, to an emerald producing country in Central or South America. Often a third-party payment is involved. Cross-border trade is typically financed through a letter of credit. The issuer of that letter, for example, a bank that finances trade, is paid up front; when the goods reach their destination, accompanied by bills of lading and customs paperwork, the letter of credit is honoured. A genuine or fictitious shipment of goods effectively moves the money. With the massive levels of international trade, authorities are challenged to spot TBML (see citations in Cullen Commission 2022, 14).

Corporate legal vehicles can obfuscate the money trail. A simple trust can hide the true owner of an asset. Making the trustee a lawyer adds a layer of confidentiality. Offshore trusts in the right jurisdiction can take advantage of local rules: short limitation periods, high burdens of proof to open up the trust, and the refusal to recognize foreign production or seizure orders. Trusts settled with a triggering flight clause move assets automatically to another jurisdiction upon the receipt of an injunction from a court or a search warrant (Simser 2008, 17). While the law in Canada is slowly changing, there has traditionally been scant attention paid by the government to the owners of private corporations; a number of provincial jurisdictions and the federal government are now implementing an ownership registry system (see Policy Challenges below).

Prevention and Detection

Countries around the world have implemented anti-money laundering (AML) regimes: regulatory barriers designed to impede and discourage those money launderers. FIUs are central to the policy approach. Canada's FIU model includes a number of basic elements:

- FINTRAC has a regulatory oversight role for several actors in the legitimate economy vulnerable to money laundering: Reporting Entities (REs) which include financial institutions and in FATF nomenclature, and, in FATF nomenclature, Designated Non-Financial Businesses and Professions (DNFBPs).
- REs have a number of regulatory responsibilities thrust upon them. They must develop an AML program that includes control measures designed to achieve regulatory outcomes. That program must include a methodology to ensure the reporting entity knows their customer (KYC). Who are they? How do they conduct business? KYC helps the RE to distinguish between legitimate and suspicious transactions.
- REs must follow prescribed client identification procedures. A prospective launderer should not be anonymous; identity verification poses a barrier. The FIU also has an information disbursement function. Where laundered assets find their way into the REs system, law enforcement should be able to follow the money trail.
- REs must keep certain types of records. The FIU audits REs compliance. The REs' records provide an audit trail for law enforcement.
- REs have mandatory reporting obligations. Large cash transactions must be reported ($10,000 or more in cash, either in a single transaction or multiple transactions within 24 hours). There are similar rules for virtual currency. Reporting is required for electronic fund transfers of $10,000 or more, either out of or into Canada, and either in a single transaction or multiple transactions within 24 hours. Casinos must report disbursements of $10,000 or more

in the course of a single transaction or multiple transactions within 24 hours. In 2018–19, FINTRAC received large cash transaction reports to a value of $10,055,099 and $17,627,947 in EFTs. There are also reporting obligations for cross-border currency movements requiring travellers to declare if they are carrying in excess of $10,000 cash or negotiable instruments. Finally, terrorist property reports are mandated.[3]

- REs are also required to file STRs (suspicious transaction reports). An STR is required where the reporting entity has "reasonable grounds to suspect that the transaction is related to the commission or attempted commission of a money laundering or terrorist activity financing offence." (FINTRAC 2022) Unlike EFT or large cash transactions, there is no minimum threshold for STRs. In 2018–19, 235,661 STRs were reported but the FIU has not reported on their value (which leaves part of the money laundering story untold).

- The FIU analyzes that information and if based on their discretion, certain thresholds are met, the agency must make information disclosures to law enforcement. In Canada, many of the disclosures respond to voluntary information reports (VIRs). By filing a VIR, police advise the FIU of their interest in a certain target. If an FIU analyst is satisfied that disclosure is merited, then information about the target will transmit back to law enforcement. Alternatively, the FIU can decide that privacy interests outweigh law enforcement's need for disclosure and refuse to provide information (Simser 2020).

FINTRAC's information gateway role, that is, the disclosure to law enforcement, tax authorities, and national security agencies, is critical to the enforcement role discussed in the next part of this chapter.

Enforcement and Remedial Measures

Money laundering is criminalized: an accused can be charged, prosecuted, and convicted of the offence. Criminal asset forfeiture can be sought at sentencing (or in absentia for a fugitive who has been accused). Sanctions against Russian oligarchs can be enforced through asset forfeiture under federal legislation (for example the Special Economic Measures Act, 2019). Depending on the predicate offence, policing and prosecutions can occur at the federal or provincial level. Authorities in eight provinces and one territory can launch a civil asset forfeiture proceeding; the courts can forfeit the proceeds and instruments of unlawful activity, including money laundering; charges or convictions are not a precondition to such a civil law proceeding. All enforcement and remedial measures share a common challenge: access to actionable information. As we shall see, Cullen suggests that our institutions are not fit-for-purpose to meet this challenge.

The FIU as Information Gateway

The FIU is an information gateway. FINTRAC compiles information from REs. REs are chosen based on a risk assessment of their perceived vulnerability to money laundering activity. FINTRAC as an information gateway navigates between privacy rights and the informational needs of law enforcement. The FIU is statutorily required to act "at arm's length" and be "independent from law enforcement agencies and other entities to which it is authorized to disclose information." (PCMLTFA, Part 4) FINTRAC is required to have a biennial audit conducted by the Office of the Privacy Commissioner. The FIU must protect privacy interests against unauthorized disclosures. Most importantly. FINTRAC may only disclose to law enforcement where they determine that there are reasonable grounds to suspect that the information would be relevant to the investigation or prosecution of a money laundering offence or a terrorist financing case. There is a weakness in this system. Arm's length officials in a distanced federal agency have an imperfect lens on the predicate criminal activity underlying money laundering. The Cullen Commission stated that the federal anti-money laundering regime is not effective. FINTRAC collects massive quantities of data but shares back insufficient qualitative information (Cullen 2022, 200).

To address this weakness, law enforcement and national security agencies can alert the FIU to their interest in a particular investigatory matter by forwarding a voluntary information report (VIRs) to FINTRAC. Members of the public can also make a VIR. In 2018–19, 2,754 VIRs went to the FIU. For example, a VIR might indicate an investigative interest in specific actors suspected of money laundering or terrorist financing. In 2018–19, FINTRAC provided 2,276 disclosures to law enforcement. FIN-TRAC's compliance role includes compliance examinations of reporting agencies and guidance to various businesses subject to their regulatory regime. In 2018–19 there were 497 compliance examinations of REs.

The challenge with the VIR process, however, is that the FIUs' role is largely reactive. Many activities could paint a picture for investigators: a bank might file an STR on trade activities of their client that seem anomalous (a TBML indicator); a client may instruct their bank to undertake uneconomic activities (back-to-back wire transfers across several jurisdictions). An FIU analysis of the aggregate of these activities might well identify actors higher up the criminal food chain. The Cullen Commission report gives testament to our collective failure to identify and interdict professional money laundering businesses.

Open-Source Information Gateways

The FIU is not the only information gateway available to investigators. There are open-source research options. A seasoned investigator will create a profile of their target: names, aliases, dates of birth, marriages, divorces, spouses, ex-spouses, girlfriends, boyfriends, children, maiden names, and nicknames. Social media (Facebook, Twitter, and LinkedIn) and tools such as the "Wayback Machine"[4] can draw a picture. Corporate registries can be searched (Wadlinger et al. 2018). Determining beneficial ownership of companies and trusts has traditionally been a tremendous challenge in Canada, although this is starting to change with beneficial ownership registries (see Policy Challenges below). Private databases can sometimes provide helpful information (the Yellow Pages, Dunn and Bradstreet, LexisNexis, TransUnion, and so on). Finally, certain types of property link to publicly available registration systems. Land is the most typical of this type of asset, but vehicles, airplanes, and watercraft have registries. Lenders may register their security interests against property (e.g., in each province's Personal Property Security Act registration system; Simser 2008).

International Information Gateways

If assets linked to Canadian criminality have moved offshore, law enforcement have several options to obtain the relevant information. By statute,[5] Canada can work with a foreign government where a Mutual Legal Assistance Treaty (MLAT) exists. MLAT requests tend to be ponderous, bureaucratic, and very slow. FINTRAC has reciprocal sharing arrangements with other FIUs around the world. Non-treaty requests can be made through networks, like the Camden Asset Recovery Inter-Agency Network (CARIN) and the Egmont Group. Experienced investigators have their own networks and can often get a colleague in Tokyo or New York to quietly procure a title search for them.

Taxation: A Limited Information Gateway

The Canada Revenue Agency (CRA), Canada's federal tax authority, can disclose information to law enforcement under limited circumstances. The CRA can be a vital partner in financial crime investigations, furnishing critical information which supports asset identification and an undeclared income. A criminal with no reported income and significant assets is a rich target for law enforcement. CRA can take their own enforcement measures. Alternatively, the Income Tax Act permits the CRA to disclose to law enforcement relevant taxpayers' information where criminal proceedings have been commenced by the laying of charges. There is also a Criminal Code process where ongoing investigations can obtain disclosure (even if no charges have been laid). In either instance, disclosures are limited to a category of very serious crimes, including offences related to drugs and criminal organizations.

Judicially Authorized Disclosures

An investigator can lay an "information to obtain" before a judge, who can issue a search warrant or information-gathering order based on the affidavit evidence. An investigator can also seek a restraint order against assets. In some instances, civil forfeiture authorities can seek the assistance of the court to obtain evidence and information. A warrant may reveal account transactions showing that money has been wired to another account; a warrant on that account can reveal further trails, all of which need to be pursued. Two important practical things to consider for any of these options: they are labour-intensive and time-consuming. Poorly resourced law enforcement renders these tools prolix.

Using Information to Disrupt Money Laundering

Scriptwriters created a catchphrase in the 1976 Watergate thriller *All the President's Men*: follow the money. To that end, what can law enforcement do next? There are three broad options:

- Money laundering is criminalized activity. A federal or provincial prosecutor can seek a conviction and in sentencing, criminal asset forfeiture.
- Several provinces have civil asset forfeiture laws.
- There are various regulatory devices available in specific contexts: customs agents can seize and administratively forfeit smuggled cash; tax authorities can attribute and then levy taxes against undeclared income.

There are several enabling information gateways. Investigators can conduct open-source searches, conduct surveillance and interview witnesses. The FIU can make disclosures. Investigators can use warrants. Civil forfeiture authorities have statutorily enabled flows of information that comply with privacy laws.

Money Laundering Criminalized

Several Criminal Code (the Code) offences are relevant to a money laundering case. The possession of proceeds of crime is an offence for one. While often applied to the possession of stolen goods, this provision would also capture proceeds. With fewer elements to prove and the same penalty, this possession offence is more frequently used than the money laundering offence. The Code's money laundering offence has the following key elements:

- that the accused dealt with property or the proceeds of property;
- that the property was obtained by crime;
- that the accused knew or believed that the property was obtained by crime; and,
- that the accused intended to conceal or convert the property (Code, s.462.31).

In 2019, amendments were introduced to capture recklessness (see citations in Cullen Commission 2022, 41). That is, an accused who was willfully blind or reckless to the origin of the property can be found to have committed an offence. Dealing with the property includes an accused who "uses, transfers the possession of, sends or delivers to any person or place, transports, transmits, alters, disposes of or otherwise deals with, in any manner and by any means." (Code, s.462.31) The courts have held that Parliament intended to "cast a wide net" to prohibit the laundering of the proceeds of crime (*R. v. Tejani*). In *R. v. Daoust*, the courts have stated that the purpose of the money laundering provision in the Code was to prevent offenders from placing their proceeds of crime beyond reach of the law enforcement.

Criminal Asset Forfeiture

Under the Code (and the Controlled Drugs and Substances Act), a prosecutor can, as a general matter, seek forfeiture of two types of property: proceeds of crime and offence-related property (ORP).[6] A proceed is property (or benefit or advantage) obtained or derived directly or indirectly from the commission of a designated offence. Designated offences extend beyond money laundering to include all federally indictable offences as well offences designated (or excluded) by regulation. There is a dual criminality provision: if property in Canada derives from an offshore offence, that property is forfeitable as long as the offshore predicate offence would have been a designated offence had it been committed in Canada. In other jurisdictions, ORP is known as an instrument or instrumentality and only invoked in prosecutions by indictment. That is, property used to commit a crime, typically an indictable offence.

Fine In Lieu

Where an offender has placed proceeds of crime beyond the reach of a sentencing court, the court shall presumptively order a fine in an amount equal to the value of that property or part of that property. Where the offender willfully defaults on payment of the fine the court must impose a term of imprisonment; the scale of punishment depends on the value of the property that cannot be forfeited. This scale ranges from up to six months for fines less than $10,000 to between five and ten years for fines of $1 million or more.

Civil Asset Forfeiture

Civil asset forfeiture, also known as non-conviction-based forfeiture (NCB), is a "remedial statutory device designed to recover the proceeds of unlawful activity as well as property used to facilitate unlawful activity" (Simser 2011, 1-1). There are eight provinces and one territory with civil forfeiture laws. While each system has its own unique features, generally, the province is statutorily empowered to bring a proceeding against any type of property (*in rem*). In garden-variety civil lawsuits, a defendant is a person (or company). In a civil forfeiture proceeding, the property itself is the defendant. Generally, two types of property, proceeds and instruments, can be subject to a proceeding. Proceeds of unlawful activity are items of property that have, as their provenance, unlawful activity. Anyone with a known claim to title receives notice and has statutory grounds to contest. If the province establishes that the origin of the property is in unlawful activity, the court is empowered to extinguish the title and forfeit the property to the province. Civil forfeiture authorities rely on statutorily authorized information gateways. Provincially regulated law enforcement has authority to share information; federally regulated (and foreign) law enforcement generally shares under a statutorily mandated memorandum of understanding.

Policy Challenges

As noted, Canada's AML system is subject to periodic evaluation by the FATF (2016), an international body. The most recent Mutual Evaluation Report for Canada occurred in 2016 and identified a number of challenges:

- Lawyers, law firms, and Québec notaries are largely exempt from AML laws, creating a significant loophole. The issue is complex: the Supreme Court of Canada ruled in 2015 that efforts to include lawyers in the AML program were unconstitutional. Self-regulatory bodies that oversee lawyers have some cash reporting measures, but in an AML context, they are not particularly robust.[7] A working group consisting of law societies and the federal government is currently considering the issue. The Cullen Commission observed that while lawyers are exposed to significant money laundering risks, the self-regulating bodies offered the best way to manage those risks (Cullen 2022, 1174).

- As discussed, Canada's FIU receives a broad range of reported information, including STRs and VIRs, but there is a structural limit to their analysis: FINTRAC cannot push back and request further disclosures from reporting entities. Those who have worked on a financial crime case know that each level of disclosure broadens possibilities: is this actor connected? Is this account relevant to the scheme? Does the disclosure reveal new vectors, new actors, and new areas that demand further inquiry? This seems asymptotic, with each new disclosure opening further lines of inquiry. The Cullen Commission observed that the federal system compels massive quantities of data while producing a very modest number of intelligence packages, which if delivered late provide even less qualitative value (Cullen 2022, 210).

- Canada has a robust and concentrated financial services industry, where compliance is serviceable, but FATF notes that we lag when it comes to DNFBPS.[8] FINTRAC needs to improve regulatory efforts to encourage compliance.

- Legal persons and arrangements, like corporations and trusts, are poorly regulated particularly when it comes to transparent beneficial ownership. Legal responses are starting to emerge. In 2021, trusts resident in Canada must file beneficial ownership information with tax authorities, even if they report no income. Recent amendments require federal corporations to retain a beneficial ownership register and there are ongoing efforts in the provinces and territories. Companies can be incorporated federally, but 91 percent of private entities are incorporated across the ten provinces and three territories (Department of Finance 2018). A broader beneficial ownership registry is in development by the federal government and Cullen recommends that provinces adopt it. (2022, 39) The risk-based AML regulatory system, through KYC, requires REs such as financial institutions and securities dealers to collect beneficial ownership information for trusts and private companies; REs must know their customer. The federal government is building a company registry that is expected to be online in 2023 (Cullen 2022, 1106).

- Finally, FATF notes that law enforcement results on money laundering prosecutions and asset recovery are not commensurate with money laundering risks for a country like Canada. The Cullen Commission found that law enforcement needed to step up their activity at all levels to "follow the money" (police, prosecutors, and civil forfeiture professionals; Cullen 2022, 1656–1620).

Early Policy Responses

Regulations have been enacted augmenting approach of FINTRAC to virtual currency activity, prepaid cards, as well as foreign money service businesses.

- "Fintech" is an abbreviation capturing the emerging financial technology and platforms that are competing with, and disrupting, the more traditional financial services offered by brick-and-mortar financial institutions. From an AML perspective, fintech introduces new risks, particularly through offshore currency exchanges, virtual currencies, and the use of prepaid cards. Virtual currencies and open loop prepaid cards (which run on a payment network and are not restricted to use by a single merchant) can operate outside of the traditional financial system. These vectors impair the FIU's ability to produce financial intelligence. Now, prepaid payment products are treated as bank accounts for the purposes of the regulation (e.g., akin to the customer due diligence required when an account is opened). The regime for prepaid cards has been modestly amended, adding exemptions for certain closed loop cards. Crowd funding has been brought into the AML regime.

- FINTRAC does not directly regulate virtual currency. However, virtual currency dealers are now reporting entities, where they will be treated similarly to money service businesses. As REs must comply with FINTRAC's regulatory oversight, which will include the requirement for compliance programs. Virtual currency is given an interesting definition. In 2018, the definition was narrower (a digital currency that was not a fiat currency); now virtual currency is "a digital representation of value that can be used for payment or investment purposes." Virtual currency excludes fiat currencies but includes something that can be readily exchanged for funds or another virtual currency or a private key of a cryptographic system that enables access. In other words, the definition not only includes conventionally understood virtual currencies used for payments, like Bitcoin, but also investment-based items like security tokens. Regulated entities must maintain a virtual currency ledger for transactions of $10,000 or more.

- Foreign money service businesses (MSBs) are now regulated entities; these are enterprises that do not have a place of business in Canada but provide business directed at Canadians. Again, this is a recognition that the internet and new payment methods present a risk to be exploited by money launderers. The Vancouver Model involved an MSB that deliberately flew beneath the radar of FINTRAC. On the third floor of a nondescript office building in Richmond, cash deliveries were received daily, put through a money counter and then handed over to gamblers (see citations in Cullen Commission 2022, 2).

- There are changes to reporting requirements for STRs, electronic funds transfer reports, record keeping, and identification requirements.

The government acknowledged that these regulations were meant, in part, to address deficiencies identified by FATF.

Implementing these changes will be challenging:

- There is significant value in trying to capture offshore MSBs and virtual currency dealers as regulated entities. Effectively capturing them will be challenging. How will the FIU meet their regulatory objectives? What happens if the offshore entity sublimely ignores the entreaties of Canada's FIU? FINTRAC is not without options. Multijurisdictional finance is interrelated, and many other countries share Canada's aspirations. There are formal networks, like the Egmont Group,[9] that FINTRAC can access.

- Thresholds that make sense in the real world do not apply to the virtual world. For example, virtual currencies appeal to consumers because they are frictionless and low cost. Ten thousand dollars in cash is physically bulky. Bitcoin is not.

- A 2019 Senate report has recognized the complexity of open banking and the interplay between fintech and traditional financial institutions. Despite some statutory protections, after an initial consent, Canadians don't have very much control over their personal data when it is held by a financial institution. This is a barrier to innovation for emerging fintech disruptors who want to offer platforms that are faster and cheaper than the traditional offerings of financial institutions. FINTRAC's proposed regulations recognize the need to oversee the AML risk in this area, but it remains to be seen whether that scheme is fit for purpose.

The Cullen Commission

The final 1,800-page report of the Cullen Commission produced 101 recommendations:

- The status quo is neither sustainable nor acceptable. Canada's AML system is not effective and the RCMP's inattention since 2012 has allowed unchecked money laundering growth.

- Cullen acknowledged that British Columbia took many positive steps as a result of Dr. German's work and interim recommendations (for example, requiring source of funds in a casino).

- Cullen has recommended that the province create an AML Commissioner and a dedicated money laundering intelligence and investigation unit. Law enforcement should mandate "following the money" in all cases for profit-based crime. Asset forfeiture should be pursued more vigorously. Civil forfeiture should include an unexplained wealth provision. Where the director of the program proves to the court that a respondent has unexplained wealth that cannot be accounted for through legitimate income, the onus will shift to a respondent to explain the provenance of their assets. If the respondent refuses, a rebuttable presumption arises that their property is a proceed of unlawful activity and thus forfeitable.

- Certain sectors remain vulnerable to money laundering and AML policy improvements are required. Those sectors include real estate, private lending, realtors, mortgage lending, chartered professional accountants, banks, credit unions, and luxury goods. Money service businesses should be regulated by British Columbia. Cullen made recommendations about how the federal government ought to implement a corporate registry system that includes transparent links identifying beneficial owners. Dr. German notes that there is a localized form of trade-based money laundering (TBML) whereby criminals use dirty money to pay the debts of legitimate businesses in exchange for a cheque or negotiable instrument (a variant on the black-market peso exchange; German 2019, 254–55). Cullen called TBML a pervasive but poorly understood money laundering method that requires further attention (Cullen 2022, 1446).

Other Policy Responses

What other policy options are available?

- In 2015, the UK piloted JIMLIT, the Joint Money Laundering Intelligence Task Force. JIMLIT brings together a variety of actors: law enforcement and national security personnel, regulators and tax authorities, and private actors including forty financial institutions (banks, the Post Office, MoneyGram and Western Union). Section 7 of the Crimes and Courts Act, 2013 provides a safe harbour; anyone can share information with the National Crime Agency (NCA).[10] This allays the concerns of banks, who were worried about client lawsuits. JIMLIT enabled Barclays Bank to disclose the existence of numerous bank accounts that had unusual amounts of cash moving into them. A series of coordinated civil recovery actions were brought at the same time, closing ninety-five accounts (see citations in Cullen Commission 2022, 32). In Canada, there is a money laundering bankers' control group among financial institutions, FINTRAC and the RCMP which is a long way from the sophistication of JIMLIT.

- Covid-19 has accelerated the use of digital payments. The pandemic has one expert predicting that 67 percent of global payments will be digital by 2025; prior to Covid-19, the prediction was 57 percent (Gringoli et al. 2020, 1). This will increase pressure on non-cash focused AML techniques. At the same time, the pandemic has placed pressure on our economy and financial institutions: one worries that cost-cutting in banks could affect AML and compliance programs in this environment.

- Big techs pose risks beyond those presented by fintech. Fintech operates in the financial system; large technology firms, ranging from Alibaba to Facebook and Google, are not currently significant players in the financial system, but they could be with their low-cost structure and massive customer reach that can be scaled up to disrupt the sector. The Bank for International Settlements noted in their 2019 annual report that big techs present opportunities: for example, data analytics allows efficient assessments of creditworthiness of customers, including the unbanked. That said, there are risks. The 2019 FINTRAC Annual Report notes that public policy needs to anticipate challenges, not only from a financial regulation perspective but also from a consumer protection, data privacy, and competition (anti-trust) perspective.

- From an AML perspective, payment services are of great interest. Many payment services, such as Apple Pay, Google Pay and PayPal, are overlay systems that rely on existing infrastructure (credit cards). Some services, like Alipay in Asia and M-Pesa in Africa, require users to settle payments directly on that big tech firm's proprietary system. This is an area that regulators are watching closely. Facebook's proposals around Libra, a permissioned blockchain cryptocurrency, and Calibra, the e-wallet, have been the subject of considerable attention, particularly by the United States Congress.

- Cryptocurrency presents some risk. Bitcoin is volatile and, compared to a fiat currency like the dollar, relatively shallow. So-called stable coins present similar challenges. That means for smaller transactions, the transaction needs to settle very quickly to mitigate the risk of volatile swings in value (e.g., of Bitcoin). For high quantity money launderers, like a kleptocrat, there's not enough available cryptocurrency to easily move the millions (or billions) stolen from a state treasury (Simser 2015). Cullen has recommended that virtual asset service providers be regulated provincially (Cullen 2022, 1411).

- Finally, technological developments will continue to offer opportunities and present threats, particularly as distributed ledger technology, artificial intelligence, extended reality, and quantum computing evolve. Regulators of all stripes will be challenged to stay abreast of technology's dynamism, particularly when regulated intermediaries are disrupted by technology.

The challenge money laundering poses to society is a mirror of the challenge that organized crime poses: a test of our values and the importance of rule of law. The 1,800 pages of the Cullen Commission's final report provide a roadmap that British Columbia can follow. We don't yet know how other provinces will react and we certainly don't know what the federal reaction will be. If policymakers want to seriously address money laundering, intergovernmental cooperation will define our collective success or failure.

Notes

1 Jeffrey Simser, Toronto, Canada. The views expressed in this chapter are personal and do not reflect the views of his employer prior to his 2022 retirement, the Government of Ontario nor the Ministry of the Attorney General. The author is grateful for the sharp editorial assistance of my friend Colleen Carson, LL.B, my long-suffering friend Stephen Sterling and the thoughtful comments of Rachael Simser, M.A. Any errors or mistakes are mine alone.
2 Government approval can be obtained for larger transactions.
3 Countering the financing of terrorism is a deeply complex matter in its own right and beyond the scope of this chapter.
4 An archival index hosting older versions of web pages dating back to 1996.
5 Mutual Legal Assistance in Criminal Matters Act
6 There are dozens of forfeiture mechanisms in the Code and an even greater number in regulatory statutes.
7 For example: Part III of By-law 9 of the Law Society of Ontario requires lawyers to not accept more than $7,500 in cash from clients. Beyond the basic prohibition, which seems patently susceptible to evasion, there's no reporting to the FIU.
8 DNFBPs typically include casinos, real estate agents, and dealers in precious metals/gems.
9 The Egmont Group is a body consisting of 165 Financial Intelligence Units (FIUs).
10 Section 462.47 of the Code could similarly be used.

References

Aichinger, Ilse (Austrian poet). 2018. Quoted in Manguel, *A Packing My Library*, 140. New Haven: Yale.

Bank for International Settlements Annual Economic Report. 2019. https://www.bis.org/publ/arpdf/ar2019e.htm.

Confronting Money Laundering and Terrorist Financing: Moving Canada Forward, Report of the Standing Committee on Finance Nov. 2018, 42nd Parliament, 1st Session.

Cullen Commission. 2022. (www.cullencommission.ca) heard testimony from a number of experts in 2020 including some cited in this chapter: Hoffmann, J. (February 24, 2020); Hughes, J. (February 24, 2020), Lord, S. (May 29, 2020), Levi, M. (June 5 and 8, 2020); Schneider, S. (May 25–27, 2020); and Wainwright, R. (June 15 and 16, 2020). The final report was delivered in June 2022.

Department of Finance. 2018, February 7. Reviewing Canada's Anti-Money Laundering and Anti-Terrorist Financing Regime. https://www.canada.ca/en/department-finance/programs/consultations/2018/canadas-anti-money-laundering-anti-terrorist-financing-regime.html.

FATF. 2016. *Anti-Money Laundering and Counter-Terrorist Financing Measures – Canada - Mutual Evaluation Report September 2016*. https://www.fatf-gafi.org/publications/mutualevaluations/documents/mer-canada-2016.html.

———. 2018. *Professional Money Laundering*. http://www.fatf-gafi.org/publications/methodsandtrends/documents/professional-money-laundering.html.

FINTRAC. n.d. Data, including their 2018–19 Annual Report can be found at: https://www.fintrac-canafe.gc.ca/intro-eng. FINTRAC's website also provides guidance documents, for example on STRs: https://www.fintrac-canafe.gc.ca/guidance-directives/transaction-operation/Guide2/2-eng.

German, P. 2018, 2019. *Dirty Money* (March 31, 2018 and Part 2 was issued in March 31, 2019). https://news.gov.bc.ca/files/Gaming_Final_Report.pdf. https://news.gov.bc.ca/files/German_Report_luxury_cars.pdf.

Gringoli, V., G. Williams, J. Ott, and T. Olsen. 2020. *The Covid-19 Tipping Point for Digital Payments*. https://www.bain.com/insights/the-covid-19-tipping-point-for-digital-payments/.

Levi, M. 2013. *Money-Laundering Typologies: A Review of their Fitness for Purpose*. Ottawa: Government of Canada.

Simser, J. 2008. "Money Laundering and Asset Cloaking Techniques." *Journal of Money Laundering* Control 11, 15.

———. 2011. *Civil Asset Forfeiture in Canada*. Toronto: Canada Law Book.

———. 2015. "Bitcoin and Modern Alchemy: In Code We Trust." *Journal of Financial Crime* 22, no. 2: 156–169.

————. 2020. "Canada's Financial Intelligence Unit: FINTRAC." *Journal of Money Laundering Control* 23, no. 2: 297–307.

Standing Senate Committee on Banking, Trade and Commerce. 2019. *Open Banking: What it Means for You.* https://sencanada.ca/en/info-page/parl-42-1/banc-open-banking/.

Sterling, S. 2015. "Identifying Money Laundering." *Journal of Money Laundering Control* 18, no. 3, 266–292.

U.S. Government Accountability Office. 2020. *Report to Congressional Requesters: Trade-Based Money Laundering* (April). https://www.gao.gov/assets/710/705679.pdf.

Wadlinger, N., C. Pacini, N. Stowell, W. Hopwood, and D. Sinclair. 2018. "Domestic Asset Tracing and Recovery of Hidden Assets and the Spoils of Financial Crime." *St. Mary's Law Journal* 49, no. 3, 611–612.

Cases and Statutes

Canada Criminal Code, RSC 1985, c C-46
R. v. Daoust, 2004 SCC 6.
R. v. Tejani, 1999 CanLII 3765 (Ont CA) U.K. Crimes and Courts Act, 2013.

Contributors

SANAA AHMED is an assistant professor of law at the University of Calgary, where she teaches courses on money laundering and criminal law. Her research takes an interdisciplinary approach to money laundering and terrorism financing regulation and focuses on the intersection of law, public policy, and economics. Through a critical appraisal of questions of power at the national and transnational level, Ahmed's work examines the regulatory, constitutional, and governance issues at the heart of global regulation.

JOHN CASSARA had a twenty-six-year career as a United States intelligence officer and a U.S. Department of Treasury Special Agent. Assigned overseas, he developed expertise in trade-based money laundering, value transfer, and underground financial systems. Since his retirement, he has lectured in the United States and around the world on a variety of transnational crime issues. He has authored numerous articles and six books including *Trade-Based Money Laundering: The Next Frontier in International Money Laundering Enforcement*.

GARRY CLEMENT is a financial crime prevention expert and advocate; he joined VersaBank in London, Ontario as the Chief Anti-Money Laundering and Chief BSA Officer in 2022. Garry relies on his thirty-four years of policing experience, having worked in roles as the National Director for the RCMP's Proceeds of Crime Program, working as an investigator and undercover operator in some of the highest organized crime levels throughout Canada. During Garry's policing career, he received numerous awards and commendations for his investigative abilities. Garry has published numerous articles on the state of policing in Canada.

ARTHUR J. COCKFIELD (1967–2022) was a professor at Queen's Universi-ty Faculty of Law where he was appointed as a Queen's National Schol-ar. He received fellowships, external research grants, and awards for his tax research, including the Douglas J. Sherbaniuk Distinguished Writing Award. He served as a legal consultant to organizations that include the OECD, the United Nations, the World Bank, the Department of Justice, the Department of Finance, the Canada Revenue Agency, the Office of the Auditor General and the Office of the Privacy Commissioner of Canada.

CAROLINE DUGAS has more than twenty years of experience in the bank-ing industry. She completed her Bachelor of Finance and her graduate degree in financial crime with the University of Sherbrooke. In addition, she has completed several courses related to securities. To further develop her skills in the financial crime sector, she graduated in 2021 with a Mas-ter's Degree in Counterterrorism from Liverpool John Moore University.

JAMIE FERRILL is the Discipline Lead of Financial Crime Studies and Lec-turer in the same at the Australian Graduate School of Policing and Se-curity, Charles Sturt University, and co-Editor-in-Chief of Salus Journal. She has nearly a decade of law enforcement experience, having worked for Canada Border Services Agency prior to commencing an academic ca-reer. Jamie holds a PhD from Loughborough University (UK), a Master's in Homeland Security Leadership from the University of Connecticut (US), and a Bachelor's in Criminal Justice from Mount Royal University (Canada). She has held a visiting research fellowship at the Academy of International Affairs NRW in Germany. A political sociologist, Jamie re-searches threats to national and economic security; her current focus is on border governance, transnational cooperation and collaboration, and organizational processes.

CAMERON FIELD is a vice president with the Vidocq Group and consults on financial crimes, anti-money laundering and white-collar crime. Prior to that he was the intelligence lead for the Bank of Montreal Anti-money Laundering team for five years. Before working in the private sector, he served thirty-two years with the Toronto Police Service. During this time, he was the Officer in Charge of the Corporate Crime Team of the Organized Crime Enforcement Service. Field is a frequent speaker at financial crime events internationally and has published in many industry and law enforcement periodicals. He received a BA in Justice Studies from the University of Guelph and an MSc in Criminology from the University of Leicester in the UK. He is also a certified anti-money laundering specialist from ACAMS.

MICHELLE GALLANT is a professor at the Faculty of Law, University of Manitoba. She is a former Associate Dean (Research and Graduate Studies), a past Executive Director of the Manitoba Legal Research Institute and was a member of the Manitoba Law Reform Commission for more than ten years. Michelle teaches courses on taxation law, philanthropy and law, property law, and the international and domestic governance of tainted finance. She was a member of the Research Council affiliated with the 2022 Public Commission of Inquiry into the use of the Emergencies Act. Her research and scholarly work attends to money laundering law, civil forfeiture regimes, terrorist financing, philanthropy and law and taxation law.

PETER GERMAN, KC, is Chair of the Advisory Board of the Vancouver Anti-Corruption Institute. A lawyer and member of the Ontario and British Columbia bars, he served as the RCMP's Director General Financial Crime and as Deputy Commissioner. He has a PhD in Law from the University of London, focused on asset recovery, and is the author of *Dirty Money* reports prepared for the Attorney General of BC. Dr. German practices law and is a consultant on criminal justice matters.

RHIANNA HAMILTON is a researcher coordinator working with Queen's University's Institute of Intergovernmental Relations. Her research interests include transnational environmental crime (for example wildlife trafficking), money laundering, sex trafficking, cryptocurrency-based money laundering, and the gendered dynamics of financial crime.

TODD HATALEY is a professor in the School of Justice and Community Development at Fleming College. He is a retired member of the Royal Canadian Mounted Police. During his tenure as a federal police officer, he conducted investigations into the cross-border smuggling of drugs, weapons and humans, money laundering, as well as organized crime, national security, and extra-territorial torture investigations. Dr. Hataley is also an adjunct associate professor at the Royal Military College of Canada. His research currently focuses on the management of international boundaries, money laundering, Indigenous policing, and transnational crime.

CAITLYN JENKINS is a Political Studies student at Queen's University. Her research interests include transnational money laundering and terrorist financing, bipartisanship in the Canadian government, civic engagement, foreign policy, and the role of non-state actors in shaping international institutions and norms. Caitlyn is a research assistant for the Institute of Intergovernmental Relations at Queen's University where she pursues projects on the relationship between transnational money laundering and cryptocurrency and on the nature of financial crime in the Canadian economy. Caitlyn is also the acting co-Editor-in-Chief of *Politicus*, Queen's undergraduate politics journal.

CHRISTIAN LEUPRECHT is Class of 1965 Distinguished Professor in Leadership in the Department of Political Science and Economics at the Royal Military College of Canada, Editor-in-Chief of the *Canadian Military Journal*, Director of the Institute of Intergovernmental Relations in the School of Policy Studies at Queen's University, and Adjunct Research Professor in the Australian Graduate School of Policing and Security at Charles Sturt University. An elected member of the College of New Scholars of the Royal Society of Canada and a recipient of RMC's Cowan Prize for Excellence in Research, he has held visiting fellowships at the School for Advanced International Studies at the Academy of International Affairs NRW in Germany, Johns Hopkins University, Flinders University in Australia, the Hanse Wissenschaftskolleg in Germany, the University of Grenoble in France, and Yale University. He is the author of *Intelligence as Democratic Statecraft* (Oxford University Press, 2021).

DAVID MAIMON is professor in the Department of Criminal Justice and Criminology at Georgia State University (GSU) and the director of the Evidence-Based Cybersecurity research group. He is also a Chief Science Officer at VIDOCQ. Prior to joining GSU, David held academic positions in the Department of Criminology and Criminal Justice with the University of Maryland, and in the Department of Sociology with the University of Miami. Over the years, Dr. Maimon worked with numerous governmental agencies and private sector organizations on various cybersecurity and anti-fraud related projects. His research interests include cyber-enabled and cyber-dependent crimes, computer hacking, computer networks vulnerabilities to cyberattacks, and decision-making processes in cyber space. His research has led to numerous scientific publications. In 2022, he also co-authored the book *Evidence-Based Cybersecurity: Foundations, Research, and Practice* published with Routledge (Taylor & Francis). David earned a PhD in Sociology from the Ohio State University in 2009.

KATARZYNA (KASIA) MCNAUGHTON obtained her PhD in law from Queen's University, Kingston in June 2022. Her thesis (under the supervision of Professor Arthur Cockfield) examined the role of financial intelligence units (FIUs) in international anti-money laundering (AML) law and policy. In particular, she conducted an in depth, comparative study of national models of FIUs from ten, selected, Western (Canada, Denmark, Netherlands, Luxembourg, United States) and Eastern (post-Soviet) countries (Estonia, Latvia, Lithuania, Poland, Ukraine), and produced a critical assessment of the current international law approach to fight money laundering. Katarzyna has a Law degree from Poland (University of Gdansk), and holds a master's degree in criminology, law and society (University of California Irvine) and an L.LLM. from Chapman Fowler School of Law.

DENIS MEUNIER is a former Deputy Director of the Financial Transactions and Reports Analysis Centre of Canada (FINTRAC) and former Director General of the Criminal Investigations Directorate at the Canada Revenue Agency (CRA). Denis has worked as a Technical Assistance Expert with the International Monetary Fund (IMF) in several countries on anti-money laundering (AML) capacity building; as an instructor at the University of Ottawa; and now is an independent AML consultant. Denis has been an active volunteer for Transparency International Canada, a non-governmental organization focused on anti-corruption, and served as a Board member of that organization. Denis has testified at several Parliamentary Committees on AML legislation reform and has advocated for a publicly accessible registry of beneficial owners of corporations and trusts.

PIERRE-LUC POMERLEAU is a partner at VIDOCQ, responsible for assisting clients in growing their business and innovating while managing risks and protecting their assets. Before joining VIDOCQ, Pierre-Luc was a vice president at the National Bank of Canada, overseeing the Financial Crime and Corporate Security Division, including data analytics and innovation. Pierre-Luc earned a PhD in Business Administration with a specialization in Homeland Security from Northcentral University, an MBA from the Université de Sherbrooke, and a bachelor's degree in criminology from the Université de Montréal. He also holds various security and financial crime professional certifications, among them CPP, PSP, PCI, CFE, CAMS, CCCI and CFCI certifications. In 2020, he published his book *Countering Cyber Threats to Financial Institutions: A Private and Public Partnership Approach to Critical Infrastructure* with Palgrave Macmillan. His latest book *Evidence-Based Cybersecurity; Foundations, Research, and Practice* was published by Routledge (Taylor & Francis) in June 2022.

STEPHEN SCHNEIDER is a professor of Criminology at Saint Mary's University in Halifax. His areas of interest include organized crime, financial crime, and corporate crime. He is the author of five books, including the best-selling *Iced: The Story of Organized Crime in Canada*.

PAMELA E. SIMPSON currently works within the TD Fusion Intelligence Team as a Senior Information Security Analyst, focusing on intelligence collection, production, and process automation and enablement. Prior to joining TD, Pam worked with BMO as Strategic Cyber Threat Intelligence Analyst within the Global Information Operations Centre. Here, she focused on strategic reporting of state-sponsored cyber threats and ransomware. During her time with BMO, Pam also served as the private sector lead on the Scientific Executive Council for the Human-Centric Cybersecurity initiative, which leverages a transdisciplinary group to help create a more inclusive digital society. During her master's in international relations at Queen's University, she focused on anti-money laundering and terrorist financing, co-publishing an article entitled "Tracking Transnational Terrorist Resourcing Nodes and Networks" in the *Florida State University Law Review*. She was also provided the opportunity to study financial crime related to initial coin offerings and distributed ledger technology at the University of Sydney Law School.

JEFFREY SIMSER served as a lawyer and legal director at the Ministry of the Attorney General in Toronto, Canada for more than thirty years before retiring in 2022. He is one of Canada's leading experts on asset forfeiture and money laundering law. He holds law degrees from Queen's University at Kingston and Osgoode Hall Law School. Mr. Simser is the author of two books, *Civil Asset Forfeiture in Canada* (loose-leaf) and *Canadian Anti-Money laundering Law: The Gaming Sector*. He is currently working with co-authors on another book, *Money Laundering in Canada*. He has published dozens of peer-reviewed articles. Mr. Simser was twice qualified as an expert witness at the Commission of Inquiry into Money Laundering in British Columbia (the Cullen Commission). Mr. Simser has provided training and support to law enforcement and to jurisdictions across Canada and around the world (including the Democratic Republic of the Congo, the Philippines, Guatemala, and Kenya).